Collins

CAPE® REVISION GUIDE
CARIBBEAN STUDIES

T0312369

Kevin Thompson, Marjorie Lawson-Downer, Andrea St John, Eartha Thomas-Hunte

Contributors: Cait Hawkins, Diana Josan, Teasha Levy-Manfred, Kathleen Singh, Nicola White

Published by Collins
An imprint of HarperCollins*Publishers*
The News Building, 1 London Bridge Street,
London, SE1 9GF, UK

HarperCollins*Publishers*
Macken House, 39/40 Mayor Street Upper,
Dublin 1, D01 C9W8, Ireland

First edition 2017

10 9 8 7 6

ISBN 978-0-00-815728-9

www.collins.co.uk/caribbeanschools

A catalogue record for this book is available from the British Library.

Typeset by QBS Learning

Printed and bound in the UK by Ashford Colour Press Ltd

Publisher: Elaine Higgleton
Commissioning Editor: Lucy Cooper
Development Editor: Cait Hawkins
Managing Editor: Sarah Thomas
Project Manager: Alissa McWhinnie
Copy Editor: Mary Hobbins
Proofreader: Lucy Hyde
Answer Checker: Catherine Dakin
Artwork: QBS Learning
Cover design: Kevin Robbins and Gordon MacGilp
Production: Lauren Crisp

MIX
Paper | Supporting responsible forestry
FSC
www.fsc.org   FSC™ C007454

This book contains FSC™ certified paper and other controlled sources to ensure responsible forest management.

For more information visit: www.harpercollins.co.uk/green

Image Credits: Chapter Opener 1: Michaeljung/Shutterstock; Chapter Opener 4: Kamira/Shutterstock; Chapter Opener 8: Merc67/Shutterstock; Chapter Opener 12: Maxisport/Shutterstock; p94: DeAgostini/Getty Images; p128: Education Images/UIG/Getty Images; p158: Tropicalpix/E+/Getty Images; p162: TRISHA SCOTLAND/NEWZULU/Alamy Live News

Maps: Sheena Shanks

Contents

Introduction

Purpose of the Revision Guide

The purpose of this Caribbean Studies Revision Guide is to support candidates as they prepare for the Caribbean Examinations Council CAPE® Caribbean Studies examination. It has been written by practising teachers of the examination.

It should be noted, however, that in order to gain full benefit from the content provided, particularly on approaches to the Module 3 School-Based Assessment (SBA), students are advised to make full use of this guide from the outset of their studies and not exclusively in the final stages of preparation for the examination.

Organisation of the Revision Guide

The Revision Guide has been organised around the structure of the Caribbean Examinations Council CAPE® Caribbean Studies examination. This ensures complete syllabus coverage in terms of content and the stated syllabus objectives, which are outlined at the beginning of each chapter. However, bearing in mind the interdisciplinary nature of the course and the fact that the content should necessarily be approached in a non-linear way, the guide has in-built features to ensure clear and comprehensive cross-references between content sections. In addition, the guide contains guidance on how to approach all three papers of the examination as well as the SBA.

The Revision Guide is organised into four sections:

Section 1: Research and Examination Techniques
- Chapters 1 and 2 cover the content requirements of syllabus Module 3: Investigating Issues in the Caribbean. It also provides practical support for students in preparation for and production of the research project required for the SBA.
- Chapter 3 provides guidance and support for students in approaching Papers 01, 02 and 03/2 of the examination, with advice on writing essay-style answers and on tackling multiple choice questions.

Section 2: The Caribbean Region
- Chapters 4 and 5 cover the content and objectives of sections 1–2 of syllabus Module 1: Caribbean Society and Culture. These chapters focus on defining the Caribbean and its identity and on how the historical perspective has resulted in today's Caribbean in terms of society and culture in particular.

Section 3: Impacts on Caribbean Society
- Chapters 6 to 11 cover the content and objectives of sections 3–8 of syllabus Module 1: Caribbean Society and Culture. These chapters focus on how specific factors have influenced the formation of Caribbean society, culture and identity.

Section 4: Issues in Caribbean Development
- Chapters 12 to 19 cover the content and objectives of sections 1–8 of syllabus Module 2: Issues in Caribbean Development. These chapters focus on defining development, identifying issues in the development of the Caribbean and investigating various aspects of the Caribbean region that influence and/or are affected by these issues.

Key Features of the Revision Guide

The Revision Guide incorporates a number of key features designed to reflect the multiplicity of experiences within the Caribbean region, the interdisciplinary nature of the approach and content of the course and the structure and nature of the final examination.

These key features are:

- Key Terms – Key Terms boxes provide a concise definition or explanation of key terms used and their specific application to the experience of the Caribbean region where appropriate.
- Did you know? – The Did you know? feature presents mini case studies or additional or more in-depth information on specific issues or events, often specific to a certain part of the Caribbean region.
- Quick Facts – Quick facts boxes in the margins provide snippets of additional information pertinent to the main discussion and which can be used to illustrate or extend key points.
- Exam Tips – Exam Tips boxes give advice on how to approach aspects of the examination or to apply areas of content to specific types of questions or tasks.
- Making the Connection – Making the Connection boxes highlight areas of cross-disciplinary or cross-sectional aspects of content by providing clear links to content contained within other chapters or sections of the Revision Guide.
- Check Your Knowledge – the Check Your Knowledge feature in each of the chapters covering Module 1 and 2 syllabus content provides an essay question similar to those set in Paper 02 of the examination, along with some guidance on how to respond to it.
- Multiple-choice Questions – each chapter (except Chapter 3) concludes with a set of multiple-choice questions which reflect the nature and scope of those set in Paper 01 of the examination.

Research and Examination Techniques

Chapter 1

Purpose, Sources and Principles of Research

By the end of this chapter you should be able to:

- explain the nature and purpose of research;
- identify and access sources of information for your project;
- apply selection criteria to available sources;
- understand the principles behind referencing;
- be aware of different referencing styles;
- adhere to basic principles for maintaining ethical standards in conducting research.

In this chapter you will be reminded of some of the major concepts and principles which you will need to understand and apply when conducting research for your own project. As you know, this is 40 per cent of your final grade for Caribbean Studies. This chapter lays the foundations by assisting you in planning your investigation, which is a wonderful opportunity to deepen your understanding of the area of Caribbean regional and diasporic experience that you have selected.

Nature and Purpose of Research

Definition and Purpose of Research

Research is:

- the process of collecting data using a calculated and methodical method, and the analysing and interpreting of that data in order to identify the cause of or arrive at a solution to a problem;
- a rigorous and focused quest to gather knowledge and understanding of any social and physical phenomena;
- a consistent, rational and systematic study of or enquiry into a problem or a phenomenon, through the application of the scientific method;
- geared at providing answers to questions, solutions to problems, and enlightenment for unexplained phenomena.

There are two fundamental reasons why research is conducted.

1. To acquire information about something that you do not know, for example:
   - to extend knowledge of life and our environment;
   - to find solutions to problems;
   - to provide purposeful data for sensible decision-making and for the creation of policies and procedures;
   - to provide explanations of unknown phenomena;
   - to help to improve knowledge and the ability to handle situations.

2. To gather evidence, for example:
   - to verify and test existing facts and theories;
   - to extend information in various fields of knowledge.

Did You Know?

Pure research (or basic or fundamental research) is undertaken to increase our understanding of the world around us. It is focused on generating new ideas, theories or principles.

Applied research is geared to finding solutions to practical problems and to advance the human condition.

Forms of Knowledge

Key Terms

The forms of knowledge are traditional, experiential and scientific.

- **Traditional knowledge** – knowledge that has been gained through tradition or narration. It is oral knowledge which is usually transferred from generation to generation. The Caribbean has a rich oral tradition, where indigenous peoples preserved their practices and aspects of their cultures by passing on their knowledge to their descendants. Knowledge about the earliest inhabitants of the islands was gained through word-of-mouth. Not much of the Taino and Kalinago cultures was recorded during Spanish colonisation, which is why the preservation of aspects of their culture through traditional knowledge is so valuable.

- **Experiential knowledge** – knowledge which one arrives at based on personal experience of an occurrence or event. When someone has had an experience that provides him with specific knowledge, he can be seen as an authority on that issue. Within the Caribbean, people's identities are usually shaped by experiences such as the power under which they were colonised, the African heritage of enslaved people, the cultures of the indentured immigrants, and the legacies of the indigenous people. Such knowledge is valuable in research because it provides a benchmark against which other knowledge can be measured.

- **Scientific knowledge** – knowledge arrived at as a result of methodical study, and organised around generally established principles. It is based on empirical evidence and is geared at providing an understanding of the natural world. It is acquired through the scientific process, namely:
  - making observations
  - formulating questions
  - collecting applicable data
  - analysing the data
  - formulating conclusions.

Quick Facts

The difference between pure and applied research:

Increasing the knowledge base of a particular field of study is the single most important goal of pure or basic research, while for applied research it is to utilise information from the knowledge base (put forward by pure research) to formulate solutions to specific problems.

Examples

One of the following cases is an example of the application of **experiential knowledge**.

a. Gavin lives in Woodlands, Montserrat, with his mother and three younger sisters. His father migrated to Dubai four years ago and the family has not heard from him since. Gavin attends Montserrat Secondary school and is in the eleventh grade. However, he wants his mother to allow him to quit school and get a job at a bauxite plant so that he can help out the rest of the family.

b. Michael is a student at Roxborough Secondary school in Tobago and finds that when there is political unrest in his community it affects his attendance and academic performance, so he proposes the erection of boarding facilities for students who live in volatile communities.

Case **a** does not show the application of experiential knowledge because, while Gavin faces the problem of choosing to support his family or continuing school, his request to his mother is not channelled towards a wider application of his own experience. It is focused on his and his family's needs, not the wider community.

Case **b** shows the application of experiential knowledge because:

1. It is based on Michael's first-hand experience of the political unrest in his community.
2. He has evidence that this political unrest has affected his academic performance and attendance.
3. His experience has led him to focus on others who might also face this dilemma.

The following situation illustrates the application of **traditional knowledge**:

> The residents of Boundbrook in Portland, Jamaica, have had limited access to piped water for years, and have improvised by continuing the age-old practice of harvesting rainwater for their recreational and agricultural use. In recent times, water shortage, due to drought and a decline in water catchment basins in the county of Surrey, has led the government representatives to propose the resurrection of the harvesting of rainwater on a large scale and for long-term viability. The representatives have sought the assistance of the Boundbrook community to assist them in the building of a traditional rainwater gathering structure.

Explanation:

> The knowledge about rainwater harvesting utilised here is traditional because it has been gained through tradition and practice. The residents of Boundbrook have built, repaired and maintained the catchment structures for generations and have become skilled at it. It is a tradition for the community and the residents are the ideal candidates to provide support for those who would wish to embark on this venture.

Check Your Knowledge

1. Explain the significance of experiential knowledge.
2. Give an example of the use of traditional knowledge.
3. List the steps involved in scientific knowledge.

Answers:

1. Experiential knowledge involves the application of a person's previous experiences, perception and understanding, and therefore is significant because it provides the benchmark against which an individual can measure his own experiences.
2. Seeking the assistance of the indigenous people of Costa Rica in collecting plant extracts and identifying their purpose, since the indigenous people have been using these plants in the treatment of their ailments for generations.
3. See the Key Terms box above.

Systematic Enquiry

Enquiry is seeking answers to questions to which you do not know the answers, and is usually geared at increasing knowledge. **Systematic enquiry**:

- is the practice of gathering and then rationally analysing information in order to provide explanations for issues, obtaining new knowledge or solving a problem

- utilises the **inductive-deductive approach**, where the process of **reasoning** is used to draw inferences from the findings of a study or arrive at a conclusion
- involves two important elements – the collection of data and the analysis and interpretation of the collected data.

Key Terms

Reasoning – the application of logic to arrive at a considered conclusion. The two main types of reasoning are:

- **Deductive reasoning**: Reasoning from the general to the specific. A logical relationship is established from the perspective of general knowledge (a major premise and a minor premise), which is then used to predict a specific observation or conclusion.
- **Inductive reasoning**: A two-stage process method that consists of first a specific observation and then out of this the prediction of a general principle.

Inductive-deductive approach – involves the construction of a **hypothesis** from observed **facts**, then deduction and verification are used to arrive at a conclusion.

Facts – provable observations that are taken to be true.

Hypothesis – an educated guess or tentative assumption based on previous knowledge and observation.

Quick Facts

The process of **deductive reasoning**:

A major premise is a statement from which a conclusion can be drawn and is assumed to be true.

A minor premise is a specific case associated to the major premise.

Example:

Major Premise: Jamaica produces runners who are gold medal winners.

Minor Premise: Usain Bolt of Jamaica is the world's fastest runner.

Conclusion: Usain Bolt is a gold medal winner.

Generation of New Knowledge

New knowledge is generated constantly, because of:

- the huge amount of scientific research being undertaken to discover new knowledge;
- the need to find solutions to both ongoing and new problems;
- people's tendency to challenge existing knowledge and accepted truths, especially if they believe in the value of their new ideas;
- the fact that changes and advances in the world necessarily generate new situations and problems, which in turn open up opportunities for generating new knowledge.

Reliability and Validity in Research

The value of research is hinged on its reliability and validity. **Reliability** in quantitative research refers to:

- the degree to which the results of a study can be replicated and the results are consistent;
- the extent to which the measurement tools used produce consistent and stable results in repeated testing;
- the absence of internal bias or manipulation of the results when the measurements are replicated.

Example

Applying reliability to a research topic:

Do remittances benefit students of Cotton Ground, Nevis, whose parents have migrated to the USA?

If this research was done 20 years ago, six years ago and two years ago, and is to be undertaken by a researcher today, the results yielded should be consistent. This is because each time the research was done it would be replicated by using a similar measurement tools and approaches (questionnaire, interviews, etc.).

Validity refers to how well a test measures what it is supposed to measure, and to the level of a researcher's confidence that their results are free from bias, mistakes or even deliberate deception. Measurements and observations, and the instruments used to collect them, such as questionnaires or surveys, cannot be valid unless they are reliable and accurate.

Problem Solving

Problem solving is a process that applies reasoning and decision-making skills to arrive at a solution. There are five basic steps to problem solving, once you are aware of the problem:

1. Define the problem in general terms.
2. Select a particular problem. In essence, select a specific area of the problem.
3. Identify possible solutions.
4. Evaluate all the plausible solutions in order to choose the most suitable one.
5. Devise a plan of action to implement the selected solution.

Did You Know?

How to improve validity in your research:

1. Have clearly defined goals and objectives. Define the variables so that they are measurable elements.
2. Align your assessment measures to your goals and objectives.
3. Ensure that difficult or confusing wording has been eliminated.

Example

Applying problem solving:

Developers propose to erect an all-inclusive hotel with an international conference centre in Bartica, Guyana, but the local citizens object to the project because they would like to preserve the integrity and character of the town.

Step 1 Define the problem – this is the broad issue being faced by the people of Bartica.

- Controlling development in Bartica; preserving the integrity and character of the town of Bartica.

Step 2 Select the problem – this is the specific area which is of concern to the residents.

- How can development be controlled in Bartica, Guyana?
- How do the people of Bartica preserve the integrity and character of the town?

Step 3 Identify possible solutions – which solutions can adequately address the issue?

- Withhold building permits indefinitely.
- Propose legislation that stipulates eco-friendly and historically appropriate construction.

- Re-zoning the town to exclude hotel construction from areas of historical, architectural or environmental significance.
- Designate areas as green spaces and historical sites.
- Enact ordinances that determine the style and design of all buildings.
- Levy fines on investors who erect buildings in the country that contravene the ordinances of the towns.

Step 4 Choose the most appropriate solution – why is this the most feasible option to pursue?

- Investment in the form of buildings that will enhance the tourism industry is always welcomed as it has long-term implications for employment, revenue and development. With these benefits in mind, the most appropriate solution would be to allow the development, but first have legislation that stipulates eco-friendly and historically appropriate construction. On one side, the investors get to build their hotel and conference centre which should lead to returns on their investment, especially as this resort would definitely be an attraction for those who are eco-friendly. On the other side, the town would preserve its integrity and character, local employment would rise and the country's gross domestic product (GDP) would increase.

Step 5 Devise a plan of action to implement the selected solution – putting the recommendation into practice:

- After collection and analysis of relevant information and data, the findings presented support the need to preserve the integrity and character of the town's architecture. It is recommended that the erection of the proposed hotel and conference centre be permitted only if adjustments are made to align the original design to a new proposed structure so that they conform to the preservation laws of the government agency that regulates their building.

(While this is a simplified version to approaching your research project, it can definitely provide you with a starting point.)

Check Your Knowledge

1. Which of the following would be suited for pure research?
    A. Should pollution standards be eliminated in the cement industry of Jamaica?
    B. Are hereditary traits transmitted by DNA sequence in reproductive cells?
    C. How effective are the penicillin antibiotics in the treatment of typhoid fever for the residents of Jacmel, Haiti?
    D. Are male middle-aged bus drivers more likely to develop poor circulation than female middle-aged bus drivers?

Answer:

A and C – the focus in both instances is to increase our understanding, and answer scientific questions.

Quick Facts

Researchers use both primary and secondary sources of information. Primary sources are first-hand sources of information which have not gone through any process of interpretation. Secondary sources are sources in which the information from primary sources has been processed or interpreted in some way.

Making the Connection

The use of primary and secondary materials is discussed in detail in Chapter 2 'Research Practice'.

2. Which of the following would be suited for applied research?
   A. Treatment of diabetes among the sugar factory workers of GuySuCosugar, Guyana.
   B. Has West Indies cricket promoted the economic development of the Caribbean?
   C. Do bacteria interfere with the normal life function of birds?
   D. Does exposure to violence in the media influence students' abilities to resolve conflict?
   E. The implementation of laws to regulate the number of animals hunted and killed each year.

Answer:

A, B and D – these topics seek to find solutions for, or answers to, specific problems or questions.

Sources of Information

Identifying and Accessing Sources

The box below summarises the main sources from which a researcher collects information.

Key Terms

Archives – collections of records, documents, photographs or other material that give information about events or issues of historical significance.

Existing literature – literature that has already been generated on the topic that the researcher is investigating, such as textbooks and reports. This includes literature that reviews, assesses and evaluates the writings on a specific topic or issue.

Internet sources – online sources or materials which provide information that are accessible over the internet. Online journals and online sites established by universities, scholarly organisations and scientific societies are acceptable internet sources for research.

Minutes of meetings – written documentation of formal proceedings that are captured at official meetings. They contain information on who attended and the decisions made at these meetings.

Newspaper reports – reports that have been published in a newspaper and give detailed accounts of, or information on, an event, issue or situation.

Oral histories – historical information that has been gathered from people through interviews and conversations and recorded to provide evidence about the past.

Criteria for the Selection and Use of Sources of Information

When selecting sources, each needs to be specifically examined and assessed in terms of relevance, degree of validity and adequacy for purpose.

Table 1.1 **Selection and use of sources of information**

Source	Types	Selection criteria	When to use	Disadvantages
Archives	• Government agencies' public records • Research organisations • Businesses and commercial organisations • Hospitals and healthcare providers • News media	• Relevance to research topic • Availability of the source as the main element of research • Availability of the needed data • Creation of other areas of focus • Completeness of format and preparation • Clarification it brings to the research	• There is the need to make comparisons with similar populations • To get a complete picture of a phenomena • To present information about past activities • To identify areas of need and concern • They present information from the source • When time and resources are constraints	• Data may not be up-to-date (archives are usually updated every five years) • Data usually based on a large population sample • May be time consuming to search for relevant/necessary information
Existing literature	• Books • Ebooks • Scholarly articles • Peer-reviewed journals • Statistical and other reports	• Provision of background information • Stability of the information • Depth of coverage on a topic • Date of publication	• To get background information about a topic • To get an overview of main ideas • To get historical facts	• The time to write and print a book can cause information to be outdated • Facts can be incorrect • The information is revised, leading to change in content
Internet sources	• Databases • Websites	• Current nature and accuracy of information • Current nature of content and links • Reviewed information	• When the information lays the foundation for deeper analysis • When the information has not been tampered with	• Information is at risk of being biased, inaccurate and incomplete • Difficult to establish credibility of sources
Minutes of meetings	• Verbatim minutes • Action minutes • Closed-door meeting minutes	• Recording of events • Availability of factual and chronological events • Recording of motions and actions • Provision of trends over time	• Togather information about actions taken • To collect data on attendees	• Lengthy discussions not included • Records may be incomplete • May contain classified information which cannot be made public
Newspaper reports	• Local news • National news • International news • Commentary • Epaper	• Relevance to the topic being researched • When summaries of key studies are needed • Presents key facts about an issue	• They provide information that can lead you to other sources • They provide recommendations for reform and problem-solving strategies	• Do not provide detailed study results • Some newspapers require a fee to access their information • Can sensationalise events or facts to create a 'good story'

(continued)

Table 1.1 *continued*

Source	Types	Selection criteria	When to use	Disadvantages
Oral histories	• Audio recordings • Video recordings • Transcripts • Eyewitness accounts	• Untapped perspectives shared in historical record • Quality of evidence for understanding about people's past • Provision of viewpoints on changes and constancy in values and traditions • Provision of insight into specific groups (ethnic, religious) • Clarification of folklore	• To learn more about people's way of life • To get information about overlooked groups • To get insight into a culture's traditions	• Depend on the memory of the participant • Information is limited to the history of a particular city, country or area • Information is geared at the criteria established by the agency that commissioned it
Visual images	• Maps • Before and after Pictures • Video tapes	• Provision of information about real-life situations • Showcasing of new perspective on the issue • Conveying missing detail • Capture of applicable visual images	• When they represent the issue • To show changes over time	• Open to subjective interpretation • Permission of the participants may be difficult to acquire

Figure 1.1 **Choosing your sources**

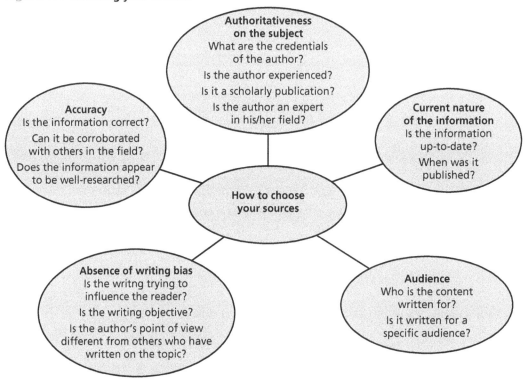

The diagram in Figure 1.1 summarises the important things to focus upon when collecting information to substantiate your research and to meet the required criteria in terms of degree of validity, adequacy and relevance, always bearing in mind the fundamental question: do the source findings relate to the hypothesis or problem?

Internet Sources

It is very important that you are vigilant in the selection of your sources to ensure that you have used appropriate ones to validate your research. While online sources can prove to be invaluable, a researcher must use some important criteria in addition those applied to other sources to select which of them are appropriate for inclusion in their **literature review**.

Figure 1.2 **Criteria for using internet sources**

Authorship
Can the author be identified – is their name on the page?
What are his/her qualifications?
Does the author provide contact information?
(A website with an unnamed author should be avoided.)

Motive
What is the author's purpose in writing this?
Which audience is the information intended for?
Is the author affiliated to an organisation?

Accuracy
Can the information be verified?
Are there grammatical, typographical and spelling errors?
(The presence of these can be an indication that the writing has not been created by an established authority or been reviewed.)
Is there evidence that the information has undergone review?

Objectivity
Is there evidence of bias?
Is the author impartial and unbiased?
Does the writer use emotive words to influence readers?

Currency
Is the creation date provided?
Is the information updated regularly? When was the last time? Is it up-to-date?

Links
Are the links on the site current?
Do the links lead to dead ends?
Are the links related to the topic?

> **Key Term**
>
> **Literature review** – an analytical and detailed review of the existing literature that relates to a particular field of study. See Chapter 2 'Research Practice' for more information on this.

> **Exam Tip**
>
> A critical approach is important in examining information found on the internet. It is recommended that you print out the information that you plan to include in your research and document the date of access, website address and other key details.

Referencing Style

In the writing of any research, it is extremely important that the researcher acknowledges the sources from which he or she has gathered information. In some instances, you will be citing the work that you used, in other cases you will be paraphrasing. As you will need to include information about all these sources in the **bibliography**, it is best to familiarise yourself with the means of citing sources. There are three major referring styles used for citing sources. These are the **American Psychology Association (APA)**, **Modern Language Association (MLA)** and **Chicago Manual of Style**.

Key Terms

Bibliography – a compilation, arranged alphabetically, of the sources that the researcher consulted in the process of conducting his or her research.

APA – the organisation, American Psychology Association, which is credited with one of the writing formats used for essays, publications, books and papers. This is the reference style used in Social Sciences.

MLA – Modern Language Association is the creator of the MLA writing style, which provides researchers with guidelines for writing and acknowledging the works of others.

Chicago Manual of Style – a guide for structuring citations, and using grammar and language in writing. It establishes the criteria for academic publishing in the Humanities.

Exam Tip

As you research and collect information from your sources, input the information into your document by utilising the 'Manage Sources' option on the 'References' Section of Microsoft Word. This will help you to save key information about your sources.

With advances in technology and the efforts to make people work smarter, there are programs on the computer that make referencing so much easier than ever before. Microsoft Word offers the built-in option of References on the task bar for writers to utilise. It allows you to create a bibliography, manage sources and insert citations using the style that is required by your course. Be sure to familiarise yourself with this option so that you can use it when writing your research.

The Bibliography

Quick Fact

The difference between a bibliography and a list of references:

A bibliography contains details of all sources consulted in the preparation of a piece of writing while a list of references contains only those sources actually referred to in the writing.

When you are researching in preparation for writing, make a note of all the sources you consulted. Later on, in compiling your **bibliography** you should be sure to include them, even if you do not actually reference them in your report. Listing all the sources you used in your research is an indication of the depth of your research. The bibliography shows:

* that you have read extensively on your topic;
* that you did some research;
* the sources from which you gathered information;
* when the information you are using was published;
* the publishers who are credited with making the sources available.

Example

The importance of a range of credible sources to show depth of research.

Problem:

A Caribbean Studies student became interested in doing research on the topic of the trustworthiness of people who become couples after meeting on Instagram. He only found information from one reliable source. The other sources he found were tabloid newspapers. His lecturer told him that people who write tabloids are not concerned with the truth but with sensationalism. He also told him that when there is no likelihood of corroboration, it fails the triangulation test, so he should think long and hard before pursuing this topic for his project.

Solution:

Ideally, the respondent should pursue another topic or another angle for his research project. For example, he could investigate if blind or online dating leads to marriage. However, he would need to seek other sources such as books on blind dating, online dating and dating in the 21st century in order to provide him with a broader information base as his bibliography would be limited and might not have enough credible authors for the literature review.

As sources of information, tabloids are inadequate; the researcher needs to look at why the stories were generated, and if there is support for their claims. The researcher should be seeking sources that represent expertise in the field as he should be focused on achieving accuracy in his data, not getting anecdotal information.

The Appendix

Research papers are usually long detailed documents with only the essential information included. However, researchers may see the need to include some additional documents which will supplement their research by providing a greater understanding of it. This is what the appendix is, a supplement to a document, such as a research project, in which you will find supporting information. The appendix is usually placed at the end of the document.

Materials that might be included in the appendix are: maps, graphs, tables, statistics and explanations, photographs, drawing, raw data, correspondence, transcripts of interviews, sample calculations, questionnaires/surveys (with the results being presented in the main part of the research).

There are some points to consider when selecting which documents to include in the appendix:

- Is the information very detailed and will it be difficult to summarise?
- Does including it in the body of your research make the project appear poorly structured?

Styles for Referencing, Bibliography and Appendices

There are some fundamental differences among the three main referencing styles. Each organisation has made resources readily available for everyone to use, and they constantly update the information to accommodate the changing times. So, nowadays, there are guidelines on how to reference blogs, webpages and so on, which are new sources of information, in addition to the traditional sources such as books and journals.

APA – Referencing and Bibliography

The American Psychological Association (APA) sets out some key requirements for referencing, writing the bibliography and the appendices. For **text citation**, the APA utilises the author-date method of citation. This means that the author is listed by last name, and date of publication within the text.

Quick Fact

Triangulation is a technique used in research that makes use of two or more sources or methods to help validate data. If the various sources or methods lead to the same conclusion or result, validity is increased.

Exam Tip

Think of the appendix as a dumping ground for information that, if absent from the research, will not affect the fluency of the presentation or the understandability of it. Remember, the information in the appendix is not absolutely necessary; research will not suffer from it being omitted.

Exam Tip

The title 'Appendix' is used when only one appendix is included. When writing more than one they should be labelled Appendix A, Appendix B, Appendix C and so on.

Quick Facts

Online sources are usually given a **digital object identifier (DOI)**, which is a unique alphanumeric string that has been assigned to any article that has been published electronically and is available for access: doi:XXXXXX. The DOI is typically found on the first page of the journal article near the copyright notice.

The guidelines to follow for referencing are:

- Include a quote or to summarise an author, you must include the page number or paragraph number.
- Direct quotes that are fewer than 40 words must be incorporated in your text. Use quotation marks to separate the quote.
- Direct quotes that are more than 40 words must be separated from your text and presented as an indented block of text. You **do not** use quotation marks in this case.

The table below sets out the APA style for references and bibliographies.

Table 1.2 APA style for references and bibliographies

	Referencing text	Bibliography
One Author	**Format** Last name (Year of publication) (Last name Year of publication, Page) **Example** • Taylor (2014), traces the history of workers conflict in the Caribbean … • In 2014, Taylor presents an in-depth examination on the impact of labour policy on income inequality … • This has been identified as a major effect of labour policy on income (Taylor 2014, 142).	**Format** Last name, First initial. (Year of publication). *Title*. Location of publisher: Publisher **Example** Taylor, O. (2014). *Broken Promises, Hearts and Pockets: A Century of Betrayal of the Jamaican Working Class*. Kingston: Arawak Publications
Two or more Authors When a work has more than two authors, all the names must be cited the first time, and afterward only include the first author's last name followed by et al.	**Format** Last name and Last name (Year of publication) (Last name & Last name Year of publication) **Example** • Haralambos and Holborn (2013), define culture as … • McChesney, Covey and Huling (2012) explain that leaders can only achieve extraordinary goals … • McChesney et al. (2012) explain further that success … • … that enable goals to be prioritised (McChesney et al. 2012)	**Format** Last name, First initial, & Last name, First initial. (Year of publication). *Title*. Location of publisher: Publisher **Example** Haralambos, M. & Holborn, M. (2013). *Sociology Themes and Perspectives* (8th Edition). UK: Harper-Collins McChesney, C., Covey S., & Huling, J. (2012). *The 4 Disciplines of Execution: Achieving Your Wildly Important Goals*. New York: Free Press
Journal article and other sources If the source is available online, add the DOI or URL to the end of the reference.	**Format** Last name, Year of publication **Example** One main condition of alcoholic liver disease is cardio vascular disease (Gao & Bataller, 2011),	**Format** Last name, First initial. (Year). Title of article. *Journal Title*, volume number(issue number):page range. doi: xxxx or URL **Example** Gao, B. & Bataller, R. (2011). Alcoholic liver disease: Pathogenesis and new therapeutic targets. *Gastroenterology*, 141(5):1572–85. doi:10.1001/jama.2012.82
Online newspaper articles	**Format** Last name (Year of publication) **Example** Connelly (2015) quoted a retired educator who claims that the education policies are lacking …	**Format** Last name, First initial. (Year, Month Day). Title of article. *Newspaper Name*. Retrieved from URL **Example** Connelly, C. (2015, September 27). Bernard: More of the same from education policies. *Newsday*. Retrieved from http://www.newsday.co.tt/news
Website	**Format** Name of article, year **Example** Marginalised or privileged? Why boys underachieve in Caribbean schools, 2000	**Format** Name of article (Year, Month Day). Retrieved from name of website: URL **Example** Marginalised or privileged? Why boys underachieve in Caribbean schools (2000, August 30). Retrieved from the Aldis website: http://www.eldis.org

MLA – Referencing and Bibliography

The MLA provides guidelines for formatting your writing as well as references. For MLA formatting there are some basic rules that apply:

- Using a standard font such as Times New Roman, size 12.
- Double-spacing throughout the paper.
- Setting margins of one inch for top, bottom and both sides.
- Using indentation for paragraphs.
- Numbering pages consecutively, placing it in the top right-hand corner.
- Double-spacing within each citation and between each citation.
- Having a page titled 'Work Cited'.

Table 1.3 MLA style for references and bibliographies

Source	Bibliography
Book with one author	**Format** Author's last name, First name Middle initial. *Title*. Location of Publisher: Publisher, Year, Print. **Example** Taylor, Orville W. *Broken Promises, Hearts and Pockets: A Century of Betrayal of the Jamaican Working Class*. Kingston: Arawak Publications, 2014, Print.
Book with two or three authors	**Format** Author's last name, First name Middle initial, Author's last name, First name Middle initial, Author's last name, First name Middle initial. *Title*. Location of publisher: Publisher, Year, Print. **Example** Haralambos, Michael and Holborn, Martin. *Sociology Themes and Perspectives (8th Edition)*. UK: HarperCollins, 2013, Print.
Electronic book (Ebook)	**Format** Author's last name, First name Middle initial. *Title*. Location of publisher: Publisher, Year of publication. Electronic publisher. Web. Day Month Year of access. **Example** Blackmar, Frank W. *The History of Human Society*. New York: Charles Scribner's Sons, 2006. The Project Gutenberg EBook. Web. 7 January 2016.
Website	**Format** Author's last name, First name Middle initial. *URL title*. Publisher or sponsor of site (use n.p. if this information is not available). Date of publication. (n.d. if no date is available). Web. Day Month Year of access. **Example** Curley, Robert. *Which Caribbean islands are the safest, most dangerous?* About.com. August 2015. Web. 16 February 2016.

Quick Fact

When no date has been provided for a publication that you retrieved from the internet, use the abbreviation **n.d.** where you are required to include the year.

Exam Tip

Each reference style has its own set of guidelines, so it is important that you consistently follow the format for the referencing style you choose and are aware of how specific punctuation, such as commas, colons and full stops, is used.

Did You Know?

The difference between an online book and an ebook:

An online book is one that is only available for reading online. This book can only be accessed virtually; no hard copy is available, and it is read much like a printed book.

An ebook, on the other hand, is an electronic version of a book that can only be accessed for reading on a dedicated e-reader such as a handheld device (tablets, Kindles, iPads) or a computer.

The table below shows the way to reference some types of source and also how to address the bibliography.

Table 1.4 **Chicago Manual of Style references and bibliographies**

Source	Reference	Bibliography
Book with one author	**Format** Author last name, Year of publication, Page number **Example** The history of workers conflict in the Caribbean has been traced … (Taylor 2014, 103)	**Format** Author's last name, First name Middle initial. Year of publication. *Title*. Location of publisher: Publisher. **Example** Taylor, Orville W. 2014. *Broken Promises, Hearts and Pockets: A Century of Betrayal of the Jamaican Working Class.* Kingston: Arawak Publications.
More than one author	**Format** (Author's last name and Author's last name Year of publication, Page number) **Example** The idea that the family structure has evolved is evident in the way the family today is being defined, (Haralambos and Holborn 2013).	**Format** Author's last name, First name and Author's last name, First name. Year of publication. *Title*. Location of publisher: Publisher. **Example** Haralambos, Michael and Holborn, Martin. 2013. *Sociology Themes and Perspectives (8th Edition)*. UK: HarperCollins.
Journal article	**Format** (Author's last name Year of publication, Page number) **Example** (Nicholson 2009, 65)	**Format** Author's last name, First name. Year of publication. "Title." *Journal name* Volume number (Issue number): Page number(s) **Example** Nicholson, Maxine. 2009. "The persistent practice of folk forms worship among the Mennonites of Belize." *Journal of Religion and Health* 4 (2): 63–69. For an online journal, add the URL: Lake, David. 2002. "Rational extremism: Understanding terrorism in the twenty-first century." *Dialogue IO* 1 (1, January 2002): 15–29, http://journals.cambridge.org/article_S777777770200002X

For the Chicago Style, there are a few things you should remember:
- URLs must be cited for online sources.
- A list of sources cited (bibliography) should be included and titled 'References'. This should be placed at the end of the text.
- The general format for text citations is (Author Last Name, Year of Publication, Page number).
- The citation should usually be placed at the end of the sentence, but before the punctuation mark.
- It uses footnotes (notes printed at the bottom of the page to explain further, cite references, or add a comment).
- Newspapers are rarely included in the list of references. All information related to them should be in the body of the work in parenthesis. The format would be (*Newspaper Name*, Day Month Year of Publication, Section, Page number).

Principles of Ethical Conduct

Ethics are:
- the set of moral and honourable principles that guide the actions of the researcher;
- values and behaviours that help in the protection of individuals and communities, and maintain the trust of stakeholders.

In conducting research, the researcher must be aware of the ethical aspects of research and must apply the appropriate ethical standards. They must strive to be objective and ethically neutral so that they are not influenced in the collection of data, and in arriving at conclusions.
The researcher:
- should be knowledgeable about what is required of him or her in carrying **ethical research**;
- should make use of logical reasoning to make intellectual and truthful decisions about the research;
- should ensure that the outcome of the research also adheres to ethical standards of research.

Maintaining Integrity Throughout the Research Process

In order to maintain an ethical standard of behaviour throughout the research process and **research integrity**, Wayne C. Booth, Gregory G. Colomb and Joseph M. Williams, in their book *The Craft of Research* (2nd edition, Chicago: University of Chicago Press, Chicago, 2003, p.286) advise researchers not to:
1. **plagiarise** or claim credit for the results of others;
2. **falsify** sources or **fabricate** results;
3. use **data manipulation** to serve their own needs or ends;
4. submit data whose accuracy they have reason to question, unless they raise the questions;
5. conceal objections that they cannot counter;
6. caricature or distort opposing views;
7. destroy or conceal sources and data that are important for those who follow.

Consent of Research Subjects

Consent to participate in any research project should be informed and voluntary. This means that the participants must be made aware of the research process that they will be a part of, and that they willingly agree to the terms and conditions as stipulated by the researcher and give their **informed consent**.
To ensure informed consent, the researcher must outline:
- the purpose of the research;
- the procedures involved in the research process;
- the amount of time that is required of the participant;
- a description of the risks if any that the participant will be exposed to;
- a statement giving the assurance of confidentiality;
- names of contact persons associated with the research project;

Quick Fact

Stakeholders are individuals who have a vested interest in the research. These would include the researchers, the participants, the communities where the research was conducted and all the people who are a part of the research directly or indirectly, on whom the research will have an impact.

Key Terms

Ethical research – research that is designed and conducted lawfully, is valid and reliable and protects the rights of the research participants.

Research integrity – the application of good research practices and conduct.

Plagiarise – to take credit for another person's ideas, writings, results or procedures, and passing them off as your own.

Data manipulation – the handling, recording and reporting of data to conceal the real findings in order to deceive others.

Fabricate – to create data or results and then record and report these data or results as though they are true.

Falsify – to manipulate materials, methods or processes, or to alter or omit data or results so that the published research is not a true representation of the research carried out.

Informed consent – involves ensuring that the participants are made aware of the procedures, risks and benefits that are a part of the research. Once the participants are made aware of these issues, they must give their consent to participate in writing.

- a statement of participation being **voluntary**;
- a statement indicating that at any point the respondent has the right to withdraw without being penalised.

There may be instances in which gaining informed consent is impossible, impractical or pointless. Some instances are:

a. when having the participants provide written consent can put them at risk; for example, if the researcher is collecting information on the drug smuggling practices in a named city;

b. when the participants can be compromised; for example, in the collection of information on research relating to 'the effectiveness of undercover police officers infiltrating the narcotics trade in a named town';

c. when the research is being done on 'public behaviours'; for example, in collecting information on 'the types of lewd behaviours that participants engage in during Carnival'.

The option to take part in any research is left to the participant being recruited, and he or she should be informed that their participation is voluntary. In many instances, participants' consent is sought, but they are not made aware of the fact that they have the option to not participate, or that they can withdraw at any time in the research process. This should be clearly stated when seeking any participation.

Key Term

Voluntary participation – a principle which allows people to choose whether, how and when to be a part of a research project.

Example

An example of seeking informed consent and clarifying the voluntary nature of participation:

> Your consent to participate in this survey requires that you read and agree to the following:
>
> Your participation in this survey is voluntary. Your responses are completely anonymous and will be held in the strictest confidence. No identifying information will be divulged and there are few, if any, risks to you. All responses will be compiled and the results analysed as a group. Refusal to participate will not affect you.
>
> In addition:
> - you may stop responding at any point without penalty
> - you can choose not to answer a question without consequence
> - you can contact the researcher at johndoe@capecxcstudent.com, if you have any questions or concerns about the research.
>
> Please select one of the options below. Thank you.
>
> ☐ I agree to participate in this study.
>
> ☐ I do not agree to participate in this study.

Key Terms

Confidentiality – keeping identifying information about participants a secret so that it is not available to anyone, especially those who are not directly involved in the research.

Privacy – the right of an individual to limit access to information about himself (physical, intellectual and behavioural) to others.

Respect for Privacy and Confidentiality

In conducting any research, the biggest concerns are dealing with the issue of **confidentiality** and **privacy**. The need to ensure the privacy and confidentiality of participants is critical to ensuring the integrity of the research practice. Some research topics may be of a sensitive nature and the information divulged can be sensitive, personal or even damaging.

These types of information must definitely be safeguarded. Such sensitive information has been provided because the respondent believes he or she can trust the researcher. This expectation of non-betrayal means that the researcher has the responsibility to maintain the relationship of trust. To maintain confidentiality, researchers should create procedures that enable **anonymity** in data collection and that any identifiable data are removed immediately after analysis. In this way they are carrying out a duty to care for the wellbeing of the participants and not exposing them to any **risk of harm**.

Key Terms

Anonymity – the guarantee that participants will remain unidentified throughout the study. Ensuring that there is no way to link a participant's response to his or her identity.

Risk of harm – when the researcher puts the participants in danger (physical, psychological or to their reputation) as a result of their participation in the project.

Figure 1.3 Benefits of maintaining confidentiality

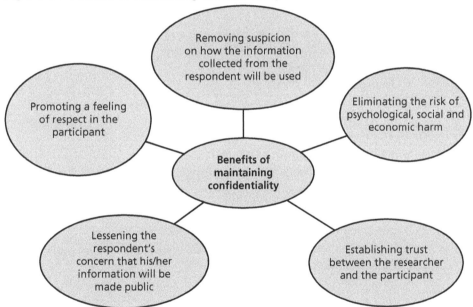

In order to maintain privacy and confidentiality, the researcher should:
- reduce who has access to the data;
- set up data so that any link between the respondents and the identifying information that they provide is erased;
- undertake investigation with a process that does not compromise ethical standards;
- take care in deciding whether or not to record sensitive information;
- be aware that anonymity and privacy are to be respected at all times.

Integrity and Transparency of the Research Process

Research integrity is adhering to responsible codes of conduct in undertaking all aspects of the research process. It involves following the accepted and established professional codes of research. Research integrity covers:

- **Honesty:**
  - in the acknowledgment and use of contributions to the research;
  - in your intentions for the research results, the collection of data, and in presenting the findings;
  - in ensuring authenticity and truthfulness at all stages of the research process;
  - in all aspects of the research project.
- **Care and respect:**
  - in the protection of respondents who are involved in the research project;
  - caring for animals involved in the conduct of the research;
  - in the sharing of information and resources, and in interaction with other researchers.
- **Transparency:**
  - in providing clarity when conflicts of interest arise or are about to arise;
  - in data collection and interpretation;
  - in sharing negative results if that is the case;
  - in drawing conclusions and presenting the results.

  Transparency serves to provide:
- the opportunity for researchers to analyse the work of others, a precondition of any work done by researchers;
- encouragement for excellence in observation, theory and procedural aspects of the research process;
- clarity for others who seek to collect and analyse data, in the process of which they are able to acquire new skills and devise new techniques.

In research, data transparency is important because it provides those outside the research project with access to evidence or data that has been used to support the claims made by the researcher.

Avoidance of Plagiarism

What is considered as **plagiarism**? There are many ways in which people tend to steal the work of others.

Key Term

Transparency (or **Research Transparency**) – the principle that researchers are obligated to present the data, theory and methodology upon which their conclusions have been based so that other researchers are able to scrutinise their work to arrive at an understanding of the proposed theories and authenticate them.

Key Term

Plagiarism – (or literary theft) is the act of passing off work of others as your own without giving credit to the source that provided it.

Figure 1.4 Acts of plagiarism

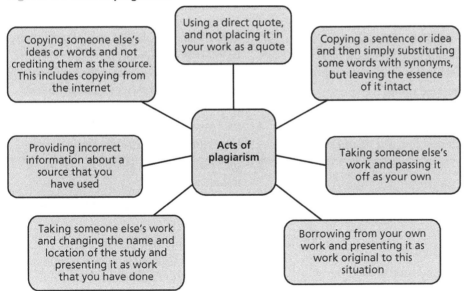

Plagiarism is a very serious offence and can have far-reaching effects on the persons involved. Penalties can be:

- legal – being taken to court and fined for copyright violations;
- academic – being given a failing grade, being expelled from the institution and being blacklisted.

Acknowledging your sources is the surest way of avoid allegations of plagiarism. The best way to do this is to document all the sources that you have gathered information from.

Multiple-choice Questions

1. A group of students went on a field trip to Devil's Hole Cave in Trinidad, where one of them observed a proliferation of empty bottles that littered the cave. He wants to do research on preventing the continued dumping of waste there and preserve the eco-system.

   Which means of gathering information for a possible research problem did he utilise?

   A. Oral knowledge
   B. Traditional knowledge
   C. Experiential knowledge
   D. Scientific knowledge

2. Systematic enquiry allows for

   A. the creation of rules and standards to guide the research
   B. thorough investigation into an issue to build on or disprove earlier findings
   C. the improvement of a problematic situation through creative research
   D. the collection of adequate background information to identify problems

3. A researcher uses an observation checklist to capture the number of students who are dropped off at school late every day. The researcher became bored and tired of waiting outside the schools, and then began to tally the make of the vehicles (cars, SUVs, etc.). When he came to collate his data, he included what he had observed. This is a threat to validity because

   A. the experience of the researcher changed the standard and influenced what was supposed to be measured
   B. the researcher did not capture any data related to his research topic
   C. an observation checklist was inadequate to collect the data he needed
   D. a researcher should always be interested in his subjects

4. A student undertaking a research project read this statement to a prospective participant.

   'I am interested in collecting information about industrial waste disposal in your neighbourhood. If there are questions you do not wish to answer, please indicate your reluctance and we will move on to the other questions in the questionnaire.

   Also we can stop at any point if you feel uncomfortable while you are participating in this research.'

   The researcher conveyed that the respondent's participation is voluntary by telling the prospective participant that

   A. the researcher wants to collect information about industrial waste disposal
   B. there are some questions that he might not answer
   C. he will feel reluctance to answer some of the questions
   D. the researcher will stop the research if the respondent expresses being uncomfortable in participating at any point

5. When a researcher lists all the sources he consulted for his bibliography, it shows

   I. that he used numerous sources for his research
   II. the authorship and age of the publications
   III. the researcher's interest in the topic
   IV. the appendix with the supporting information.

   A. I and II only
   B. I and IV only
   A. I, II and III
   B. II, III and IV

6. A student used a quote by Professor Barry Chevannes about the marginalisation of males, but could not find the card he had created with the referencing information. He believed the quote contributed a lot to his topic so he included it. However, to get around the problem of citing the source, he credited the quote to David Plummer because he had also written on the topic and the student had the relevant information about him on hand. This is an example of

   A. taking someone else's work and changing the name and location of the study and presenting it as work that you had done
   B. providing incorrect information about a source that you had used
   C. crediting the writer for his ideas, but ignoring his contribution to the research
   D. borrowing from your own work and presenting it as work original to this situation

7. Transparency is important to the research process because
   A. it allows other researchers to access the data and the methodology used in order to authenticate the results derived
   B. it shows that the researcher did not fail to conduct his research in a professional manner
   C. it ensures anonymity and privacy in research
   D. an awareness of the requirements of the research process is important to the integrity of the research

8. Archives are good sources of information for research because they
   A. are historical records that have been accumulated over time about past events
   B. support the research process through triangulation
   C. place facts into context and are readily accessible
   D. extend the literature review by adding variety to the sources

9. Which of the following is a hypothesis?
   A. The tourism sector and a high employee turnover rate.
   B. Having dogs as pets in a home causes children to have allergic reactions.
   C. Why do people overindulge in alcoholic drink?
   D. There are many causes of work related stress.

10. The American Psychological Association (APA) uses
    A. the text citation method of listing the author's last name, and date of publication within the text
    B. a page titled 'Work Cited'
    C. the general format for text citations, which is Author's Last Name, Year of Publication, Page number
    D. endnotes and footnotes to cite references and provide information

11. Which of the following is not a disadvantage of oral history:
    A. It is subject to what the participant remembers.
    B. The information is limited to the history of a particular area.
    C. Recorded interviews about historical events are primary source documents.
    D. Information not transcribed from the audio tape and video tapes can be lost.

12. One way to ensure the privacy of the participants in a research is to
    A. collect demographic questions separate from the directed questions
    B. set up the data to disguise any connection between the respondents and the information that they provide
    C. design a waiver for the participants to sign, giving the researcher the right to disclose any information
    D. rewrite the questions so that the responses presented are similar

13. Changing or omitting the results so that the research does not yield the truth about the study is an example of
    A. fabrication   C. concealment
    B. plagiarism   D. falsification

Chapter 2

Research Practice: methods, application analysis and presentation

By the end of this chapter you should be able to:

- identify a research problem;
- formulate relevant research questions and/ or hypotheses;
- understand the purpose and importance of the literature review;
- evaluate existing information about the problem;
- identify and apply appropriate methods of enquiry;
- identify and apply appropriate methods of sampling;
- present data in a variety of appropriate forms;
- apply appropriate techniques to analyse data;
- discuss your findings and draw reasoned conclusions;
- make relevant and practical recommendations.

This chapter provides practical information on planning and carrying out your investigation into Caribbean issues and in producing the report which you need to submit for the School-Based Assessment part of your course.

The Research Problem

A research problem is the topic you would like to investigate, to address or to study. It is a statement on an area of concern, something that needs improvement or an issue to be investigated and/or resolved. This statement presents the problem in a neutral way – it does not say how to do something or offer any kind of view or solution. Your research problem should be a topic that is of some interest to you and one which is, to some extent, familiar to you. Identification of the research problem is the first stage in the research process.

Identification of a Research Problem

There are many issues in the world that need corrective actions and the implementation of policies. In general, society is beleaguered by numerous problems and they need to be studied to find solutions. Chief among them are social inequality, resistance to diversity, poverty, discrimination, epidemics, unemployment and religious intolerance. The Caribbean is an area that has its share of social issues which need addressing.

There are three basic sources from which a research problem is derived:

1. Your own interest.
2. A modern or contemporary interest.
3. The existence of different views in an area which invite investigation.

Exam Tip

Research Problem Selection

The CAPE® syllabus has provided you with a wide range of issues from which to you can investigate. Popular ones over the years have been:

- Pollution
- The impact of the media on culture
- Sports and the regional/national economy
- The impact of dancehall music on society
- Causes and consequences of migration
- Traditional/modern medicine
- The effects of crime on society
- Folk forms of worship
- Technology on Caribbean society
- Natural and human disasters

There are many issues in the Caribbean which have yet to be investigated, so it should not be difficult for you to select from the proposed themes in order to arrive at a topic.

The choice of topics is very wide and you should be able to find an issue in your country, city, town, community or school to research. Start by being more observant and reflective, and be on the lookout for things that catch your attention or cause you concern.

Figure 2.1 Ways of identifying a research problem

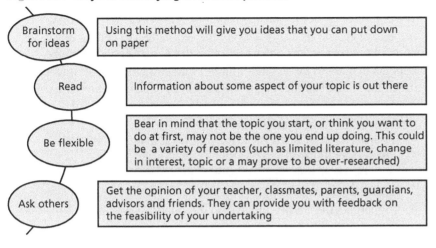

What are the elements to focus on in the selection of the research problem? Asking yourself the following questions can lead to the selection of your research problem:

- How can my research improve the standard of living in society? (The goal of social research is to find solutions for societal problems.)
- Which societal problems are the most pressing and require the attention of researchers?
- Which of these problems need an urgent solution?
- Do I want to dedicate the time, effort and commitment to undertake this research?
- Can my research findings and recommendations make a difference?

Check Your Knowledge

Lance lives in Speightstown, Barbados, and is concerned with the residents' practice of improper garbage disposal along the coast and poor farming practices that include the use of chemical fertilisers and pesticides, and he knows that this is bad for both the environment and humans. On which topic(s) could he conduct his research?

I. An investigation into the effect of the environment on residents in Speightstown.

II. An investigation into how improper garbage disposal affects the residents in Speightstown.

III. The use of chemical fertilisers is responsible for the poor crop yield for residents in Speightstown.

IV. Examine to what extent residents' poor farming practices affect the water supply system of residents in Speightstown.

A. I and III only

B. II and IV only

C. I, II and III

D. II, III and IV

The correct answer to this is B. These two research topics, II and IV, relate to the case that he is interested in. I is an incomplete idea and does not express a research problem, while III is a hypothesis.

Significance of the Study

The Significance of the Study is usually referred to as the 'Rationale'. It is the explanation or justification of the worthiness of conducting that particular research. It is a description of the work's importance, the benefits that are to be derived from the study and the overall impact that it will have. The Significance provides a brief explanation of why your research topic is worthy of study and why it may have a significant impact on the body of already existing research.

The researcher must consider the following in presenting the Significance of the Study:

- How the study will fill knowledge gaps in that area or promote further research.
- The impact the study will have on the public as well as those in the field of research.
- The practical benefits to be derived.
- The influence it might have on public policy.

Example

The researcher sees that every student has an electronic device that they use while travelling on the bus to school, but their conversations tend to show how ignorant they are of the dangers of using these devices to post information. This is cause for alarm as there is a generation of young people who appear to have little understanding of the repercussions of the inappropriate use of technology.

Recent laws have made it illegal to post videos, comments or pictures which are deemed to be cyber-bullying, sexting, sextortion, gang violence, acts of terrorism and pornography. The fact that students' lives can be ruined because of their ill-thought out actions is cause for concern. The researcher feels that this topic needs to be investigated and it is for this reason that he has decided to analyse the effects of posting inappropriate information over the internet on students' academic careers.

Literature Review

No research is complete without a **literature review**, which is the foundation of research because it summarises the findings or assertions of previous research. A literature review is:

- a critical analysis and summary of a published body of knowledge;
- the researcher's conclusions about the topic.

In conducting research, there are numerous authentic sources from which you can gather information for your literature review. The main sources from which you should gather information are textbooks, statistical reports, archives, minutes of meetings, newspaper reports, internet sources and oral histories. You will definitely need to read widely when constructing a literature review.

Benefits of conducting a literature review:

- Allows the researcher to gather current findings about the research topic.
- Provides greater understanding of an unfamiliar topic.
- Gives new ideas that can be utilised by the researcher.
- Prevents the researcher from doing what has already been done.
- Allows the researcher to identify flaws and problems of previous research.

Key Term

Literature review – an evaluative report of existing literature related to an area of study. It should summarise, evaluate and compare the literature, provide a theoretical base for research and help determine the nature of the research.

- Highlights conflicts between the views of different authors.
- Provides the researcher with options in the selection of possible approaches.

Once the literature review has been completed, the researcher should:
- have a solid foundation of knowledge in the area;
- have a clearer understanding of where their research will go and what questions they need to pose;
- know the experts he will need to consult if questions about the topic arise.

To summarise, the purpose of the literature review is to:
- identify and discuss the sources that have contributed to your research topic;
- define, refine, establish and focus your research topic;
- provide information about the viewpoint your research will take;
- draw attention to inaccuracies in previous research;
- justify your research by showing there has been previous interest in the area and by highlighting gaps in the previous research which your research can help fill.

> **Exam Tip**
>
> It is important to understand that for a literature review you must do more than write a summary listing what each source has advanced; rather, you should synthesise the information as a whole in order to provide your perspective on it. In essence, you must identify what is relevant, what is questionable and what is lacking from the existing literature.

Research Objectives

So, you have selected a research problem, now what? The next step is to identify the objectives of your research.

Writing Research Objectives

Research objectives, which summarise or describe what is to be achieved in the project, are used as statements of purpose for the study. These objectives provide you with the HOW of your research topic. In essence, how do you intend to achieve the aim of your research? There are two types of objectives, general and specific.

> **Key Terms**
>
> **General objective** – the stated intention of a study that expresses what the researcher expects to achieve by the study in general terms and why. This is your **Problem Statement**.
> For example: To investigate the effectiveness of warning labels on cigarette packages to deter teen smoking.
> **Specific objectives** – objectives that describe the variables which are to be measured by the study. They are logically connected parts of the general objective and systematically address the various aspects of the problem.
> For example: To determine if the warning labels catch the attention of the consumers; to identify the understandability and clarity of pictorial messages and symbols.
> **Problem Statement** – the statement that guides the general purpose or aim of the research project.

> **Exam Tip**
>
> Consider having one general objective for your research, which is your Problem Statement. From that general objective, you then generate specific objectives or research questions.

A formulated research problem provides a description of the intention of your investigation in the form of a **Problem Statement**, while the research objectives give a precise description of the specific actions you will take in order to achieve this goal. A research objective channels the investigation of the variables in the research.

Research objectives:

- need to be clear and succinct statements;
- are either formulated or refined after the literature review has been written, and are often directly informed by the literature review;
- narrow the focus of the study – this prevents the researcher from collecting data that are not relevant to the problem being studied;
- provide specificity – they ensure that the research is geared at a specific area of a theme;
- guide the information – they organise the study into clearly defined parts.

Formulating Objectives from the General to the Specific

Key Terms

Understanding the different terms and how they relate:

Term	Definition
Problem Statement	A statement that provides the general objective, purpose or aim of the research project. It is a researchable problem that is to be investigated. For example: *To investigate factors associated with violence against female employees in the hotel industry.* It can be written as a question: *Does income influence the eating patterns of students in a named high school?*
Statement of the Problem	An expansion of the Problem Statement, where the variables and relationships are explained. It acts as a guide for the researcher and the readers, so that they can see the direction that the research is taking, and it shows what is being investigated and what is not. From the Statement of the Problem, you are able to formulate the Research Objectives and/or Questions.
Research Objectives	These are precise statements specifying the key issues that will be the focus of the research project. Generally, a research project has a general objective and several specific research objectives. General Objective example: *To examine whether limited gender laws are associated with increased violence against female hotel employees.* Research objectives can also be framed as research questions.
Research Questions	Instead of providing research objectives, the researcher can use research questions. The major difference is that the key issues to be focused on are stated in the form of questions, for example: *Has the lack of gender laws contributed to increased violence against female hotel employees?* Specific Objectives: *Have gender laws been enacted in the country in the past 10 years?* *What are the violent acts committed against female hotel employees?* *Is there a connection between female workers feeling unprotected legally and the acts of violence committed against them in the hotel industry?*
Research Hypotheses	Research objectives can also be stated in the form of hypotheses. A hypothesis is the prediction of an association between two or more variables, usually predicting the effect of an independent variable on a dependent variable. **Independent variables** are measurable and are not influenced by the other variables that are being measured, while **dependent variables** depend on the independent variables. For example: *Increased violence* (independent variable) *against female hotel employees is associated with the lack of gender laws* (dependent variable).

Creating Specific Research Objectives and Questions

Specific research objectives and questions are very important, and must be included in your research project. They:

- focus the study;
- guide your research;
- determine the approach;
- guide the mode of investigation;
- determine the analysis;
- define the reporting;
- are related to your research purpose.

Research objectives can be expressed as research questions and vice versa. Below are some examples.

Research objectives	Research questions
To examine how the education reform policies in St Kitts address the needs of students in Cayon.	Do education reform policies in St. Kitts address the needs of students in Cayon?
To explore how hip hop videos of foreign artistes influence the style of dress of teens in West Caicos.	Do the hip hop videos of foreign artistes influence the style of dress of teens in West Caicos?
To examine how students' involvement in the performing arts influence their decision to pursue further study abroad.	Are students involved in the performing arts more likely to pursue further study abroad?

The Research Hypothesis

A **hypothesis** is a statement which predicts the cause-and-effect relationship between two or more variables.

A research hypothesis can be:
- an educated guess of conditions of a phenomenon;
- a prediction of a relationship between two variables;
- a tentative statement of a solution to a problem;
- a tentative point of view;
- a preliminary explanation;
- a proposition not yet tested.

A hypothesis is a specific statement that relates to a problem, presenting the answer as 'yes' or 'no' depending on the outcome of the research. For this reason, it is a useful tool to help focus general research problems for meaningful analysis.

Types of Hypothesis

- **Descriptive hypothesis** – describes a behaviour in terms of the specific characteristic so that it provides a goal for observation. It seeks to measure the behaviour. For example:

    Observance of Rastafarian customs influences the vegetarian eating patterns of the believers.

- **Working hypothesis** – is subject to adjustment and alteration as the investigation progresses. For example:

    There is a strong relationship between teens' attention span and the cereals they eat for breakfast.

Exam Tip

The following exercise will help you develop research objectives.

1. Using the recommended areas of investigation in the syllabus, choose a research topic that you have an interest in and develop a suitable general research objective or problem statement.

2. Develop three specific objectives for that research topic.

3. Change your research objectives into research questions.

Quick Facts

There is the tendency to confuse theories with hypotheses. Hypotheses are ideas and it is after those ideas have been tested that you can then arrive at explanation of those findings, which are referred to as theories.

Then

> *Teens who eat a heavy breakfast are more attentive than students who eat cereal for breakfast.*

- **Null hypothesis** – makes a prediction of no relationship or no significant difference existing between groups or variables. Usually this hypothesis is written as, 'There is no relationship (or difference)' between the groups.
  For example:

  > *There is no relationship between the students who pass more than six CSEC® exams and the involvement of their parents in their school life.*

- **Alternative hypothesis** – a prediction about the anticipated result, which is based on previous literature and studies about the topic. It is usually the hypothesis that the researcher wants to prove to be correct. For example:

  > *There is a relationship between students who pass more than six CSEC® exams and the involvement of their parents in their school life.*

In general, hypotheses are used only in quantitative research, not when conducting qualitative research.

Writing a Hypothesis

When you write a hypothesis, it must:
- make a prediction;
- be formulated in simple terms that are easily understood;
- identify at least two variables, an independent and a dependent variable, and make a clear distinction between them;
- provide the opportunity for refutation; this means that the results of the study can be open to being proven false;
- correspond to existing knowledge;
- seek to provide an acceptable explanation of fact.

The hypothesis is usually written after the research problem has been stated and the **literature review** has been conducted. It is then that you will be able to identify possible relationships between variables and the conditions that you want to test.

Example

Identifying variables

Let us practise identifying the dependent and independent variables, by using the statement provided.

(Remember: An **independent variable** is constant and unaffected by the other variables, while the **dependent variable** is dependent on other factors and is the one that is expected to change as a result of experimental manipulation of the independent variable(s).)

An investigation into how the hip hop videos of foreign artistes influence the style of dress of teens in West Caicos, Turks and Caicos.

The hip hop videos cause a change in teens' style of dress.
  independent variable   *dependent variable*

and it is not possible that

<u>teens' style of dress</u> could cause a change in <u>hip hop videos.</u>
   dependent variable   *independent variable*

Look at another example:

An investigation into the causes of violence against female employees in the hotel industry in Martinique.

The <u>causes of violence</u> cause a change in <u>female employees.</u>
   independent variable   *dependent variable*

and it is not possible that

<u>female employees</u> could cause a change in <u>causes of violence.</u>
 dependent variable   *independent variable*

Methods of Enquiry

Data collection is an integral part of any research project. It is the method by which the researcher collects information in order to answer their research questions. The data collection method selected can determine whether the results can be accepted or invalidated, depending on its suitability for purpose. In collecting data, the onus is on the researcher to decide:

- which data he will need to gather;
- how he will gather the data;
- when he will gather the data;
- who will collect the data.

Quantitative and Qualitative Research Methods

There are two major **methods of enquiry**, **qualitative** and **quantitative research**.

Key Terms

Methods of enquiry – the methods utilised in the collection of data for analysis.

Quantitative research – a method used in the collection and statistical analysis of numerical data, which is used to explain a specific phenomenon.

Qualitative research – a method of data collection which uses observation and interpretation to get a better understanding of the world. The results are often presented in a narrative or descriptive form.

Table 2.1 **Comparing qualitative and quantitative research**

	Qualitative	Quantitative
Purpose	Provides information about the 'human' side of an issue, such as beliefs, opinions, behaviours, intentions, emotions and relationships	Collection of numerical data which are then analysed statistically in order to be used to explain a specific phenomenon
The approach used	Observation and interpretation	Measurement and testing
Characteristic of the sample	Small samples, which are often in their natural setting; non-representative; purposeful	Large samples used to provide widespread results; precise and random representative sample
Data collection method	Unstructured; no constraints or stipulations; spontaneous responses	Structured responses; categories are provided from which respondents must choose
Examples of data collection methods	Interviews • Key informant • Semi-structured • Individual Focus group discussions Participant observations/field notes Logs, journals, diaries	• Random sampling surveys • Structured interviews • Population census • Questionnaires • Observation checklists
Researcher involvement	Intimately involved; trust emphasised; results are subjective because it involves examining and reflecting on perceptions, values and attitudes	Uninvolved, detached; results are objective because they measure the frequency, range and scale of a phenomena
Goals	To develop understanding of realities; have a concern or issue resolved; to understand social processes	To test theories; establish facts; predict relationships between variables; provide statistical descriptions of phenomena
Questions to answer	How? Why?	What? How many?

Qualitative Methods

The three most common qualitative methods are:

Focus groups	**In-depth interviews**	**Participant observation**
• effective in drawing out data on the cultural customs of a group • produce general ideas about issues of concern to the cultural groups or to the subgroups represented	• ideal when data on individuals' personal histories, experiences and perspectives are being investigated • especially appropriate for the study of delicate topics	• suitable for accumulating information on naturally occurring behaviours in their traditional environments

Quantitative Methods

The three most common quantitative methods are:

Survey/Questionnaire	**Observation schedule/ checklist**	**Document analysis**
• suitable for collecting homogeneous data from a large population • typically poses questions to bring about responses about facts, qualities, behaviours, inclinations, traits and attitudes	• suitable for gathering information about people, events and places using a checklist to identify frequency of a phenomenon	• suitable for obtaining relevant documented information that will help in the validation of facts in the research • especially important for the literature review

Surveys and Questionnaires

Table 2.2 The advantages and disadvantages of surveys and questionnaires

Advantages	Disadvantages
Allow for complete anonymity	Low response rate
Can be inexpensive to administer	Administered under the assumption that all respondents are literate
Easy to compare and analyse the information gathered from them	There is the risk of not getting careful feedback
Yields a lot of information	The wording of the questions can result in biased responses
Many sample questions already exist	Some responses may be incomplete
The questions can be created as open-ended and close-ended depending on the information that the researcher is seeking	The respondents have the option to complete or not complete the questionnaire
Close-ended questions are easy to analyse	Open-ended questions are time consuming to analyse
There is no interview bias	
Is administered to a large number of respondents	

The Structure of a Questionnaire

In constructing a questionnaire, there are three areas to focus on:
1. the introduction;
2. the demographic data;
3. the format of the questions.

In the **introduction**, you need to include:
- the title of the study;
- a brief summary of your school, class and course being studied;
- the purpose of the study that is tied to the questionnaire;
- the length of the questionnaire;
- a guarantee of confidentiality.

Example

Demographic data

Using the research topic, *An investigation into the causes of declining sales in craft items in the Castries Market, St Lucia,* the researcher has decided to interview vendors in the Castries Market, therefore these demographic data will be important:

Please tick the response that applies to you

Age: ☐ 17–21   ☐ 22–26   ☐ 27–31   ☐ 32–36   ☐ 37–41

☐ 42–46   ☐ 47–51   ☐ 52–56   ☐ 57–61   ☐ 62–66

☐ 67–71   ☐ 72–76   ☐ 77–81   ☐ Over 81 years old

Gender: ☐ Male   ☐ Female

Education   ☐ Primary School   ☐ Secondary School   ☐ Bachelor's

☐ Post-Graduate   ☐ Other (Explain) _____

Key Term

Surveys – methods of collecting information from a sample or fraction of a population that is being studied. The most common forms of surveys are telephone interviews, mail survey and in-person interviews.

Quick Facts

In today's world, advances in technology have brought about a change in the administration of questionnaires. In addition to face-to-face, telephone and pen-and-paper, there are now computerised questionnaires. These web-based surveys are administered online as the participants respond to the questionnaires by using the internet to access them.

The **format of the questions** should follow a basic structure:
- The first question should be a close-ended question: a Yes or No response.
- General questions precede specific questions.
- Questions considered as sensitive placed at the end of the questionnaire.
- Questions grouped according to topic.
- Instructions on how to answer should be placed before the questions.
- Questions that have rating scales should have the scale placed before the questions.

Example

Rating Scale Questions

Questions

Please indicate how much you agree with the following statements by choosing one response. To indicate your answer, please tick the box that corresponds with your response.

	Strongly disagree	Disagree	Neutral	Agree	Strongly agree	Unable to rate
Most of the participants' costumes leave nothing to the imagination.						
The Carnival participants who wear masks behave more outrageously than those without masks.						
The government does not do enough to censor the mode of dress during Carnival.						

Focus Groups

The intention of **focus groups** is to get feedback in the form of perceptions, opinions and attitudes, by facilitating discussion and comments about the topic being studied.

Typically, a focus group:
- lasts one to two hours
- has between six and 12 participants
- is led by a moderator or facilitator who poses open-ended questions
- provides the researcher with insights which he gathers from listening to the group
- is non-structured, allowing for the study of people in their natural setting.

Key Term

Focus groups – groups of individuals selected and assembled to provide insight into themes or ideas that the researcher wishes to investigate.

Table 2.3 **The advantages and disadvantages of focus groups**

Advantages	Disadvantages
The views and experiences of a selected group of individuals are gathered through structured discussion	Participants' reactions may be different if they become self-conscious of the setting
Provides shared insight into the participants' common perception of everyday life	The discussion may be dominated by one or two members of the group
Might be quickly arranged and relatively inexpensive	Might be difficult to arrange around the schedules of the selected participants and could prove to be expensive
A quick means of gathering thoughts, impressions and perceptions	Unnecessary information, which bears no relevance on the topic, may be provided
Allows for the examination of participants' reactions to each other	Analysing the responses can be difficult
An efficient way to collect information that has much significance and range	

In-depth Interviews

Table 2.4 Advantages and disadvantages of in-depth interviews

Advantages	Disadvantages
Provides more detailed information when compared to other data collection methods	Requires a highly trained interviewer who does nothing to influence the responses
Can provide important information, especially when used in conjunction with other data collection methods	The results cannot be used for generalisation. This is because small samples are chosen and the random sampling methods are not utilised
Provides a more peaceful atmosphere for data collection	An interest in the phenomena may lead to biased interview responses
Ideal for use when respondents are not comfortable sharing information in a group setting such as a focus group	The interview process (conducting the interview, transcribing and analysing the results) can be very time consuming

Did You Know?

There are three key principles to bear in mind when conducting in-depth interviews.

1. Ask factual questions before asking opinion questions. For example, ask 'What are the major features of J'ouvert?' before you ask 'What do you think about activities that take place during J'ouvert?'

2. The questions asked should be open- not close-ended. For example, do not ask 'Has J'ouvert evolved over the years?' Rather, ask 'How has J'ouvert changed over the years?'

3. When necessary, use probing questions. For example:
   - Would you give me an example?
   - Could you explain further?
   - Could you elaborate on that?
   - Is there anything else?

Participant and Non-participant Observation

Table 2.5 Advantages and disadvantages of participant observation

Advantages	Disadvantages
Allows for the observation of natural behaviour	The researcher can become biased and attached, losing his objectivity
The researcher develops a close relationship with the respondents. This leads to acceptance and inclusion in activities which provide him with an up-close perspective	Close association to the subjects can lead to biased interpretation of data
Immersion in the group allows for a better understanding of the respondents' feelings	The researcher's presence can lead to an artificial environment
The researcher has the opportunity to view and participate in various activities – scheduled and unscheduled	The researcher faces the challenge of simultaneously collecting data and participating
Provides direct information	It is very time intensive

Key Term

In-depth interviews – involves conducting interviews with a select group of individuals. The researcher probes aspects of the participants' feelings, attitudes, beliefs, and so on, with a view to discovering the respondent's perspective on an issue, situation or idea.

Key Terms

Observation – a systematic method of data collection. It is the observation or examination of people in their natural settings and then methodically recording those results.

Participant observation – the process in which a researcher studies people in their natural setting by observing and participating in the activities so that they can learn about them, by blending in and becoming a part of the setting before removing themselves in order to analyse and process the data.

Non-participant observation – the qualitative process of observation in which the researcher observes the subjects, but is separate from them and does not participate in the activities.

Table 2.6 **Advantages and disadvantages of non-participant observation**

Advantages	Disadvantages
The researcher is objective and neutral	The researcher's findings tend to be subjective; he does not have the opportunity to seek clarity of events and activities
Allows for careful analysis of all aspects of the phenomena	The researcher is only able to observe what he sees; complexities are off-limits because the researcher is on the outside
Respondents are more willing to share secrets and weaknesses with strangers	An awareness of being observed can lead participants to become uncomfortable; this can cause 'unnatural' information

Key Terms

Primary sources – first-hand sources of information that have not been interpreted.

Secondary sources – sources of information or material that were derived from primary sources.

Quick Facts

It is useful to think of primary sources of data as data that have been gathered from the information source and have not yet undergone analysis.

It is useful to think of secondary sources of data as data that have been collected over time and undergone at least one round of analysis before being presented.

Check Your Knowledge

One disadvantage of participant observation is that:

A. The researcher has to rely on memory, and this can prove to be difficult in capturing all the important data.

B. It provides direct contact with the subjects.

C. The researcher develops a close relationship with the respondents.

D. An awareness of being observed can cause the respondents to generate 'unnatural' information.

A is the answer to this. As an active participant the researcher must ensure that he is not conspicuous, therefore not taking copious notes would help. This is why he has to rely on his memory and this may lead to some key information being forgotten or omitted.

Use of Primary and Secondary Materials

Data can be collected from two sources.

1. **Primary data collection** involves the use of experiments, surveys and direct observations to gather information. Primary data is also data that the researcher collects himself. For example, interviews, observations and life histories are primary data.

2. **Secondary data collection** involves collecting information from documents or electronically stored information. These are data that already exist. Collecting data from a secondary source is often referred to as 'data mining'. The census of any country, such as that from the Statistical Institute of Jamaica (STATIN), is a common source of secondary data.

Table 2.7 **Sources of data collection**

	Primary sources of data collection	Secondary sources of data collection
Definition	Sources of information that provide first-hand evidence, information that has not been interpreted; it is data created by a witness or participant of an event	Sources of information or material that analyse, evaluate and interpret information contained in primary sources or even other secondary sources
When to use	• To get the original conclusions of previous researchers • To facilitate for your own analysis of information rather than depending on the interpretation of others	• To uncover historical or background information about a topic • To expose the researcher to the perspectives, interpretations and conclusions of others
Examples	Autobiographies, oral histories, speeches, manuscripts, interviews, surveys, court records, websites, art, music, translation of an original document, memoirs, diaries, opinion polls, treaties, maps, photographs, government records, letters, correspondences, eyewitnesses, first-hand newspaper and magazine accounts of events, opinion polls, emails, scientific data transcripts, artefacts of a period	Books, biographies, literature reviews, dictionaries, encyclopaedia, newspapers, magazines, commentaries, reviews (art, music, movie, theatre), websites (can also be primary sources)

Sampling

Part of the process of conducting research is the collection of primary data, which requires that you:

1. identify your **target population**;
2. select your representative **sample**;
3. make your findings, which are then generalised to the target population.

Target Population

The target population is:

- the population that the researcher wants to generalise to;
- the population from which the researcher intends to select the sample in order to make a generalisation of findings;
- the entire group from which the researcher wishes to draw implications.

For example, a researcher's target population is the families who live along rivers in Guyana, and so he collects information on families who live along the Essequibo River in Guyana. What the researcher has done is used the accessible population.

Sample Selection

Sample selection is necessary because we cannot study the entire population due to constraints such as lack of feasibility and cost. Imagine undertaking a research on the factors that contribute to people having respiratory problems in an island such as Saba. It would not be feasible or cost effective to study the entire population of over 1,900 citizens. Instead it would be best to choose a sample, from St Johns or The Bottom. The findings would then be generalised to the entire population.

Figure 2.2 **How sampling works**

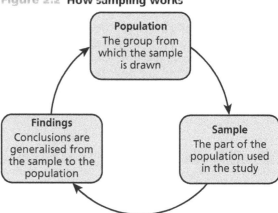

The utilisation of a sampling method in research is essential because of how useful it can be in providing key data. It is best to use a sample when:
- the population is very large, and using a sample would capture a true representation of that population;
- the population is homogenous or has similar characteristics;
- the researcher is short of time and money.

Probability and Non-probability Sampling

In order to identify the size of your sample, you will need to select an appropriate sampling method. There are two types of sampling method:
1. Probability Sampling
2. Non-probability Sampling.

Probability Sampling

In **Probability Sampling**:
- Conclusions can be drawn about the population from which the sample has been selected because it provides a representative sample.
- There is the 'equal probability of selection', which means that there is the same likelihood of selection for every **element** in the population.

Key Terms

There are six types of probability sampling:

1. Simple Random Sampling	4. Cluster Sampling
2. Systematic Random Sampling	5. Multistage Sampling
3. Stratified Random Sampling	6. Multiphase Sampling

Figure 2.3 **The basic steps in sampling**

Step 1. Define the target population All the people who make up the population from which the sample will be drawn	EXAMPLE The Population Tourists who visit St Eustatius
Step 2. Select the Sample Frame A list of the population is where you would get your sample from. A subset of the population is chosen	The Sample Tourist couples who travel to St Eustatius to hike on The Quill
Step 3. Choose a Sample Technique The means by which the sample is chosen is needed. The two methods are Probability and Non-probability Sampling	Sample Technique – Non-probability Sampling Purpose Sampling used as the researcher has handpicked the couples based on their experience of hiking on The Quill trail

1. **Simple Random Sampling** – every member of the sample is selected from the total population in such a way that every member has the same probability of being chosen.
   The steps involved in Simple Random Sampling are:
   a. define the target population;
   b. create a **sampling frame**;
   c. assign a unique number to each element in the population;
   d. determine the sample size;
   e. select the sample size randomly.

Key Term

Sampling Frame – a complete list of all the members of the population that the researcher wishes to study.

Did You Know?

There are three ways in which sample elements can be selected.

- The Lottery or 'Blind Draw' Method – numbers representing each element are placed in a vessel and shuffled. The numbers are pulled out until the sample size has been selected.
- Table of Random Numbers – the numbers are arranged randomly in a table and the researcher blindly selects a starting point and systematically selects numbers from the table until the sample size has been chosen.
- Random Number Generator – a computer program selects the sample in a random manner.

The sampling method is appropriate when the population is small and homogenous. The benefits are:
- it allows for the selection of the greatest number of possible samples;
- every element has the opportunity to be chosen;
- the elimination of bias that comes with using a table of random numbers.

Example

A student wants to conduct a research into the types of crimes people in the North East Division of Trinidad are arrested for. The report shows that 300 people have been arrested in 2014. This will be his population and he will randomly select 30 people for his sample, which he will use to gather information on the types of crimes that they have been arrested for.

2. **Systematic Random Sampling** – this technique organises the target population so that the elements can be selected. The researcher randomly selects the first item and then the 'nth' elements, which are chosen at regular intervals. To do this:
   - the researcher selects a random point at which to begin;
   - then the researcher choses his interval, which is constant, and this is the progression that he uses to select his sample.

Example

A researcher is conducting a study on the effect of students' sleeping habits and their use of electronic devices. The researcher has 230 students at St Martin High School in St Vincent and the Grenadines from which he will choose his sample of 20. The researcher follows these steps:

a. The random starting point he selects is 9.
b. He then choses an interval of 11. Consequently, he selects the following individuals for his sample – 20, 31, 42, 53, 64, 75, 86, 97, 108, 119, 130, 141, 152, 163, 174, 185, 196, 207, 218, 229.

3. **Stratified Random Sampling** – this sampling technique divides the population into different strata or subsets (usually homogenous and without overlaps). The sample is then selected from each stratum or subset.

   The steps in Stratified Random Sampling are:
   a. define the target population;
   b. pinpoint the number of strata and the classifications, such as single-parent household or two-parent household;
   c. develop a sampling frame;
   d. divide the sampling frame into the strata (the strata must have no overlap);
   e. assign a distinctive number to each element;
   f. determine the sample size for each strata;
   g. randomly select the determined number of elements from each stratum.

   In Stratified Random Sampling, determining the size of the strata can be done using:
   a. proportionate stratified sampling – sampling where the representative number of elements in each stratum is proportionate to the target population, so that the sample size from each stratum represents the population size in each stratum;
   b. disproportionate stratified sampling – the disproportionate allocation of the representative number of elements in each stratum of a target population. This does not allow the elements an equal chance of being selected for the sample.

Example

A researcher was investigating the quality of CSEC® passes for high school students in Jamaica. He decided to look at three strata – all-boys, all-girls and co-educational institutions. He then selected his sample in proportion to the number of schools. He found six all-boys, seven all-girls and 17 co-educational institutions. He needed to select a sample of 50 students, so he used the ratio of 6:7:17. Figure 2.4 provides an outline of the final sample that the researcher would use for this research.

Figure 2.4 **Stratified Random Sampling example**

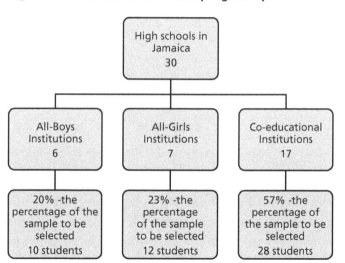

Did You Know?

If the researcher in the example had chosen a disproportionate sample within the strata, he would have used a percentage that was *not* in proportion to the number of schools. Look at the example below to get a clear understanding of proportionate and disproportionate stratified sampling:

You are looking at the relationship between the appointment to government positions and the recipients' political affiliation in St Lucia. The political parties, St Lucia Labour Party (SLP) and the United Workers Party (UWP) are the two dominant parties. The population comprises 51 per cent SLP supporters and 49 per cent UWP supporters. You want a sample size of 100 and you intend to stratify on the basis of political affiliation.

- For proportional stratified sampling, you would randomly select 51 SLP supporters and 49 UWP supporters from the population.
- For disproportionate sampling, you would randomly select 50 SLP supporters and 50 UWP supporters from the population.

4. **Cluster Sampling** – a sampling technique in which groups or clusters of the population are chosen for analysis. In Cluster Sampling, the population is divided into clusters or subgroups, following which a random sample of the subgroups is selected and all the members of the selected clusters are surveyed. Cluster Sampling is best used when the population that the researcher wishes to sample is large. One of the most common methods of clustering is a geographical cluster. This sampling, also known as area sampling, is useful when the population is widespread as it treats population within local areas as clusters, which makes them easier to manage.

Did You Know?

Drawbacks to Cluster Sampling

Similarities in characteristics can lead to cluster sampling being less efficient because during the design stage the selected sample can be over or under represented. The end result is a sample that does not truly represent the population.

Limited clusters can lead to a large portion of the population being omitted and this can lead to a high sampling error.

The Steps in Cluster Sampling are:
1. Identify and define the population.
2. Identify the size of the sample needed.
3. Identify and delineate the cluster.
4. List the clusters.
5. Estimate the average number of population per cluster.
6. Determine the number of clusters needed for the research.
7. Randomly select the clusters needed using the table of random numbers.
8. Include all the elements for the selected clusters.

Example

A researcher planned to conduct research on how housing developments affect the environment in the Dominican Republic.

- The researcher divided the country into cities with new housing developments, which represent the clusters – A: Santo Domingo, La Vega, Santiago; B: Salcedo, La Romana, San Francisco de Macorís; C: San Pedro de Macorís, Moca, Puerto Plata, Higüey; D: Pedernales, Hato Mayor, Isla Soana.

- Next, he selected a number of clusters using random sampling – Sample A: Santiago La Vega, Santo Domingo, and Cluster D: Pedernales, Hato Mayor, Isla Soana.

- The researcher samples all the elements from each cluster.

You will notice from Figure 2.5 that, from the four original clusters, two clusters are chosen and all the elements of the selected clusters are used in the sample.

Figure 2.5 How cluster sampling works

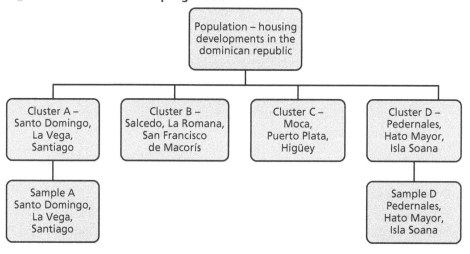

5. **Multistage Sampling** – this technique is a kind of cluster sampling in which samples are selected at different stages, reducing the sample at each stage of the selection of the sample. It differs from the other sampling techniques because it uses more than one stage.

Quick Facts

The difference between Cluster Sampling and Multistage Sampling:

In Cluster Sampling the researcher selects the primary units and then selects all the elements from the secondary unit, while in Multistage Sampling only some of the elements from the second stage are selected.

Figure 2.6 How multistage sampling works

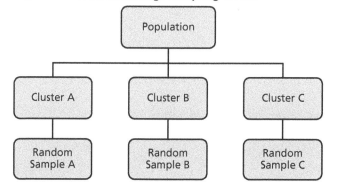

Example

A researcher wishes to collect a sample for his research, 'An investigation into the relationship between where teens live and their performance in sporting activities in St Lucia'.

- First, the researcher randomly selects the quarters that St Lucia is divided into: Canaries, Gros Islet, Dennery, Vieux Fort and Mixoud.
- From each area, he randomly selects a village.
- Next he randomly selects some of the homes with teens in sports and arrives at his sample.

6. **Multiphase Sampling** – also known as double sampling, this is a technique in which the sample units are selected at different stages. Some information is collected from the entire sample, while another set of information is taken from a sub-sample.

Example

A researcher conducted a research on causes of the evolution of music in Trinidad and Tobago. In the first phase the researcher selected his sample from musicians who play all music genres in the countries. In the second phase, he selected Calypso musicians to yield information on how the tradition has changed.

Non-probability Sampling

Non-probability sampling:

- cannot be generalised back to the population to answer 'how many'-related research questions;
- may be subjected to bias in the selection of the sample;
- has no set means of allowing an element being guaranteed selection.

1. **Convenience Sampling** – in Convenience Sampling the elements are selected on the basis of availability and convenience. Also known as grab sampling, accidental sampling or opportunity sampling. The sample is drawn from prospective respondents who are:
   - nearby;
   - readily available.

Example

A researcher conducted research on the religious groups in St Croix and, because he lives close to the St Paul's Episcopal Anglican Church, he interviewed the church goers who pass his home to attend the church.

However, by conducting the survey at this church only, the researcher has not chosen a representative sample of the group.

2. **Purposive Sampling** – this sampling, also called Judgment Sampling, uses a method of selection in which the researcher's personal judgment is utilised in selecting the elements of the sample. Sampling is done based on unique and specific criteria that relate to the research. The selection of the elements is based on the most appropriate and on convenience. Only the regular elements qualify;

those that fall under the description of extreme are eliminated. It is best to use purposive sampling when:
- the sampling unit is small;
- there is the need to address urgent issues;
- the researcher has a definite understanding of the population.

Example

A researcher investigated students at a named high school who are known to supplement the financing of their education by selling snacks on the school compound. The students selected are those who supplement the financing of their education by 'selling snacks' and because they meet the criteria outlined by the research.

3. **Quota Sampling** – this is a sampling method of collecting representative information from a group. In quota sampling:
   - the population is separated into mutually exclusive subgroups;
   - the researcher then uses personal judgment as to the selection of the elements;
   - the selection of the sample is non-random;
   - the members of the sample group have some common characteristics;
   - the common characteristics may be related to age, gender, income, education, etc.

Example

A researcher is planning to conduct research on the relationship between the socio-economic status of students and the type of schools that they attend. There are 3,500 students, with 1,600 in the lower class, 1,200 in the middle class and 700 in the upper class (based on the income levels of their parents). The researcher wants a sample of 70 students, so he plans to use quota sampling with 32 from the lower class, 24 from the middle class and 14 from the upper class.

(The researcher selected this sample based on the relative proportions of the subsets.)

4. **Snowball Sampling** – a sampling technique that uses references to identify and select respondents. The researcher collects information from those identified as possible participants and gathers information from them about others who fit the criteria. This technique is used when:
   - it is difficult to identify the members of that particular population;
   - the elements of the population are difficult to get to;
   - the research is exploratory in nature.

Example

A researcher conducted research on street children and how they get an education. Her initial respondents were two young ladies who live on the streets but still attend school. She asked them to refer others to her, who they knew were in the same situation as themselves. Since official records were likely to be incomplete or inaccurate given the transient nature of the population in question, the researcher would not have had information on all the students who are living on the streets nor would she have had easy access to that population, this technique was the most suitable.

Forms of Presenting Data and Techniques for Analysis

Presenting Data

In research, there is usually the need to include statistical data that they have collected from primary sources. There are three fundamental ways to present this data. Information can be included by:
1. presenting the information in tabular form;
2. using the information in a graph or chart;
3. incorporating the data in the text.

The form you use to present data is dependent on:
- the volume of data you have to present;
- how complex the data are;
- the topic you are conducting the research on;
- the audience you are presenting the data to.

Tabular Presentation of Data

A table is a diagram that has columns and rows that contain organised data. Tables:
- are useful to show comparison between data;
- present small amounts of alphanumeric data.

1. **Frequency Distribution Table** – this presents the value of an element and the number of times that value appears.

Key Terms

Some types of tables used to present data are:
- Frequency Distribution Table
- Cumulative Frequency Distribution
- Stem and Leaf Plots

Example

A researcher has collected information on the topic 'An investigation into the relationship between texting and students' poor performance in English Language'.

The researcher collected the results of 75 students at Maryville Comprehensive High School who sat English Language at CSEC® level in 2014. The table below is a frequency distribution table showing the passes in English Language.

Figure 2.7 Table showing the frequency distribution of CXC® passes in English Language

Passes obtained	Tally	Frequency of passes
1	IIII	4
2	ʇʜʇ ʇʜʇ III	13
3	ʇʜʇ ʇʜʇ ʇʜʇ ʇʜʇ ʇʜʇ III	28
4	ʇʜʇ ʇʜʇ ʇʜʇ II	17
5	ʇʜʇ ʇʜʇ III	13

2. **Cumulative Frequency Distribution Table** – this type of table indicates the frequency of occurrence of particular values of a data set. In this table:
   - its usefulness is in determining the number of occurrences that fall above or below a value in the data set;
   - it shows the frequency of the occurrences over the different categories;
   - the cumulative frequency, or running total, is arrived at by adding each frequency;
   - the last value must add up to the total of all the observations.

Example

A researcher collected data on 105 respondents and the distance that they travel to school each day. Her results were:

Kilometres travelled daily: 8, 10, 3, 7, 6, 10, 4, 8, 10, 5, 8, 6, 10

She presented the data in a cumulative frequency table.

Figure 2.8 **Cumulative frequency table of the distance that students travel to school daily**

Distance travelled	Frequency	Cumulative frequency
3	1	1
4	1	1 + 1 = 2
5	1	2 + 1 = 3
6	2	3 + 2 = 5
7	1	5 + 1 = 6
8	3	6 + 3 = 9
10	4	9 + 4 = 13
Total		13

3. **Stem and Leaf Plot** – a graphic means of displaying rank order and the shape of the distribution of data. It is best used when the data are not numerous. It is useful in the identification of outliers or extreme values in the data.

   A Stem and Leaf Plot, when turned on the side, resembles a bar graph or a histogram. You are able to easily identify the median and the mode from this simple graph.

   Creating a stem and leaf plot is similar to creating a frequency table in that it is grouped.
   - Construct the stem and leaf plot.
   - Place the **stem units on the left side** of the vertical line. These are usually the first digits of the numeric result.
   - Place the **leaf units on the right side** of the vertical line. These are usually the last digit of the numeric result.

Example

The following data were collected about 20 students' fitness level, specifically their performance in one-minute sit-up exercises.

78 89 47 94 76 60 76 65 49 91 96 74 49 93 70 86 40 63 67 108

Figure 2.9 **Stem and Leaf Plot showing total number of sit-ups that each student completes in one minute**

STEM	LEAF
4	0 7 9 9
5	
6	0 3 5 7
7	0 4 6 6 8
8	6 9
9	1 3 4 6
10	8

Graphic Presentation of Data

Charts and graphs are graphic representations of data. They are useful tools for presenting, summarising and exploring numerical data. Large amounts of data are ideally presented in graph form, while a table would be ideal to present a smaller collection of data. Graphs generally have an x-axis (horizontal) and a y-axis (vertical). The type of chart or graph used to present the data is determined by:

- what they need to show;
- the amount of data to be displayed;
- the trends and patterns that need to be illustrated;
- the correlation between variables;
- the frequency of the occurrence of the event;
- the comparison that needs to be made.

Regardless of the form you use to present data, there are some key elements that must be included:

- A title, which should provide all the information that the reader will need to understand the data.

For graphs:
- the x-axis title, which must be clearly labelled and should identify the category or value;
- y-axis title, which must be clearly labelled and identify the unit of measure for the data.

For charts:
- the key or legend, which must identify the colours, patterns or symbols used to represent the data.

1. **Bar graphs or bar charts** – these are graphic displays of **discrete data**. They are columns on graphs. They are used to:
   - compare the number of different discrete groups, by representing categories such as genres in music – Calypso, Reggae, Rock, Hip Hop, Rap, Pop;
   - illustrate the frequency of categories;
   - show change over time, such as rainfall totals in January, February and March.

Key Terms

The types of charts or graphs used to present quantitative data are:
1. bar graphs or bar charts
2. histograms
3. line graphs
4. pie charts
5. pictographs
6. maps.

Key Term

Discrete Data – data that can only have values and are counted. They can be categorical (such as gender) or numeric (such as weight of students).

Bar graphs can be drawn horizontally or vertically.

Example

Research conducted yielded the following results for the denominations of 75 students of Island Harbour in Anguilla.

Baptist	5	Seventh Day Adventist	14
Jehovah's Witness	7	Pentecostal	12
Presbyterian	11	Non-denominational	8
Anglican	10	Other	4

Did You Know?

Frequency Polygons are a graphical device for understanding the shapes of distributions. They are similar to histograms, but are especially helpful for comparing sets of data.

Figure 2.10 **Bar graph showing the denominations of students of Island Harbour, Anguilla**

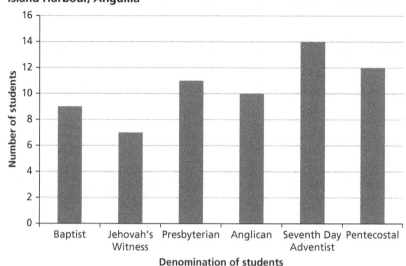

Key Term

Continuous data – data that can be measured. It has an infinite number of possible values within a selected range, such as temperature range.

2. **Histograms** – histograms are a special kind of bar graph that are used to organise and display large sets of quantitative data. They display **continuous data**, set in regular intervals along the x-axis, using bars with no space between the columns. In addition to a title and x- and y-axes, a histogram must contain:
   - the bars – the height and the width are extremely important. The width of each bar (on the x-axis) must be equal and represent the length of the interval. The height of each bar (on the y-axis) represents the frequency or number of times the value occurred;
   - the legend – this provides information about the source of the data and how the measurements were gathered.

3. **Line Graphs** – these are graphs that use line sections to display data results over time.
   Line graphs are ideal for revealing trends over time. They:
   - show categories or data that are grouped;
   - show time-series data, such as increases in the minimum wage over time;
   - reveal trends and relationships between data;
   - show relationship more clearly than tables;
   - compare trends in different groups of a variable.

Quick Facts

The difference between a bar chart and a histogram:

A bar chart has separate columns which are defined on the x-axis by a **categorical variable**, where no measurement is involved, while on the histogram the bars represent a **quantitative variable**, in which ordering and measuring take place.

Example

Research conducted on the number of artistes penalised in Trinidad and Tobago for the lyrical content of their songs over the past 10 years yielded the following results:

Year	2004	2005	2006	2007	2008	2009	2010	2011	2012	2013
Number of artistes penalised	12	17	13	19	24	25	18	22	27	21

Figure 2.11 **Line graph showing number of artistes penalised for lyrical content**

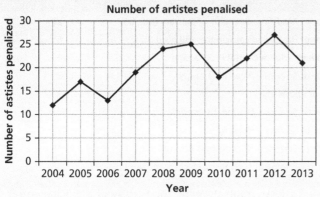

4. **Pie Charts** – charts that graphically depict parts of a whole as 'slices of pie' using data where the total is 100 per cent. Pie charts are best used:
   - when the data categories are relatively small;
   - to emphasise general findings.

Key Terms

Categorical variable – a variable that takes one finite or fixed value.

Quantitative variable – a numerical value (single or a range) or variable that can be measured.

Example

Research was conducted on the methods of solid waste management practices in Belize. The data collected was tabulated and then presented in a pie chart to show the proportion of practices utilised.

Waste management practices	Landfill dumping	Incineration	Recycling	Waste combustion to generate power	Composting
Percentage of responses	41	27	18	9	5

Figure 2.12 **Pie chart showing solid waste management practices in Belize**

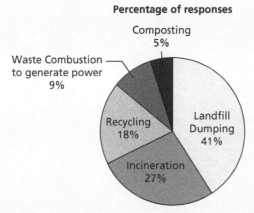

5. **Pictographs** – also called pictograms, these are graphs that display data using symbols, icons or pictures. Pictographs are variations of bar graphs, and should be used carefully as they can misrepresent data. It is important that they are visually accurate in order to be effective.

Example

A researcher collected data on the genders of students that enrolled in the Faculty of Medical Sciences at the University of the West Indies, Mona, in 2014:

Programme	Males enrolled	Females enrolled
Bachelor of Medicine, Bachelor of Surgery (MB, BS)	23	37
Bachelor of Basic Medical Sciences (BB Med Sci.)	65	45
DDS Undergraduate Dental Programme	15	19
Bachelor of Science – Physical Therapy	35	21
Doctor of Pharmacy	39	48
Bachelor of Science – Diagnostic Imaging	12	23
Bachelor of Science – Nursing	27	68
Bachelor of Science – Nursing Post RN	19	47
Advanced Diploma in Diagnostic Medical Ultrasound	43	31

Figure 2.13 **Pictograph showing the Faculty of Medicine enrolment of students by gender**

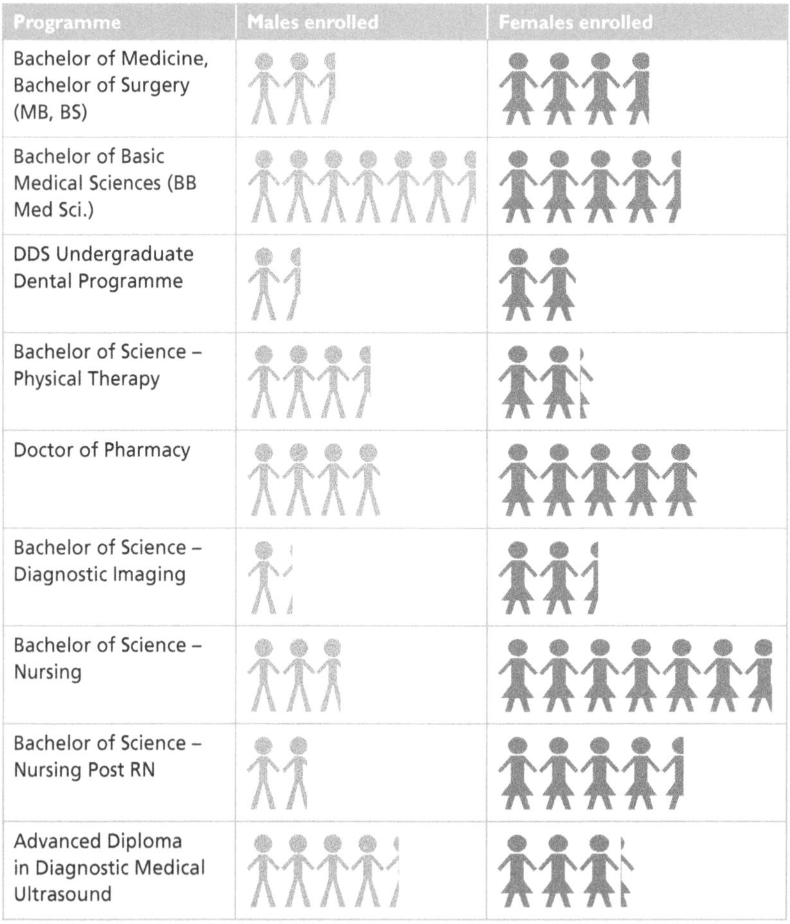

6. **Maps** – geographic representations of information that cannot be captured using other statistical data. Maps:
   - present areas, boundaries, locations and names of places;
   - help to create and present spatial patterns and distribution of data;
   - can identify distributions;
   - provide a large amount of information quickly and comprehensively;
   - compare different areas;
   - validate findings.

Example

Figure 2.14 Map of Castries, St Lucia, showing the international franchises that have established fast-food businesses

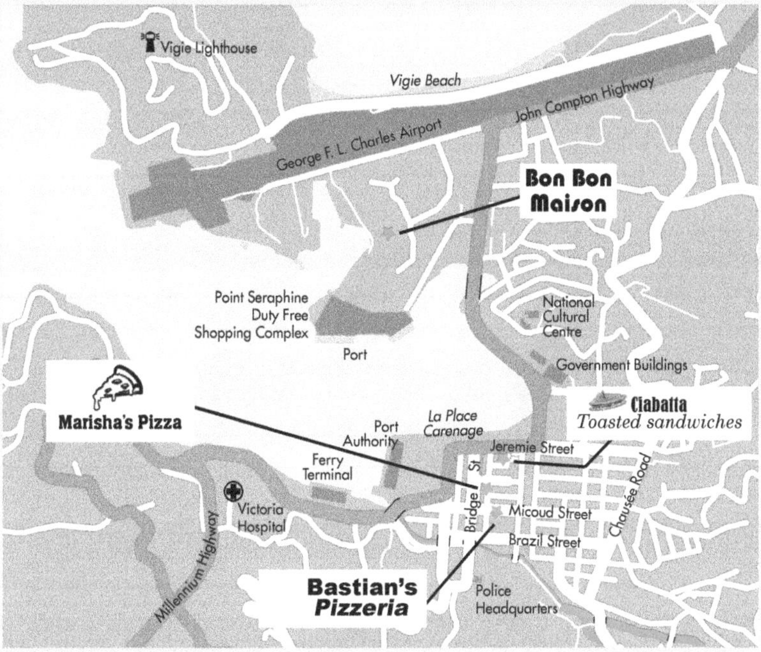

Textual Presentation of Data

Data can be presented textually by arranging them into sentence and paragraph form. The researcher uses words to convey pertinent information. Textual presentation:
- utilises statements to present and describes numerical data;
- focuses the readers' attention on important data;
- complements tabular data;
- highlights the most striking aspects of data.

Exam Tip

In presenting data, ensure that:

- all tables and figures are accompanied by textual data that explain the key findings;

- figures and tables do not repeat each other, that is, they should not be presenting the same information;

- there are no stand-alone tables and figures, they must be mentioned in the text.

Example

From the data collected, it was revealed that 80 per cent of the male respondents indicated that they practise more than 16 hours per week, compared to 55 per cent of female students.

Selection of Appropriate Forms to Present Data

The selection and use of modes of data presentation are determined by:
- the quantity of data to be presented;
- the objective of the research;
- whether the data is proportionate or absolute; discrete or continuous.

Figure 2.15 **When to use forms of data presentation**

Bar graphs
- To compare grouped data, such as results of an exam
- To compare categories, such as academic courses that students take at a community college
- To compare amounts in a single time period, such as weekly rainfall totals for the month of May

Histograms
- To show frequency, such as types of crime committed
- To represent grouped continuous variables, such as time students spend on the internet

Line graphs
- To show changes of continuous variables over time, such as yield of the crop of cayenne pepper over seven years

Pie charts
- To show differences in categories that are small in number, such as types of entertainment that married couples enjoy
- To represent data as parts of a whole, such as faculties and the percentage of students that enroll in them

Pictographs
- To show general differences between categories such as bottles of soda that students drink

Frequency polygons
- To compare grouped data that is continuous, such as weight of athletes

Stem and Leaf Plots
- To represent ungrouped data, such as the number of bottles of water that respondents drink weekly
- To present original data values, such as the number of songs dance hall artistes release in a year
- To compare two sets of ungrouped data, such as grades that male and female students score on a Biology test

Techniques for Analysing Data

After data have been organised into tables, charts, graphs and text, the researcher's next step is to analyse the data. Data analysis refers to the examination of data to unearth key findings, such as relationships, **trends**, **patterns** and **anomalies**. These findings apply meaning to the statistics revealed in the research process. Data analysis involves:
- collecting useful and useable information;
- description and summary of data;

- the identification of relationships between variables;
- the identification of differences between variables;
- the revelation of any significant change in the dependent variable or variables;
- making comparisons between variables;
- uncovering external factors that may have affected the dependent variable or variables;
- identifying potential reasons for the findings;
- laying the groundwork for possible solutions.

There are some important questions that you should focus on when preparing to analyse your data. Figure 2.16 provides some of the questions that you should seek to answer as you attempt to identify the relationships among data.

Figure 2.16 **Focus questions for analysis of data**

Identifying Trends

Identifying a trend involves asking the question, 'Has there been a change in the data?' This is then followed up with the next question, once the first has been answered, 'Is the change a normal change or a variation?' The process involves:

- assessing if there has been a decrease or increase over time;
- comparing the before and after of a time period;
- investigating the reason behind the change;
- making predictions based on the results.

Key Terms

Anomalies – deviations from the normal results in data; unusual results or results that fall outside of the normal ranges within a group.

Pattern – the evident repeated nature in which a series of results or data are yielded; a set of data that are yielded in a specific form.

Trend – the gradual change of a condition or an output over time; the general movement of an output or element.

Example

The results of a research on the use of aerial spraying to combat mosquito breeding and its effect on children with respiratory ailments show the following:

Year	2010	2011	2012	2013	2014	2015
Number of times aerial spray carried out	12	18	12	18	24	12
Children with respiratory ailments	26	35	21	40	56	28

The results were displayed on a line graph and the following trends were discovered:

- There is a direct relationship between the number of times that aerial spraying occurred and the number of children who developed respiratory problems.
- Generally, as the number of times aerial spraying occurrences increased, the number of children who develop respiratory problems increased.
- The years 2013 and 2014 show an unusual increase in the number of children who developed respiratory problems. This appears to be a departure from the general trend.
- The high number of 40 and 56 children being affected in these years may be attributed to more children being born in the area those years, or more families with children moving there, therefore more children would be affected.

Finding Patterns

Patterns are yielded when:
- there is a link between variables or results;
- the variables reveal a sequence such as when one variable influences another.

Example

A research was conducted on the relationship between students' performances in mock exams and the amount of time they spend studying. The pattern that was revealed was that the more hours students spent daily studying, the greater their chances of performing well on their mock exams, and ultimately their CSEC® and CAPE® examinations. In essence, the pattern shows that a change in one variable causes a change in the other variable, and in this case there is a positive correlation between students' study time and performance in exams.

Anomalies

Anomalies mean that some data are unlike any of the other data. Anomalies are readily identified because they stand out from the other values when presented.

Example

A student conducted a research on how effective security systems are to deter burglaries in an upscale community. The results showed a general decline in break-ins as more home owners installed surveillance security systems. One home, however, had an increase in the number of break-ins within a six-month period. This anomaly raised the question as to why thieves were still targeting this particular home.

The Categorisation and Comparison of Data

The **categorisation** and **comparison** of data are important because they allow the researcher to organise and reduce the data while keeping the meaning of the results. The ways to do so involve:

- organising themes and patterns into logical categories;
- assigning labels to the data;
- depicting the major ideas;
- identifying relationships;
- identifying themes and patterns.

1. **Categorisation** – this is the process of dismantling the data into groups or categories before compiling them to find the answer to the research questions. Categorisation aids in identifying patterns and themes in the data:
   - identifying the modal score;
   - showing relationships among categories of data.

2. **Comparison** – when comparing data, to derive the average and the range, we use measures of central tendency: the mean, the mode and the median.

Key Terms

Categorisation – this involves placing the data into groups based on categories, whether they are pre-set or created.

Comparison – this refers to the calculation of data and displaying them to show similarities and differences in results.

Key Terms

Measures of central tendency

The Mean – the mathematical average of a set of numbers. This is arrived at by adding the value of all the numbers and then dividing the result by the total number of scores. The mean is simply the average of the data.

Example: In conducting a research on students who attend evening school and plan to re-sit the CSEC® English A and Mathematics examinations, a researcher collected the ages of 10 respondents: 16, 21, 19, 22, 17, 18, 21, 21, 19 and 16.

The mean is calculated by adding the ages: 16 + 21 + 19 + 22 + 17 + 18 + 21 + 21 + 19 + 16 = 190

and then dividing the total by the number of scores: 190 ÷ 10 = 19

The average age of the respondents is 19 years old.

The Mode – this is the most frequently occurring value. To find the mode you simply select the value that occurs most often.

Example: Using the example above (16, 21, 19, 22, 17, 18, 21, 21, 19 and 16), we see that the mode is 21 years old because it occurred more frequently than any other value.

The Median – the middle score of the range of numbers.

Example: To find the median, we must first arrange the values from lowest to highest. The ages above are arranged in rank order, so the numbers would look like this: 16, 16, 17, 18, 19, 19, 21, 21, 21, 22

The Median would then be 19. Note that since the set of numbers is even (10), we need to get the average of the middle numbers. In this case it is 19 + 19 = 38, then 38 ÷ 2 = 19

In quantitative research, there is the need to analyse the results, and the measurements that the researcher might focus on, including comparing results. One way to do this is to triangulate the data. Triangulation is bringing the data that relate to the same issue together from the various sources in order to compare or contrast them. It is combining several sources of data. One major benefit of triangulation is that the use of several sources provides greater accuracy and acceptance of the results.

Example

Triangulation

You collected data using a questionnaire on the socio-economic status of people who purchase houses in Long Island, Nassau. Your sample was 20 residents. You also collected information about the price of the homes from realtors. In addition, you collected information on the number and price of houses sold, and the income of the purchasers from public records. The prices of 10 homes ranged from $200 000 to $1 500 000.

Your hypothesis is 'The price of homes in Long Island shuts out the lower class families'.

To triangulate, you use the income levels of the respondents and compare the results with the prices of the houses in the neighbourhood and the number of homes bought by people within the various income levels.

Data Analysis and Presentation

In the presentation of data, some results yielded can be statistically important or are not significant at all. In the analysis of data, it is key to look for:
- obvious findings – those findings that are immediately noticeable;
- differences – marked increases or decreases in the frequency of events;
- changes – significant changes in the dependent variables;
- patterns – results that are consistent;
- correlations – establishing if there is a connection between variables and the causes of the connections.

The means by which you present your data will determine how you will analyse your results. This simply means that you should be able to identify trends in the data and provide possible reasons for them if your research was focused on changes over a period of time.

Figure 2.17 Forms of data presentation and their connection to data analysis techniques

Data presentation	Data analysis techniques
Bar Charts	Identify patterns, relationships and comparisons
Histograms	Identify patterns, relationships and comparisons
Line Graphs	Identify trends over time
Maps	Identify spatial pattern, distribution patterns
Stem and Leaf Plot	Identify distribution patterns, anomalies, comparisons; Find median and mode
Pie Chart	Identify patterns and percentages, make comparisons
Pictograph	Identify multiple sets of data for comparison

Key Term

Conclusion – discusses the meaning of the results beyond what they show statistically. It gives an interpretation of the findings and a summary of what can be drawn from them.

Example

Sample Data Analysis

'It is possible that since 75 per cent of the respondents indicated their preference for taking local and regional vacations, they believe that the tourism sector is affected by the growing number of terrorist acts at international vacation sites. It could also be because the local and regional tourism sectors make their offers more attractive and provide better value for money, as opposed to the international tourism sector.'

Conclusions and Recommendations

Summary of Findings

Main findings Compared to Research Objectives

The main findings from your research project should be clear, logical and comprehensive. The main findings must be presented so that they can be followed, either by going backwards to arrive at the research questions or going forward to the **conclusion** without any confusion.

The interpretation of the results:

- involves restating the research topic and comparing and contrasting the findings with the research questions;
- explains what the data mean in relation to the research questions;
- discusses whether or not the findings support the hypothesis;
- incorporates the results with those of other researchers.

Areas of Contention in Relation to Research Objectives

In the discussion of findings, it is important to present a description of the trends, patterns and anomalies. The key findings of the data, and more importantly the 'whys', are necessary in the discussion. Focus should be on the connection between and among the variables, and comparing the groups or categories in the research. The following key findings should be described:

- unexpected results;
- emerging trends;
- minor findings.

New and Interesting Findings, if any

The research may yield new or interesting findings, so the researcher needs to present them in the study. Show how the findings substantiate, reject, contradict or add to the existing evidence, and discuss the implications of the data. Highlight the key findings in your discussion and say how the results impact the understanding of the research problem.

Limitations of the Research

Limitations are the restrictions or constraints that were evident in the research. Limitations refer to the problems encountered in conducting the research. The areas where they occur are usually:

- the sample size;
- data collection procedures;
- the measurement;
- access to sample.

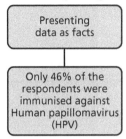

Figure 2.18 The difference between presenting data as facts and interpreting data

Presenting data as facts

Only 46% of the respondents were immunised against Human papillomavirus (HPV)

Interpreting data

The findings indicate that the drive to protect residents against HPV is not suffficient as a great number of the community run the risk of being infected with the virus. Additionally, the efforts to address the isssue of the shortage of vaccine indicate a lack of preparedness on the part of the health ministry to combat this growing problem.

Example

Stating limitations

'One limitation of this research was the size of the sample. Despite having a large population in the community, only a very small representative sample was willing to participate in the research process.'

This could have an effect on the researcher's ability to generalise the results to the population.

Areas for Further Research

In this area, do not include statistical data, rather, simply provide a summary of the findings and highlight what was unearthed in conducting the study. Make suggestions for further study by looking at the questions that were raised from carrying out the study.

Example

Recommendation for further research

'Researchers need to undertake a more intense research to determine the factors that influence the recent change in the mode of the male style of dress. They need to determine what has caused the change in attire in recent years, and then determine what types of males purchase the specific clothing that has become popular today.'

Exam Tip

The conclusion and recommendations must be based on the results that were yielded in the analysis of data. Your data collection instrument should have addressed the issues and it would be from those results that you would draw conclusions and make recommendations.

Recommendations

The recommendations are policies that address the key findings of the research or can be seen as actions to be implemented to address the problems found in the research project. They are based on the results of the research project. There are two types of recommendations that should be made:

1. Policy recommendations, which are related to the key findings in the research. The recommendations are guided by the results of the research project.
2. Recommendations for further research, which are recommendations for future research undertakings based on the results of your research.

Multiple-choice Questions

1. Data can be presented in
   A. text, patterns and correlations
   B. tables, graphs and texts
   C. frequencies, text and summary
   D. charts, summary and continuous data

2. Percentages are useful for showing
   A. relationships and comparisons between categories of responses
   B. examples of calculations and the results yielded
   C. measures of central tendency such as the mean and mode
   D. trends and patterns which are evident in the data

3. A researcher was able to observe the actions of participants as they reacted to the new traffic patterns in a city for a two-week period. This was not enough time to identify all the actions of the participants. A much longer time would have given a more accurate result of how the participants dealt with the changes. This situation is an example of
   A. discussion of findings
   B. limitations
   C. recommendations
   D. data presentation

4. Tables are ideal for presenting data when
   I.   the data set contains very few numbers
   II. showing a single category of information
   III. the data need to be easily understood
   IV. the tables have titles which provide details about the content in them.
   A. I and III only
   B. II and III only
   C. I and II only
   D. I, III and IV only

5. Information on a questionnaire that requires the respondent's age, income, education and employment status are classified as
   A. close-ended questions
   B. demographic data
   C. confidential data
   D. preliminary questions

6. A reporter took some pictures of the Soufrière Hills volcanic eruption in 1995, and had also written a letter to his family describing what he saw and experienced. These were preserved and are now on display at the Montserrat National Museum. A student uses these in his research. These would be examples of
   A. secondary sources
   B. background information
   C. primary sources
   D. tertiary sources

7. An example of a probing question that can be used in an in-depth interview is
   A. Have you lived in the neighbourhood more than two years?
   B. Could you elaborate on what are the causes of gun violence in the neighbourhood?
   C. Do you know anyone who I can ask about the car stealing ring?
   D. What two methods do students use to cheat on exams?

8. One disadvantage of participant observation is that
   A. the researcher has to rely on memory, and this can prove to be difficult in capturing all the important data
   B. it provides direct contact with the subjects
   C. the researcher develops a close relationship with the respondents
   D. an awareness of being observed can cause the respondents to generate 'unnatural' information

9. Tertiary sources of data collection
   A. are the original data sources and have not been altered or interpreted
   B. are print and electronic materials that share information
   C. provide evidence of a phenomena written after it has been investigated
   D. provide information that has been gathered from primary and secondary sources and arranged and presented in a convenient manner

Chapter 3

Examination Techniques

By the end of this chapter, you should be able to:

- recognise cue words in multiple-choice questions (MCQs);
- use strategies to eliminate incorrect responses in MCQs;
- identify key terms and concepts in questions that will need to be discussed when writing your essays;
- identify the topic and the command or directive words in each essay question;
- organise and communicate ideas clearly and logically;
- present written evidence to illustrate a range of phenomena that relate to the Caribbean;
- use words and phrases that link your ideas and provide for transition from one paragraph to the next.

Introduction

The purpose of this chapter is to provide you with general tips and strategies for taking Papers 1 and 2. It also provides advice on approaching Paper 03/2. It will give you the skills needed to approach the examinations successfully by describing how to answer the multiple-choice questions (MCQs) effectively and how to write answers to essay questions.

Paper 1 is a multiple-choice paper with 45 questions spanning the three modules. The aim is to test your knowledge and understanding of the main concepts and issues across the syllabus.

Paper 2 comprises four sections with Sections A and C testing Module 1 and Sections B and D testing Module 2. You are required to answer four questions, one from each section.

Overview of the Examination

Writing in an examination is very demanding; you have studied and you believe that you can give your best in the examination room. To ensure that you achieve success, and score at least a passing grade, the following recommendations will help you. Figure 3.1 provides various tips to help you in your preparation for the exam.

Figure 3.1 **Before the examination – preparation tips**

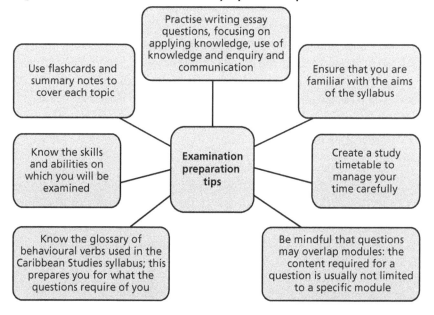

Additional Reading

To prepare adequately for the CAPE® Caribbean Studies examination, you must be well-read. To achieve this:

- ensure that you use this comprehensive revision guide;
- cover the recommended readings outlined in the syllabus;
- read from multiple sources so that you have different perspectives on a topic;
- access past papers that you can use to practise;
- practise paraphrasing key ideas so that you enhance your writing skills and expression.

Did You Know?

Making the Connection

Throughout this revision guide, 'Making the Connection' boxes can be found. These are important in assisting you to see the interconnectedness of topics in the chapters. When you see these pointers, make sure you cross reference and see how the topics interrelate.

Paper 1 – Multiple-Choice Questions (MCQs)

Here are some tips to consider when answering MCQs:

- Read the question in its entirety before you look at the responses.
- Read the question more than once to understand what the test item is asking.
- Read every response before choosing your answer.
- Highlight important words in the questions and in the responses provided; remember to underline the key terms.
- If, after reading the question, you are unable to identify the correct response, apply the process of elimination:
  - Eliminate distractors/options you know are incorrect.
  - Apply the True and False technique to the responses to help narrow down your final choice.
  - Look closely at responses that do not fit with the grammatical structure of the stem; they tend to be incorrect.
  - Look for clues in both the phrasing of the questions and in the response options provided.
  - When a question appears to have more than one response that seems to be correct, ask yourself if the response you think is right completely addresses the question.
  - Remember that if the response to a question is only partially true, then the likelihood that it is incorrect is very high.
- Look out for questions where all the responses appear to be correct. These take more time to eliminate the incorrect responses. (See the next section for more information on dealing with this type of question.)
- Choose the most suitable response from the remaining options if necessary.

- If you find that you cannot answer a question within a minute or less, it is best to skip the question and return to it afterwards.
- Once finished, check that you have answered all the questions because you may have left one out.

Example of an MCQ with options

1. When a researcher lists all the sources he consulted for his Bibliography, it shows
   - I. that he used numerous sources for his research
   - II. the authorship and age of the publications
   - III. the researcher's interest in the topic
   - IV. the Appendix with the supporting information
   - A. I and II only
   - B. I and IV only
   - C. I, II and III
   - D. II, III and IV

Answer:

Questions such as the example above require that you choose a combination of responses before selecting **A**, **B**, **C** or **D**.

The correct answer is **A**. The Bibliography shows the authors and the date of publication of sources in addition to indicating the number of sources that the researcher consulted.

A knowledge of what the stem relates to, in this case what the purpose of the Bibliography is, ensures that you can eliminate some of the responses. For example, option III, the researcher's interest in the topic, cannot be determined by the number of sources consulted, and option IV, the Appendix, with supporting information, has nothing to do with a Bibliography other than it may be referenced in it.

Making the Connection

The MCQ example is one that might be written to address part of the content of Module 3 of the exam syllabus, which is covered in Chapter 1 'Purpose, Sources and Principles of Research'.

Exam Tip

Steps in answering MCQs:

- It is important that you read the entire question and all the possible answers. When reading, highlight the important details.
- Next, eliminate the answers that you know are clearly incorrect.
- Then, look at the remaining answer(s) and re-read the question to ensure that you are left with the most appropriate response(s).
- If you have more than one answer, it is time to draw on your analytical skills to decide which answer is the best fit.
- Only then should you make a choice, and hopefully it is the right one.

Questions Where all the Responses Appear to be Correct

There are times when you will be presented with questions where all the responses appear to be correct. These are called umbrella questions and tend to take more time to arrive at the correct answer. The key to answering this question is to analyse the question to see exactly what it is asking you to answer.

Example

This is an important aspect of cultural expression in the region, which is tied to colonialism, religion, folklore and culture and is used to portray liberty and celebration.

a. J'ouvert

b. Caribbean Festival

c. Junkanoo

d. Crop Over

Answer:

At first glance, all the responses appear to be correct. However, the question is asking for the cultural phenomenon that is tied to colonialism and is an expression of celebration. Responses **a, c** and **d** are all <u>examples</u> of this cultural phenomenon, not the phenomenon itself, and all fall under the umbrella of **b.** Caribbean Festival.

The most appropriate answer would therefore be **b.**

Paper 2 – Essay Questions

Paper 2 comprises eight essay questions that test the objectives in the modules. You are required to answer four questions – one from each section. The questions focus on areas in Module 1, Caribbean Society and Culture, and Module 2, Issues in Caribbean Development.

These questions require high-order thinking skills and the application of these to the writing of your essays.

Exam Tip

Higher-order thinking skills refer to:

- **Application** – you apply the knowledge, principles and facts that you have garnered.
- **Analysis** – you make inferences, analysing and evaluating information to draw conclusions on the motives.
- **Synthesis** – you compile and incorporate salient facts to formulate ideas.
- **Evaluation** – you make judgements, considering ideas and critiquing viewpoints and issues based on specific principles and presenting your perspective.

In writing your responses to Paper 2, these are the skills that you will need to apply and upon which your essays will be graded, as outlined in the Caribbean Studies CAPE® syllabus:

- **Knowledge and Comprehension** – what you know; providing knowledge concepts.
- **Use of Knowledge** – how you use what you know; citing applicable examples and elaborating on the topic.
- **Enquiry and Communication** – how you express what you know, present arguments and detailed discussions and draw conclusions.

Know that in this paper you are required to:
- present facts and explain concepts and ideas;
- present arguments supporting or refuting concepts, issues, theories and processes;
- display an understanding of knowledge.

Exam Tip

To master the enquiry and communication requirement, it is important that you present your points clearly and link and draw attention to the main points by using transition words.

Some transition words to use in your essays:
- To contrast – *on the other hand, in contrast, however*
- To express result – *consequently, therefore, as a result, hence, thus*
- To give examples – *such as, for example, for instance*
- To add information – *additionally, moreover, not only … but also, in addition, also*
- To conclude – *in conclusion, to summarise, in summary, as can be seen*
- To clarify – *in other words, as has been noted*

As students preparing for higher education, the expectation is that you will:
- demonstrate your knowledge of content and concepts;
- show the application of that knowledge when responding to examination questions;
- communicate your ideas and arguments logically and coherently.

Guidelines for Writing Caribbean Studies Essays

1. Read the questions carefully and underline the key terms and concepts in the question so that you can refer to the important points to address in writing your essay.

2. Pay close attention to the requirements of the questions so that you provide the requisite responses.

3. Pay close attention to the phrasing of the questions (the rubric). Know what the questions are asking you to do. The wording of the questions determines how much and what type of information you need to provide. You should be aware of the command words listed in the CAPE® Caribbean Studies syllabus – 'Glossary of behavioural verbs used in the Caribbean Studies Examination' (see the Did You Know? box on command words).

4. You must approach each question with the understanding that no ONE section of a MODULE stands alone. All parts of the syllabus are interconnected.

5. No question will test your knowledge of ONLY ONE SECTION OR PART OF A SECTION in a module.

6. Students MUST use Caribbean examples to support all their points. To gain full marks, you must provide examples to support your points and arguments.

7. You are expected to apply your knowledge of the Caribbean territories in your responses. This means that in presenting information your responses SHOULD NOT be restricted to your territory of origin.

8. Organise your points and supporting details in a logical manner, according to your plan.

9. Do not include irrelevant information to lengthen your essays. Strive for clarity and cohesion in your writing.

10. Calculate the right amount of time to spend on each question and stick closely to your schedule. The essay questions in each part of the exam carry different marks (20 or 30) – therefore divide the exam time allocated accordingly.

Did You Know?

Command Words

The 'Glossary of Behavioural Verbs used in the Caribbean Studies Examination' outlines what is required of you for each command word. For example:

- **Analyse** is asking for a full and methodical examination of the parts of a process, situation or theory, and then that you draw your conclusions.
- **Assess** expects you to give reasons for the importance of something such as a process, relationship or approach.
- **Describe** is asking that you write a lengthy answer; you explain key concepts and issues, and give logical arguments using applicable examples, without necessarily drawing a conclusion.
- **Discuss** means that you should write an extended answer in which you define key concepts, state the situation, explore related issues and concepts, use examples to illustrate the arguments for and against, but do not necessarily come to a definite conclusion.
- **Evaluate** expects your answer to weigh up the evidence and give a judgement based on the provided criteria.
- **Examine** expects you to write an extended answer defining key concepts, stating the situation, explaining the issue(s) and exploring related concepts and issues.
- **Outline** means that you are being asked to provide only the main points or features, and omit the details.

Exam Tips

- As you read the questions, identify and number the tasks that each one requires. Once you have done that, make notes about each part. As you write your essay, refer to each task and ensure that you have answered the question in its entirety.
- Questions may require that you provide answers which are specific to a time period or to a specific group. Do not ignore this stipulation as it will jeopardise the marks that you can score.

Example

Question:

Discuss the impact of two intellectual traditions which have influenced the development of the Caribbean.

[20 marks]

In answering this question, you should:

1. Define the key terms in the question – intellectual traditions, development, the Caribbean.
2. Identify what is being asked of you by 'discuss' and what is meant by 'influenced' in the question.
3. Select and define the two intellectual traditions you will be writing about: Pan-Africanism, Négritude, Rastafari, or Garveyism.

Exam Tip

Be sure to note the marks awarded for the questions. Based on the section, the question can be worth either 20 or 30 marks. Use this as a guide in writing your answer. Questions which are awarded 30 marks require higher-order thinking and application of knowledge.

Making the Connection

The essay question example is one that might be set to address part of the content of Module 2, Section 6, of the exam syllabus, which is covered in Chapter 17, 'Intellectual Traditions' in this book.

4. Establish the background to the historical experiences identified based on the intellectual traditions selected.

5. Discuss how intellectual tradition number one began, and has since influenced the development of the Caribbean – provide at least three points and explain each in detail clearly, making sure to look at both positive and negative aspects of development in the Caribbean.

6. Discuss intellectual tradition number two as for number one, above.

7. Communicate your ideas logically, addressing the highlighted areas and developing your arguments.

8. Summarise your points and write a comprehensive conclusion that reiterates your stance.

Applying exam criteria to your answer:

Knowledge and Comprehension	• Definition of development, the Caribbean, intellectual traditions – Pan-Africanism, Négritude, Rastafari, Garveyism. • List founder(s) or pioneer(s) of the intellectual traditions you are writing about. • List reasons for the development of the intellectual traditions. • Identify the Caribbean territories influenced by these movements.
Use of Knowledge	• Explain how great or how limited the intellectual traditions chosen have been on the social, political and economic development of the Caribbean, either in a positive or negative way. • Identify how key figures of the movements influenced the political, economic and social climate of the Caribbean. • Explain that some countries, such as Jamaica, in an effort to implement the practical aspects of intellectual traditions, such as Pan-Africanism, Marxism and Neo-Marxism, needed financial support to achieve the desired economic stability and so were forced to embrace austerity measures from the IMF. • Discuss how Caribbean writers rose to prominence on the regional and international scene. • Explain whether each movement was a success or a failure, and give reasons.
Enquiry and Communication	• Communicate by offering a well-structured answer in which the key issues or points of the essay are outlined as well as a definition of key terms/ concepts. • A position on the 'view' must be offered and this position developed by illustrating Caribbean examples to demonstrate the impact of these intellectual traditions on development. • The essay should close with a conclusion based on the analysis.

Sample Introduction:

The Caribbean can be defined as the territories that have a shared history of colonialism, the encomienda system, slavery, indentureship and independence and may share a similar political system. It is the region in the Americas which comprises the Caribbean Sea, its islands and the surrounding areas. The experiences of the Caribbean territories have led to the emergence of intellectual traditions – which refers to the thoughts and ideas that emerged due to these shared experiences and have led to political, cultural and intellectual advances within the region. These traditions reinforce the value and contribution of the forced and voluntary migrants to the Caribbean. Some key intellectual traditions have evolved out of this, namely, Pan-Africanism, Négritude, Rastafari, Garveyism, Indo-Caribbean thought, Neo-Marxism and Caribbean Feminism.

Sample Supporting Paragraphs (on one of the traditions):

Pan-Africanism is a philosophy based on the belief that African people and people of African descent share common bonds and objectives. It promotes unity to achieve these objectives, and unity among Black people, and Black Power, is an important part of its philosophy. As well as unity, it advances the feeling of self-worth and pride among African people in addition to an appreciation of African values. Its origins were in combating the oppression and enslavement that came with colonisation and slavery. The Pan-Africanist movement was said to have started in the mid-1800s by African Americans, Martin R. Delany, Alexander Crummel and Edward Blyden, who were an abolitionist, a religious leader and an activist, respectively.

It was in the 1940s, however, that the Pan-African movement gained traction. It is important to note that Henry Sylvester Williams is credited with coining the idea of Pan-Africanism, but the real credit lies with radical men like W. E. B. Du Bois and Marcus Garvey, who truly established this movement. With their advocacy, the objectives and beliefs of the Pan-African movement found a place on the international scene.

Pan-Africanism has led to the promotion of Black pride within the Caribbean. This is seen in the people's identification with and support of an African mode of dress, the acceptance of African religious practices, such as revivalism, and the use of drums and up-tempo beats in traditional religions. People have embraced their ethnic origins and cultural expressions, which have been seen in natural hair styles, African jewellery and the use of authentic fabric to make clothing. Evidence of Pan-Africanism can also be seen in the birth of other movements, such as Garveyism and Rastafari.

Exam Tip

You will notice that the introduction:

- defines the terms – Knowledge;
- provides a background for the development of the intellectual traditions – Use of Knowledge;
- lists the intellectual traditions – Knowledge.

Exam Tip

Note that in the first two paragraphs:

- the term 'Pan-Africanism' is defined;
- the reason for the birth of Pan-Africanism is explained;
- the historical perspective is presented;
- the founders of the movement are identified.

Exam Tip

Note that:

- the promotion of Black pride in the Caribbean is elaborated upon;
- the last sentence in the paragraph introduces the other intellectual tradition to be discussed.

Making the Connection

Pan-Africanism and other intellectual traditions are described in detail in Chapter 17, 'Intellectual Traditions'. There, you will also find more information on Pan-Africanism to use in answering this question, such as: increased awareness of the plight of Black people, movement towards socio-economic and political independence, greater international cooperation among Black peoples and the sharing of strategies.

Exam Tip

Checklist for answering essay questions:

- Demonstrate your knowledge of concepts.
- Apply that knowledge to your answer.
- Respond to the command words in the question.
- Organise and develop your content and ideas.
- Give background information.
- Define key terms.
- Present arguments.
- Provide examples where relevant.
- Structure your paragraphs.
- Use formal writing.

Exam Tip

To receive a good score for Enquiry and Communication, you must:

- Communicate by giving a well-structured answer in which you outline the key issues or points of the essay as well as a definition of key terms.
- Have a clear introductory paragraph presenting the ideas you are going to write about; outline the main points of discussion here.
- Be able to discuss the impact of two specific intellectual traditions on the development of the Caribbean. You must develop each point by drawing examples from Caribbean countries to show the link between the two traditions and development in the Caribbean.
- Present your arguments logically and clearly, and demonstrate a good use of writing skills. You must possess the necessary skills to convey or express ideas effectively by:
  - good use of vocabulary – your choice of words must be applicable to the question and show depth of knowledge about the topic;
  - sentence structure;
  - writing proper paragraphs.
- Show correct spelling and grammar – basic skills such as subject/verb agreement, correct spelling of words and punctuation are important.
- Sequence your ideas clearly by outlining and presenting the responses to include the use of transition words.
- Reach a clear conclusion based on your analysis. The essay should end with a conclusion that summarises the main ideas and your position or view. Do more than restate the key points of the discussion; present implications for the arguments you have presented.

Paper 03/2

Paper 03/2 is the alternative to the School-Based Assessment (SBA), and is written by private candidates. As a private candidate you do not submit an SBA, but will write Paper 03/2 that tests the skills developed by students who have submitted the SBA. The paper is based on Module 3, Investigating Human and Social Development in the Caribbean. The paper comprises two sections where three questions are presented. You will be required to answer two of these.

- Section A has ONE compulsory question, which is based on a case study.
- Section B has two structured questions and you will be required to answer ONE of them, based on your own investigation.

Section A: Compulsory Question on a Given Case Study

This section comprises a case study summary with a number of questions organised under subheadings that refer to different aspects of the research process. The example below gives an excerpt from a case study and the question on methods of data collection that goes with it.

Exam Tip

The questions in both sections of this paper contain information broken down into numerous segments and sub-sections. It is recommended that you clearly **label** the questions and segments when giving your answers. For example:

d. Limitations

(i) Two reasons why the researcher had a problem collecting data in the community were that the citizens were very resistant to strangers coming in and the illiteracy rate among the residents was very high, so that there was a great number of incomplete questionnaires.

(ii) The limitation that the illiteracy rate among the residents was very high, causing a great number of the questionnaires to be incomplete, would affect the findings of the research by reducing the data results, so that there is the threat of bias in the results.

Example

Excerpt from a case study:

> Research was conducted on the effects of the Soufrière Hills volcanic eruption in 1995, to identify ways in which the former residents have adjusted to life after this catastrophic event. Data from government records indicate that 60% of the Montserratians had relocated to other territories within the Caribbean, while 30% had relocated to North America. A few of them, 10%, had returned to the island, hoping that another eruption will not occur any time soon.

In conducting the interview, 60 questionnaires were distributed evenly to the three areas of location for the people of Montserrat – North America, Montserrat and territories in the Caribbean.

(b) Method of data collection

(i) Outline ONE disadvantage of using disproportionate stratified random sampling in this research.   [2 marks]

Sample Answer:

One disadvantage of using disproportionate stratified random sampling in this research is that it does not allow the elements an equal chance of being selected for the sample. The portion allocation for the places of relocation is not equal to the ratio for the number of questionnaires issued to each group.

Exam Tip

The key to answering the questions on this paper is to know the principles of social research. This question requires that you know the methods of data collection and their advantages and disadvantages. Be sure to apply your answer in a concrete way to the question being asked. The second sentence in the sample answer does that.

Section B: Investigation on a Given Topic

For Section B, you must select one question, and your responses should be based on the topic that you have investigated as part of your course. You are expected to conduct your investigation on one of a choice of topics suggested for the year that you are sitting the examination.

The questions address the application of different areas of the research process to the given topic. You can be asked to identify challenges, strategies that were utilised or ways in which recommendations can be implemented. Your answers should be focused on applying research skills to the topic.

The Caribbean Region

Chapter 4

Location and Definition of the Caribbean

After revising this topic, you should be able to:
* locate the Caribbean region and name the territories;
* identify and list the sub-regions of the Caribbean;
* identify the Caribbean territories in relation to the Caribbean Sea, Atlantic Ocean and continental land masses;
* define the Caribbean region in the following ways:
  a. geographical
  b. geological
  c. historical
  d. political
  e. diasporic.

Objectives

Locate and define the Caribbean region and its diaspora.

Quick Facts

The American Mediterranean Sea is the combined water bodies of the Caribbean Sea and the Gulf of Mexico. This area includes Cuba, Hispaniola, Jamaica and Puerto Rico, which separate the American Mediterranean from the Atlantic Ocean.

Geographical Location of the Caribbean Region

The Caribbean is the region in the Americas which comprises the Caribbean Sea, its islands and the surrounding areas. The region is southeast of North America and the Gulf of Mexico, east of Central America and to the northwest of South America. Some of the islands of the Caribbean border or are located in the North Atlantic Ocean. The Caribbean region has over 7 000 islands and islets and also includes some territories located on the mainland of South America. The land area is roughly 1 063 000 square miles (2 754 000 sq. km). According to a United Nations estimate, the population of the Caribbean at the beginning of June 2016 stood at 43,465,216.

Figure 4.1 Map showing the Caribbean in relation to the rest of the world

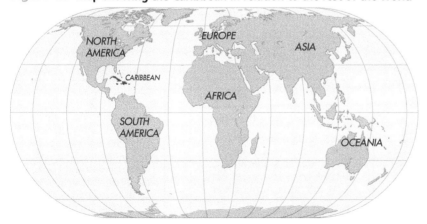

The Caribbean is divided into four sub-regions, see Figures 4.2 to 4.6.

- **The Lesser Antilles**, which is made up of the three smaller islands groups: the Windward Islands, the Leeward Islands and the Leeward Antilles. The Lesser Antilles is a double arc of islands that stretch from the Virgin Islands to Trinidad.
- **The Greater Antilles** refers to the four largest islands in the Caribbean: Cuba, Hispaniola (Haiti and the Dominican Republic), Jamaica and Puerto Rico.
- **The Mainland Territories** of the Caribbean include Belize, Suriname, Guyana and French Guiana.
- **Other territories** in the region include the Cayman Islands, The Bahamas and Turks and Caicos Islands.

Figure 4.2 Map of the Caribbean identifying the sub-regions

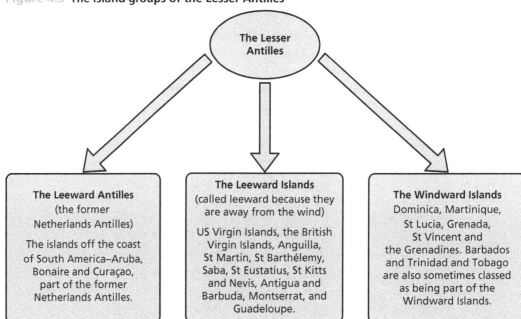

Figure 4.3 The island groups of the Lesser Antilles

The Lesser Antilles

The Leeward Antilles
(the former Netherlands Antilles)

The islands off the coast of South America–Aruba, Bonaire and Curaçao, part of the former Netherlands Antilles.

The Leeward Islands
(called leeward because they are away from the wind)

US Virgin Islands, the British Virgin Islands, Anguilla, St Martin, St Barthélemy, Saba, St Eustatius, St Kitts and Nevis, Antigua and Barbuda, Montserrat, and Guadeloupe.

The Windward Islands
Dominica, Martinique, St Lucia, Grenada, St Vincent and the Grenadines. Barbados and Trinidad and Tobago are also sometimes classed as being part of the Windward Islands.

Figure 4.4 Map of the Windward Islands

1:6 600 000   Barbados and Aves are not part of the Windward Islands

Figure 4.5 Map of the Leeward Islands

1:6 600 000

Figure 4.6 Map of the Leeward Antilles

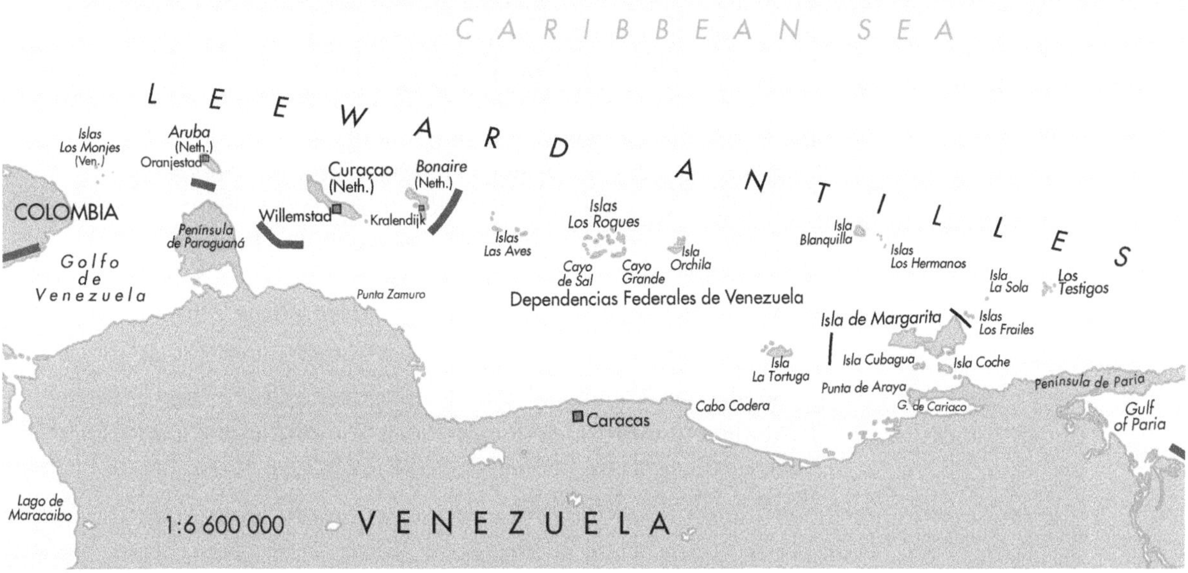

1:6 600 000

Quick Facts

The term Caribbean is an elusive or abstract concept and there is no one specific definition that can be applied to it. The definition can be from the political, geographical, geological, historical or diasporic perspectives.

Defining the Caribbean Region and its Diaspora

Exam Tip

Problems defining the Caribbean

There are several different ways to define the Caribbean. A geographical definition, for example, includes The Bahamas, Turks and Caicos Islands and Guyana, even though they do not have coastlines on the Caribbean Sea. A standard definition cannot be applied to the Caribbean, so, when being asked to define it, you need to pay attention to the structure of the question. Read the question carefully to get an understanding of whether you are being asked for a political definition, a historical one or another.

The Geographical Definition

Defined geographically, the Caribbean is the area 'washed by' the Caribbean Sea, and often described as the Caribbean Basin. It comprises the Lesser Antilles, the Greater Antilles, the mainland territories of Central and northern South America, and other territories such as the Cayman Islands, Turks and Caicos Islands and The Bahamas.

In practice, however, things are more complicated. First, The Bahamas are not 'washed by' the Caribbean Sea and so do not fit into the strict geographical definition, yet they are accepted as part of the Caribbean. Second, Panama, Columbia, Belize, Venezuela, Costa Rica, Nicaragua and Honduras are situated on the mainland of Central America, but are still included as part of the geographical definition of the Caribbean because they are washed by the Caribbean Sea. Third, the mainland territories of Suriname, Guyana and French Guiana are located on the mainland of South America and border the Atlantic Ocean, which means that geographically they are considered South American and so are excluded from the *geographical* definition of the Caribbean.

However, these countries, the mainland territories of Suriname, Guyana and French Guiana, share the linguistic, historical and demographic features of Caribbean countries rather than their Latin or Central American neighbours that are not categorised as part of the Caribbean, even though they are washed by the Caribbean Sea. This means, first, that 'washed by the Caribbean Sea' is not a concrete definition. And second, while there are certain common characteristics that define the Caribbean, the term 'Caribbean' is fluid.

The 'geographical' Caribbean has the following boundaries:
- North – Cuba, the Dominican Republic, Haiti, Jamaica and Puerto Rico
- South – the coast of Columbia, Venezuela and Panama
- East – the Lesser Antilles chain of islands
- West – Belize, Costa Rica, Guatemala, Honduras, Mexico and Nicaragua.

So, the only commonality of the geographical Caribbean is that the territories are washed by the Caribbean Sea. And, as we have seen, this means that territories normally considered to be part of the Caribbean are excluded by this definition.

The Geological Definition

The **geological** Caribbean refers to the area defined by the Caribbean Plate that shares similar seismic, tectonic and volcanic features. The territories of much of the eastern Caribbean, have been formed from the impact of plate tectonics. The area is characterised by the Lesser Antilles archipelago, which developed from tectonic activity along the destructive plate margin at the eastern edge of the Caribbean Plate. The Caribbean Plate interacts with the Nazca and Cocos Plates to the west and the North American Plate to the east and north and the South American Plate to the south.

Key term

Geology/geological – geology is the study of the Earth involving the the Earth's structure, features and the materials it is made of, in addition to the composition of those materials.

Did You Know?

The island of Montserrat was formed as a result of the geological feature called plate tectonics. The destructive plate boundary between the North American Plate and the Caribbean Plate in a west-south-westerly direction led to the emergence of the volcanic island Montserrat, which is an island of the Antilles Island Arc.

The boundaries of the geological definition of the Caribbean are as follows:

- The western edge of the Caribbean Plate lies in the Pacific, just beyond the coasts of Honduras, Costa Rica and Panama. Yet, the geological boundary determines the Caribbean to extend only as far as the Western or Pacific coastline of Central America.
- The northern edge of the plate is determined by the line of the Greater Antilles, which leaves Belize, Cuba and The Bahamas as outside of the region.
- In the south, the line of the plate runs through Trinidad, northern Venezuela and Colombia, causing Guyana to be classified as extra-regional.

Quick Fact

The Lesser Antilles lie along the eastern boundary of the Caribbean Plate where its most distinct feature is the active volcanic arc. The islands here are volcanic in origin.

The historical definition

The historical Caribbean refers to the countries that have shared experiences of European **colonisation**, **slavery**, **indentureship** and the **plantation system**.

The four leading colonial powers in the Caribbean were Spain, Holland, France and Britain, which colonised the territories from the early sixteenth century onwards. Other colonial powers that claimed various territories in the region at different times were Denmark, Sweden and Portugal. The common colonial influences on the territories of the region led to similar historical and cultural experiences across the region:

- The colonial powers for the most part implemented large-scale agricultural production on plantations and imported labour first in the form of slavery and later under the indentureship system.
- The indigenous populations were adversely affected by colonisation through displacement, disease and forced labour practices amounting to slavery, which all resulted in their near extinction.
- Individual territories also retained close ties to their specific colonial power, such as in language and religion. For example, Guyana and Jamaica are former British colonies and maintain many aspects of the British culture; Suriname and Aruba were colonised by the Dutch and their influence is still evident today.
- The European powers used colonisation, slavery, the **encomienda system** and the plantation system to sustain the economic wealth of Europe. These systems shaped the shared history of the Caribbean nations.

Making the Connection

Chapter 5, 'The Historical Process', examines the shared historical experiences of the Caribbean region in more detail.

Key Terms

Colonisation – the settlement of a group of people who seek to take control of territories. It usually involves large-scale immigration of people to a 'new' location and the expansion of their civilisation and culture into this area.

Slavery – a legal institution in which individuals are owned by others who control every aspect of their lives, including what they do and where they live. Enslaved people are forced to work without pay because legally they are chattel, or property. Slavery arrived in the Caribbean after Britain introduced the plantation system which demanded high levels of labour. The origins of most of the enslaved who were brought to the Caribbean were in West Africa.

Indentureship – a system where a labourer was contracted to work for a stipulated period of time, in exchange for passage and subsistence. At the end of this term he was given land, cash and also had the option to return to his homeland. The first group of indentured East Indians (over 230 Indians) arrived in Guyana on May 5th, 1838, after the abolishment of slavery in the British Caribbean.

Plantation system – a system of cultivation based on large-scale farming units or plantations to achieve agricultural mass production, usually of a few commodity crops – mainly sugar in the Caribbean. Plantation economies rely on the export of cash crops as a source of income.

Encomienda system – a system under which natives of conquered lands were given to an explorer or conquistador by the Spanish Crown. The objective was to guarantee economic and political order in the areas conquered by the Spanish. It was a system designed to control and regulate all aspects of American Indian life.

Countries that experienced colonisation were influenced by their colonisers' cultural traits. It is for this reason that the languages, cultural practices, religions and economic activities of Caribbean territories and states reflect those of their colonial powers. Thus, although colonisation is a shared feature of the 'historical' Caribbean, within this there are also fundamental differences between the territories. Some territories have been colonised by different powers. For example, Spain had control of Puerto Rico from 1493 until it was granted autonomy in July 1898, only to be taken over by the United States in October of that same year. Table 4.1 shows the territories of the region and their main colonial powers.

Table 4.1 **Caribbean territories and the main colonial powers that have influenced them**

Colonial power	Caribbean territories colonised at various times
Spain	The Spanish empire initially claimed all of the Caribbean and most of Latin America. The influence of Spanish culture is most strongly felt in Cuba, Venezuela, Dominican Republic, Puerto Rico
Britain	Anguilla, Antigua, Barbados, Bermuda, St Kitts, The Bahamas, British Guiana, British Honduras, Cayman Islands, Dominica, Grenada, Jamaica, Montserrat, Nevis, St Lucia, St Vincent, Tortola, Trinidad and Tobago, Turks and Caicos Islands, the Virgin Islands
France	Dominica, Guadeloupe and Martinique, Haiti, St Barthélemy, St Kitts, St Lucia, St Martin (northern half), St Vincent, Tobago
Holland	The Netherland Antilles (Aruba, Bonaire, Curaçao, Saba, St Eustatius, and St Martin (southern half)), Tortola
United States (US colonisation came later than European)	Puerto Rico, Virgin Islands, Cuba

The Political Definition

Political definitions of the Caribbean refer to the socio-economic and other groupings found in the region. For example, one political definition might relate to the countries that share – or have shared – a similar political system, of which there have been three dominant types: **independent states, associated states** and **colonial dependences** (or **dependent territories**).

Key Terms

- **Independent states** – countries which previously were under colonial rule but are now self-governed. These are also known as sovereign states. They are: Antigua and Barbuda, The Bahamas, Barbados, Belize, Bermuda, Haiti, Cuba, Jamaica, Dominica, Dominican Republic, Grenada, Trinidad and Tobago, St Kitts and Nevis, St Lucia, St Vincent and the Grenadines.

- **Associated states** – the former British colonies in the Eastern Caribbean (Antigua, Grenada, Dominica, St Vincent, St Lucia and St Christopher- Nevis-Anguilla) that from 1967 enjoyed a semi-independent political status: their defence and external affairs were handled by Britain, while they maintained control over their own constitution. Over time the associated states became independent.

Quick Fact

Associated states, which were under the United Kingdom from 1967–1981, enjoyed the freedom of being in control of their constitution. All except Anguilla opted to become independent Commonwealth countries. Anguilla opted to become a British colonial dependency. This means that there are no associated states in the Caribbean today.

- **Colonial dependencies** (or **dependent states / territories**) — countries that are not independent and enjoy the rights and privileges of the country that governs them. They are: the territories of Great Britain — Montserrat, British Virgin Islands, Anguilla, Cayman Islands, Turks and Caicos; the territories of the Netherlands — Netherland Antilles; the territories of the United States — Puerto Rico, US Virgin Islands; and the territories of France — Guadeloupe, Saint Martin, Martinique, St Barthélemy.

Quick Facts

The Commonwealth Caribbean refers to those former colonies of Britain that have a shared history of colonialism, slavery, indentureship and independence. Also called the Anglophone Caribbean, these countries are part of the global group of countries called the Commonwealth of Nations, which is largely made up of territories of the former British Empire.

Did You Know?

The history of Saint Christopher-Nevis-Anguilla is complex. This three-island union was initially a crown colony and later became a colonial dependency. It became an associated state on 27 February 1967. In 1971, Anguilla separated, leaving the union of St Christopher and Nevis. St Kitts (St Christopher) and Nevis became independent in 1983 and Anguilla reverted to a colonial dependency.

There are also modern political socio-economic groupings in the Caribbean. For example:
- The Association of Caribbean States (ACS) is a union of almost all nations located on the Caribbean Basin (plus El Salvador, located on the Pacific Ocean), whose aim is to promote consultation, cooperation and concerted action among all countries of the Caribbean.
- The Caribbean Community (CARICOM) is an organisation of 15 Caribbean nations and five dependencies or associate members whose main purpose is to promote economic integration and cooperation among members. Their membership includes Guyana and Suriname, both in South America; Belize in Central America; and The Bahamas, Bermuda and the Turks and Caicos Islands (the latter two are associate members) from the Atlantic.

Quick Facts

Guadeloupe, Martinique and French Guiana are not considered part of the political Caribbean. They are departments of France, a status that makes them officially French territory even though they are located in the Caribbean. Likewise, the BES islands (Bonaire, St Eustatius and Saba) are provinces of the Netherlands.

Another way to politically define the Caribbean is in terms of a shared history of colonial rule. The countries that are included in the definition depends on the perspective taken. For example, the political Caribbean *for Britain* during its colonial rule could be described as either of the following:
- The Windward and Leeward Islands, and Dominica, Trinidad, Barbados, British Honduras, Bermuda, The Bahamas, British Guyana and Belize, or
- The West Indies Federation.

Whereas, for other European powers, during their colonial rule the political Caribbean could be defined as any of the following:
- The French West Indies
- The Dutch West Indies
- The Spanish West Indies
- US colonies including Puerto Rico and the Virgin Islands.

Did You Know?

The term 'West Indies' was first used by Europeans to distinguish the region from the East Indies (Asia), but later acquired political significance with the establishment of **The West Indies Federation**. This was a short-lived political federation established between 1958 and 1962 with the objective of uniting the territories under British colonial rule and ultimately bringing about political independence of the region. Despite its collapse, there is still a joint West Indies cricket team (which includes Guyana).

The Diasporic Definition

The **Caribbean diaspora** refers to the migration of Caribbean people to many countries of the world. These people, despite now living elsewhere, still identify themselves in some way with the Caribbean region. In this way, the Caribbean can be defined as a transnational community extending to these overseas communities.

There are three aspects of the diaspora:
* Individuals or groups from the region who have migrated to other areas outside of the Caribbean, but still consider their original country as home.
* Individuals and groups who have a connection to the region in general (natives, descendants or some other affiliation), and are influential and committed to its economic development (as opposed to assuming a specifically nationalistic approach to development focused on their home territory).
* Descendants of people from the region who have been born outside the Caribbean and yet identify themselves based on the first generation's heritage.

Check Your Knowledge

Explain the concept of the Caribbean diaspora and describe ONE period in history which can be attributed to the establishment of it.

Demonstrate an understanding of the following terms and concepts by defining and using them correctly:
* diaspora;
* Caribbean diaspora;
* migration;
* cultural identity;
* ethnic group consciousness.

Explain the different aspects or definitions of the terms 'diaspora' and 'Caribbean diaspora'.
* The term diaspora means the migration or dispersion of a people from their homelands that are either voluntary like the East Indian Indentures or mid-20th-century economic migrants to the UK, or forced like the enslaved Africans.
* The Caribbean diaspora refers to:
* the transnational communities that have been established outside of the Caribbean region which have migrants who still regard their original country or region as their home

Key Term

Caribbean diaspora – the people of the Caribbean who, even though they have established themselves outside of the region by migrating to other countries (mainly the United Kingdom, the United States and Canada), still retain strong familial, emotional, cultural and economic ties to the region.

Making the Connection

The diasporic communities and their ties to and influences on the Caribbean region are discussed in Chapters 11 'Caribbean–Global Interactions' and 14 'Globalisation and Development'.

Exam Tip

'Explain' requires statements on what happened and how and why it happened, along with elaboration of terms, concepts and approaches.

'Describe' requires a lengthy answer in which you explain key concepts and issues and give logical arguments. You must use detailed examples, but **not** necessarily draw a conclusion.

Making the Connection

Chapter 5 'The Historical Process'

Chapter 10 'Arts and Popular Culture'

Chapter 11 'Caribbean–Global Interaction'

- the offspring or descendants of individuals who were born in another country or region, but who shape their identities based on the identity of the initial transplanters and on what they see as their point of origin, i.e. the Caribbean region. - individuals and groups who maintain strong collective identities based on their point of origin, who define themselves as the diaspora and take an active interest in the Caribbean, though not necessarily viewing this as their main source of identity.
- For the most part in the case of the Caribbean, it is economics that have caused migrants to move away from their homelands in search of better employment, salaries and standard of living.
- This migratory movement has led to the creation of the Caribbean diaspora in Canada, the United Kingdom and the United States.

Establish the time period of the Caribbean diaspora you will discuss. The following are some examples:

- The post-emancipation migration of workers within and to peripheral areas of the Caribbean looking for work (to Venezuelan oil fields, Cuban plantations, the construction of the Panama Canal)
- The late 19th and early 20th-century economic emigration to the US: after the abolition of slavery in the US, many Caribbean people were attracted by the new opportunities this offered
- The expanding World War 2 war economy and post-war economic growth attracted migration to both North America and Europe, especially to Britain where schemes were set up to attract workers from the Caribbean to help with the post-war rebuilding effort
- Political and economic upheaval in Cuba and Haiti, in particular in the late 20th and early 21st century, led to many political and economic migrants entering the US.

Describe the time period of the Caribbean diaspora you have chosen. The post-war migration of workers to the UK:

- During the 1950s, a large number of people from the Caribbean migrated to Britain, encouraged by recruitment campaigns by the British government and the British Nationality Act of 1948, which afforded free entry into Britain for all Commonwealth citizens, leading to a mass exodus within the region. The United States, on the other hand, had introduced some restrictive immigration policies that served to deter settlement there. (Later, however, a large number of Caribbean nationals who had made Britain their home migrated to Canada and the United States.)
- At the same time, economic problems in the Caribbean, mainly due to the shrinking agricultural sector, created hardships and resulted in limited employment opportunities in the region.
- Many of these migrants were young women who went to train as nurses in the newly established British National Health Service while many men took on jobs in the transport sector (bus and train drivers, bus conductors, etc). Later, teachers were also recruited from the Caribbean.

Briefly explain other effects of the Caribbean diaspora at this time:

- It resulted in the preservation of a strong ethnic group consciousness and a commitment to the economic and political development of their homeland. For example, a sense of cultural identity and celebration is seen in the festivals such as Caribana in Toronto, the Notting Hill Carnival in London and the West Indian and Puerto Rican Day Parades in New York, which promote national and ethnic pride.
- Economic development is seen in the remittances that members of the diaspora send to the region, and the savings and investments that they channel into their countries and ultimately the region.

A possible conclusion is to summarise your main points discussed in the essay.

Multiple-choice Questions

1. The four distinct areas of the Caribbean are
    A. the Leeward Islands, the Leeward Antilles, the Independent States and the mainland territories
    B. the Lesser Antilles, the Greater Antilles, the mainland territories and the other territories, such as the Turks and Caicos Islands
    C. the ABC islands, the Netherland Antilles and the Leeward Islands and the islands of Turks and Caicos, The Bahamas and the Cayman Islands
    D. the Greater Antilles, the Leeward Islands, the mainland territories and countries of South America

2. The plantation system introduced by the British involved
    A. the encomienda system, which was used to support the British colony's need for free labour
    B. the annihilation of the early settlers and the destruction of their villages
    C. the enslavement of Africans and later the indentureship of Chinese and East Indians to maintain systems of production
    D. a political and agricultural system based on the Westminster system of Britain being commissioned

3. Guyana, Surinam and French Guiana are considered to be a part of the historical Caribbean because they
    A. are part of the dependent states of the kingdom of Netherlands since they were colonised by them
    B. are mountainous and rugged territories, with volcanic eruptions causing damage to historical buildings and monuments
    C. make up the countries in the earthquake zone, where seismic and volcanic activities often occur
    D. share a commonality of the past and of cultural experiences, which are as a result of being ruled by specific European countries

4. A boundary of the geological Caribbean refers to
    A. independent states such as Jamaica, Trinidad and Guyana
    B. the north line of the Greater Antilles
    C. the Windward Islands of Martinique, St Lucia, Grenada, and St Vincent and the Grenadines
    D. the archipelago that developed along the Caribbean Plate

5. The Lesser Antilles comprises
    A. the Windward Islands, the Leeward Islands and the Leeward Antilles
    B. the Windward Islands, the Greater Antilles and the Netherland Antilles
    C. the Netherland Antilles, Turks and Caicos Islands and the Leeward Antilles
    D. the mainland territories, the Leeward Islands and the Netherland Antilles

6. Workers, especially the highly educated ones, who migrate to countries outside of the Caribbean and secure an enhanced standard of living, establish transnational communities and then actively contribute to the national and regional development of the Caribbean region that they have left behind are considered to be part of the
    A. regional development
    B. transnational network
    C. Caribbean diaspora
    D. labour export phenomenon

Chapter 5

The Historical Process

Syllabus Objective

Analyse the impact of the historical process in Caribbean society and culture.

After revising this topic, you should be able to:
- describe and explain migratory movements to and patterns of settlement within the Caribbean to 1838 and recognise their significance to the historical development of the region;
- describe and explain migratory movements both into and out of the Caribbean from 1838 to the present, including diasporic communities, and assess how these have an impact on the region;
- explain the development and impact of various systems of production, especially forced labour, and their legacies;
- assess the different ways Caribbean people have responded to oppression through various forms of resistance;
- understand the various movements in politics, the economy, society and culture leading up to independence.

The Caribbean can be defined in many ways. This chapter is concerned with the historical definition. The history of the Caribbean can be divided chronologically into different historical periods, but running through them are some common themes that connect people's experiences and the legacies of these through time. The main themes are:
- **migration** of different groups into, within and out of the region and their cultural and social impact;
- **oppression** through conquest, colonisation and imposed systems of production, including forced labour;
- **resistance** to this oppression.

The Chronology: An Outline

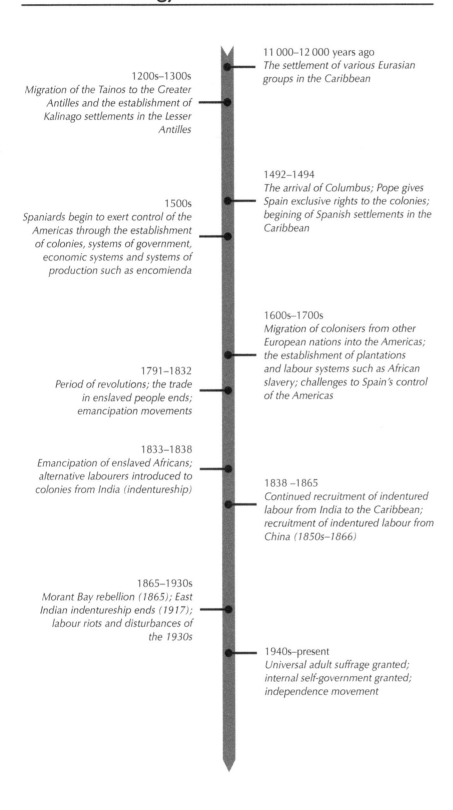

11 000–12 000 years ago
The settlement of various Eurasian groups in the Caribbean

1200s–1300s
Migration of the Tainos to the Greater Antilles and the establishment of Kalinago settlements in the Lesser Antilles

1492–1494
The arrival of Columbus; Pope gives Spain exclusive rights to the colonies; begining of Spanish settlements in the Caribbean

1500s
Spaniards begin to exert control of the Americas through the establishment of colonies, systems of government, economic systems and systems of production such as encomienda

1600s–1700s
Migration of colonisers from other European nations into the Americas; the establishment of plantations and labour systems such as African slavery; challenges to Spain's control of the Americas

1791–1832
Period of revolutions; the trade in enslaved people ends; emancipation movements

1833–1838
Emancipation of enslaved Africans; alternative labourers introduced to colonies from India (indentureship)

1838 –1865
Continued recruitment of indentured labour from India to the Caribbean; recruitment of indentured labour from China (1850s–1866)

1865–1930s
Morant Bay rebellion (1865); East Indian indentureship ends (1917); labour riots and disturbances of the 1930s

1940s–present
Universal adult suffrage granted; internal self-government granted; independence movement

Migratory Movements and Patterns of Settlement to 1838

The Caribbean is thought of as a place of 'migratory peoples'. What are the origins of the people that make the Caribbean so diverse?

Amerindian Migration and Settlement

Figure 5.1 Amerindian migrations and settlement in the Caribbean region to c.1500

← Migrations
○ Kalinago people today
Scale 1 : 157 000 000

Reasons for the Migration

It all started with the movement on foot of the ancestors of the Amerindians from **Eurasia** to the Western Hemisphere, through the Bering Strait between what are now Alaska and Russia. They left their homelands to migrate eastward during the fourth Ice Age, around 18 000 to 16 000 years ago, when most of Europe was frozen over.

The Ice Age led to a shortage of vegetation for animals and thereby a shortage of meat for these nomadic, hunter/gatherer tribes, who then migrated eastwards in search of food, following the migration of the woolly mammoth, a main source of meat for them.

Did You Know?

The land bridge theory explains the Amerindian migration into the Americas by proposing that North America was joined to Eurasia by a land mass that extended across the Bering Sea, which providing them with a path to the Americas when exposed by lower sea levels. The ice bridge theory, on the other hand, asserts that the Bering Sea was frozen over during the fourth Ice Age, thus forming an ice bridge that provided the path to the Americas. The ice bridge theory is more widely used as it explains why migration occurred during the fourth Ice Age.

This, however, was not one massive migration of all the people that faced hardships during the Ice Age. Eurasia is a large territory that was the dwelling place for many different racial and cultural groups. Different groups crossed over into the west at different periods.

Many of these groups settled on the North American continent. Some travelled further and eventually settled in Central America, while others continued onwards to South America. Subsequently, they developed different cultural practices based on the resources available to them that further distinguished them from each other.

Amerindian Society and Culture

The Tainos

The Tainos of the Greater Antilles mostly settled in Cuba, Hispaniola, Jamaica and The Bahamas. It is generally believed that they migrated to the Caribbean from the Orinico Valley basin of Venezuela around AD 600–700, because of the frequency of flooding and hurricanes in that region along with competition from other groups for territory, and that their later and eventual settlement in the Greater Antilles was possibly due to being pushed further northwards by the Kalinagos.

The Tainos, who were not as advanced in pottery-making technology as the Maya and Aztecs (who made large storage containers for food and water), settled along the coastal regions of these larger islands close to fresh water. They needed ready access to both flat land, for the growing of cassava, and to the sea, for fish and other seafood. Strategically, they also preferred a commanding view of all incoming sea traffic because, unlike their mainland counterparts the Maya and Inca, they did not have a standing military and needed to be aware of incoming enemies to prepare for conflict and/or evasive action.

Quick Fact

Nomadic groups are tribes of wandering hunters and gatherers constantly searching for animals to hunt and crops to forage for food. These hunter/gatherer groups developed this lifestyle because their technology did not afford them the capabilities to make pottery and other clay containers (they were a pre-ceramic culture) to store water and food or the ability to preserve foods for long periods.

Exam Tip

Here, we are mainly concerned with the Tainos of the Greater Antilles and the Kalinagos of the Lesser Antilles islands. However, the Maya of Belize and Mexico and the Inca of South America are also discussed because various definitions of the Caribbean do include these mainland territories.

Life for the Tainos included constructing makeshift palm houses (homes they would evacuate for inland caves in the event of a hurricane) in complex settlements with plazas and other public structures, having a political system based around one inherited leader, the Cacique, and an informal economy centred around agriculture and fishing. They established this lifestyle as the Caribbean islands were not as expansive as the mainland and the only real threat to Taino existence came from the Kalinagos of the Southern Lesser Antilles islands.

Quick Fact

Though it is generally said that the Tainos settled in the Greater Antilles while the Kalinagos settled in the Lesser Antilles, they in fact shared the islands of Puerto Rico and Trinidad. It should also be noted that the Tainos of the Greater Antilles were not homogenous, but different groups with varying cultural practices and distinctive histories.

The Kalinagos

The Kalinagos mostly settled in the Lesser Antilles islands, which are even smaller than the Greater Antilles, and their generally hilly geography and rocky coastal regions provided less agricultural space. It is for this reason the Kalinagos posed such a great threat to the Tainos, whom they raided for agricultural produce and enslaved. In fact, they spoke an Arawakian language, presumably derived from captives. The focus of their society was more on warfare and trading than the Tainos, and it was generally more fluid with elected rather than inherited leaders.

Did You Know?

It is argued that the more fluid, warlike society of the Kalinagos, as well as their mountainous geographical location away from the main areas of Spanish settlement, enabled them to better resist the Spanish than the Tainos. The Tainos did actively, but unsuccessfully, resist the Spanish, who, after the decline of the Taino population, then turned their attention to the Kalinagos as a source of labour for their encomienda system. The Kalinagos embarked on many years of guerilla warfare and, as a result, remnants of their culture, such as basket weaving and the dug-out canoe, have survived.

Exam Tip

The Tainos and Kalinagos have been referred to in the past as 'uncivilised'. As students of history, we must recognise that it is not our place to be **ethnocentric**, which is the act of judging other cultures based on the standards, customs and, often, the assumed superiority of one's own culture.

The Maya and Inca

The Maya settled mainly on the interior areas of Central American territories, such as Mexico (the Yucatán Peninsula), Belize, Honduras and even Guatemala. Like the Inca, who settled in South American territories such as Peru, Ecuador, Central Bolivia and Colombia, the Maya had a standing army as a result of their larger population and territories they had to defend from other groups.

Both Maya and Inca also had complex political systems, with the Maya choosing to elect their leaders while the Inca had a hereditary system where leaders rose to power based on family ties, supported by complex religious beliefs that validated leaders and their privileges. Both societies were also highly stratified, with systems to protect individual ownership of property, and had economies based on large-scale agriculture that both groups had the land space to support.

The Amerindian Cultural Legacy

Figure 5.2 **The Amerindian cultural legacy**

Amerindian invention	How/why adopted by Europeans	Today's usage
Cassava cakes	These cakes made of cassava/yuca flour did not spoil as easily as European wheat bread and helped to sustain the Europeans while they travelled in and out of the Caribbean.	Called 'bammy' in many Caribbean territories (other names include 'ereba', 'casabe') and traditionally eaten with fish (just like the Tainos did). A main source of income for many rural Caribbean farmers who sell them to hotels and locals alike.
Taino 'barbecue' (meat cooked on a grill made of green sticks called 'barbacoa', with indigenous habanero (scotch bonnet) peppers, allspice (pimento) and an assortment of indigenous herbs)	This method of cooking preserved the meat for long periods.	Jamaican jerk chicken and pork is a direct derivative of Taino barbecue.
Hammock	Installed on ships as a means of cheap bedding for sailors, and in trees to keep explorers off the ground and away from insects and other crawling creatures.	Used in homes in rural areas to relax or sleep. Many have been installed in major hotels and tourist attractions for relaxation.
Extraction of dyes from woods	The dye industry became a major Caribbean economic activity for many Europeans. This accompanied the increased cultivation of cotton in the Americas to fuel large European clothing factories.	The use of wood dyes is not widespread throughout the Caribbean as a commercial activity. The tradition is still continued by many high schools that teach students how to extract and apply these dyes as part of their course work.
Tobacco cultivation and smoking	Became a major cash crop for the European colonies (later to be largely replaced in many areas of the Caribbean by sugar). It was grown on large farms and often rolled into cigars and exported. Tobacco smoking became a symbol of the wealthy in Europe.	Its cultivation is still a very important industry in some Caribbean countries, such as Cuba.
Cacao cultivation and chocolate making	Chocolate was an important product to the European colonial economies up to the 20th century.	Agro diseases have led to a decline in cacao cultivation in the Caribbean. However, it is still produced in the region. Until 2009 the Dominican Republic led the world in 'Fairtrade-certified' cacao production and it remains a key producer.
Words such as hurricane, canoe, barbecue, hammock, tobacco, cannibal, cay (or key), barracuda, maize, cassava, cacao, manicou, agouti and savanna Place names and names of natural features in Trinidad and Tobago, for example, include Arima, Tunapuna, Mucurapo, the Caroni and Oropuche rivers, the Taman and Aripo mountains	Specifically Caribbean or American terms passed into common usage, a process facilitated by the use of Amerindian translators.	Many Amerindian words have become part of the language of Caribbean people and beyond, even if we are unaware of their origins.

European Migration and Settlement 1492–1700s

The European voyages of discovery of the late 15th and early 16th centuries, and the subsequent migration to the Americas from Europe, had a profound and irreversible effect on the Caribbean region and its indigenous population.

Reasons for the Migration

- The political, economic, cultural, technical and religious situation in Europe at the end of the 15th century and through the 16th century all contributed to the arrival and settlement of Europeans in the Americas.

Quick Fact

New maritime technologies included:

- compasses for determining direction
- sextants and astrolabes for calculating latitude and longitude
- more advanced maps
- better equipped ships such as the Portuguese caravel, which combined European and Arabic rigging making it easier to sail across and into the wind.

Key Terms

The Renaissance – often dubbed 'The Rebirth of Knowledge', a period in 15th-century Europe when citizens developed a renewed interest in scientific knowledge and the arts. This was largely brought on as a result of the invention of the printing press.

The Treaty of Tordesillas – an agreement between Spain and Portugal in 1494 dividing the known and as yet unknown territories outside Europe between them by an arbitrary line through the Atlantic, with Spain receiving territory to the west of it. As the line dissected Brazil, this went to Portugal, with the rest of the Americas being apportioned to Spain.

Hegemony – the political, economic or military predominance or control of one state over others.

Indentured servant – a labourer who paid for their passage to the New World by working for an employer for a fixed term of years.

- The European culture of maritime exploration exploded into fierce rivalry between Spain and Portugal with each attempting to discover the fastest sea passage to the wealth of the Far East. This coincided with the **Renaissance**, which, among other things, helped bring about more advanced sea-faring technology that made long-distant voyages more viable.
- The Portuguese explored the possible southern and western route along the African coast and found a route around the tip of Africa in 1488, while Spain financed Christopher Columbus' attempt to find an alternative route to the east by sailing westwards across the Atlantic.
- The internal politics and mindset of Spain also had a part to play. The Christian 'Catholic Monarchs' had recently succeeded in expelling the Muslim Moors from Spain in the *reconquista*. Further expansion and conquest was viewed as a necessity, as a means of increasing Spain's wealth and power to ward off any future Moorish challenges and as a way to expand and export the missionary zeal sparked by this religious conflict.
- Unsure and doubtful that Columbus' venture would prove successful, Spain sent three ships with limited human resources. This journey, in 1492, led to the first fateful encounter between the indigenous peoples of the Western Hemisphere and the Europeans.
- The Pope, worried that the discovery of a 'New World' would escalate Spanish–Portuguese rivalry into war, brokered the **Treaty of Tordesillas** between them in 1495.
- The discovery by Colombus of gold and precious stones in the Americas resulted in a rush of Spaniards to the region, including the Caribbean. These were mainly ordinary people fleeing poverty at home. At first, however, they came mostly to plunder and make their fortunes, not to settle. As the migration continued after the first spate of arrivals, Spaniards began to settle. Most Spanish settlement was in mainland South America, but in the Caribbean they settled mainly in the mineral-rich, larger islands of the Greater Antilles, more suited to large-scale agriculture and strategically placed to contribute to Spanish expansion.
- The desire of other European countries to end the Spanish **hegemony** over the region and its wealth grew as the 16th and 17th centuries progressed because of Spain's political rivalry with France and France's political and religious rivalry with Protestant England and the Netherlands. As a result, these countries financed expeditions, which were essentially illegal and contrary to the Treaty of Tordesillas, in an attempt to establish a foothold for themselves.
- In the Caribbean, for the most part, these other European states eventually managed to establish themselves and to settle in those areas (mainly the Lesser Antilles islands) of little or no interest to Spain because they lacked mineral wealth and vast tracts of agricultural land, or were not of strategic importance.
- Subsequent intense political and religious rivalry then went on to fuel a continued impetus behind colonisation, settlement and economic development in the region as European states and their citizens vied for control.
- Many of the early European settlers were labourers displaced by war, famine, poverty and other hardships. They were contracted as **indentured servants** on farms growing tobacco and other cash crops.

Did You Know?

There is an argument that the *reconquista* resulted in the evangelical nature of Spanish colonisation and their intolerance and suspicion of other religious influences, and that this, too, accounts for the religious ethnocentrism that is a feature of Caribbean cultures today, where even West African religious influences are taboo among some Christian West African descendants. The counter argument, however, suggests that Spanish Catholicism was better able to incorporate and tolerate native beliefs than the Protestantism of the Dutch or the English, resulting in the emergence of **syncretic** religions, such as Santeria in Cuba.

Effects of the Migration

The conquest and control of Caribbean and American territories, once solely inhabited by indigenous peoples of the region, started with Columbus naming the first group of islands he encountered San Salvador (modern day Bahamas) in 1492. This was the first American territory claimed by the Spanish.

1. **Cultural effects**
   * The Treaty of Tordesillas granted Spain almost unrestricted control over the Caribbean for over a century. This gave the Spanish freedom of choice of where to settle and establish their colonies. Thus, Spanish cultural influence (such as language, place names, Roman Catholicism and architecture) is most strong in the islands of the Greater Antilles, in particular Cuba, Santo Domingo and Puerto Rico.
   * The subsequent changing and fluid political make-up of the region, with some territories changing hands over and again, often reflecting the changing balance of power in Europe, resulted in a diverse admixture of European cultural influences both across the region and within territories themselves. Trinidad, for example, has Spanish, French and British cultural influences, while Dominica passed from the French after many years of colonial rule to the British.

2. **The decline of the indigenous populations**
   * One of the most devastating effects that the coming of the Spanish and then other Europeans had on the Americas was the **genocide** of various Amerindian groups. For example, the 1516 Spanish census in Hispaniola recorded only 12 000 indigenous people compared to 3 million in 1496.
   * The Spanish introduced the *encomienda* system in which indigenous Amerindians were expected to pay tribute to the Spanish and to labour in their fields and mines, in exchange for 'protection' and instruction in Christianity (specifically Roman Catholicism). The overly harsh implementation of this system is thought to be one of the factors behind the decline in the indigenous population.
   * Other factors behind the steep fall in the indigenous population were a declining birth rate, wars in which they attempted to expel Europeans from their territories and succumbing to diseases, such as smallpox and syphillis, which were brought by the Europeans. Some found it difficult to cope with the food shortages and the unsettled nomadic lifestyle they now had to adjust to, and died of

Quick Fact

European governments would covertly sanction, and even financially back, 'Lord Proprietors' to undermine Spanish influence in the colonies by illegally settling there. They also unofficially sanctioned acts of 'piracy' committed by their own citizens against the Spanish treasure fleets.

Quick Fact

The first permanent British colony in the Caribbean was on St Kitts in 1623 (though they had already established a colony in Bermuda in 1612). They shared the island with France, who also used it to establish its own foothold in the region in 1625.

Key Terms

Syncretic – the combination of different forms of belief or practice.

Genocide – the deliberate and systematic extermination of a national, ethnical, racial or religious group.

Making the Connection

The systems of production introduced by Europeans, including the encomienda, and the impact of these on the region are looked at in more detail later in this chapter.

Key Term

Metropole – the parent state of a colony.

Exam Tip

The mercantile system is a good example to use if you need to illustrate the extent Europeans went to in order to assert their control over, and ownership of, all aspects of colonial life. For example, in essays that ask the extent to which you believe that control by Europe of Caribbean territories still exists today.

Making the Connection

The contributions of European colonisers of Caribbean territories is looked at in more detail in Chapter 9 'Societal Institutions'.

ensuing hardships. There is evidence that many Amerindians were also hunted and killed for sport.

Did You Know?

It is often stated that the Spanish migration into the Caribbean region led to the extinction of the indigenous people and cultures. However, many would disagree that such extinction took place because many direct ancestors of these indigenous people still live in parts of Guyana, Venezuela, Mexico and even in the Greater Antilles island of Puerto Rico. There are also remnants of their culture present today.

3. **The establishment of new systems of production and economic control**
   - The establishment of large-scale agriculture in the form of plantations, and its consequences, is arguably the most influential contribution of Europeans to the region. The plantation system formed the base of an economic system where all factors of production were owned and controlled by the Europeans and a social system where the European race and culture were established as superior to all others.
   - In order to protect their interest in Caribbean economies, systems were established to ensure that only the **metropole** would benefit from its American holdings. The Spanish enlisted the **mercantile system** while the British enforced the **Navigation Acts** to ensure that all proceeds from colonial businesses benefitted their mother countries.

Key Term

Mercantile system – an economic system characterised by restrictions placed on trade between colonies and countries outside of the metropole. The **British Navigation Acts** of 1651 were derivatives of mercantilism that were direct restrictions on the use of foreign trade ships for trade between British West Indian colonies and any other European nations. The French had instituted similar laws by 1644.

4. **Political influences and legal systems**
   - The colonising countries imported their own legal systems and institutions and systems of government. Some territories, such as Martinique, Guadeloupe and French Guiana, are still officially part of France and became *départments* in 1946.
   - The 'old respresentative system' consisting of a governor supported by an elected assembly was widespread through the British Caribbean, as was the adoption of the principles of common law.

5. **The introduction of slavery**
   - Enslaved people from West Africa were first introduced to the Caribbean to work in Spanish mines and on Spanish estates to replace the dwindling indigenous population.
   - In 1518, Spain granted the Portuguese, whose legal rights in the territories of West Africa had been legitimised by the Treaty of Tordesillas and the *Asiento*, a licence to trade in enslaved people to provide Spain's growing colonies with much needed labour.

- These licences were sold to the highest bidder and, as they were highly lucrative, there was fierce competition for them, especially from the mid-1600s when demand for enslaved labourers rose with the growth of the plantation system.
- African slavery became a large business enterprise that many European countries had a stake in.
- In 1713, the right to grant the *Asiento* passed from Spain to Britain as part of a peace treaty.

Figure 5.3 The main spheres of influence of the four main colonial powers in the Caribbean

Some territories, such as Trinidad, changed hands a number of times. The table shows where the influence of each colonial power was most strongly felt.			
Spain: Cuba, Dominican Republic, Puerto Rico. Venezuela and some other mainland territories are also considered part of the Spanish Caribbean	**Britain:** Jamaica, Leeward islands, Windward Islands, Trinidad and Tobago, Barbados, Cayman Islands and The Bahamas	**France:** St Domingue, Martinique, Guadeloupe	**Holland (now The Netherlands):** Aruba, Bonaire, Curaçao, St Maarten, St Eustatius, Saba

Quick Fact

Despite the *Asiento*, there was an illegal trade in enslaved people and other commodities carried out by Spain's rivals in the region. The Guiana coastline, Aruba, Bonaire and Curaçao (ABC islands) and the islands of St Martin, St Eustatius and Saba proved ideal safe houses for the illegal enslaved people and illegal goods of the Dutch West India Company. The Spanish had little interest in these islands that would eventually form the Dutch Antilles.

Figure 5.4 Summary of the main activities and influences of the four main colonial powers in the Caribbean

	The Spanish (16th century onwards)	The British (16th/17th century onwards)	The French (16th/17th century onwards)	The Dutch (16th/17th century onwards)
Economic activities	Gold and silver mining, farming, export of cash crops, slave trade	Illegal trading along with raiding of Spanish colonial fleets; later, farming, export of cash crops, slave trade	Privateering; later, slave trade, farming, export of cash crops	Colonial raiding, illegal trading of commercial goods; later, salt mining, slave trade
Labour systems	*Encomienda*, then European indentureship and African enslavement	European indentureship, then African enslavement, followed by East Indian and Chinese indentureship	African enslavement	African enslavement
Colonial government	Crown controlled (Council of the Indies) through colonial government consisting of Viceroys, *Cabildos* and *Audiencias*	Old Representative System and, later, Crown Colony Government	Direct Rule, followed by the *Départment* system in the mid-20th century	The Dutch focused on trading and commercial activites more than on permanent settlement, which required complex governmental structures. Even so, their legal and political systems were in evidence in their colonies in the Guianas
Main tools to control and benefit from the colonies	Control of the *Asiento*; the mercantile system	Navigation Acts	Code Noir (1685) – a legal framework governing slavery and the slave trade	Trading companies, such as the Dutch West India Company, who bid for and were granted the *Asiento*
Main influences	Spanish language and place names; Roman Catholicism (including an active involvement of church orders in education); architecture	English language and place names; Anglican Protestantism; Westminster (parliamentary) system of government; legal system through common law; formal education system; plantation society and economy	French language and place names; Roman Catholicism (including an active involvement of church orders in education); plantation society and economy	Dutch language and place names; The Dutch Reform Church (Protestant)

Making the Connection

Chapter 6, 'Characteristics of Society and Culture'

Chapter 7, 'Identity and Social Formation'

Exam Tip

'**Examine**' requires a detailed study in an extended answer defining key concepts, stating the facts and exploring related concepts and issues.

Check Your Knowledge

Using examples to illustrate your answer, examine THREE major features of Caribbean society today that were a result of European migration to, and settlement in, the Americas.

Demonstrate an understanding of the following terms and concepts by defining and using them correctly:

- European
- Migration
- Colonisation
- Settlement
- Hybridisation
- Caribbean society
- Americas
- Treaty of Tordesillas
- Social stratification
- Cultural pluralism
- Slavery
- Plantation society
- Genocide

You must examine THREE of the following:

- **Socio-cultural features**: Europeans' stress on the superiority of their race and culture resulted in social stratification that still exists today, based on race and colour. The introduction of peoples of different races and cultures led to cultural diversity or pluralism. Examples of cultural features and practices introduced by the Europeans are:
  - **place names**: Spanish, French, English;
  - **language**: propagation of European forms. Standard English is still distinguished as the official language, while other forms are only acceptable in informal settings;
  - **religion**: the Christian religion, which influenced the **education system**, indoctrinated Black people to be hard working and submissive labourers. A Christian-based education system still teaches students to be hard working and subservient members of society. African religious practices, such as Obeah, are seen as taboo, while forms of European Christianity (though hybridised and adapted to the Caribbean situation) are usually accepted.
- **Education system**: Caribbean boys and girls were trained to be good colonials; boys were favoured over girls, European education models were followed and there was a lack of positive references to African, East Indian or indigenous people and their heritage. Today's education system still contains vestiges of these features:
  - European architecture
  - European **food**
  - European dance and music.
  - **Demographic features**: The near genocide of the indigenous population resulting from the introduction of the *encomienda* system, together with wars, food shortages and diseases, such as smallpox and syphilis, brought by the Europeans.
- **Economic features**: The Europeans introduced new economic features in the form of:
  - large-scale agriculture on plantations; the plantation system formed the base of an economic system where all factors of production were owned and controlled by the Europeans. To ensure that only the metropole would profit, the Spanish enforced

- the mercantile system and the British enforced the Navigation Acts. Wealth today is still concentrated in the hands of a few and the economic influence of ex-metropoles is felt through neo-colonialism;
- the introduction and expansion of slavery as a huge business. Descendants of these enslaved people form the majority ethnic group in today's Caribbean.
- **Political and legal features**: Colonising countries brought their own legal systems and institutions and systems of government. The 'old representative system' was widespread through the British Caribbean as was the adoption of the principles of common law; for example, the English introduced the Westminster (parliamentary) system of government to Trinidad and Tobago.
- A possible **conclusion** is a summary of the main ideas.

The Forced Migration of Africans 1500–1807

The Triangular Trade

The majority of African enslaved people were captured in the interior of West African states and then transported on foot to the coastal regions by African slave raiders to await embarkation on ships that would take them across the Atlantic on the **Middle Passage** of the **Triangular Trade** route.

Figure 5.5 **The Triangular Trade route**

> ### Key Term
>
> **Triangular Trade** – the trade that operated between Europe and Africa, Africa and the Caribbean and from the Caribbean back to Europe. This trade formed the hub of commercial activity in many European port cities.
>
> **Middle Passage** – The leg of the Triangular Trade route between Africa and the Caribbean.

Figure 5.6 The enslaved people were tightly packed below the decks of large cargo ships owned by European slave-trading companies

Figure 5.7 The enslavement of Africans 1500–1870

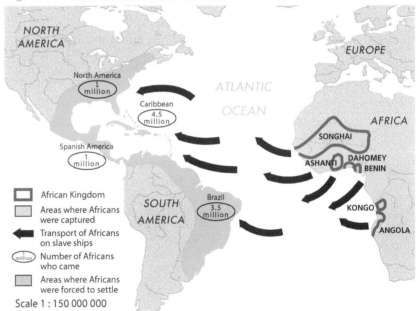

Many Africans died on the three-month voyage to the Americas, but around 10–15 million arrived, with 4.5 million being forced to settle in the Caribbean.

Reasons for the Forced Migration

After the decimation of the Amerindian population in the Caribbean and Central and South American mainland territories of Spain, there was a need for a reliable and cheap source of labour to cultivate cash crops on the newly established plantations.

The original Caribbean cash crops of tobacco and cotton declined because of competition from North American states. As a result, 'King Sugar' led to the growth of large-scale plantation economies by the mid-1600s. Sugar differed from tobacco in that it required much more extensive cultivation to be economically viable, requiring a much larger workforce.

Europeans believed that African labour suited this purpose for the following reasons:

- The Africans had already established a slave trade to support the need for cheap labour on the continent, aided by the relatively high degree of cultural and political fragmentation there, and the Europeans had already made contact and established a system of trade with the West Africans.
- African forced labour was about two times cheaper than European indentured labour (which was in quite limited supply anyway) and at least four times cheaper than European free labour would have cost.
- Many Europeans were of the view that African labourers were well-suited to plantation labour because they were already accustomed to the harsh tropical weather and vigorous labour in Africa. It was a common belief that they would make a more durable workforce than the Amerindian or European labourers.
- Plantation labour was intensive. The average enslaved person had a lifespan of around 7–9 years on a typical sugar plantation, thus labour had to be easily replenished and Africa could provide an endless source with vast populations on its west coast alone.
- Trade with Africa had already been established, making the trade in humans a matter of simple exchange of European goods such as rum, clothing, old muskets and glass beads for enslaved Africans.

Effects of the Forced Migration

1. **The growth of the plantation system and increased sugar production**
   - The transportation of Africans to the Caribbean led to the growth of the plantation system, based around large-scale farming units and the establishment of a social class structure where Europeans rose to the top as the wealthy owners of production and the Africans were strategically positioned at the bottom.
   - The large-scale production of sugar, that this forced migration facilitated, generated considerable wealth for the European colonial powers and satisfied the increased demand for sugar in Europe. (Sugar was Britain's largest import by the mid-18th century.)
2. **The introduction of new cultural practices and influences**
   - The African people were constantly reminded of their position in society by the many restrictions placed on them by the ruling **plantocracy**. This made it nearly impossible for African cultural forms to transition into Caribbean society. The Europeans were wary of these practices and banned most, fearing a hidden agenda of rebellion and dissension. As a result, new cultural forms were born in the context of the 'New World', which emerged from the mixing of European and African traditions.
   - The Africans, now a disadvantaged group, developed a unique culture as a means of coping with and surviving the harsh realities of enslavement. These cultural symbols are still evident in Caribbean language, religion, music and dance forms. Modern examples of the African influence in modern Caribbean culture are: the existence of the religious movements Santeria, Vodou and Obeah; the heavy influence of the drums in music; and the dependence on herbal traditional medicine, especially among rural communities.

Quick Fact

The relatively high degree of cultural and political fragmentation in Africa contributed to the conditions that made it conducive to the supply of enslaved labour. Generally, African rulers allowed and even supported the trade by providing the Europeans with slave raiders and guides willing to pillage villages belonging to rival communities for human commodities. They received numerous European goods in exchange for human cargo.

Key Term

Plantocracy – a term used to to describe the ruling class of plantation society that owned the main means of production (land and labour).

Some African-derived traditions are still taboo and restricted in the Caribbean because of the continued negative perception attached to these beliefs. One example can be found in Jamaica, where the Obeah Acts (1760 and 1898) render the practice illegal. Obeah is a religious practice of African origin that involves the use of herbal medicines for healing and to make contact with ancestral spirits. Many planters thought the practice to be uncivilised, dangerous and ungodly. These labels still brand the practice today.

3. **The establishment of new social norms as a result of 'plantation culture'**
   * The institution of the extended family was the African tradition most affected by the European restrictions. Marriage and even loose family structures were prohibited for enslaved people in most British Caribbean colonies. White people only allowed copulation among Black people for the purposes of breeding. On most plantations, children did not get the chance to meet their fathers. Some scholars have argued that the tradition of absentee fathers and common law relationships in the Caribbean are the result of this plantation culture.
   * A noticeable result of Africans coming to the Caribbean is the racial stratification that is still evident many decades after slavery ended, and the distrust and tensions in society it generates.

4. **Demographic change**
   * Territories of the British, Dutch and French, where plantations were first established, saw the influx of a dominant African segment of their population. The Spanish introduced plantations later into their colonies and so, here, the African segment of the population is not so dominant.
   * Another change to the demography of the region was the increase in numbers of those of mixed race – at the time termed, '**mulattos**'. This term is offensive.

Key Term

'**Mulatto**' – a person having mixed ancestry – a White parent and a Black parent. The term is old fashioned and not in use today.

It is extremely offensive as its meaning is linked to the word mula or mule.

Quick Fact

The British abolished the slave trade in 1807, but slavery itself was not abolished in British territories until 1834. The Dutch and the French later followed the British lead, but slavery was only finally abolished in Cuba in 1886.

Making the Connection

* Chapter 6 'Characteristics of Society and Culture'.
* Chapter 7 'Identity and Social Formation'.
* Chapter 9 'Societal Institutions'.

Check Your Knowledge

"The forced migration and enslavement of African people in the Caribbean has left them detached from their original culture and led them to appreciate and accept the culture of the Europeans."

With the use of examples from the Caribbean, discuss the extent to which you agree with this statement.

Demonstrate an understanding of the following terms and concepts by defining and using them correctly:

* Forced migration
* Enslavement/slavery
* Cultural diversity
* Cultural pluralism
* Culture
* Cultural imperialism
* Cultural erasure
* Assimilation
* Enculturation
* Cultural/ethnic hybridisation
* Culture of resistance

You must debate the extent to which there is:

1. **a sense of detachment from original African culture;**
2. **an appreciation and acceptance of the culture of the Europeans:**
   - Establish how colonialism, slavery and plantation society negatively impacted on the cultural practices of Africans. During slavery African cultural practices were illegal resulting in a degree of detachment.
   - New cultural forms were developed from the mixing of European and African traditions. Africans therefore developed a unique culture as a means of coping with and surviving the harsh realities of enslavement.
   - Show that the degree of acceptance and appreciation is debatable, especially since cultural practices were forced upon them by their 'masters'. Some passively resisted and others were more overt in their resistance.
   - Discuss the extent to which the following may occur to show varying levels of detachment, appreciation and acceptance of the culture of Europeans:
     - **Creolisation** – the original cultural practice underwent a change and became different. The new creolised form, which may be similar in appearance, is different in nature and context from the original. A gradual (and ongoing) historical process that gave birth, in the Caribbean, to new art forms.
     - **Acculturation** – an essential part of the Creolisation process as it permits the creation of a new, unique 'mix' of cultural elements that define the Caribbean.
     - **Cultural assimilation** – a process of active participation of various ethnic groups that allows their cultures to be fused together into one dominant cultural expression. It usually involves the acceptance and active participation by various cultural groups towards acceptance of the dominant cultural expression that identifies with all.
     - **Cultural hybridisation** – when original cultural practices merge to create a new accepted culture.
     - **Syncretism** – the merging of separate traditions (e.g. religious) to create a more accommodating form accepted by the wider society.
     - Stress the **cultural imperialistic** ideology of assimilation and superimposition of ethnocentric norms and values, that is the European culture in Caribbean society, with varying degrees of hybridisation (for instance, immediate change of names to European ones, change in diet, change from traditional ancestral worship to Christianity).

Give examples of how:

- some **African cultural practices** are still apparent in Caribbean **language**, **religion**, **music** and **dance** forms, such as the religious movements Santeria, Vodou and Obeah; the heavy influence of the drums in music; and the dependence on herbal traditional medicine;
- Africans were detached or separated from the institutions of **family and marriage**; marriage and family structures were banned for enslaved people.

Consequently, absentee fathers and common law relationships in the Caribbean are the result of the plantation culture.

Summarise your points in a comprehensive **conclusion** that reiterates your stance.

Migratory Movements Within and Outside the Caribbean, 1838–Present

Figure 5.8 Migration to the Caribbean c. 1830 to c. 1920

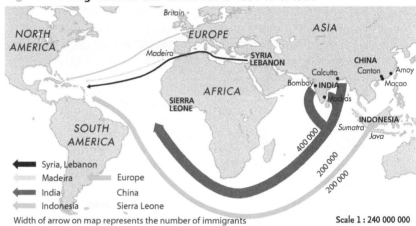

Width of arrow on map represents the number of immigrants

Scale 1 : 240 000 000

Asian Migration

Reasons for the Migration

The abolition of slavery in British territory in 1834 led to a frantic search by the plantocracy to identify another source of cheap and readily available labour. This was especially true in the larger colonies, where labourers took advantage of what was ample underused land to earn their own livelihoods away from the plantations, from peasant farming and animal husbandry.

The planters believed the formerly enslaved people would now charge unreasonable sums for their labour, so the introduction of competition in the labour market, in the form of willing immigrants, would keep the cost of labour in check. These labourers had to be easily replenished (like the Africans), hence the labour recruiters turned their attention to the heavily populated and poverty stricken regions of Asia, in particular China and India. The idea behind the scheme was the system of indentureship whereby passage to the colonies was provided in return for a set period of work.

Initially, the governments of these countries endorsed the scheme and encouraged the poor to embark on it, which would in turn relieve the pressure on them to care for their poor. The government of India even saw it as a way to rid the country of some of its **untouchables**.

After complaints of abuses of their labourers, the Chinese government ended the scheme abruptly, which led the recruiters to depend solely on India. When many recruiters started resorting to aggressive and illegal tactics, such as kidnapping and forging immigration documents to meet their shipment quotas, in 1917 the Indian government also stopped the scheme.

Key Term

Untouchables – the name given to any member of the lowest caste in Hindu society. The caste system of India was a rigid social structure based on the Hindu religion. This term is offensive.

Did You Know?

An European indentureship scheme started in the Caribbean in the 16th century when labourers were brought in to supplement the declining Amerindian labour source. An extension of this system emerged after slavery ended, when labourers from Ireland, Scotland and Germany were recruited to work on Caribbean plantations. This system lasted from 1834 to 1841. Approximately 5 000 European indentured labourers went to Jamaica, while around 200 found their way to St Kitts. The system failed because many Europeans disliked the rigors and restrictions of plantation labour and walked away from their contracts. Many descendants of these indentureship programmes still exist in parts of Jamaica named after their homeland; there is Irishtown in the St Andrew Hills, and German Town, also called Seaford Town, in the hills of Westmoreland.

Effects of the Migration

1. **Demographic impact**
   - The larger British colonies of Jamaica, Guyana and Trinidad received the largest number of Asian immigrants, and their legacy and influence are still prominent in these areas today. More than 400 000 thousand East Indian immigrants entered the Caribbean between 1838 and 1917, and approximately 20 000 Chinese immigrants came between 1852 and 1893.

2. **New cultural input**
   - East Indians brought with them new religions – Hinduism and Islam – as well as their own language and cultural practices. The Chinese tended to integrate more with the existing culture.
   - The Dutch brought Indonesians from Java to their colony of Suriname, where they now comprise around 15% of the population, thus adding to the racial and cultural mix of the region.

3. **Economic effects**
   - The arrival of the Asian indentured workers helped boost the sugar production industry, especially in Guyana, but resulted in a depression in wages as demand for other workers necessarily decreased. This coincided with a general economic downturn in the region.
   - The Chinese fostered economic diversity through their introduction of rice cultivation in Guyana, where rice production is still a major part of the economy.

4. **Social impact**
   - Racial tensions increased in the regions that received the most Asian immigrants. Conflicts arose as a result of competition for work, lands and women. Female workers were not as valued as men by the recruiters and so only a small number arrived on the scheme.

The Caribbean Diaspora

Before most Caribbean countries gained independence, citizens could travel relatively freely, for example for work or education, to other territories belonging to the same metropole. After 1838, this included now free formerly-enslaved people within the British territories.

The financial means for poorer Caribbean citizens to travel was provided by the emergence of credit unions, partner plans, colonial banks and other financial institutions, and, by the 20th century, technological advances in transport and communications made travelling via sea and land cheaper, faster and more efficient.

Figure 5.9 Emigration from the English-speaking Caribbean, c. 1850–present

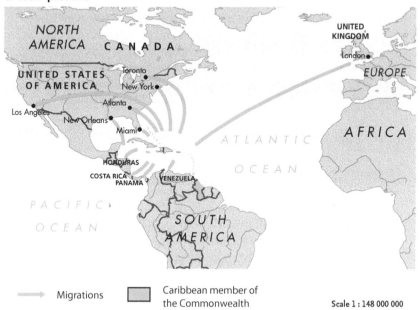

Migrations   ▢ Caribbean member of the Commonwealth   Scale 1 : 148 000 000

Movement of People Within the Caribbean

Towards the end of the 19th century, the labour market was swelled by formerly-enslaved people and many territories in the region also felt the pinch of an economic downturn. Many workers therefore went to seek employment in other parts of the region.

- In 1884 a slump in the price of sugar led to a wage freeze in Santo Domingo (now the Dominican Republic), and a subsequent labour shortage was filled by migrant workers from the Leeward Islands. These English-speaking Black people were often victims of racism, but many remained in the country, finding work in the docks, railway construction and sugar refineries.
- Many Caribbean nationals went to work on big projects, such as the Panama Canal (1903–1914), in order to avoid working on the plantations. Jamaicans, Barbadians and West Indians from Spanish, Dutch and French islands toiled together in Panama on what became a multinational project.
- There was also an abundance of work in the newly established Cuban sugar plantations, and on banana estates in Honduras and Costa Rica.
- The oil industry in Venezuela attracted many Caribbean nationals seeking jobs outside agriculture, as did the oil refineries of the Dutch islands of Aruba and Curaçao, along with their emerging tourist industries.

Migration Outside the Caribbean

In the 20th century many Caribbean nationals travelled outside the region to Europe, the United States and Canada. Early 20th-century Caribbean immigration in New York transformed the Harlem area of the city, which became the location for the international headquarters of Marcus Garvey's Universal Negro Improvement Association (UNIA).

Many also travelled during and after the Second World War to aid in the war and the rebuilding effort. This migration then led to many of their relatives joining them later as word of better opportunities spread throughout the Caribbean.

Migrant flows were affected by the immigration laws of the 'host' countries. For example, the Immigration Act of 1924 attempted to curb the flow of migrants to the US; the 1962 Commonwealth Immigration Act in the UK also introduced restrictions on Commonwealth migration.

Europe, the United States and some Caribbean states hosted a number of political refugees from Cuba and Haiti. The political restrictions and violence in these states pushed citizens to leave for more secure, liberal nations.

Effects of the Migration

The most noticeable impact of the migration of Caribbean peoples the world over is the formation of **diaspora** communities. These communities are very evident in cities such as Bristol and London in England, New York and Miami in the United States, and as far north as Toronto, Canada, where a 2001 poll suggested that there are more than 200 000 people of Caribbean descent living in the city.

Diaspora communities can be very influential, even influencing laws and elections in host countries. The Cuban people of Florida, for example, are said to have had a major influence in determining every United States presidential election since 2000.

One of the greatest impacts of the migratory movement of Caribbean nationals within and outside the region is the inflow of remittances to their remaining family and other dependants. This inflow of goods and money for dependent children led to the coining of the term 'barrel children' – children who received food and clothing from their parents instead of direct care. However, the downside to this type of migration is that many families can be disrupted as parents and spouses live abroad, sometimes for long periods.

The migration of uneducated and unskilled labourers enabled many to learn skills abroad that they put to use in their home countries upon their return. While the migrants did not exactly receive formal education or training in these skills, what they learnt from experience was enough for many to utilise back at home.

Migration eased the pressure on Caribbean governments to provide employment for their citizens. On the other hand, migration also resulted in a brain drain from home countries as many skilled and educated workers, such as teachers, nurses and doctors, left for higher wages in host countries. In Jamaica, for instance, the labour force decreased by 10% between 1970 and 2000.

Migration acted as a form of cultural exchange, where the music, language and literature of home and host countries expanded with the back and forth movements of migrants.

Making the Connection

Marcus Garvey and the UNIA are discussed in detail in Chapter 17 'Intellectual Traditions'.

Quick Fact

Almost a million people migrated to Britain; the largest migration was between 1945 and 1962. One of the first large groups arrived on board the *Empire Windrush* from Jamaica in 1948.

Key Term

Diaspora – the Caribbean diaspora refers to societies and living spaces outside of the region, where Caribbean people converge and form communities reminiscent of their homeland territories.

The Development of Systems of Production and Responses to Oppression

Systems of production were utilised by all racial and national groups in the Caribbean with each group having its own distinctive style of providing food and surplus goods for trade and use. This section focuses on the development of these, and how a few ill-conceived systems led to the oppression, and sometimes genocide, of Amerindians, Africans and Asians.

Slash and Burn

What is Slash and Burn?

The **slash and burn** technique of agriculture was employed by the Tainos and Maya centuries before the coming of the Europeans to grow maize, peppers and other provisions. The method not only clears the land in preparation for planting, but also gets rid of pests. The ashes left behind after the burning act as a type of fertiliser, and even pesticide. After prolonged cultivation on these slash and burn plots, the land is left to rest for periods of up to eight years in order to replenish the soil.

The Legacy of Slash and Burn

Poor peasant farmers adopted this technique of farming especially in the period after slavery and it is still employed today among those farmers with limited technology and resources to clear, fertilise and fumigate agricultural lands.

The Encomienda System 1520s–1720s

What was the Encomienda System?

The **encomienda system** was a policy adopted by the Spanish in the early 16th century for use in their American colonies. It operated as a system geared towards establishing Spain's cultural, social and racial superiority and dominance in the New World by subjecting the original inhabitants of the Americas to Spanish leadership and education. Tainos, Kalinagos, the Maya, and even the highland Inca, were subjected to the system.

After the Treaty of Tordesillas (1494), Spain needed to populate the Americas to effectively make them an extension of the kingdom. The Crown therefore offered grants of land to its citizens. The conquistadors who helped with the *reconquista* in Spain in the late 1400s were the first to receive land in the Americas. The awardees of these parcels of land were also given the responsibility to care for and protect the indigenous people, who, in turn, should repay the Spaniards, known as *encomenderos*, by giving their service as labourers or providers of agricultural produce.

It was these Spaniards' responsibility to provide the Amerindians with food, clothing and shelter along with the requisite religious and cultural instructions that were tied to the system. Many of these *encomenderos*

Key Terms

System of production – all the functions required (input, process, ouput) to create an end product.

Slash and burn – the clearing of agricultural plots by burning trees and other types of vegetation.

Quick Fact

Though widely practised in other parts of the world, the original inhabitants of the Caribbean are widely regarded as the pioneers of this technique in the region.

embarked on missions to find mineral wealth in the Americas using their grants of indigenous labourers as miners, while others established profitable large farms growing cash crops for export to European markets.

Many *encomenderos* forgot their duties to protect and instruct the Amerindians, and instead focused on their goals of obtaining wealth. Thus, widespread abuses of the indigenous people ensued:

- Labourers were often given impossible tasks to find gold in territories where there was little or no gold.
- They were made to toil at an unnatural pace for long periods to provide food for the growing Spanish population.
- Many were overworked, cultivating cash crops such as tobacco on larger farms than they were used to.
- They were subjected to harsh punishments.

Resistance and Responses to the Encomienda System

The encomienda system came under much pressure from high profile colonisers such as Dominican friar Antonio Montesino and Bartolomé de las Casas, who both recognised and reported the abuses of the Amerindians to the Spanish Crown. Reports were made of how the Amerindians were hunted for sport, punished unreasonably by cruel means and that they were dying at alarming rates because of these abuses.

The Spanish government attempted to regulate the encomienda system through the Laws of Burgos (1512–13) and the New Law of the Indies (1542), but these failed as they were met with resistance from the colonists who did not want to be told what to do with 'their labourers'.

The Amerindians tried to fend for themselves by forming bands of rebel groups that hid away in the mountain regions of the Caribbean territories. The harsh interior conditions proved too difficult for most of these former coastal dwellers and many died of starvation.

Many also succumbed to battles fought with the Spanish, and those who were captured died of the harsh punishments meted out. It is also reported that many opted to commit infanticide to save their children from the abuses before committing suicide themselves.

The system eventually came to a legal end in 1720 following the rapid decline of the indigenous population. By this time many had died of European diseases or the hardships that came with the European colonisation.

The Plantation System 1640–present
What was the Plantation System?

The **plantation system** is the longest existing system of production in the history of the Caribbean. It is the only system of production that spanned the period from the arrival of the Spanish to post-slavery.

Sugar and tobacco were the main crops grown on Caribbean plantations. Tropical conditions proved to be ideal for growing them. This, coupled with high demand in Europe resulting from growing industrial economies, brought many wealthy investors to the region who were looking to establish plantations.

Key Term

Encomienda system – indigenous Amerindians were expected to pay tribute to the Europeans (in gold, silver, crops, foodstuffs or other goods) and to labour in the fields and mines in exchange for 'protection' and instruction in Christianity.

Quick Fact

The encomienda system is often labelled as 'slavery'. This is not strictly true as, though it may resemble chattel slavery as a system of forced labour, it was not in legal terms considered a form of slavery.

Did You Know?

Today, little is known of the Amerindians as most of their history died with their people. Much of what remained of their culture and race merged with other cultural forms. Those that marooned themselves in the mountains, for instance, formed unions with the first Africans of the Caribbean that also ran to the hills to escape forced labour institutions.

There was little competition in the market because mercantile and navigation laws prevented trade with competing colonies. For example, Spain would only buy and trade goods with her Spanish colonies and prohibited other European nations from doing so. The principles of the mercantile system adopted by European states with regard to their colonies also dictated that the manufacture of goods from raw materials should be carried out domestically. Therefore, the colonies could only produce raw materials, not manufacture finished products. Crops were exported to European mother countries to be used as raw material to support European industries. For example, sugar was used to make sweets and baked goods and as a sweetener for beverages, tobacco was exported for cigar-making and cotton was extensively used in the European garment industries.

The plantation system, and in particular the cultivation of sugar, required large amounts of human labour and cheap labour sources were vital to the viability of these large farms that on average would be approximately 150 acres in size. The typical plantation needed about one labourer per acre for optimum production, hence the average labour-intensive plantation utilised 150–160 labourers for various tasks.

The Caribbean plantations were self-sufficient for the most part, with plantation managers even encouraging the labourers to grow their own food in a bid to cut costs. A typical plantation in the Americas had living quarters for the labourers equipped with garden plots known as 'provision grounds' for growing food, though flour, rice and salted meats had to be brought in.

Most sugar plantations had a sugar factory to process the cane into raw sugar. This was usually in a central location for efficiency, and wood for fuel was harvested from forested areas on the plantation.

All costs were kept to a minimum to ensure maximum profits. During slavery, labourers received meals and yearly clothing allocations. After slavery, employees were responsible for their own living expenses and had to pay the planters rent for plantation housing.

Plantation labour was harsh and intense, so much so that on many plantations life expectancy for enslaved people was only 7–9 years. Labour was just as intense in the post-slavery era as plantation owners did their best to coerce labour from their paid employees in order to get 'value for money'.

There were no gender-specific tasks on the typical plantation; labour was divided according to the age and health of the labourer. Planters were only concerned with maximising efficiency, hence women worked alongside men. Children and the elderly or sickly did lighter tasks, such as weeding of the fields and animal husbandry.

Plantation workers were often subjected to hot and inhumane conditions in the fields and sugar factories. They worked throughout the day and an overseer would try to ensure that production was not slowed regardless of illness among workers, adverse weather conditions or fatigue.

Labourers who disobeyed instructions or tried to abscond from their duties were often punished harshly. The enslaved were beaten or even killed for resisting their masters, while paid labourers were denied wages or had the benefits that came with their contracts rescinded.

The plantation system was also a means of social control because those who laboured were subject to its rules and regulations. For instance, the enslaved Africans were not allowed to leave the plantation without the permission of their masters.

How is Plantation Society Reflected in Modern Caribbean Life?

The table below highlights the general similarities between modern Caribbean societies and the former plantation society.

Exam Tip

The table lists general similarities between modern and plantation societies. In order to answer an essay question on this in the exam, you will probably be required to think of similarities and differences with your own local experiences.

Figure 5.10 Similarities between modern society and the plantation society

Plantation society	Modern Caribbean society
Domination of agricultural landscape by plantations	Continued dominance of sugar plantations in, for example, Guyana, Trinidad, Jamaica, Belize, Cuba and Dominican Republic
White control of the means of production (land, factories, machinery)	Control of means of production (land, factories, machinery) predominantly by White or mixed race people
White/mixed race ownership of businesses (plantations) and mixed race people being given preferential labour in the plantation great house	While education has levelled the field to some extent, ownership of, and managerial positions in, businesses and industries controlled by the private sector and important civil servant posts seem to still be reserved for the White and lighter-skinned upper classes while menial labour is done by a large number of Black staff
Black/African culture discouraged and often suppressed	Still typically the case in the modern Caribbean, where in many territories African religious practices such as Obeah are still taboo (even illegal), while various forms of European Christianity (albeit hybridised and adapted to the Caribbean stuation) are widely accepted European languages are still recognised as the official language of most territories in the Caribbean, while forms of language that incorporate elements of African languages, for example patois in Jamaica, are only acceptable in informal settings
White people lived apart in the plantation great house while Black people were relegated to poor housing facilities with little or no sanitation	In most Caribbean territories, the upper classes (mostly consisting of White and mixed race people, who own the means of production) control and own the most preferred property. While there has been some progress towards a more equitable situation and many Black people have moved up the economic ladder through education, employment and entrepreneurship, there are still more poor Black people living in slum and ghetto areas than other groups
Christian-influenced education system that taught Black people to be hard-working and subservient and submissive labourers	A Christian-based education system still teaches students to be hard working and subservient members of society as it is the 'Godly' thing to do. These desired behaviours are enforced through a strict system of punitive sanctions and reward systems
Laws, political system and a militia established to protect the wealth and property of the White plantocracy	The laws of many Caribbean countries still seem to protect the property and interests of the upper classes disproportionately. Caribbean prisons are filled with members of the lower classes while most 'white collar' crimes that the upper class tend to commit are punished with light sentences and fines

Resistance and Responses to the Plantation System

There were many forms of effective resistance to the plantation system, both under slavery and after. For example, plantation workers often feigned illness in order to escape labour. Plantation workers also used language barriers to their advantage by pretending to misunderstand the instructions of their overseers. Labourers would even maim animals used in production or destroy plantation equipment in order to stall work.

After the abolition of slavery, many formerly enslaved people tried to find ways to avoid having to continue to work on the plantations. In larger territories, such as Guyana, Jamaica and Trinidad, where more land was available, they were able to set themselves up as peasant farmers, often squatting on free land but also forming cooperatives to buy large tracts of land where they grew food for subsistence and sale. On smaller islands, such as Barbados and Antigua, however, their options were

Making the Connection

Slavery underpinned the plantation system for more than 200 years. Not surprisingly, therefore, responses and resistance to the plantation system during and just after the slavery era were inextricably linked to slavery, which is examined in more detail in the next section.

Key Term

Chattel slavery – also called traditional slavery, is so named because people are legally treated as the 'chattel' (personal property) of the owner and can be bought, sold, traded and inherited as any other 'goods'. It is the least prevalent form of slavery in the world today.

Quick Fact

The children of White planters and Black enslaved women, known as 'mulattos', were often used as house enslaved labourers. This was because many White people did not think it appropriate for these fair-skinned enslaved people to be working alongside the darker enslaved in the fields as it made them seem equals.

limited and they often had little choice but to enlist to continue working on sugar plantations as paid labourers.

Partner plans, building societies and credit unions also emerged out of the need for many plantation labourers to escape its oppressive environment. For many, these financial institutions enabled the latitude to own homes, finance the education of their children and start businesses away from the plantations.

African Slavery 1500s–1838
What was Chattel Slavery?

Chattel slavery was the form of slavery used in the Caribbean. Most European traders and planters viewed it as an economic system; it involved the ownership and use of mainly West African people as labourers on plantations, the suppression of their rights and the imposition of new norms that meant them adhering to and carrying out the instructions of their 'masters'. Slavery was also a condition passed on through birth – children born to enslaved people were also enslaved – something different from other forms of forced labour.

The owners of the enslaved people, many of whom were White (though it was not uncommon to find 'mulatto' owners), used methods such as 'seasoning', which was the use of religious instruction and punitive sanctions, as a way to break the enslaved into desired habits that would make them easily manipulated and productive workers.

Most enslaved Africans were used on Caribbean plantations as cultivators of cash crops, such as sugar. There were also those who worked as artisans or skilled labourers, and some that performed duties in households and in factories.

While the labour in plantation great houses was not as physically intense as field labour, those who worked in the plantation houses faced the psychological stress of having to learn their masters' preferences so they could satisfy all their requests. Many females also had to withstand their masters' sexual advances. Women were seen as objects by their masters and were sometimes subjected to unwanted sexual advances. Many planters felt that they had a right to do with the enslaved women as they pleased because they were their chattel/property. If an enslaved woman should become pregnant by her master, she was often subjected to cruel forms of abortion that left many seriously injured or dead.

Enslavement of Africans, like *encomienda*, also served the purpose of emphasising European hegemony and social and cultural superiority. The enslaved were constantly reminded of their lowly status through the restrictions placed on their interactions with White people and White culture: the enslaved were not allowed to dress like the White people did; they were not allowed to carry swords, as this was a sign of status; nor were they allowed to socialise or speak to White people unless they were directly addressed.

Resistance to Slavery

Resistance to slavery took several forms:
* non-violent resistance
* flight, or 'maroonage'
* violent resistance and revolt.

1. **Non-violent resistance**
   - This included acts such as deliberate loss or sabotage of tools and machinery, malingering (feigning illness), pretending not to understand orders, mocking the White masters, and so on. More extreme forms took the shape of inducing abortions, to deny owners a stock of future enslaved people, and suicide.
   - African cultural practices were actively discouraged, but the enslaved's response to this was to create their own forms of hybridised religion and culture, and retain their language and oral and musical traditions where possible.
   - Non-violent resistance, coupled with resilience in the face of extreme adversity, though it did not majorly affect the workings of the plantations, did at least give the enslaved some feeling of empowerment over their lives.

2. **Flight**
   - Running away was an option, especially where there were areas of mountainous terrain that made pursuit difficult. Runaway enslaved sometimes joined forces with pockets of indigenous groups who had previously fled to remote areas to escape the early European colonisers.
   - They established 'Maroon' communities, mainly located in Jamaica, Suriname, Haiti, Grenada, St Lucia and Cuba, and were able to retain less-diluted African cultural influences than on the plantations.
   - The guerrilla warfare of the Maroons has been credited as a major factor in the success of the Haitian Revolution and elsewhere they respresented a thorn in the side of the plantocracy through their mere existence, not to mention raids on plantation estates, and a beacon of hope for the enslaved community.

3. **Violent resistance and revolt**
   - Forms of violent resistence resulted in severe punishment, but individual or plantation-level acts of violence against the White minority did occur. On occasion, but not often, resistance led to wider revolt and even wholesale revolution, such as in Haiti in 1791.
   - The only successful uprising was in Haiti, which resulted in the Republic of Haiti being governed by Black people from in 1804. This provided inspiration for other later, though unsuccessful, enslaved rebellions and grist to the mill for **abolitionists** who used it as a scare tactic to show what could happen in other colonies if slavery continued. Though later revolts failed, they all added to the strength of this argument and the Christmas Rebellion in Jamaica is thought to be the one that finally convinced the British authorities that emancipation was a necessity.

Figure 5.11 **Major rebellions of the enslaved**

Colony and name of rebellion	St Domingue/ Haiti: Haitian Revolution	Barbados: Barbados Rebellion	Guyana: Demerera Rebellion	Jamaica: Christmas Rebellion/ Baptist War
Colonial ruler	France	Britain	Britain	Britain
Main leaders	Toussaint L'Ouverture, Jean-Jacques Dessalines and Henri Christophe	Bussa and Nanny Grigg	Jack Gladstone and his father, Quamina	Samuel 'Sam' Sharpe
Date	1791–1804	1816	18–19 August 1823	1831–1832
Main causes	Disenfranchisement of the Haitian 'mulattos' by Haitian and metropolitan White people – all non-White people were excluded from most White privilages and cultural practices. Enslaved populations of more than 500 000 felt the c. 24 000 White people treated them inhumanly	An attempt to overthrow the British planters, gain freedom and take control of the island	About 10 000 enslaved people protesting poor treatment and the desire for freedom. Enslaved people mistakenly thought they were legally freed by Britain and were being illegally detained by their masters	The belief King William had granted emancipation led to c. 60 000 enslaved in revolt demanding more freedom and a working wage
Outcome	Escalated into war with France and 350 000 were killed by 1804. Victory for the rebels resulted in most White people being expelled from the colony and the first Black-led republic in the Caribbean. Black enslaved culture became the dominant cultural form	One quarter of the island's sugar crop was destroyed and nearly 1 000 rebels were killed. More than 200 were tried and executed	The rebellion was brutally crushed and approximately 250 enslaved were killed	More than 500 enslaved people and 14 White people were killed, and the economic damage was estimated at more than £1.5 million at the time

Quick Fact

Despite the failure of the later revolts of the enslaved people, their leaders, such as Sam Sharpe and Quamina, have entered the pantheon of national heroes, with streets and monuments being dedicated to them after independence.

Other Responses to Slavery

African slavery was condemned in both the Americas and Europe for its unChristian nature, its infringements of basic human rights and the cruelties unleashed on the enslaved. The system eventually ended in the British Caribbean with the passing of the Emancipation Act in 1833, with the enslaved in most colonies being set free by 1834.

Did You Know?

There are many interpretations of why the system of slavery came to an end. Different arguments that have been made over time include the role of the abolitionists, the role of the enslaved themselves in revolting and resisting, the question of whether slavery was or was not profitable any more and a shift in metropolitan economic policy away from mercantilism to free trade.

Some enslaved people continued to live on the plantations for an extended four-year period of partial enslavement, called the **Apprenticeship system**. This ended prematurely in some colonies, but lasted the full four years in others. Full freedom was granted in all British West Indian colonies in 1838.

The peasantry proved to be an important response to African oppression and enslavement among the former enslaved populations, especially in the larger Caribbean territories where land was available. After emancipation and the end of Apprenticeship, many Black people refused to remain on the plantations and there resulted a sharp increase in numbers of small-scale farmers engaged in the growing of crops such as sugar cane, bananas, ground provisions and an assortment of fruits. They also engaged in charcoal burning, fishing and hunting to diversity their earnings.

Availability of land was an issue and many in smaller colonies had no choice but to remain as labourers in the plantations, at least for the short term. Elsewhere, **peasant groups** used various legal and illegal means to gain access to plots. The most common method used was by squatting on 'idle' land (unoccupied and unused land) that either belonged to the state or private owners. In a bid to thwart squatting, colonial authorities implemented heavy fines and even imprisonment in some cases.

Peasant farmers often pooled their funds and formed cooperative groups to purchase large plots of land that was then divided and shared. The local authorities then implemented laws restricting large cooperatives from purchasing land. The most successful method employed by the former enslaved was to purchase land through missionary church groups. These groups, such as the Baptists and the Moravians, would use church funds to purchase large plots of land, and then sell it to the freed Black people in smaller, more affordable parcels. These plots were used to establish clusters of peasant farming communities that were called 'free villages'. Usually these lands were located in the hilly interior and proved difficult to farm. Importantly, though, they were situated out of the reach and watchful eye of the authorities.

Peasant farmers had little access to tools and additional labour to clear the often densely forested and hilly lands for agriculture. They resorted to traditional solutions. The slash and burn technique of farming was used to clear land for farming and also as a means of getting rid of harmful pests. The ash left over from the process also acted as a cheap fertiliser.

Key Terms

Abolitionist – an adherent of abolitionism, which was the movement to end the slave trade and set all enslaved persons free.

Apprenticeship system – a four-year transition period after emancipation during which the working hours of enslaved people and the wages they received for additional work were legally enforced.

Peasant groups – bands of formerly enslaved people who cooperated in various ways to achieve independence from the plantations by creating small farms outside the plantations to raise animals and grow crops for subsistence and small-scale commerce.

Check Your Knowledge

Using examples to illustrate your answer, discuss THREE ways in which the slash and burn technique aided in establishing economic independence among freed Black people up to the 20th century.

Demonstrate an understanding of the following terms and concepts by defining and using them correctly:

- Slash and burn technique
- Economic independence
- Peasant farming
- Free villages
- Freed Black people
- Crown lands
- Squatting
- Cooperatives

Outline and describe the slash and burn technique as a system of production and who were the pioneers of this technique centuries before the coming of the Europeans.

You MUST discuss THREE of the following economic activities among freed Black people that can be linked to the slash and burn technique:

- Peasant farming:
  - **Freed Black people**, especially in larger countries (such as Guyana, Trinidad and Jamaica) where lands were available, and who did not want to be tied to work on the plantations, established peasant farming, which allowed them to become economically independent.

- Poor peasant farmers had little access to tools and additional labour to clear the land for agriculture. They adopted traditional solutions, such as slash and burn. Its advantages were: it demanded limited resources and technology; it eradicated harmful pests; and it provided cheap fertiliser in the form of ash left from the process. This technique is still used today among farmers.

- In the smaller countries, such as Barbados and Antigua, there were limited opportunities for economic independence, as there was less available land, and many freed Black people continued to work as paid labourers on the sugar plantations.

- They used legal and illegal ways to gain access to plots by squatting on 'idle' land belonging to the state (Crown lands) or private owners or pooled their funds and formed cooperative groups to buy large plots of land that was then divided and shared. They also received financial help and support from missionary groups and abolitionist groups, who provided land to establish free villages.

- **Animal husbandry**: freed Black people who acquired land that they cleared by slash and burn, used it for animal husbandry. They cooperated to achieve economic independence from the plantations by creating small farms to raise animals and also fished and hunted to increase their earnings.

- **Selling produce**: freed Black people also used land cleared by slash and burn to grow crops for subsistence and small-scale commerce. They engaged in charcoal burning and squatted on Crown lands to grow crops, such as sugar cane, bananas, ground provisions and fruits, to sell in the local markets. This resulted in them becoming self-sufficient and economically independent.

- A possible **conclusion** is to summarise the main points.

Indentureship Schemes

What was the Indentureship System?

The **indentureship** system of production became widespread in the years following the ending of African slavery in 1834. It was most prevalent in the larger British colonies after the failed attempts to recruit and use European indentured labourers and the ending of Apprenticeship in 1838, when full freedom was granted to the African enslaved.

At this time in the British Caribbean, it involved the recruitment of labourers from China and India to work on plantations on a contractual basis. These contracts, binding for approximately 4–5 years, provided the planters with a large pool of labourers during the post-slavery era. The immigrants were recruited with the promise of a good life and a steady income in the Caribbean. They were also promised benefits, such as free passage back home at the end of the contractual period or a parcel of land, as a reward for their service. Most ended up in the larger British colonies of Jamaica, Trinidad and Guyana where many formerly enslaved people had left the plantations to engage in peasant farming on the land that was available there.

The scheme is often compared to slavery because of the intense labour required on the plantations and the abuses and breaches of the original contractual arrangements between immigrants and planters. Many immigrants were overworked and grew tired of the many restrictions, especially rules restricting their movement both on and off the plantation. There were instances of planters forcing labourers to remain as their workers by extending contracts by a year or more as punishment for tardiness or illness and being absent from work during the contracted period.

Resistance and Responses to the Indentureship Schemes

- Many of the labourers who were part of the schemes became increasingly frustrated with their strained relationship with the planters and abandoned their contracts prematurely to work for their peers who had settled and started their own businesses. For example, many Chinese labourers started laundries and shops where they used fellow Chinese as workers.
- It was planter policy to segregate Asian and African workers under the principle of divide and rule. Asians and Africans were housed separately, were given different jobs (for example, African-Guyanese foremen overseeing Asian-Guyanese cane cutters) and were subject to different working conditions and restrictions aimed at keeping the Asians on the estates. This, along with the fact that the arrival of the East Indians effectively resulted in lower wages, and an East Indian tendency to strictness in observing their own cultural norms, led to friction between the two communities, especially in Guyana and Trinidad where it spilled over into racial clashes. The legacy of this remains in the politics and economy of Guyana, especially, which are stratified along racial lines.
- Reports of abuses and comparisons to slavery did nothing to promote the system in the eyes of potential migrants or their governments. The Chinese government withdrew its endorsement of the scheme relatively early on and the scheme effectively ended in 1917 when the Indian government also pulled out.

Key Term

Indentureship – the state or period of being a servant bound to service for a specified time in return for passage to a colony.

Summary of Labour Systems, c. 1500 to c. 1917

Figure 5.12 **Comparison of forms of labour used in the Caribbean from the 16th to the 20th century**

	Encomienda	African slavery	Indentureship
Period of implementation	Early 16th century to early 18th century	16th century to 19th century	17th century to early 20th century
Application	Used by the Spanish to acquire labour for work in mining and agriculture	Used by all European colonies to provide labour for all aspects of plantation life and production	Used in British, French and Dutch colonies, but mainly by the British as agricultural labourers on plantations after the abolition of slavery in 1834
Labourers' place of origin	The Americas: Central and South America and the Caribbean	The Gold Coast/ West Africa: Ghana, Benin, Senegal, Angola, Senegal, Nigeria	Europe: Ireland, England, Scotland, Germany, Portugal; Asia: China, India, Indonesia
Reason for the system	Established to bring the Amerindians fully under the jurisdiction and influence of Spain and Christianise them while exacting labour in return for this 'protection' and religious 'instruction'	Established to solve the labour problem that arose as a result of the declining indigenous populations; shift to sugar production required more labour	Established as a solution to the perceived labour problems that would ensue after full freedom was granted to enslaved Africans
Entitlements of the labourers	Labour for religious and cultural instructions from the Spanish. Labourers were bonded for 6–8 months	Enslaved Africans were legally the chattel of Europeans and provided free labour until they died or were set free	Indentured servants worked for a wage until their five-year contracts ended
Cruelties of the system	Amerindian culture was suppressed; labourers were overworked, killed for sport, punished inhumanly; the population was brought to the brink of extinction	African culture was suppressed; objectification of labourers; labourers lived and worked in harsh conditions and were punished inhumanly; descendants of the enslaved faced a legacy of poverty and low social status as an effect of slavery	Unhealthy and inhumane working conditions with strict regulations; workers were cheated out of contractual entitlements and wages
How it ended	Ended in the 1720s by the Spanish government because of reported cruelties and failure of the *encomenderos* to adhere to laws established to protect the labourers	The slave trade was made illegal in 1807 by the British government and African slavery officially ended in 1834 (British) with full freedom in 1838; The system was abolished for a combination of factors: abolitionist movement; fear of rebellion; economic considerations; changes in trade policies	Effectively ended in 1917 when the Indian government no longer allowed recruiters to export labour; also came at a time of decline in the importance of sugar to the Caribbean economies and an increasing glut of labour in the colonies

Movements Towards Independence

In other parts of the Caribbean, many territories achieved independence through revolution (for example, Haiti) or wars of independence (much of mainland Latin America). In the British Caribbean, however, independence was achieved through a gradual process of decolonisation resulting from the efforts of Caribbean peoples to push for greater rights and freedoms.

Discontent Among the Colonists

Long before political enfranchisement, adult suffrage and internal self-government was sought by the majority; many White owners of working capital in the Caribbean sought to be independent of the oppressive rules, taxes and economic control of their colonial rulers.

Most colonies faced extensive taxation from their metropoles. The metropole gained extensively from customs duties on goods going in and out of the colonies, and also from direct taxation on property and through the granting of licences. Many felt that, as tax payers and the sole investors in the colonies, they should have more of a say in how their colony was operated and how their taxes were put to use. Colonial legislative bodies, called **local assemblies** in the British Caribbean, often clashed with the governors and government bodies appointed by their metropole. The members of these assemblies were White landowners who had little vested interest in implementing laws and policies to help support the majority of the population.

The demise of the local assemblies and the **Old Representative System** was brought about by the Morant Bay Rebellion in 1865 in Jamaica. The rebellion had two important consequences: first, it helped convince the government in Britain of the need for constitutional reform in Jamaica; second, it alarmed the local assembly enough for it to decide to place its powers in the hands of central government. As a result, **Crown Colony rule** was implemented in Jamaica in 1866. Other colonies soon followed.

Many Black people thought the removal of the oppressive assembly would ameliorate the harsh conditions of joblessness and poverty that they faced, but in reality nothing really changed, as members of the nominated council under Crown Colony rule were from the same landowning and merchant classes who had made up the assemblies. It could be argued that Crown Colony rule curtailed the growing opportunities for Black people as it was imposed at just the time when some were starting to pull themselves out of poverty and could have begun to play a representative role in colonial government.

The Movement Towards Political Independence
Towards Political Enfranchisement

With the exception of Haiti, Black people were effectively excluded from meaningful political participation until the middle of the 20th century. However, during this period a number of experiences and influences came to bear which worked to promote the idea of **political enfranchisement**.

These included:

- Migration within and outside the Caribbean from around the turn of the 20th century, which exposed people to new and different experiences, philosophies and ideas.
- Soldiers returning from the First World War, who had been fighting for the 'motherland' and who had experienced racism in Europe, had been exposed to radical political currents and were diassatisfied with returning to unemployment at home.
- The Great Depression caused even greater economic and social hardship, resulting in a number of protests, strikes and riots across the region in the period 1929–38. Outlets for migration were also closed off as countries, such as the United States, imposed restrictions on immigration.
- The emergence of the trade union movement was a means to highlight all that was wrong within the colonial workforce, including racial disparities in the distribution of jobs, and ruling White disinterest. Trade unions became advocates for the working classes, dedicated to promoting better working conditions and improvements to health and

Key Terms

Local Assembly – in British Caribbean colonies, this was the legislative branch of what was originally intended to be 'representative government' (the other two branches were the Governor, representing the Crown, and the Council). After emancipation this became a misnomer because the majority of citizens – the formerly enslaved,, along with many 'mulattos' and White servants – were excluded by the required property qualifications from both membership and voting.

Old Representative System – the form of government originally established in British colonies, of which the local assemblies were part, along with a governor and council.

Crown Colony rule – this was effectively direct rule from Britain. The representative assembly was replaced by a nominated legislative council chaired by the governor.

Political enfranchisement – freedom from political subjugation; the ability of a nation to determine its own affairs.

Quick Fact

The Morant Bay Rebellion was a protest by Black labourers against the colonial government's neglect of Black people, which ended in violence after the governor ordered the crowd to disburse and they refused.

Quick Fact

Trade unions had their origins among liberal-thinking middle-class Creole White people. The colonial rulers allowed them as a way of appeasing the workers and lessening the likelihood of discontent and dissatisfaction, but in fact they became part of the main thrust towards independence.

Making the Connection

Garvey, Pan-Africanism and other ideologies and their proponents are discussed in Chapter 17 'Intellectual Traditions'.

Key Terms

Franchise – in political terms, the right to vote in public elections.

Universal adult suffrage – the system whereby voting rights are granted to adults (initially aged over 21, but later reduced to over 18) irrespective of their race, sex or social class. Prior to this, the right to vote in the Caribbean was determined by the amount of wealth or property a man held, and women were not allowed to vote at all.

Political party – an organised group of people with roughly similar political aims and opinions that seeks to get its candidates elected to public office.

education. They were also a mouthpiece for those, such as Captain A. A. Cipriani in Trinidad and Tobago, who were critical of Crown Colony rule.

- Trade union leaders became immensely popular among the masses, with many, such as Norman Manley (Jamaica), Alexander Bustamante (Jamaica) and Uriah Butler (Trinidad and Tobago), going on to form political parties.
- The development of ideological currents in the 1920s and 1930s that promoted anti-colonialism, Black consciousness and Black pride. A major proponent of this was Marcus Garvey through his UNIA, which had chapters throughout the Caribbean, and his newspapers, such as *Negro World* and the *Blackman*. There were also movements for independence in the diaspora, such as the Jamaica Progressive League in New York.

The labour unrest of the 1930s, combined with looming Black radicalism, prompted the British government to set up the Moyne Commission (also known as the West India Royal Commission) in 1938. The commission recommended some consistutional reforms, such as a wider **franchise** and lower qualifications for candidates, but its main recommendation was that a colonial fund be established to take care of the needs of the colonial working class. It was, however, overtaken by the events of the Second World War and the progressive thinking that it unleashed and, even before the war had ended, the dismantling of Crown Colony rule and the route to self-determination for the Caribbean began.

Universal Adult Suffrage and Internal Self-government

The process of dismantling existing political systems in the Caribbean occurred at different times in different colonies, but the outline was broadly similar, with the first step being the introduction of **universal adult suffrage**. This finally heralded the dawn of mass politics in the Caribbean and it was first put into effect in elections in Jamaica in 1944 (followed by Trinidad and Tobago in 1945, Barbados in 1950 and British Guiana in 1953). Many Caribbean citizens saw the franchise as a way of expressing their dissatisfaction with the neglect of their suffering under colonial rule, and further saw it as a way of electing representatives that would lobby for the amelioration of their plight.

Mass politics involved the creation of **political parties**, and many of these grew out of the trade union movement and had the same leaders. The People's National Party (PNP) of Jamaica, for example, grew out of the National Workers' Union (NWA) and was led by Norman Manley, while the Jamaica Labour Party (JLP) grew out of the Bustamante Industrial Trade Union (BITU) led by Alexander Bustamente. Other parties across the region at independence included the Barbados Progressive League, led by Grantley Adams, the People's Progressive Party, led by Cheddi Jagan (Guyana), and the People's National Movement, led by Eric Williams (Trinidad and Tobago).

As well as the extension of the franchise, the system of **internal self-government** was also progressively established in which the complete authority of the governor under Crown Colony rule was gradually replaced by increasing the powers of elected members of government, including the appointment of ministers of individual departments and a chief minister from among these elected members. As the traditional make-up of the various legislative bodies was increasingly challenged by members elected by the majority of the population to represent and protect their needs and rights, the mindset of the old colonial political system was eroded to be replaced by new thinking where colonialism had no place.

At the same time, post-war financial pressures on Britain's own economy, coupled with greater willingness to divest itself of its colonial possessions, came into play through a general trend of **colonial disengagement**.

Did You Know?

There was a school of thought in Britain that the Caribbean colonies were too small to be individually self-governing and this was one of the ideas behind the West Indian Federation (WIF). The WIF came into being in 1958, but was short-lived for many and complex reasons to do with suspicions both between colonies and of Britain's motives behind it. After Jamaica left in 1961, British colonies pushed for individual independence.

The Achievement of Political Independence

The, by now, inexorable move towards independence, coupled with the British realisation of the economic damage continued protests against central rule would cause in the region, culminated in the granting of independence, first for the 'big four' – Jamaica and Trinidad and Tobago in 1962, then Barbados and Guyana in 1966 – followed later and over time by smaller colonies, such as St Kitts (1983).

Did You Know?

Not all British colonies opted for independence. The colonies of Montserrat and Cayman, for example, chose to remain colonies of Britain, while Grenada, Dominica, Antigua, St Lucia and St Kitts, along with St Vincent, opted to accept associated statehood status in 1967 instead of independence. Most of these colonies would later gain independence, ending with Barbados in 2021.

Economic Independence?

Hand-in-hand with the movement towards political enfranchisement went attempts to achieve some sort of **economic enfranchisement**, which would ultimately form the base for a degree of economic independence. Because the large-scale systems of production chiefly connected to the plantation system were in the hands of colonialists and big businesses whose interests were tied to the colonial power, the opportunities to achieve this tended to be of a small, entrepreneurial nature. All this was against a background of a general decline in sugar production and the failure to find suitable alternative large-scale cash crops.

Entrepreneurial Activities to Help Achieve Economic Enfranchisement

While political enfranchisement lay ultimately in the power of the authorities to grant, a degree of economic enfranchisement was directly

Key Terms

Internal self-government – the situation where the Chief Minister (or Premier/ First Minister) and the Cabinet of a colony are in control of all the domestic matters, except defence and foreign affairs.

Colonial disengagement – the process by which a colonial power gradually divests itself of direct responsibility for its former colonies. With respect to the mid-20th century Caribbean, this occurred within a context of a general recognition of the right to national self-determination and of a global anti-colonial movement that saw independence being achieved elsewhere, including large former British colonies such as India.

Making the Connection

The WIF is looked at in more detail in Chapter 15 'The Integration Movement'.

Quick Fact

Most former colonies still recognise the British monarch as their head of state. The exceptions are Guyana (which became a republic in 1970), Trinidad and Tobago (1976) and Dominica (1978).

Key Term

Economic enfranchisement – the situation when a group of people or a country achieves the ability to determine how it develops its systems of production.

Making the Connection

The political make-up of the Caribbean is looked at in more detail in Chapter 4 'Location and Definition of the Caribbean'.

Making the Connection

The sections 'Resistance and responses to the plantation system', 'Other responses to slavery' and 'Resistance and responses to the indentureship schemes', above, provide more detail on some of these entrepreneurial activities.

accessible to the poorer classes through a variety of entrepreneurial ventures, including:

- the establishment of peasant groups and free villages to acquire and cultivate land away from the plantation system. They were able to diversify away from the main plantation crops into other crops, such as rice, bananas, cocoa, coffee and arrowroot;
- migrating and seeking jobs outside their home states in order to send home remittances;
- the establishment of small family businesses, such as shops and laundries;
- their involvement in savings societies and partner plans to acquire the financial means to set themselves on the path to economic enfranchisement.

It can be argued that while most Caribbean territories did achieve political independence, economic independence has been elusive – the major resources are still owned by foreign companies and local elites, and so full economic enfranchisement is something of a misnomer.

Multiple-choice Questions

1. The Treaty of Tordesillas was meant to :
   A. Prevent an escalation of the Spanish and Portuguese rivalry
   B. Divide Europe between Spain and Portugal
   C. End Spain's hegemony over the Americas
   D. Draw an arbitrary line between Spain and Portugal

2. Which of the following is NOT a consequence of the Treaty of Tordesillas?
   A. The undermining of Spain's hegemony in the Western hemisphere
   B. Genocide of the Kalinagos
   C. The introduction of the encomienda system
   D. The unofficially sanctioned acts of piracy by several European governments

3. The first British colony to be permanently settled on in 1623 was
   A. Bermuda
   B. Trinidad
   C. Jamaica
   D. St Kitts

4. Enslaved people from West Africa were first introduced to the Caribbean to work on
   A. Spanish tobacco estates
   B. Spanish sugar plantations
   C. Spanish cotton fields
   D. Spanish mines and estates

5. The *Asiento* in 1518
   A. Gave Portugal the licence to trade in enslaved people
   B. Gave Britain the right to trade in enslaved people
   C. Legitimised Portugal's rights to the West African territories
   D. Allowed the Dutch to become the main trader in enslaved people in the 16th century

6. The first indentureship scheme was started in the 16th century because
   A. There was a decline in the Chinese workforce
   B. The Chinese government stopped the scheme abruptly
   C. There was a dwindling Amerindian labour force on the estates
   D. The East Indian government stopped the scheme after reports of abuse of East Indians

7. Identify which of the following territories received most Asian immigrants
   A. Jamaica, Guyana, Trinidad
   B. Trinidad, Guyana, Grenada
   C. Trinidad, Guyana, Antigua
   D. Jamaica, Guyana, Barbados

8. In an attempt to curb migration from the Caribbean in the early 20th century, the United States established
   A. The Immigration Act on Commonwealth Countries in 1924
   B. The Immigration Act of 1924
   C. The Commonwealth Immigration Act in 1924
   D. The Act against illegal Immigrants in 1924

9. In 1938, the West India Royal Commission (Moyne Commission) was set up to
   A. Aid planters and enslaved Africans in the smooth transition to freedom
   B. Investigate trade union leaders
   C. Investigate labour unrest in the 1930s British West Indies
   D. Encourage the smooth transition from colonial to self rule

10. The practice of universal adult suffrage in the Caribbean was first seen in 1944 in
    A. Trinidad
    B. Jamaica
    C. British Guyana
    D. Barbados

Chapter 6

Characteristics of Society and Culture

After revising this topic, you should be able to:
- identify and discuss the elements and characteristics of Caribbean society:
  - a shared common purpose
  - a defined territorial space
  - continuity over time and space
  - citizenship within a state;

- identify and discuss the elements and characteristics of Caribbean culture:
  - learnt behaviour common to all humans
  - customs and traditions
  - norms and values which provide a guide to behaviour
  - institutions which prescribe behaviour
  - gendered practices.

How Can Society and Culture be Defined?

Key Terms

Society – generally speaking, in geographical terms, a society is a group of people that originates from a common place or a group that calls a particular location 'home'. A society can also be defined sociologically as involving the sharing of certain values and attitudes that serve as standards by which behaviours are measured and controlled.

Culture – the way of life, including aspects of lifestyle, products, ideas and symbols, common to members of a specific society, community or organisation. Like society, the concept of culture involves a number of meanings or aspects that work on different levels.

A **society** is not usually defined only by political borders on a map, but also by the similarities among the group that are used to identify them. Groups made up of members of a society may migrate to other places because of wars, shortages in food, natural disasters or even political and religious differences and thus transport their society with them. These general similarities in lifestyle, practices, products, values and beliefs are collectively known as **culture**.

When it comes to values and beliefs, the concepts of society and culture overlap – a sense of belonging (to a society) leads to the formation and reinforcement of shared values and beliefs (culture), while adherence to and sharing a set of values and beliefs in turn increases a sense of belonging.

The culture of a society has characteristic traits that can be used to identify those who belong to that society. A deeper interpretation encompasses the customs and generally accepted social behaviour of a group of people that is drawn on as a means of communicating and transmitting the history, values, ideals, beliefs and the future goals of a society. Being able to associate with and feel like part of a group or society based on its culture is referred to as **cultural identity**.

Types of Culture

Cultural forms can be categorised into material (tangible) culture and non-material (intangible) culture. Figure 6.1 shows examples of this.

Figure 6.1 Examples of material and non-material culture

Material culture	Non-material culture
Skills, products, processes and practices such as: • architecture • dress and jewellery • cuisine • technology • child-rearing practices • farming practices • religious practices • festivals • artistic creations (such as art, music and literature).	Values, ideas and beliefs such as: • language • moral codes and ethics • norms and roles • societal institutions including family and religion and the attitudes and beliefs enshrined within them.

Key Term

Cultural identity – the feeling of belonging, usually based on one's self-perception, to any kind of social group that has its own distinct culture.

Making the Connection

The Arts and popular culture in the Caribbean are investigated in Chapter 10 'Arts and Popular Culture'.

Did You Know?

Culture has many meanings on many different levels. It is a way of life, embedded within the values and norms of a society, and involves shared meanings and a shared understanding of those meanings through symbols, beliefs and ideas. Culture also encompasses artistic creations and expressions such as popular music, festivals and traditions. Various terms have been coined to express different types of culture. Some examples are:

• Popular culture – mainstream culture based on the tastes of ordinary people rather than elite culture or high culture (for example, popular music forms rather than classical music).

• Folk culture – localised and traditional aspects of everyday life, usually in a defined rural area.

• Other types include youth culture, cyber or internet culture, subculture, mass culture, ideal culture or real culture.

Exam Tip

All the characteristics of society and culture described in this chapter can be used both individually, to provide specific meanings of the two terms that can be applied to particular contexts, and collectively combined to produce full and rounded explanations of the terms.

Characteristics of Society

Shared Common Purpose

Society is often defined as a group of people who share common experiences, interests, objectives and values. In the Caribbean, the people of the various territories share a common history of colonialism, slavery (or other oppressive work conditions) and the plantation system. These shared experiences have given rise to a commonality in culture,

Key Terms

Cultural diversity – the existence of a variety of cultural forms, based on race, ethnicity, religion and other beliefs or values within a society.

Plural society – a society consisting of two or more distinct ethnic or racial groups who retain their cultural traditions and even their own dwelling spaces. Though these groups interact with each other, they retain their separate identities in fundamental areas such as food, religion and family life.

Quick Fact

The diaspora is not physically contained within the area known as the geographic Caribbean. However, they have preserved elements of their Caribbean cultural identity, which allows them to still be viewed as members of Caribbean society.

Making the Connection

Geographic definitions of the Caribbean are investigated in Chapter 4 'Location and Definition of the Caribbean'.

norms and value systems that help to structure people's interactions and relationships. For example, in the Caribbean, racial discrimination is not promoted and the principle that all persons have equal opportunities to improve their standing in society is also generally accepted.

Despite this 'big picture' commonality, however, the Caribbean can be viewed as **culturally diverse**, or even as a **plural society**. Plural societies transcend the uniformity that usually defines a society. Many different groups operate under the one societal umbrella, acknowledging and accepting each other while also understanding and viewing each others' cultural practices as 'normal'. For example, Christian, Rastafarian, Hindu and Islamic people understand that they share a common space in the Caribbean and are governed by a broad but common set of values that enable this shared society to function. However, where conflicting views of the common purpose exist, there have developed deep-seated tensions within societies.

A Defined Territorial Space

A basic characteristic of society is the sharing of a physical space by a group of people who have a similar cultural identity (common and distinctive beliefs and ways of doing things). This physical or territorial space can be used to define the area where a society exists. For example, Caribbean society is often identified on a map as those countries/states whose shores are washed by the Caribbean Sea (although there are also broader definitions of the Caribbean Region). It is a geographic characteristic of society.

Continuity Over Time and Space

The existence of a group and the most permanent aspects of their culture within a space over a particular period of time is also a characteristic of societies. For example, Mexico is a physical space or society where specific forms of language, dance and cuisine have been identifiable in that space of Central America since the coming of the Spanish. This is in contrast with the Haitian migrants who fled to Jamaica after the violent political ousting of President Jean-Bertrand Aristide and who have not been present long enough or in great enough numbers in the country for one to be able to say that a Haitian society has been formed within that space.

Citizenship within a Space

This aspect of society identifies the group of people native to a state or country, of which they are citizens or nationals. This is a political characteristic of society. Nationals are part of a society through their birthright. They were born in the territory in which the society exists and have government-issued documentation to verify this. This also serves to formalised their membership of the society in some way. Their proven descendants can also claim citizenship and thus membership of that society.

Citizens do not necessarily live within the 'space', however. Some may have migrated for work or study. Also, there are those who reside within the 'space' but are not citizens of it.

Illegal immigrants may also be considered part of a society, but not as a national or a citizen. For example, Korean and Chinese illegal migrant workers who operate businesses in Jamaica are not citizens of the country, but over time they have become accustomed to and take part in Jamaican cultural practices and are considered part of Jamaican society.

What makes 'Caribbean Society'?

The Caribbean can be defined as a society. There are a number of indicators that can be used to do this:

- A common history of colonisation by European powers such as the British, Spanish and French. Despite Caribbean countries having attained independence, these European colonisers have left their legacies in societal institutions such as family structure, education and religion, as well as a cultural legacy (such as language, architecture, food, sport or dress).
- A common geographic location of those territories belonging to it.
- A commonality in race, ethnic heritage and migratory patterns of its inhabitants starting with the Amerindians and continuing with the Europeans, the Africans and the Chinese and Indians.
- Shared language and forms of communication (dependent on the influence of the European colonisers).
- Similarities in religious influences and beliefs that help to form the general value systems of the groups that make up the society.

Any complete and comprehensive definition of Caribbean society must include the space called the diaspora: this is any area outside of the Caribbean where there is a strong presence of Caribbean natives acknowledging and practising Caribbean culture. Thus, Caribbean society can also be a sizeable group of Caribbean nationals/citizens who share a cultural identity and a common purpose living outside the realms of the Caribbean Sea (for example, the African-Caribbean diaspora in London; the Haitian diaspora in Miami).

Characteristics of Culture

Learnt Behaviour

Culture shapes our behaviour and culture is learnt – we are not born knowing how to behave. **Enculturation** is the process by which culture is passed on from one generation to the next, and from one society to another. It is part of a complex web of communication (voluntary and involuntary) called **socialisation** that tells the members of a society what are accepted behaviours and what is unacceptable. The teaching of basic, socially accepted behaviours such as not cursing in public, sitting upright in a chair and even proper grooming and hygiene practices are all things we mostly learn through primary socialisation (behaviour learnt through the family) and, later, secondary socialisation (behaviour transmitted through formal institutions such as schools or churches).

Did You Know?

The citizen of a state or territory is usually an individual who is either a native or naturalised immigrant. They are considered part of the society of the state of which they are a citizen. By extension, they are also considered part of any societal grouping, based on politics or otherwise, to which their state belongs. For example, all Guyanese citizens are part of both Guyanese and Caribbean society.

Making the Connection

Societal institutions in the Caribbean are discussed in detail in Chapter 9 'Societal Institutions'.

Key Terms

Enculturation – the process whereby an individual learns their group's culture, through experience, observation and instruction, and gradually assimilates its practices and values.

Socialisation – the process through which individuals learn the behaviours required of them from other members of a society (primarily the family) who communicate, express and transmit the society's values, customs, belief systems and laws.

Making the Connection

Chapter 9 'Societal Institutions' looks at the role of the family and education in the socialisation of children in particular.

Key Terms

Cultural values – commonly held standards within a society that dictate what is regarded as being of worth and what is considered acceptable and unacceptable behaviour. For example, the right to personal property is upheld as a value in the Caribbean and so stealing is abhorred.

Beliefs are convictions and are usually based on values, scientific facts, religion, superstition or past experiences. Christianity, for instance, represents a major belief system in the Caribbean.

Norms – common, acceptable and expected ways of behaving that are generally imbued within a society.

Did You Know?

Culture is passed on and learnt through the use of symbols such as language and value systems. Cultural symbols are verbal and non-verbal, unwritten and written indicators of the material and non-material things that a society values. Cultural symbols such as language and general behaviours can be used to express ideals and ideas that a society think are important. For example, language, which is probably the most important cultural symbol, is used to pass on the history of a society, communicate the laws of a society and even the religious beliefs of a society. Language can also be used to show a society's disapproval of certain traits that deviate from accepted normal behaviour and values. Traditional dress or meals, national flags showing specific colours, a history syllabus, feast and celebrations, gestures such as the giving of gifts, hugging and kissing, and even the drinking of alcohol at certain events such as wakes are all examples of Caribbean cultural symbols.

Cultural practices eventually become ritualistic behaviours or customs that seem normal to all in a society; even subgroups that may not share the same beliefs accept the cultural practices of their region as normal behaviour. These practices or 'normal behaviours' are termed cultural norms. For example, church attendance on a Sunday by Christians is deemed an acceptable and normal behaviour which even non-Christians have become accustomed to witnessing.

Customs and Traditions

Customs and traditions are expressions of culture that are based on practices that have been passed on from generation to generation. Traditions and customs are important parts of our Caribbean society as they preserve and maintain Caribbean cultural identity.

These customs and traditions help to determine in the minds of Caribbean citizens what they stand for, while at the same time enabling other societies to identify people from the Caribbean. Examples of cultural traditions are dance, arts and crafts, festivals and celebrations, and even rituals that form parts of religious and superstitious beliefs.

Norms and Values

Both **values** and **beliefs** act as guides of acceptable social attitudes and behaviour that help to form what is considered normal behaviour, or **norms**. Adherence to norms usually brings with it rewards such as praise, acceptance or advancement while those who go against norms can find themselves disadvantaged, criticised and open to ridicule. Thus, Christians, for example, engage in rituals that have become customary, such as attending church on a Sunday and praying before meals, because they are seen to be actions that will be rewarded in some way.

Shaking hands upon greeting friends, family and even strangers, refraining from certain acts that are considered cruel or strange, and refraining from eating certain foods because they are considered unclean or unusual are all considered cultural norms.

Value systems and norms are upheld and protected by sanctions (positive and negative) and laws. A very basic example is theft: those who steal are often ostracised by their community and theft is an illegal act. Values and norms can change over time, however. Many Caribbean territories have laws, which outlaw any act deemed to be homosexual. These laws were enacted at a time when homosexuality was viewed as a criminal act the world over. Nowadays, the views of many have changed and The Bahamas was the first Caribbean country that abolished these laws, thus decriminalising same-sex relationships.

Institutions that Prescribe Behaviour

Societal institutions, such as religion, the justice system, education, the economy and the family, are an important part of the socialisation process. They serve to teach and influence what is accepted as normal behaviour and help determine the value placed on particular attitudes and behaviour. They also play a significant role in determining and meeting out the sanctions and rewards associated with values and norms.

Did You Know?

There is a theory held by a school of thought referred to as functionalism that social institutions are important because they promote social solidarity, even among groups that hold views that are contrary to the general practices of the society they exist in. An alternative view, that of the conflict theorists or Marxists, is that institutions serve to preserve, reinforce and perpetuate the unequal and hierarchical structure of society.

Societal institutions are the main defenders and upholders of a society's cultural forms as they perpetuate their usage among, and reinforce their value and significance to, members of that society. In the modern world, globalisation seems to be an irresistible force and with it often comes **cultural imperialism**. In the Caribbean, for example, North American cultural traits and patterns have become pervasive and can easily be identified in food, entertainment, literature language, religion and other cultural forms.

It is the institutions of religion, family and education in the Caribbean that continue to promote and protect local forms of culture in the face of this cultural incursion. Likewise, the extent to which indigenous and African forms of culture have been retained in the region is mostly due to these institutions, in particular the family.

Gendered Practices

Gender is a factor that determines one's identity – who we are. A significant cultural influence exerted by societal institutions, especially the family, is on gender ideologies and gendered practices. For example, gender roles and behaviours are transmitted and practised within all types of Caribbean family, African, East Indian, European and Chinese, from a young age. Children observe and emulate the behaviour of adults in the home.

The education system also aids the perpetuation of traditional gendered practices in the choice of subjects at both secondary and tertiary levels that students tend to make, either on their own account or because of the choices offered them. Girls tend to the arts and 'caring' subjects while boys are directed, intentionally or not, to more technical or scientific subjects. In this way, education reinforces the norms, values

Quick Fact

Values and norms can be changed over time if non-conformist behaviour gradually erodes adherence to the status quo. For example, it has now become the norm for women to seek and hold public office with the support of a large part of the population whereas this was once inconceivable to most.

Key Term

Societal institutions – intangible bodies that exist within society and which represent established or standardised patterns of rule-governed behaviour. They include family, education, religion and economic and political institutions.

Making the Connection

Chapter 9 'Societal Institutions' looks at the societal institutions of the family, education, religion and the justice system in the Caribbean in detail.

Key Term

Cultural imperialism – also referred to as **neocolonialism**, the culture of a large and powerful country having a great influence on another, less powerful country.

and beliefs about gender roles already learnt in the family environment. This in turn influences the employment opportunities open to certain genders, notwithstanding the traditional family roles of the woman/mother as the caregiver and main child rearer and the man/father as the provider and protector.

Check Your Knowledge

Explain, in detail, THREE ways in which society and culture overlap.

Demonstrate an understanding of the following terms and concepts:

- Society
- Culture
- Enculturation
- Gender

First, in your introduction, define the main concepts 'society' and 'culture'. Set the scene for your explanation:

- Culture is the foundation on which a society is built. A society occupies a space and develops a culture in order to adapt to their environmental settings. The culture becomes a guideline on how to behave and becomes enshrined from one generation to the next. It is from this view that culture and society would overlap.

Select THREE ways in which society and culture overlap. They can include, but are not necessarily exclusive to:

- Norms/values/beliefs
  - Values and beliefs act as guides for acceptable social behaviour, forming what are considered norms (acceptable behaviour). Members of a society follow the cultural norms they were socialised in. To greet with a handshake, open doors for a woman and prepare a typical West Indian Sunday lunch are considered 'normal behaviours' to be followed in order to achieve praise within society rather than being looked down on or ridiculed for not following practices that society deems 'normal'.
  - Caribbean Christians believe in going to church every Sunday, thus making it a habit or a ritual, a behaviour that is eventually deemed normal (a norm) in social life. The general acceptance and expectation of such behaviours that become routine, become part of the way of life (culture) and are eventually enshrined in the code of conduct of that particular society.
- Socialisation
  - The aim of institutions in society – social institutions – is to socialise the young on how to practise their culture within a society. This is done throughout a child's life into adolescence, so that he or she can become useful, functioning 'normal' adults. Here the overlap between the two concepts is seen again. The teaching of this from one generation to the next – a process called enculturation – is necessary for the young to become acceptable and useful members of society.

- Culture has to be learnt by each generation, and the family is the social institution responsible for starting the process. Apart from the family, religious and educational institutions continue this process, defending and upholding society's cultural forms, reinforcing values and beliefs for the continued 'normal' functioning of society.
- Respect for elders, learning how to speak, walk and dress help one to 'fit' into that society – all representing aspects of culture necessary for the continued development of a society.
- Gender roles
  - In the Caribbean, gender roles have been perpetuated from one generation to the next as a result of enculturation. Knowing one's role in society, taught by social institutions received from the culture of that society, gives genders their positions in society.
  - Gender roles and positions are therefore practised in society, becoming enshrined in the code of conduct within that society. In the Caribbean, boys are taught from a young age that they are the protectors and the ones sturdy enough for outdoor chores. This cultural norm extends to Caribbean women, where it is the norm to perform nurturing chores indoors. Any gender who does the opposite can be frowned upon for 'defying' what is considered normal.
  - The overlap here between society and culture is once again seen, where the code of conduct in society stems from what is considered a normal way of life (culture).

A brief synopsis could conclude the essay. Also state, based on your analysis of the evidence given, the degree to which the two concepts overlap.

> **Exam Tip**
>
> One of the aims of the Caribbean Studies syllabus is to examine the uniqueness of Caribbean society and culture in comparison to what is considered typical sociological theory. So, when answering questions on sociological concepts or terms, remember to use examples from the Caribbean to help form your arguments and illustrate the points you are making.

Multiple-choice Questions

1. Geographically, a society can be defined as
   - A. A group of people who follow a certain way of life in an area
   - B. A group of people that originates from a common location
   - C. A group living in various areas with similar cultures
   - D. A group with similar beliefs and values

2. Cultural diversity involves
   - A. The existence of a variety of cultural forms, based on race, ethnicity, religion and other beliefs or values, within a society
   - B. A society consisting of two or more distinct ethnic or racial groups who retain their cultural traditions and even their own dwelling spaces
   - C. The existence of two cultural forms in a defined space
   - D. Many cultures in one space with little interaction

3. Trinidadians who live in New York and continue to practise Trinidadian culture make up the
   - A. Diaspora
   - B. Trinidad culture
   - C. The cultural diversity of Trinidad
   - D. Plural society in Trinidad

4. Jamaican parents passing on the culinary arts to their children that entail the preparation of ackee and saltfish is called
   - A. Enculturation
   - B. Socialisation
   - C. Transculturation
   - D. Generation gap

5. The custom of shaking hands as a greeting is an example of
   - A. Non-material culture
   - B. Material culture
   - C. Caribbean customs
   - D. General culture

Chapter 7

Identity and Social Formation

After revising this topic you should be able to:

- define key concepts such as cultural diversity, stratification, social mobility, plantocracy, intelligentsia, middle class, bourgeoisie, working class, underclass, caste, acculturation, plural society, creolisation, douglarisation and hybridisation, 'mulatto' or 'mestizo';
- identify positive and negative effects of cultural identity and assess how different ethnic groups and cultural differences can affect and coexist in Caribbean society;
- analyse plantation society and its impact on Caribbean social stratification and education as the basis of new class formation and social mobility;
- identify processes of cultural change in the Caribbean and their impact, and apply key terms and concepts such as acculturation, plural society creolisation, douglarisation and hybridisation to these processes;
- assess and explain the role of racial admixture and colour in the formation of Caribbean society and culture;
- analyse the erasure, retention and renewal of cultural practices in the Caribbean region.

Cultural and Social Identity in the Caribbean

A society can be defined by its cultural **identity** and Caribbean society is no exception. Cultural identity is a unique blueprint that distinguishes us from other societies. Our cultural identity is composed of the unique traits of Caribbean people. These fall under broad categories of ethnicity, language, religion, customs, laws and art forms. The sum total of these factors distinguishes the Caribbean from other regions. For example, someone from North America can easily distinguish a member of Caribbean society of African descent from other people of African descent by the way they speak or the religious group they belong to. This individual may sport dreadlocks, proclaim their religion as Rastafari and speak in a Caribbean patois, and as such would not need to proclaim themselves to be Caribbean to any individual who is cognisant of Caribbean culture.

Despite there being a recognisable overall 'Caribbean' identity, however, there are present beneath this a myriad of differences throughout the region. These also make the Caribbean a unique entity in that, although its people can be considered a society, their differences are easily recognisable. We can easily identify the Amerindian, African, European and Asian cultural influences, for example, that permeate the everyday lives and the festivities of Caribbean society. There are also marked differences among Caribbean countries as each has developed in its own unique way. Geographical location, the European coloniser, size, type of government and ethnic makeup of each Caribbean state contributes to making them different, one from another.

Caribbean diasporic societies that developed outside of the Caribbean have also formed their own identity and this may even be distinct from that which exists within the Caribbean state from which they originated. Little Havana in Florida, for example, has a distinct identity, one that has marked differences from their Cuban counterparts, especially in terms of political outlook as most Cuban migrants in Little Havana are against the Marxist Cuban regime.

Figure 7.1 is a map of the Caribbean region. Looking at it in different ways can help to illustrate the different levels at which societies function in the Caribbean and some of the ways in which Caribbean society is culturally diverse.

Making the Connection

Different definitions of the Caribbean, including geographical, geological and historical, are presented in Chapter 4, 'Location and Definition of the Caribbean'.

Quick Facts

Other Caribbean diaspora communities exist in Brixton (a borough in London) and Birmingham in England; Tampa (Florida) and the Bronx and Brooklyn (New York) in the United States; and there are strong Caribbean-Chinese communities in Toronto and Montreal in Canada.

Figure 7.1 A map of the Caribbean region

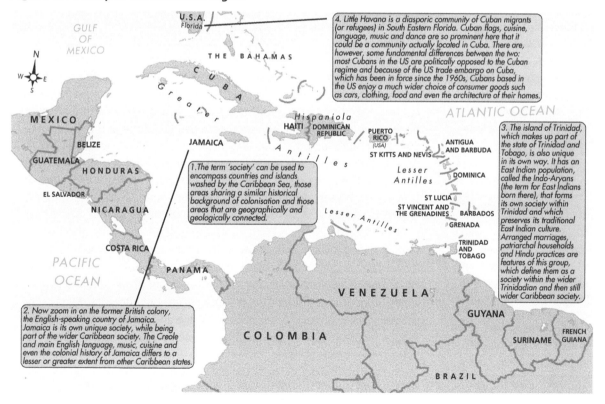

Figure 7.2 Iconic mural located in Little Havana, Florida. Notice the Cuban flags and cultural icons on the walls

Cultural Diversity

There are many and varied cultures and cultural influences evident in the Caribbean, which have given rise to **cultural diversity**. Since the early 1500s we have had a strong British, Spanish, French and Dutch presence in the Caribbean, imparting various forms of European culture. Then we had the widespread forced migration of West Africans bringing their culture from their homeland. Added to this is the Asian culture brought by the East Indians and Chinese, who have been here in numbers since the 1830s. Although their cultural presence may be the least felt, the Amerindian influence is evident, and this group has been present since before all the others. Aspects of culture in the Caribbean where diversity is evident are **race**, **ethnicity**, language, dress, traditions, beliefs, music and value systems.

These broad ethnic and racial groupings themselves can also be termed diverse. There is diversity in the array of ways in which cultural forms that are common across them are practised within them. Among Black people of African descent, for instance, there are differences in forms of language and religion resulting from the different origins of those people from a range of tribes in West Africa and subsequently the ways in which culture has evolved and been interpreted in the Caribbean. In Jamaica, for example, there are different variations of Creole depending on the cultural background of the individuals who speak it and the parish where they live.

The idea of cultural diversity implies that each group in a varied society accepts and conforms to the idea of living in a communal setting of many different groups and people.

Positive and Negative Effects of Cultural Diversity

There are both positives and equally identifiable drawbacks of living in societies that are culturally diverse. Figure 7.3 outlines the main positives and negatives of living in a diverse society, with some Caribbean examples.

Figure 7.3 **The positive and negative effects of cultural diversity**

Positive effects	Negative effects

• When different cultures mix, new cultural practices are created resulting in interculturation (the means by which the creolisation process occurs). For example, new genres of music (Chutney, Soca) have been created in the Caribbean as a result of the merging of culturally disparate musical forms. Other examples are the wide variety of foods, methods of food preparation, languages, dress, festivals and religious occasions, dances (French, British, East Indian, Spanish and African). This is the idea of unity in diversity:
 	
  • People who belong to different cultures usually have different ways of thinking and analysing issues from a variety of perspectives. Different cultures bring different experiences, which can be beneficial as they provide Caribbean society with a sound and vast knowledge base.
 	
  • Different cultural practices among the a diverse population can be shared, which means that different cultural groups can learn about each other's culture. This exposure to different cultures can lead to the development of tolerance and acceptance of different groups. People become more broad minded.
 	
  • Bigotry and discrimination are viewed as unacceptable. People are tuned to recognise discriminatory acts and readily point them out for sanctions to be applied.
 	
  • There can be a relatively peaceful co-existence of different groups within society, which can translate into an enrichment of culture. For example, many traditional festivals in the Caribbean are now shared among the various communities, to include other cultures and feature different foods and cultural craft items (for instance, during the festivities at Diwali – a Hindu festival – items from both Black and Indian culture are on display and sold).
 	
  • Cultural diversity aids tourism, which a lot of Caribbean countries depend upon to survive: tourists are intrigued by the diversity of the Caribbean and enjoy travelling to a place where multiple cultures can be experienced.
 	
  • Diversity can enhance an export market: products of significance, such as curry and spices, are marketed and sold under the diversity umbrella.
 	
  • A reputation for diversity and tolerance can encourage immigration from other communities, which can serve to further enrich society generally. Many ethnic groups migrate to the Caribbean knowing that they will be accepted, offering their skills and resources to the region. For example, Trinidad has a sizeable Syrian-Lebanese population and many Asian groups continue to arrive in Jamaica, establishing businesses on the island.
	• When different cultures mix it can give birth to new cultural practices. Therefore, there is a greater risk for erasure of cultural practices and traditions, especially of ethnic minorities or sub groups in society. For example, no one really knows the true method of preparing meats that the Tainos called barbecuing as different ethnic groups have added their own style to the mix.
	
	• The existence of different cultures can lead to racial/ethnic discrimination.
	
	• People from different cultural or ethnic backgrounds have different and inflexible views concerning lifestyle, religion and politics that can lead to tensions, strife and conflicts. For example, Hindu Trinidadians are usually against interracial marriages and this causes tension as others sometimes label this preference as racist; the Black Power Revolution in Trinidad and Tobago in the 1970s show how groups in society have expressed their dissatisfaction with the social structure. One group may struggle to gain dominance and promote their culture as real and ideal.
	
	• Different languages spoken by members of a diverse population can cause communication problems.
	
	• Issues of inferiority and superiority in terms of language, food, dress, customs, and so on, can arise.
	
	• Educational institutions often establish syllabi that mostly focus on the culture of the dominant ethnicity in a society. For example, Hindu, Rastafarian and Islamic teaching is not widespread in many schools that are largely Christian based.
	
	• Individuals may become overly sensitive and view even the simplest expression of racial pride as attempts at racism. For example, it may be difficult for White Creoles to celebrate their European heritage because of the complex historical power dynamics between colonisers and colonised.
	
	• Ethnic groups can become marginalised as they no longer reflect the stereotype of an ideal culture, such as the Chinese of Jamaica, sinhis or Gujaratis of Barbados.
	
	• Some indigenous traditions, languages and people may become marginalised over time as they find it difficult to fit into the modern diverse Caribbean society. For example, the Wai Wai and Warao people of Guyana live in the forested areas, almost forgotten by the rest of society.

Making the Connection

The historical context of the migration and settlement of different groups in the Caribbean is presented in Chapter 5 'The Historical Process'.

Ethnic and Cultural Differences in the Caribbean

The complex racial, ethnic and cultural mix that has become a main cultural trait of Caribbean society is a result of colonisation, migration (forced and voluntary) and social mobility.

Figure 7.4 The main ethnic groups of the Caribbean and their main contributions to Caribbean culture and identity

Ethnicity	Origins and how they became part of Caribbean society	Their main contributions to Caribbean culture and identity
The indigenous peoples (Amerindians)	• Originally from Eurasia • Early migrations over thousands of years before the arrival of the Europeans	• Many 'traditional' cultural forms (e.g. barbecue, hammock, canoe, place names) • The use of maize, corn and cassava in food
Europeans	• From Western Europe • Conquest and colonisation from the late 15th century • The political situation in Europe resulted in exchanges in Caribbean territories over the years	• Mainstream religion: Christianity, along with its festivals (such as Christmas, Carnival, Easter) • Mainstream languages (English, Spanish, French) and forms of Caribbean Creole that developed out of these • Laws and systems of governments • Education system and approach • Legacies of social stratification established by colonialism and the plantation system • Social norms (such as marriage, monogamy, shaking of hands as a greeting or eating with a knife and fork) • Sport and recreation (such as cricket or ballroom dancing) • The Arts (for example, classical music)
Africans	• From West Africa • Forced migration as enslaved people from c. 1500 to provide free plantation labour • Emancipation in British territories in 1834	• Hybrid religions: such as Vodou, Pocomania, Mayal, Revivalism, Rastafari • Music, dance and festivities (reggae, dancehall, calypso) • Folklore and oral traditions of story-telling • Alternative social norms, such as matrifocal families • Food, especially in the use of spices and pulses
East Indians	• Mainly from Northern India • Arrived as indentured labourers for plantations, mid 19th to early 20th centuries • Opted to stay at the end of their contracts	• Religion: Hinduism and festivals (such as Diwali); Islam and festivals (such as Eid) • Food (such as curry) • Music
Chinese	• From China • Arrived as indentured labourers for plantations, mid to late 19th century • Opted to stay at the end of their contracts	• Religion: Buddhism and other Chinese religious beliefs • Food (such as stir fry)

The mainstream forms of societal institutions, such as the family, education and religion, are all derived from the European cultural traditions. In terms of religion, in particular, many members of Caribbean society outwardly conform to the established Christian churches (both Protestant and Roman Catholic) while adhering to some of their own cultural traditions in the home. In the same way, Standard English (or French, Spanish or Dutch) is viewed as the lingua franca of business, government, education, the media, and so on, while patois tends to be spoken in everyday and for private use.

While it is not mandatory for an individual or group to subscribe to or accept all aspects of a society to become members, there must be a certain level of acceptance of the general values and belief systems of that space. For example, despite coming from a different tradition, Caribbean Hindus and Muslims for the most part accept and adhere to the legal systems of the Anglo-Christian Caribbean states in which they live. This, again, is characteristic of Caribbean society: a general tolerance and acceptance of the religious and cultural views of others. The constitution of all Caribbean countries protects its citizens against all forms of discrimination and ensures their human rights are respected.

Did You Know?

In 1937 Dominican dictator Rafael Trujillo ordered an ethnic cleansing of all Haitians living in Dominican Republic. It is believed that around 20 000 Haitians were killed during the so-called Parsley Massacre. In 2015 the Dominican government announced plans to deport all Dominican individuals of Haitian descent, as well as all Haitian citizens living in the Dominican Republic. This act has been condemned by neighbouring countries and world leaders as another ethnic cleansing similar to Trujillo's.

In the late 1980s, in Suriname, attempts to achieve better political and economic rights by the Maroon community in the interior of the country, which escalated into outright opposition to the military dictatorship, led to something akin to civil war in which many Maroons were displaced from their traditional homeland.

Where different ethnic communities exist side by side, with different cultures, tensions can arise between them. Guyana and Trinidad, for example, both have a large East Indian population that has historically been kept apart from the Afro-Caribbean community. This separateness has its roots in the plantation system when plantation owners sought to keep the communities apart in order to be able to maintain social control – following the basic principle of 'divide and rule'. The fundamental antipathy this fuelled was then exacerbated by the fact that the arrival of the East Indians drove down plantation wages and, after the end of their contracts, they were granted land – a privilege not afforded to the formerly enslaved, who also laid claim to a stronger and more established sense of 'belonging'. Having lived in relative isolation on the plantations, these East Indian communities then continued their isolated existence in their own communities established on this land, perpetuating their own cultural traditions such as the patriarchal extended family, intermarriage, culinary traditions and dress.

In Guyana, and to an extent in Trinidad, ethnic and cultural differences have extended into the political arena, with elections being contested along ethnic lines, and underlying tensions have on occasion exploded into violence between the communities as each attempts to lay claim to a sense of social and civil 'ownership'.

Having begun their existence in the Caribbean at the bottom of the social hierarchy, many Asians have managed, through the establishment of small businesses based around the combined work of family members and the acquisition of education, to render themselves upwardly mobile. In Trinidad, for example, this has been accompanied by social assimilation, with some members of the community shedding some of their cultural traditions and adopting more 'socially acceptable' ones such as the nuclear family structure rather than the traditional extended type.

Quick Fact

Indigenous, or Maroon, populations exist in relative isolation in the interiors of Belize, Guyana, Jamaica and Suriname. These communities can often be perceived by more urbanised members of the populace as backward, or even as outcasts.

Making the Connection

Chapter 17 'Intellectual Traditions' looks at concepts and ideas behind both the Afro-Caribbean and Indo-Caribbean communities' attempts to establish an identity for themselves in the Caribbean and the wider world.

Social Stratification

Caribbean society is quite paradoxical because, while it is quite diverse and hybridised, it can also be highly stratified and divided. **Stratification** is society's way of placing a value on individuals/groups. Therefore, doctors and politicians are usually high up on the social ladder of any society because healthcare and the making of policy and laws are seen as crucial. Added to that, it is commonly believed that the talents and skills required to carry out these roles are rare. To the contrary, working-class labourers are not usually high up in the social **strata** because they are considered easily replaceable as their jobs require no specialised training or talent, and their poor renumeration does not enable them to buy the influence or acquire the education or skills required for upward **social mobility**.

Did You Know?

The term 'working class' is used here to refer to people that are employees of those who own and control the systems and means of production (such as land, machinery, buildings, work schedules or industrial laws). This group usually occupies the lower social strata in most Caribbean states because they are mostly poorly paid for their labour. Another term for the working class, coined by Karl Marx in the late 19th century, is 'the proletariat'. It is important to note that, as the unpaid property of their masters, enslaved people were not considered working class.

Social stratification deals mostly with the position of whole groups on the social scale, and not necessarily of individuals. This is actually a form of discrimination as the status of individuals tends to be assessed and summed up based on general assumptions about the ethnic, racial, class or religious grouping that they belong to. For example, there is an assumption in Jamaica that some Chinese people living there enjoy wealth as a result of their business interests. This is because many own grocery stores and wholesale concerns, which has been the trend as far back as the late 1800s when Chinese ex-indentured servants used their wages to start businesses. Likewise it is also generally assumed that African Caribbeans must be of the poorer labouring class because of their history as unpaid menial labourers.

Stratification in the Caribbean is also based on the social perceptions among the population that have often formed as a result of historical experiences from the colonial period, and the plantation system in particular, which provided a model for the development of many modern Caribbean societies.

There are also instances where the social stratification systems of countries outside of the region emerge as features in Caribbean society. The East Indian caste system, for example, was brought with indentured immigrants and is still quite influential in Trinidad and Guyana, and even determines if individuals are suited for marriage or business relationships.

Making the Connection

See Chapter 9 'Societal Insitutions' for more information on family structures in the Caribbean and trends concerning them.

Key Term

Social stratification – refers to the ranking and dividing of groups in society based on ethnicity and race, class, historical background and even naturalisation/ citizenship status. The levels of social hierarchy are known as **strata**. Stratification can also be based on prestige, wealth, age, gender, caste and religion.

Key Term

Social mobility – movement of individuals or groups from one social position to another within the social stratification system in a society, usually based on wealth, occupation or education.

Quick Fact

There are three main theories that seek to explain Caribbean society: plantation society theory (George Beckford and colleagues), the plural society thesis (M.G. Smith) and the Creole society theory (Edward Kamau Braithwaite).

Did You Know?

The caste system is a rigid Hindu-based system of classifying individuals from birth based on hereditary social status. Hindus believe that people are born into their situation based on their past life or that of their parents, and so their status can never be altered. As a result, people of the lower castes are often ostracised by those of a higher caste out of fear that the misfortunes of these groups will negatively affect their own social standing. Therefore, people of a lower caste can never get married or form friendships with people from a higher caste. Those of the lowest caste are often labelled as 'untouchables', meaning that interaction with them is forbidden. This term is offensive.

Making the Connection

The social legacy of the plantation system is investigated in the next section.

Plantation Society and its Impact on Social Stratification

Did You Know?

Before the coming of Europeans to the Caribbean, social stratification among Amerindian society was largely based on inherited status, based on one's family background. For example, the cacique in Taino society was usually the son of a former cacique. The indigenous people also based stratification on religion. Religious leaders were thought to have a direct link to the deity and as such were highly respected and given privileges not afforded the average citizen. For example, the Halach Uinic in Mayan society had a strong influence on decision making.

The arrival of the Europeans in the Caribbean resulted in the establishment of the plantation system of production. The plantation was not merely a unit of production, it was an organised social system that pervaded all aspects of social, cultural, economic and political life. It can be argued that the plantation was the institution which played the most significant role in the development of Caribbean culture.

Economically, the plantation was geared to large-scale monoculture, usually of a staple crop, mostly sugar, but also tobacco, cocoa or coffee, for export to the metropole. Any needs were imported into the region from the metropole, including technology. The plantations were self-sufficient communities existing more or less in isolation. Labour was supplied in different periods by enslaved Africans or indentured labourers (mainly from Asia) who suffered hardships and oppression.

Did You Know?

The plantation society theory argues that the legacy of the plantation lived on in Caribbean society even after independence, and some would argue up to the present day. Proponents of the theory point to the perpetuation of a closed social system with power and wealth concentrated among the White people occupying the top strata and the majority of the population, Black impoverished labourers, occupying the lower strata. In addition to this social stratification, the theory also points to the pervasiveness of plantation attitudes and trends in modern Caribbean society, such as a general taste for foreign goods and a perception of their superiority derived from the plantation's reliance on imports. This perception of superiority extended to foreign culture, values, norms, beliefs and institutions, particularly those of the metropole. Likewise, as with many absentee plantation owners residing in the metropole, production in the colony up to independence was still dominated by decision-makers from outside the system and this continues with today's dominance by multinational corporations that are headquartered in the developed world.

Key Terms

Closed system – a social structure in which there is no place for mobility and the pattern of inequality in the society persists from generation to generation. An example is the Indian caste system.

Ascribed social status – a position in society based on attributes you were born with, such as race, colour and caste.

Quick Fact

In most societies money is a major determinant of one's social standing. This is usually because money is able to help an individual or group acquire the resources and means of production to control a society's industry and economy, and the education and influence needed for upward social mobility.

Key Terms

Plantocracy – a ruling class, political order or government composed of or dominated by plantation owners.

'Mulatto' – a person having mixed ancestry – a White parent and a Black parent. The term is old fashioned and not in use today.

It is extremely offensive as its meaning is linked to the word mula or mule.

Plantation Society under Slavery

During slavery, there was no social mobility in the plantation system. Plantation society was a **closed system** and an individual's **ascribed social status** was determined by race and colour. Wealth also played a part in social stratification. Wealthy White plantation owners of European origin held power, while labour was provided by enslaved Black Africans with no rights and who, under the laws of the society, were deemed the property of the owners to dispose of as they liked.

Figure 7.5 **Social stratification during slavery**

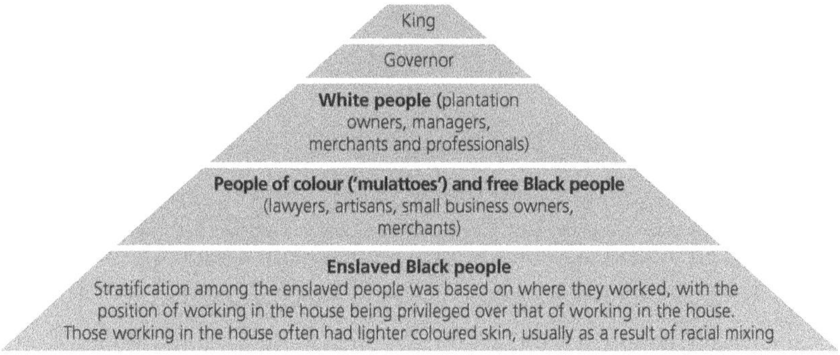

King

Governor

White people (plantation owners, managers, merchants and professionals)

People of colour ('mulattoes') and free Black people (lawyers, artisans, small business owners, merchants)

Enslaved Black people
Stratification among the enslaved people was based on where they worked, with the position of working in the house being privileged over that of working in the house. Those working in the house often had lighter coloured skin, usually as a result of racial mixing

- The monarchy (king) had ultimate control over the colonial government. Noblemen were usually appointed to important government positions, including that of governor, in Caribbean territories. These men formed the pinnacle of the Caribbean's social strata during the plantation period.
- The plantation owners and managers, along with White merchants (sellers of manufactured goods) and professionals (doctors, lawyers and high-level civil servants) formed the wealthy and professional classes that either migrated from Europe to live in the Caribbean or were Creoles (White people born in the Caribbean to European parents). They occupied the upper end of the social strata and were known as the **plantocracy**. This class in the Caribbean comprised the property owning set that was allowed to vote and could be part of the colonial government as local assemblymen of the British Caribbean, or the White plantation class that controlled the local government of other parts of the region, such as St Domingue/Haiti before the 1791 revolution. Many European-born plantation owners were absentee landlords, leaving Creole White people effectively at the top of the hierarchy.
- Below them were free people of colour ('**mulattoes**') and free Black people. This was a relatively small group and its members were artisans, lawyers, shopkeepers and owners of small businesses. They aspired to European culture and values. Among the free people of colour there were complex subdivisions based on one's degree of Whiteness as well as wealth, education and connections to White people. Even White people who were poorer than people of colour were still positioned above them in the hierarchy, by virtue of race.

Did You Know?

In pre-revolutionary Haiti (then called St Domingue) the White plantocracy refused to accept wealthy 'mulatto' planters and professionals in their social circles because they were of mixed race. These wealthy 'mulattoes' were barred by law from dressing in White fashions, playing White games and even sitting in the front pews in church, which were reserved for White people.

- The bottom of the hierarchy was occupied by the enslaved Black people and people of colour. These were the labourers that were the **chattel** of the plantation owners. Stratification also occurred within this group, dependant on skin colour and whether one assigned to the house of the field.

Plantation Society after Emancipation (1838)

Even after emancipation, social stratification remained rigidly based on race, colour and wealth until well into the 20th century. Power and wealth remained in the hands of the White few while the majority remained powerless and poor. The arrival of indentured labourers from Asia placed them at the bottom of the hierarchy, below the now freed Black people who largely worked for themselves as peasant farmers (see Figure 7.6). Although in principle they possessed more basic rights than the enslaved people before them, they suffered hardships and restrictions on their freedom of movement during their contracts. Over time, however, the acquisition of education and wealth, once their contracts had ended, allowed many members of the communities to rise through the social strata and they subsequently became established in places such as Trinidad and Guyana.

After emancipation a number of Black and mixed race people were also able to move up through the social order by means of acquired wealth. These men, especially 'mulattoes', acquired voting rights by virtue of their property holding and some became members of the local assemblies. An example is the mixed race and prominent Jamaican assembly member, George William Gordon, who was involved in the Morant Bay Rebellion. He was the self-educated son of a Scottish planter who became a wealthy businessman and landowner.

It can be argued that social stratification in today's Caribbean society is still largely based on race and wealth. It has been engrained in the consciousness of Caribbean people that White people are usually the owners of the means of production, and so most of a colony's wealth. Historically, this was the group that controlled the government and, by dint of their landholding and wealth, were allowed to participate in the democratic process. This was a right not extended to the poorer ranks of society, that comprised the majority of Afro- and Indo-Caribbeans, until universal adult suffrage was introduced from 1944 onwards. It can also be argued that the historically privileged position of White people creates preconceptions in modern Caribbean society that automatically place them at the upper end of the social hierarchy regardless of their actual wealth or any other attribute that would normally confer a high status. In the same way, the foundations for preconceptions about the position of Afro-Caribbeans in the lower strata of society, despite any improvements in status through the acquisition of wealth and/or education, can be said to be laid at the door of their history of oppression and slavery.

Quick Fact

The father of French author Alexandre Dumas was a 'mulatto' born in St Domingue. Brought to France as a child by his father and officially freed there, he suffered none of the exclusionary treatment meted out to his contemporaries of colour back in St Domingue. Indeed, he joined the army and rose to the rank of general by the age of 31.

Key Term

Chattel – personal property that can be traded, bought and sold.

Making the Connection

The plantation system of production under slavery and forms of resistance to it are examined in detail in Chapter 5 'The Historical Process'.

Quick Fact

The view that having a pale skin confers advantages, such as access to more opportunities and advancement to the higher social strata, has resulted in the phenomenon of skin bleaching or lightening, which is fast becoming a trend among young Caribbean Black people.

Independence has been argued by some to be a watershed, with people of European descent no longer viewed by the rest of society as superior; racial discrimination is not promoted, social mobility is achievable and merit has become an important factor influencing status and the acquisition of new wealth rather than colour and ethnicity. On the other hand, others disagree, pointing out the ethnic tensions that continue to exist in some territories and arguing that the factors of race, colour and wealth still play a significant role in contemporary societies.

Figure 7.6 **The stratification system of Trinidad in the period after emancipation (Post 1845)**

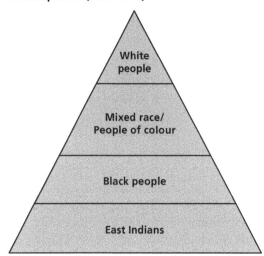

The Role of Education as a Basis for New Class Formation and Upward Mobility

Census papers, bank loan applications and even some social club applications require you to state your level of education. This helps to determine your ability to acquire wealth because your level and type of education are major factors in the job and pay scale you can achieve. This is the reason society advances educated individuals on the social ladder. There is also a high value placed on the contributions that educated individuals can make to society, whether in the field of medicine, law, engineering, business or science.

During slavery, education for the enslaved, apart from religious instruction, was viewed as unnecessary and potentially dangerous by the owners. Although some freed people of colour and freed Black people were able to acquire an education to various levels, it was only after emancipation that education started to become an important factor in social mobility, with easier access to elementary education in particular. Even so, the plantocracy did not think it was wise to broaden the outlook of labourers as they wanted them to focus on their manual tasks.

Subsequently, there was a slow but gradual access to secondary education by the former enslaved and their descendants. Education provided a means for people, largely males from the lower classes, to achieve upward social mobility via jobs in towns and in the learned professions of law, medicine, science, teaching, engineering and accounting. This emergence of talent from the lower, underprivileged classes led to the rise of a new social class within plantation society, that of educated Black people and people of colour who became local and national leaders, and role models for other Black people.

Even so, the institution of education also helped to perpetuate social stratification well into the 20th century because secondary education was still mainly regarded as the domain of the mostly White middle classes (merchants, overseers, smaller planation owners) while the children of the richer members of the plantocracy were either educated at home or in the metropole, and a basic elementary education was deemed sufficient for the majority of the population: the mostly Black and labouring lower classes. Certification was needed for many white-collar jobs, which enabled only members of the middle and elite classes to be employed in these positions.

The University of the West Indies was established in 1948. Through the acquisition of tertiary level education, African Caribbeans, along with others, have been able to access more job and leadership opportunities in the Caribbean. This has elevated many to the upper levels of the Caribbean's social strata, causing the view of Black people as poor, menial labourers to change to a more positive image of African descendants being just as capable in all areas as other ethnic and racial groups.

Concepts of Social Stratification Relevant to Caribbean Society

Terminology abounds for the various complex social strata, classes and social groupings that have been identified and defined at different times and by different schools of thought. Some of the terms that have most relevance to social formation and structures in the Caribbean region are briefly explained below.

In general terms, present-day society can be described as organised along the hierarchical lines of upper class, middle class and lower class, each of which is also internally stratified (for instance, into upper middle class and lower middle class). In broad socio-economic terms, the *upper classes* (or elites) hold most wealth (usually inherited), status and prestige. The *middle classes* comprise those in professions such as medicine and the law, those involved in business and commerce, and artisans. By dint of their position in the centre of the strata of society, the middle classes also tend to experience most social mobility – down as well as up. The lower class is also referred to as the *working class* as its members mostly comprise those involved in some sort of labour, usually unskilled. Beneath the working class is the *underclass*. This is characterised by acute poverty and usually unemployment (by definition, they cannot be members of the working class as they do not work).

Marxist theory divides society into just two classes: the *bourgeoisie* and the *proletariat*. The proletariat sell their labour to the bourgeoisie, who are capitalists and own the means of production. In Marxism, society is characterised by tensions between the two groups and the attempts by the bourgeoisie to keep the proletariat in a state of oppression.

Other theories have broadened out Marx's theory to show the existence of other classes who have little involvement in the 'class struggle'. An example of these is the *intelligentsia*, who are those who have enjoyed education to a high level and form an intellectual elite rather than one based on socio-economic power and wealth.

The terms above all imply some sort of social mobility that can be achieved on the basis of opportunities such as wealth acquisition, marriage, education and ability. Other social systems, known as closed systems, are completely rigid and allow no movement. An example of this is the **caste** system, explained previously.

In the Caribbean, a specific term has been coined to describe the political, social and economic power wielded by plantation owners and other wealthy White people in the 17th, 18th and 19th centuries: the plantocracy.

Creolisation and Hybridisation

Social stratification is a reflection of a society and attempts to define the differences within it. While attempts made at defining social groups and their members in Caribbean society during the plantation era would have been pretty easy, in modern Caribbean societies, mostly characterised by a high degree of **hybridisation** and **creolisation**, these classifications are much more difficult, some would say even impossible.

Cultural Change in the Caribbean

There are numerous theories concerning society, culture and change and how these different concepts interrelate at different times, under different circumstances and in different conditions. There are various terms for the different processes that occur when cultures come into contact and relationships are established between them. Some of these are summarised below.

As well as the plantation society theory discussed above, there are also different concepts and theories to explain the complexities of society and cultural diversity that exist in the Caribbean. One such concept is that of the **plural society** and another is the theory of creolisation expounded by Edward Kamau Braithwaite.

Key Term

Plural society – the existence of separate and distinct ethnic or racial communities within a society, which may come together for a number of common functions such as work or recreation but which preserve their own societal institutions, especially language, the family and religion. This concept also involves **cultural pluralism**, which is when discrete cultures exist side by side with little or no mixing. Cultural pluralism accepts a multiplicity of values and practices, provided they are consistent with the laws and values of the wider society. In a plural society, ethnic groups are able to peacefully coexist out of mutual respect and acceptance, but tensions and rivalries can emerge where they share societal institutions such as the political system.

Check Your Knowledge

Using examples, explain THREE features of Caribbean society and identity. Demonstrate an understanding of the following terms and concepts:

- Society
- Identity
- Caribbean
- Plural
- Diversity
- Culture
- System of production

- Hybrid
- Creolisation
- Society
- Indentureship
- Slavery
- Social stratification

- First, briefly define the concepts: society, identity, Caribbean.
- Introduce the idea of culture and society being intertwined to create a unique Caribbean identity.
- State that there are features/characteristics that identify the unique Caribbean society and that they are a result of the historical processes the islands went through.
- Individually identify and explain THREE features of Caribbean society of your choice. These can include (but are not exclusive to):
  - A culturally diverse society:
    - Various cultures exist in the Caribbean that make that society unique. The colonial history contributed to this unique feature. This includes various systems of production – the encomienda and the plantation system – and bringing in various nationalities – Africans, Europeans, East Indians, Chinese, Syrians and Lebanese. The nationalities brought with them material and non-material culture practised throughout Caribbean society today, some of which became creolised and some of which continued unchanged. Examples include culinary arts (Chinese, Indian), festivals (Divali, Carnival), dress (mix of Western, East Indian and African wear), folklore (Anansi), and language (French and Spanish words being used in the local lingua) and language (French and Spanish words being used in the local lingua). It is important to mention that people throughout the Caribbean have incorporated aspects

Quick Fact

M.G. Smith was a Caribbean poet and academic who carried out a study of societies in three Caribbean territories: originally Grenada, but then widened out to include Barbados and Trinidad and Tobago. He postulated the existence of a plural society in which various cultures and ethnicities exist out of mutual respect and acceptance without mixing or catalysing change. He also identified politics as an area where these groups can come into conflict.

Making the Connection

Chapter 5 'The Historical Process'

Chapter 6 'Characteristics of Society and Culture'

Exam Tip

'**Explain**' requires statements on what happened, how and why. Terms, concepts and approaches need to be elaborated on.

of material and non-material culture into their lives, allowing the Caribbean culture to be diverse in nature – a characteristic feature.

- Creolisation/hybridisation:
  - Creolisation/hybridisation is a feature of Caribbean society. Define these terms and give specific examples. Different aspects of the various nationalities' cultures of the slavery/indentureship era altered over time to become creolised and hybrid. This ranges from the emergence of new racial mixtures – 'mestizo' and 'dougla' (note, these terms are considered offensive), to culinary practices (West Indian style curry vs East Indian), music (Classical vs the steel pan), literature (English to West Indian), art and folklore, language (patois). All retain a hint of the original version but have been creolised to adapt to the West Indian environment.
- Social stratification/the social ladder system:
  - The social stratification system was and continues to be a feature of Caribbean society. Prior to independence in the Caribbean, one's colour, skin shade, status and wealth defined where on the social ladder one was situated. This positioned the White landowning class at the apex of the social ladder and the working class/non-White people/enslaved people/indenture workers at the base. The social ladder was inflexible and movement up the ladder by non-White people was disallowed. This changed post-independence. Social stratification is now based on merit, a defining feature of Caribbean society today. Education is universal; its free provision allows every person the opportunity to improve their social status (for instance, in Trinidad through the GATE programme). The social ladder is now flexible where movement can be upward or downward. Despite this, one aspect of the Caribbean society that cannot be erased from the minds of many is the feeling of inferiority where they continue to see the lighter shades as 'sitting' at the top of the social ladder despite the successes of non-White people in the education system: this is part of the colonial legacy, passed on from one generation to the next.
- The conclusion can comprise a brief synopsis of the three features.

Edward Kamau Braithwaite on Creolisation

In his theory on creolisation, Brathwaite opined that it is mostly determined by the response of Black and White people to their colonial situation and disposition. Cultures emerged in response to the situation that faced migrant groups in the Caribbean: White people were the masters and all other groups (especially Black people) were subservient. According to Brathwaite, this culture that emerged in the Caribbean was the first instance of creolisation.

Quick Fact

Edward Kamau Braithwaite is a Caribbean poet and scholar from Barbados. His theory on the emergence and influence of creolisation in Jamaica and by extension the Caribbean, first published in 1971, is widely used to account for the ethnic, racial and cultural variations in the region.

Did You Know?

The term 'Creole' is used in many Caribbean text books to refer to an individual of White European parentage, born and living in the Caribbean. The term was originally used by the French to describe any White person born in the colonies. In its modern application, however, which is along the lines of how it is used by Brathwaite, the term describes any person or form of culture that is native to or originated in the Caribbean as a result of the interaction between groups and races.

He describes the view of the White people as masters as a force that compelled members of Caribbean enslaved society to conform and aspire to Eurocentric views of themselves and society as a whole (religion, values, beliefs). This would eventually form the base of the creolisation of Caribbean society as Black people would now mix the culture they already held from Africa with the newly learnt European norms and values.

Brathwaite outlined the process of **acculturation** that led to creolisation among Black people in the Caribbean, started when enslaved people were given European names and taught a common language. They were also conditioned or socialised to view White culture as superior. Brathwaite argued that this socialisation of the Black people led to them seeing it as socially uplifting to emulate the traditions and culture of their masters or former masters, while engaging in African traditions was viewed negatively as a barrier to possible social and economic advancement.

Key to Braithwaite's concept of a creolised society is the idea that all cultural forms within society are mixed to differing degrees and in complex endless ways to create something new and unique. Enculturation figures in his theory as the way in which this creolised culture is passed on from generation to generation while acculturation continues to feature as an ongoing means of enriching Creole culture through non-Caribbean influences.

Braithwaite's view is that creolisation is an ongoing process. He noted that during the period of his study, the culture of the 'Euro-Creole elite' remained dominant in the mix, resulting in 'the pervasive dichotomy' that exists in Caribbean society. However, he raised the possibility of the continuation of the creolisation process to ultimately produce 'a new parochial wholeness, a difficult but possible Creole authenticity'.

Exam Tip

When using any term such as 'Creole', 'hybridisation', 'plural society' and so on, it is important to be sure of what they mean and use them correctly. In particular, you need to be aware of the distinctions in the uses of the term 'Creole', as your correct or incorrect use of it can significantly affect your grade for an essay.

Quick Fact

The term 'Creole' originally derived from the Spanish 'criollo' (lit. little child) – used to describe Spanish children born in the West Indies.

Figure 7.7 Some examples of forms of cultural hybridisation in the Caribbean

Area	Name	Location	Origins
Religion:	Myal / Pocomania	Jamaica	A form of African traditional belief system which, with the arrival of the Christian Revivalist movement in the 1860s, embraced Christianity. Out of this developed the hybrid Pocomania or Revivalism.
	Vodou	Haiti, Dominican Republic, Puerto Rico, Cuba	Africans retained their ancestral worship and incorporated it with Christian ceremonies to create a variation of voodoo which differs from the form still practised in parts of West Africa.
	Santeria (Way of the Saints)	Spanish Caribbean	Emerged as a result of the mixing of Roman Catholicism and Yoruba beliefs and traditions by African enslaved in the Spanish Caribbean. Many adherents are also practising Roman Catholics.
	Rastafari	Jamaica	The most modern of the hybridised religions, it is a mixture of Christianity and Afro-Caribbean religions in which Haile Selassie of Ethiopia was seen as the messiah and worshipped as a result. It has become a global religion.
	Kumina	Jamaica	Introduced to St. Thomas parish, Jamaica, by Bantu indentured immigrants from the Congo region around the mid-1850s. The religion has since incorporated some elements of Christianity, but it is probably one of the least diluted forms of African religious expression in the Caribbean. It is still only found in St. Thomas.
	Regla de Palo	Cuba	Developed by Congolese enslaved people in Cuba who mixed aspects of Santeria with Central African ancestral worship to create a religion often characterised by its use of magical spells and ceremonial possession.
Language:	Creole/Patois This includes the basilect (the most raw and least socially prestigious form) and the acrolect (the form considered most closely related to Standard English)	Throughout the Caribbean	Originated from a combination of two ways: – Created by enslaved Africans who deliberately created language formed to confuse Europeans. – A result of enslaved Africans mispronouncing and misunderstanding the unfamiliar words of their masters and fellow enslaved from other regions in Africa.
Race:	For racial mixing in the Caribbean, see the section below		

Quick Fact

Creolisation has played an important role in the retention and transmission of traditional values and cultural forms such as music, literature and language. In Barbados, for example, English, the official language, co-exists alongside Barbadian Creole, called also Bajan. Bajan formed through a process called linguistic creolisation.

Quick Fact

The differences between race and ethnicity: while ethnicity refers to cultural factors (nationality, regional culture, ancestry, language), race refers to an individual's physical characteristics (bone structure and skin, hair, or eye colour).

Quick Fact

Chutney is a good example of a new form of hybridised popular culture originating in the Caribbean and born out of East Indian traditions mixed with Western influences.

Quick Fact

Braithwaite views the role of 'mulattoes' as highly significant in society as they acted as 'social cement' between Blacks and White people, thus facilitating social integration.

As we can see in Figure 7.7, outlining the various examples of cultural hybridisation, there are many examples of cultural mixing and assimilation (the process by which the culture and norms of one group begin to evolve as a result of mixing or interacting with individuals living in the same society, but of a different culture).

The role of Racial Admixture and Colour in the Formation of Caribbean Society and Culture

Caribbean society and culture has formed out of waves of migrations and the cultural practices these different peoples brought to the region. Racial mixing, or miscegenation, has been a significant part of this process. Even before the arrival of the Europeans, evidence, such as the development of an Arawak-based language among the Kalinago, points to the mixing of indigenous ethnic groups; in this case probably as a result of the capture of Taino women who then taught their own Arawak language to their children born to Kalinago fathers, resulting in this language eventually becoming predominant in Kalinago society.

With the arrival of the Spanish, there began the process of racial mixing between Amerindians and Europeans, followed slightly later by the mixing of European and African, a process that continued over 300 years through the period of slavery and beyond. The arrival of East Indians, Chinese, Indonesians and others brought more to the potential mix. This mixing naturally brought with it new forms of cultural hybridisation.

Key Terms

As a result of the complexities of racial intermixing, various terms have emerged to describe different types.

'**Mulatto**' – an outdated term used to describe a person having mixed ancestry – a White parent and a Black parent. The term is old fashioned and not in use today. It is extremely offensive as its meaning is linked to the word mula or mule.

'**Mestizo**' – an oudated term used predominantly in Latin America to describe people of mixed European (originally Spanish) and Amerindian ancestry. This term is offensive.

Garifuna (or Black Kalinagos) – term used to describe people of mixed African and Amerindian descent. More specifically, it can be used to refer to the mixed race people of St Vincent, expelled from the island by the British in 1797 and exiled to various parts of Central America (Honduras, Belize, Guatemala and Nicaragua).

Dougla (or Dugla) – term historically used, especially by people of Guyana, Suriname and Trinidad and Tobago, to describe the offspring of an East Indian indentured labourer and an African enslaved or freed labourer. This term is considered offensive.

This mixing not only brought about cultural change and the emergence of new cultures, but it also resulted in a distinctive feature of Caribbean society: the large proportion of the population defined as of colour'. This definition covers a broad spectrum of skin colour that heavily impacted on society in the past and still does to some extent today. The degree to which one had White Caucasian features carried great weight, especially in plantation society under slavery. The diagram showing the structure of plantation society in Figure 7.5 reveals how skin colour affected one's social standing. Colour carried social significance not only for the free population, where people of mixed race filled the space below the White people, but also among the enslaved themselves as a result of the 'better' jobs being given to those with lighter skin colour. Indeed, the lighter the colour of one's skin, the better preference one received, in both the free and enslaved situations. Within the enslaved population, the higher value placed on light skin was a result of the social conditioning by the White people, described by Braithwaite.

In modern Caribbean society, vestiges of this perceived 'superiority' survive among all groups. However, increased social mobility is serving to erode this and to gradually blur the rigid demarcations within the structure of plantation society into which colour neatly fitted.

Erasure, Retention and Renewal of Cultural Practices

The concept of cultural change is tied into three main processes. These are **cultural retention**, **cultural renewal** and **cultural erasure**. The concepts of hybridisation and creolisation need to be understood in the context of these processes.

Key Terms

Cultural retention – the preservation of an aspect of culture. The aspect does not need to survive in its original or intact form. For example, vestiges of indigenous culture, such as elements of language, survive in various parts of the Caribbean. The barbecue has been inherited from the Tainos and, although the principles of using herbs and spices and grilling meat over a fire survive, the exact recipe and the method used by the Tainos have been eroded and altered over time and replaced by newer versions.

Cultural renewal – the return to, or rediscovery, and refreshing of elements of culture that have been forgotten, suppressed or ignored. A major example is the resurgence in interest in, and a heightening of the value placed on, the African legacy and African culture, as well as Africa itself, in the 20th century, which developed through Garveyism and the rise of Black consciousness in the form of négritude, for example. A visual element to this has been the repopularisation of African dress and the learning of African languages. A more recent trend has been for Amerindian communities in places such as Trinidad to look to identify, record and promote local instances of Amerindian cultural survivals.

Cultural erasure – the dying out of cultural practices. It can be argued that a culture in its entirety can never be completely erased because of the process of hybridisation that naturally occurs to varying degrees when cultures coexist. Thus, unidentifiable vestiges of a culture may survive unbeknownst to those who practice them.

It is usually societal institutions, such as family, religion and education, that determine the aspects of our culture that are to be renewed, erased or merged with other cultures for a hybridised mix, or retained to ensure the continuation and growth of the cultural and physical space we call society.

Quick Fact

Many of the first Asian indentured labourers intermarried into existing Caribbean communities because of a lack of females of their own community, but then, with the later arrival of more Asian women, the traditional cultural practices of that community were re-established. This could be viewed as an example of cultural renewal.

Making the Connection

You can find out more about Garveyism and négritude in Chapter 17 'Intellectual Traditions'.

Making the Connection

Chapter 5 'The Historical Process'

Chapter 6 'Characteristics of Society and Culture'

Chapter 17 'Intellectual Traditions'

Exam Tip

'**To what extent**' wording requires you to evaluate something by measuring the degree that it is reliable, valid or useful.

Check Your Knowledge

To what extent can it be argued that Caribbean society is built solely on hybridised cultural forms?

Demonstrate an understanding of the following terms and concepts:

- Society
- Culture
- Caribbean
- Hybridisation
- Cultural retention

- Cultural erasure
- Cultural renewal
- Creolisation
- Diversity
- Migration

First, define the concepts: society, culture, hybrid. Then state that hybrid cultures exist in the Caribbean, which emerged from traditional cultures brought by the ancestors/migrants all connected to planting export crops.

In your discussion, cover the following points:

- Migration of various groups into the Caribbean led to a mixing of cultures over time: state the types and cultures, such as East Indian (Hindu/ Muslim).

- The mixing of these cultures led to the development of new cultural forms – use terms such as interculturation, hybrid, erasure and explain them. Outline how the various migrations into the Caribbean by the Amerindians, Europeans, Africans and Asians have led to the ethnic and cultural mixing that has subsequently led to the unique hybridised and creolised Caribbean cultural identity that we share. This fact is especially true among the African descendants (who make up the majority of the Caribbean population), as their ancestors were often prevented from practising their original cultural forms as enslaved labourers on sugar plantations, hence their culture has become creolised. Prove that although the Europeans have tried to prevent integration of White and Black culture, that wall too has been breached with the ending of slavery and laws against discrimination legislated in the Caribbean in the post slavery era.

- Many subcultures have emerged as a means of protest against the notion of White superiority or as a way of attempting to renew and restore original cultural forms (Rastafari, Négritude, the Garvey movements).

- Show that even with the East Indians and Chinese constantly trying to protect their cultural forms through arranged marriages and living in close knit extended family structures and communities, cultural mixing and subsequent hybridisation is inevitable as a society grows over time. This is as a result of interracial marriages and legislation and education systems that promote ethnic cultural integration.

The conclusion can round off the argument by pointing out that recent migrations and movement of people have led to the continued introduction of new cultural forms into the Caribbean and the further hybridisation of our culture.

Multiple-choice Questions

1. A diverse society has
   A. Varied nationalities, races and religions living in one space over a period of time
   B. A society with recent migrants from many nations
   C. A society with varied cultures
   D. A society with various ethinicities

2. Which of the following is not a feature of Caribbean society?
   A. It is hybrid
   B. It is creolised
   C. It is homogenous
   D. It is diverse

3. When different cultures mix, new cultural practices are created, resulting in
   A. Interculturation
   B. Enculturation
   C. Miscegenation
   D. Mixing

4. One risk of the emergence of a hybrid culture is
   A. Erasure of certain cultural traditions
   B. Creolisation
   C. Ethnic cleansing
   D. Interculturation

5. Vodou, Pocomania, Mayal, Revivalism represent
   A. Hybrid religions
   B. Tradional African religions
   C. Cultural practices
   D. The African race

6. The term Creole was orginially used to describe
   A. French descendants born in the West Indies
   B. Fair-skinned mixed race Caribbean nationals
   C. Enslaved Caribbeans of African descent
   D. Caribbean nationals of African descent

7. The territories where those of African and East Indian descent were used against each other during the days of indentureship are
   A. Trinidad and Guyana
   B. Trinidad and Jamaica
   C. Guyana and Jamaica
   D. Guyana and Cuba

8. A 'mulatto' was an offensive term meaning
   A. A person of European and African heritage
   B. A person of European and Amerindian descent
   C. A person of European and East Indian descent
   D. A person of European and Chinese descent

9. The term 'mestizo' represented
   A. The first hybrid race of the West Indies
   B. An indigenous Amerindian culture
   C. A homogenous society in Dominica
   D. A Haitian migrant in Dominica

Impacts on Caribbean Society

Chapter 8

Geographical Phenomena

After revising this topic, you should be able to:
- define plate tectonics, identify the Caribbean plate and describe its movement and interaction with other plates;
- identify earthquake and volcano zones, and assess the impact of these natural hazards;
- assess the social and economic consequences of hurricanes;
- identify causes of soil erosion and methods of soil conservation;
- discuss the importance of coral reefs, for example in coastal protection and sustainability of the fishing industry;
- assess the social and economic impact of droughts and floods.

Caribbean countries are shaped by the physical features and **geographical processes** of the region: the landscape and how it was formed, as well as the climate. Some of these have a positive impact, but others less so. Our diverse landscape has a mixture of volcanic islands, coral islands and mainland territories, each with a complex range of terrestrial and aquatic ecosystems. Our cultural, historical and political systems and unique island culture are dependent on the natural and human resources found in each country. To observe and interpret these geographical features and processes allows us to relate them to our lives and, by so doing, control our response to future natural events.

There are five main geographical phenomena which affect people's lives in the Caribbean:
- plate tectonics
- hurricanes
- soils
- coral reefs
- droughts and floods.

Plate Tectonics

Location and Movement of the Caribbean Plate and its Interaction with Other Plates

The Caribbean Plate is a small section of crust that is found under the Caribbean Sea. This slab pushes between the North American Plate and the South American Plate. Central to the geological study of this region is the recognition that it has a prominent island arc: as the Caribbean plate moves eastwards it creates a destructive plate boundary, or volcanic zone, in the Lesser Antilles. Another volcanic zone is found in Central America on the western boundary of the Caribbean plate with the Cocos and Nazca plates.

Syllabus Objective

Assess the impact of geographical processes on Caribbean society and culture.

Key Terms

Geographical processes – events relating to the Earth's physical environment (including landforms, ecosystems, oceans, climate and atmospheric processes), how they change over time and human responses to them. For example: soil erosion, floods, climate change, volcanic eruptions, land use and migration.

Plate tectonics – a theory that explains how the Earth's outer crust moves around over the molten layer below. The crust consists of huge slabs of rock (plates) whose movement can fold mountains and influence the occurrence of earthquakes and volcanoes. In the Caribbean, most movement occurs along divergent boundaries (or margins), convergent boundaries and transform boundaries.

Figure 8.1 **Diagram of a destructive plate boundary, or subduction zone, forming a volcanic island arc (such as the Lesser Antilles)**

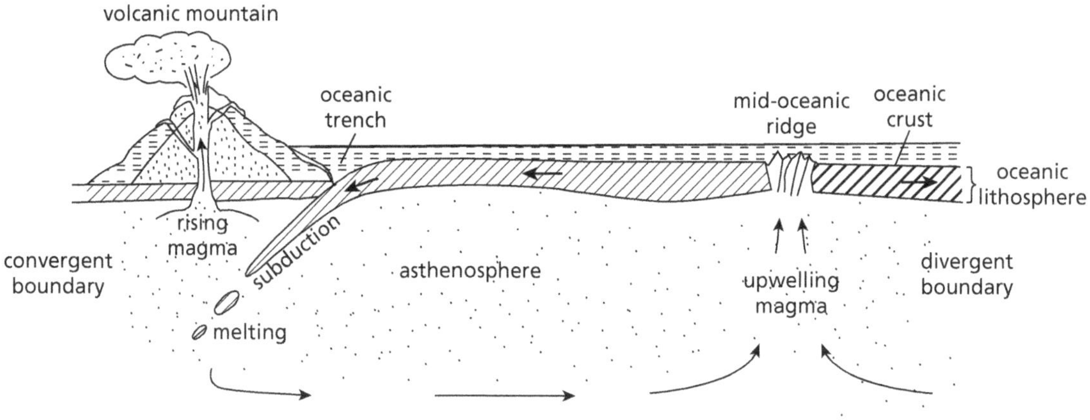

A transform fault is the boundary between two adjacent crustal plates where they move sideways past each other in a tearing action, which results in frequent small tremors and occasionally severe earthquakes. Associated with this type of fault is the Puerto Rico trench (8,400 m), which forms the deepest part of the Atlantic Ocean.

A strike-slip fault is made of large cracks, or a fault zone, that may or may not reach the surface. Strike-slip earthquake zones on the northern and southern boundaries of the Caribbean plate, where there are transform plate boundaries, have shaped the Greater Antilles (the location of the Enriquillo-Plantain Garden Fault system) and northern South America. In the Greater Antilles, the steep topography of Hispaniola (Pico Duarte in Dominican Republic is the highest point at 3,098 m) and Jamaica indicates their relatively recent uplift in geological terms.

Coral islands, such as Barbados, The Bahamas and Turks and Caicos Islands, have been created by a combination of uplift as the Caribbean plate moves and sea-level rise caused by climate change.

Figure 8.2 **Location and features of the Caribbean tectonic plate, showing the epicentre of the earthquake that hit Haiti in January 2010**

The severity of earthquakes tends to be greater to the west of the plate, in Central America, where there is most movement. Next in severity is the northern boundary while the east experiences the least movement. Volcanic activity, however, occurs only along the destructive boundaries to the west (most active) and the east (many dormant and a few extremely dangerous volcanoes).

Earthquakes, Volcanoes and the Threat of Tsunami

Key Terms

Earthquake – due to movement of the Earth's crust, pressure builds up at the junction where two plates meet. When the rocks cannot take the force, they snap into a new position and this vibration is an earthquake. Some earthquakes have a volcanic origin, occurring below volcanic vents, and are less destructive.

Volcano – an opening in the Earth's crust which allows ash, lava, steam and hot gases to escape to the surface, creating an atmosphere dangerous to plants and animals around its vent. Over time these eruptions build a cone-shaped mountain.

Tsunami – a series of high sea waves which may be the result of an undersea earthquake or, more rarely, volcanic eruption that triggers a giant landslide on the sea floor. A tsunami may be three metres or more in height and can flood coastal areas and travel up river valleys, washing people and property away.

The Caribbean people are vulnerable to the impact of **natural hazards** such as **earthquakes** and **volcanoes** because many countries are small and resources are scarce. In countries that have been affected, important political decisions have to be made and this puts leadership under pressure. Tourism also takes a major blow any time there is a natural disaster in the region because tourists view the 'Caribbean' as a whole. To help combat the negative impacts, individual countries invest in local offices and regional bodies, such as the Caribbean Disaster Emergency Management Agency (CDEMA), that coordinates **emergency management** systems.

Figure 8.3 **The social and economic impact of plate tectonics on the Caribbean**

Positive	Negative
• Soils rich in nutrients are useful to agriculture (on volcanic islands) • Attractive scenery and fold mountains, such as the Pitons of St Lucia, bring tourists • Tourist attractions, such as Sulphur Springs in St Lucia, generate income along with associated merchandise such as beauty products (such as volcanic mud face masks) • Access to: valuable minerals, including gold and silver and nickel (Dominican Republic); bauxite (Jamaica.); and oil and gas (Cuba, Barbados, Trinidad and Tobago)	• Gigantic waves called tsunamis destroy coastal areas up to 2 km inland (Port Royal, Jamaica, 1692) • Earthquakes can shake the ground and cause buildings to collapse through landslides, liquefaction or fires (Haiti, 2010; Guadeloupe, 1843) • Explosions of hot lava, ash and gases from an erupting volcano called a pyroclastic flow smother everything in their path (Martinique, 1902) • Mudflows resulting from the volcanic ash and rainfall mixing together • Poisonous gases around the volcanic vent prevent plant growth and cause acid rain

Making the Connection

CDEMA is a Community Institution of CARICOM. The role of CARICOM and its agencies in the movement towards integration in the Caribbean region is looked at in Chapter 15 'The Integration Movement'.

Key Terms

Natural hazard – the threat or loss to human systems as a result of natural processes, such as plate tectonics, extreme weather, floods and droughts, and biological processes including pests and vectors such as mosquitoes spreading viruses like dengue fever.

Emergency management – the steps that are taken before or after a disaster to minimise or solve the damaging effects and ensure sustainable development.

Quick Facts

Volcanic eruptions within the last 300 years include: Mount Pelee (Martinique, 1902), Soufrière (St Vincent, 1979), Soufrière (Guadeloupe, 1976), Soufrière Hills (Montserrat, 1995 to present), Kick 'em Jenny (under the sea, north of Grenada, 2015).

(continued)

Figure 8.3 *continued*

Positive	Negative
• Though not volcanic in origin, minerals such as oil, natural gas and asphalt (Pith Lake, Trinidad) can be created or brought to the surface by collisions between land masses • Source of geothermal energy. Schemes in Montserrat and Nevis are exploring the use of this for their large hotels	• Flash floods, caused by the removal of vegetation from upper slopes and then heavy rainfall • Damage to beaches or coastal vegetation as lava flow creates new land • Can set back development because of the cost and time needed to rebuild • Disruption to the economy if businesses and markets close • Loss of working-age people, who may migrate out of the region; for example, for economic reasons (Montserrat, 1995 onwards), for reasons of safety because of an immediate physical threat (Montserrat, 1995–97) or to escape from outbreaks of disease following a natural disaster

Earthquakes

Earthquakes are a major natural hazard and regularly occur along the plate margins. Most tremors are slight and can only be detected by seismographs, but some are stronger and can cause buildings to collapse trapping people inside (Jamaica, 1903 and 1993; Haiti, 2010). A major earthquake today causes more damage than in the past because:

- larger populations live in vulnerable areas, caused by a growth in population;
- there are now numerous high-rise buildings;
- unauthorised construction of buildings has occurred (built to poor standards);
- buildings have been built on reclaimed land or steep slopes, with weak foundations; they may collapse due to liquefaction, which is when soil behaves like a liquid during an earthquake.

Quick Fact

The islands of the Caribbean experience between 20 and 30 minor earthquakes a year. They are more frequent than hurricanes.

Making the Connection

Chapter 4 'Location and Definition of the Caribbean'

Did You Know?

In Haiti in 2010, an earthquake of magnitude 7, or 'severe', struck the capital, Port-au-Prince. At least 100,000 people lost their lives and more than 200,000 buildings collapsed (but larger figures have been given by the Haitian government). There was damage to the airport, hospitals, sea transport and communication systems. In response, more than 20 countries sent military personnel to help with the aid effort. The severity of the quake was unusual for Haiti and this was exacerbated by the weak infrastructure of this impoverished country.

Exam Tip

'**Examine**' requires a detailed study in an extended answer defining key concepts, stating the facts and exploring related concepts and issues.

Check Your Knowledge

Examine FOUR measures that Caribbean countries can implement to minimise dangers posed by earthquakes.

Demonstrate an understanding of the following concepts by defining and using them correctly:

- Earthquake
- Caribbean countries
- Disaster relief

You must examine any FOUR of the following points and demonstrate understanding by giving specific examples relevant to specific countries:

- Set up an authority to monitor earthquakes, for instance, the University of the West Indies Seismic Research Centre (English-speaking Eastern Caribbean) or Office of Disaster Preparedness and Emergency Management (ODPEM) (Jamaica).

- Establish a task force to deal with earthquake-related issues, e.g. Caribbean Disaster Emergency Management Agency (CDEMA).

- Avoid construction in earthquake prone areas.

- Pass supplementary budgets to repair damage caused by earthquakes in order to help minimise the effects of further earthquakes.

- Governments should encourage building companies and citizens to adhere to strict building codes and to construct structures to withstand the effects of an earthquake, including through legislation, because most danger to humans is posed by houses and other buildings collapsing (in 1907, Kingston, Jamaica, experienced an earthquake which destroyed 75% of homes). Preventative measures include:

  - Ensure utilities can be easily turned off by installing electricity main breaker, gas valve and main water valves. Ruptured gas mains can cause fire if sparks ignite the gas. Install fire extinguishers and fire alarms.

  - Design buildings to sway or bolt the structure to solid foundations.

  - Lightweight roofs are better: sheet metal on wooden trusses is very resilient. In the Haiti 2010 earthquake heavy concrete roofs collapsed.

  - Walls need to be reinforced: steel beams, wooden frames and reinforced concrete stand up better to ground shaking as they can sway flexibly; small windows create fewer weak spots in walls.

  - Bolt large items of furniture and other heavy items, such as propane tanks, onto the wall.

  - Impose strict building regulations for high-rise buildings to make them safer as they are potentially more at risk from the effects of earthquakes.

- The above improvements will help enable buildings to withstand the physical effects of an earthquake and minimise repairs or rebuilding.

- Plan for disaster relief assistance in areas of health, water and sanitation. This will ensure that the injured can get prompt medical attention, and there should be plans for a central location where displaced people can get food and clean water. In Haiti in 2010, 300,000 people were injured and 60% of hospitals were destroyed, so the Red Cross was forced to mount a huge response, setting up camps.

- Provide for radio or television broadcasts from local stations (for the 'all clear' and other important information, such as aftershocks, the location of aid) as a source of information as part of emergency planning for the aftermath of an earthquake because the mobile phone network may overload or not operate at all.

- Develop education programmes and awareness campaigns. For example, school evacuation drills can improve a community's preparedness (80% of schools were destroyed in Haiti in 2010), and the use of outdoor sirens is one way to inform the wider population, e.g. near the coast in case of a tsunami. More generally, signs in public places can inform the public of what to do in the event of an earthquake. They can show the closest exit and evacuation routes.

- Summarise your points in a comprehensive conclusion.

Exam Tip

A good response is one that uses examples to illustrate the individual points.

Making the Connection

Chapter 4 'Location and Definition of the Caribbean'

Chapter 12 'Concepts and Indicators of Development'

Chapter 13 'Factors that Affect Development'

Exam Tip

'**Describe**' requires a lengthy answer in which you explain key concepts and issues and give logical arguments. You must use detailed examples, but **not** necessarily draw a conclusion.

Volcanoes

Before volcanic eruptions occur, there is usually some kind of warning of increased volcanic activity, such as a tremor. In the Eastern Caribbean, along the volcanic island arc, active volcanoes have been erupting for hundreds of years. These volcanoes produce violent eruptions and acid lava, which can be unpredictable in terms of their length of eruption and degree of severity. Eruptions can vary from just a little steam to a few years of deadly pyroclastic flows. Sometimes major towns are destroyed (such as Plymouth, the capital of Montserrat, in 1995).

Did You Know?

In Montserrat, the Soufrière Hills volcano started erupting in 1995. This caused an emergency evacuation of parts of the islands, including its capital and main port, Plymouth, and then, following the permanent disruption to economic and day-to-day life on the island, led to the migration of most of the population to Great Britain, with which they had colonial ties. Following such hazards, homeless people are forced to live in tents, aid agencies are overwhelmed and rebuilding is slow because of the lack of funds to cover so many people's needs.

Tsunamis

Tsunamis have had less impact on the Caribbean region than the other types of natural hazard. The main threat would be from an undersea earthquake (Dominican Republic, 1946, 1943), or a volcanic eruption could potentially cause a tsunami (for example from Kick 'em Jenny submarine volcano, just north of Grenada).

Check Your Knowledge

Describe FOUR impacts of volcanic activity on Caribbean society and culture.

Demonstrate an understanding of the following concepts by defining and using them correctly:

- Volcanic activity
- Caribbean society
- Caribbean culture
- Natural environment

Introduce the topic by pointing out that volcanic activity is responsible for the creation of the Antilles Arc of islands.

Describe any FOUR of the following impacts of volcanoes on Caribbean society and culture:

- Describe negative impacts on the natural environment/Caribbean society and culture:
  - Poisonous gases around the volcanic vent and aid rain prevent plant growth. This leads to the destruction of the agricultural sector and export sectors.
  - Ash fallout damages plants and crops by blocking out sunlight and causes a high incidence of sickness and respiratory ailments.
  - Damage to beaches or vegetation resulting from lava flows and possible damage to coral and marine ecology affects tourism and the fishing industry.

- After effects, such as flash floods, which caused by the removal of vegetation from upper slopes and then heavy rainfall, and landslides, which may be triggered by volcanic earthquakes, create infrastructural problems, pose dangers to people and damage property and agricultural land.
- Severe climate changes can be experienced.

- Loss of life and destruction to infrastructure (housing, educational and recreational facilities, roads) causes stress to the survivors.

- Migration of people from the country at risk to other regional countries or to the metropole; for example, the Montserrat disaster of 1995 caused forced migration, both internal (to other areas of the country) and external (such as to the UK). The former led to competition for or insufficient infrastructure and social services.

- An increase in spending for local authorities and central government because there is a significant cost attached to reconstruction of the infrastructure, including roads and buildings.

- Disruption to travel and tourism.

- Rise in unemployment including the tourist industry and tourism-related businesses.

You can counter/contrast the negative points above with positive impacts on the natural environment/ Caribbean society and culture:

- Volcanic rocks over a period of time form highly fertile soils with minerals that plants require, thus encouraging agriculture in high risk areas and future abundant yields of crops.

- It makes Caribbean people aware of the nature of environmental hazards; for example, the destruction and loss that Montserrat has experienced.

- It can facilitate tourism, in particular through the creation of spectacular scenery in some countries, black sand beaches and hot springs, as in St Lucia and Dominica.

You can conclude by pointing out that some positive impacts can help balance the negatives to some extent.

Hurricanes

A **hurricane** is a large rotating severe storm that occurs in the tropics, normally between early June and the end of November. A warm sea surface temperature of 26–27°C is necessary to maintain the weather system. Other factors cause hurricanes to develop rapidly, such as a considerable depth of warm water (70 m) below the sea surface, atmospheric instability such as thunderstorms, or cumulonimbus clouds, The most dramatic atmospheric condition is the high wind speed, which must be over 119 km/h for the system to be called a hurricane (less than this and it would be a tropical storm, depression or easterly wave). The Saffir–Simpson scale of 1–5 classifies hurricanes according to their wind intensity and can be used to estimate how damaging a hurricane will be.

Key Term

Hurricane – a large rotating storm with high wind speed, storm surge and torrential rainfall, thereby causing flooding, beach erosion and power failures. A storm surge is when the wind blows the ocean ashore, creating sea levels of up to 8 metres above normal, which, if it coincides with a high tide, threatens coastal communities.

Figure 8.4 **A hurricane storm surge**

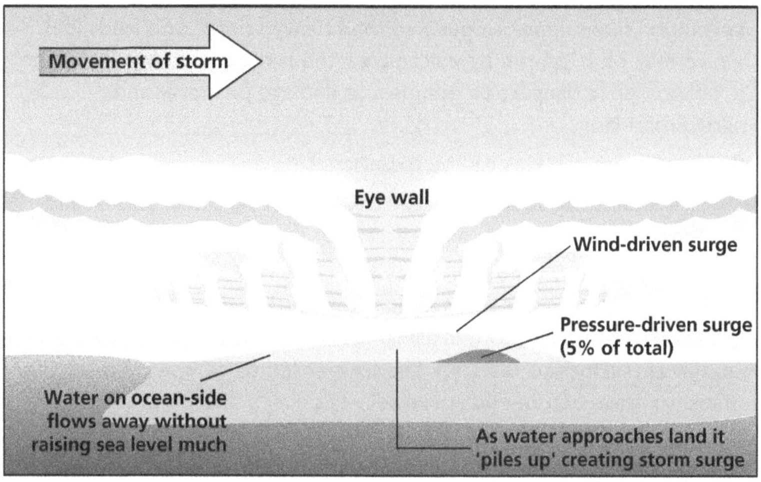

Figure 8.5 **The three levels of tropical storm**

Tropical depression	Tropical storm	Hurricane
• 62 km/hr winds or less • Thunderstorms	• 63–118 km/hr winds • Given a name and considered a threat • May cause serious damage from winds • Thunderstorms cause inland flooding • No defined eye to the storm	• 119–260 km/hr winds • Sea temperature 26°C or higher • Calm eye at the centre surrounded by towering cumulonimbus clouds • The eye wall experiences the strongest winds, heaviest rain • Anticlockwise spiral pattern of winds inwards • Waves and rip currents • Rainbands 50–300 km outwards • Inland flooding/landslides • Storm surge, 1–5 m

Hurricanes have a doughnut shape if viewed from above, with a calm region of low pressure, called the 'eye', at the centre. The weather system originates as a low-pressure trough off the coast of West Africa, travels westwards over the Atlantic and then changes direction when it reaches the Caribbean island chain, moving first north-westwards and then northwards. When a hurricane is close to land, it can cause storm surges that batter coastlines. High velocity winds and sometimes tornadoes can blow roofs off and damage windows. Torrential rain can also cause flash flooding and trigger landslides.

Did You Know?

Unlike volcanoes and earthquakesm which only occur on and around the plate margins, hurricanes can affect all parts of the Caribbean region. The potential for very strong hurricanes increases northwards as the warm Caribbean Sea and the lack of a high-pressure system to weaken the winds causes storms to strengthen. Countries to the south (including Guyana, Suriname and Trinidad) are rarely affected as they lie outside the atmospheric conditions that favour the strong wind rotation of a storm. Poorer countries, such as Haiti, are particularly at risk of hurricane damage as many people live in poorly constructed buildings.

To prevent a disaster from happening, residents must be warned in advance about the pending approach of a hurricane. This is done through a system of monitoring by meteorologists (at the National Hurricane Centre in Miami, Florida), satellites, buoys, aircraft and computer models to predict the track of the hurricane. When it seems that a hurricane will strike an area within 24 hours, a hurricane warning is issued.

Social and Economic Consequences of Hurricanes

Hurricanes and the floods that come with them are the most common natural hazard Caribbean people face and the Caribbean can expect an average of three hurricanes per year. The social and economic risks from these are increasing as the population grows and more communities and businesses are established in places known to be high-risk hurricane areas.

Governments, businesses and individual citizens can take certain actions to manage, and even lessen, the impact of a hurricane.

Figure 8.6 **Ways to plan for the impact of hurricanes**

Long-term government action	Immediate action
• Improve housing by securing roofing, storm shutters, raising electrics out of range of floodwater and installing sewer backflow to avoid water contamination	• Anchor fishing boats
	• Secure oil drums; trim trees to reduce risk of damage and injury from flying debris
• Have a system in place to evacuate areas likely to be hit by flash floods, such as settlements in river valleys	• Cover wells to prevent water contamination
• Improve hurricane defences at ports	
• Reinforce telecommunication structures and power lines	
• Plant trees and mangroves to act as a natural wind break	
• Increase awareness of the need to take out adequate insurance to help recovery	
• Educate citizens to maintain a stock of emergency supplies and how to use them	
• Plan for emergency broadcasting to keep people informed during and after	

Impacts of hurricanes:
- Threats to human life by flying debris, floodwaters and contamination of drinking water supply.
- People can become depressed from being homeless.
- Hurricanes can destroy 10–25% of property and infrastructure, and damage even more (Hurricane Ivan: Grenada, Jamaica, The Cayman Islands, 2004).
- Communications, roads and utilities shut down, leaving people cut off from emergency services and facing reductions in water and electricity supply.
- Interrupted life and livelihood as towns, schools and businesses are forced to close.
- Potential breakdown of social order with general lawlessness and looting.
- Destruction of parts of the environment, agricultural industry, forests and gardens, resulting in a shortage of local crops. Hurricanes can cause beach erosion and damage to the marine ecosystem as well

Quick Fact

The intensity and strength of a hurricane rapidly decreases once it moves over land as it is no longer fuelled by warm water.

Quick Fact

To avoid confusion if there is more than one storm, tropical storms are named once their wind speed reaches 63 km/hr.

as to the fishing and leisure industries. On the plus side, the rainfall they bring replenishes aquifers, for example in Barbados, increasing available water and relieving droughts.

- Damage to, or destruction of, port facilities. These areas are prime economic locations and attract commercial activities that may be vulnerable to disruption.
- Severe weather results in cancelled airline flights and cruise ship arrivals, which impact on the tourism industry, foreign exchange earnings and the economy.
- To avoid too great a shock to the nation's economy, disaster funds may be needed from government agencies or aid agencies.

Did You Know?

Hurricane Ivan hit the Caribbean region in 2004. Most damage was suffered by Grenada (39 killed, destruction of key buildings including a prison, looting), Jamaica (18,000 people homeless) and the Cayman Islands (resulting from intensity of the storm, about 25% of buildings were rendered uninhabitable despite strict building regulations), though Cuba also suffered more than US$1 billion of damage due to flooding caused by the storm surge. Grenada had been experiencing a period of projected growth, but the economy was hit particularly hard, with a lowering of the GDP following an acute drop in tourism and damage to agriculture. Despite aid packages, the economy remains fragile.

Responses to hurricanes:
- Promotion of the education of citizens and emergency personnel on how to prepare for the impact on themselves, their homes and communities. (This can have wider benefits, such as securing roofing, erection of storm shutters, raising electric points to above anticipated flood levels and installing a sewer backflow to avoid contamination of water.)
- Some economic activity is stimulated as citizens buy emergency items and construction materials (but some may be cheap, and of poor quality).
- The fostering of community spirit as neighbours pull together to deal with the effects.
- Foreign aid may be sent from overseas and can be used to meet the needs of people who have become homeless or in need of medical attention. Aid in the form of finance and expertise can also help with reconstruction.
- Many people mistake preparedness for having a stock of non-perishable food and beverages, but if a hurricane is severe there is a need for much more than just food. Citizens must plan for how to return their lives to normal if their home becomes damaged and they cannot return to it.

Soil

This layer of organic and mineral matter is crucial for plant growth. Humus, or decomposed vegetation and animal matter, provide the soil with nutrients which can be taken up by roots. Soil air and soil water are also necessary for a fertile and productive soil.

Soil Erosion

Soil erosion is a process caused by water, wind or ice and involves the removal of soil particles from land (particularly steep slopes), and depositing it in rivers, on land elsewhere or in the sea. High rates of erosion exist when heavy rainfall results in large raindrops that splash soil particles up and wash them down the slope and away in the floodwaters. Bare soil tends to be easily eroded because it may be dry and loose and is therefore easily washed away leaving rills and then large gullies.

Plant roots can hold soil particles together, leaf litter is essential to soil fertility and moisture retention, and tree canopies shade the soil beneath, reducing moisture loss. Additionally, vegetation slows water runoff, leading to increased infiltration and recharged aquifers.

A number of factors, including poor farming methods, can combine to increase the rates of soil erosion: over-cropping, which causes a loss of soil fertility and low crop yield; overgrazing, when there are too many animals on a small area of land; and deforestation, which is the clearing of trees for agriculture, lumber or mining. In Haiti, clearing trees on steep slopes for use as firewood, together with a lack of contour ploughing, has increased runoff and taken topsoil with it.

Key Term

Soil erosion – the removal of the topsoil from the land by heavy rainfall or wind reduces organic matter, lowering crop yields and increasing production costs. The chief cause is absence of vegetation cover, possibly because of poor farming techniques such as slash and burn and overgrazing on steep slopes.

Did You Know?

Deforestation in Haiti began under colonial rule and, later, extended with the introduction of coffee production. After the Haitian revolution, the government was forced to export timber to raise finances to pay off France and the situation was later worsened still by Hurricane Hazel in 1954. At about the same time, domestic demand for charcoal increased. Today there is a thriving black market in charcoal illegally imported from neighbouring Dominican Republic.

Soil Conservation

While soil erosion is impossible to stop completely, things can be done to slow the process down. Keeping the natural vegetation is the best idea on steeper slopes. The gentler slopes can be used for agriculture, but good farming techniques need to be practised, including crop rotation, terracing, mixed cropping, mulching and contour ploughing. Fencing off parts of the pasture for animals can keep them from overgrazing. Some farms utilise zero grazing, where animals are fed hay in stalls.

Some areas may have poor drainage and clay-rich soils that can become waterlogged and prone to landslides. These soils can be drained so that slopes can be stabilised and vegetation can grow back. Management of the amount and types of plants can be achieved by afforestation or replanting trees, which reduces wind speed and protects the soil from heavy rainfall. In Haiti the measures taken include:

- building check dams in ravines to encourage infiltration;
- making terraces, or steps, cut into hillsides;
- practising mixed cropping, so soil fertility is not lost;
- the use of alternative energy for fuels, or imported charcoal to halt the deforestation process.

Quick Fact

In 1923 more than 60% of Haiti was forested; in 2006 less than 2% was forested. An estimated 61 km² of topsoil is washed away each year.

The hilly and remote terrain in the interior of Caribbean countries can limit settlement. This is because these areas are harder and more expensive to clear. The thin soils are also not favourable to the expansion of farming here and this has historically made the flatter areas more useful, as thicker soils have formed around river valleys as alluvial deposits.

Alluvial deposits occur during a flood in a river valley when more water arrives than can be drained, so the river breaches its banks. Soil, pebbles and boulders are deposited in the channel and can cause displaced water to break river levees and flood the adjacent area. Eroded soil carried by the river spreads fresh sand and silt onto the flood plain, increasing soil fertility and making these areas prime sites for farming and settlements close by.

Figure 8.7 **In Haiti, deforestation for fuelwood, farming and wood craft has led to soil erosion on a large scale, resulting in some abandoned areas. However, some tree planting has started in small areas**

The loss of small amounts of topsoil is to be expected, but when large amounts of soil are washed away this can reduce crop yields and make agriculture less sustainable. When the local supply of food crops is reduced, there is less or none to export and so foreign exchange earnings will decline. Sometimes, to satisfy the local demand for agricultural products, expensive substitutes must be imported and this can create a trade imbalance.

Coral Reefs

A **coral reef** is a large underwater strip, or atoll, made from the skeletons of marine animals called polyps. There are hard and soft corals and colonies of these inhabit shallow water along rocky coasts in the tropical latitudes. Coral atolls exist offshore and are circular reefs enclosing a lagoon, as in The Bahamas. As sea levels were lower in the past, some

---

Key Term

Coral reef – corals are animals made of numerous tiny individuals called coral polyps. Hard corals inhabit shallow seawater and the polyps secrete calcium carbonate to create exoskeletons, forming coral reefs. They are at risk from coastal development, overfishing and nutrients from sewage and agricultural fertiliser.

reefs, such as the Belize Barrier Reef, are now far offshore and have created large lagoons for fishing and the collection of seafood, including lobster. Most reefs are fringing reefs, which grow close, and are often attached, to the shore and enclose a small lagoon. Coral polyps need sunlight, few nutrients and saline seawater to grow well, so are not found near large rivers or in polluted water.

The coral reefs absorb wave energy and, as a result, pieces may break off. This rubble is deposited on the shore, creating white sandy beaches (volcanic islands have black sand). This sheltered coastline can create wetland ecosystems and mangrove swamps, which are a breeding ground for juvenile fish. The crevices in the reef and the reef itself are home and food for a very rich marine ecosystem and the ecology is studied by many scientists. Spawning corals create the basis for a food chain for fish and small reef dwellers, which can support fishing industries and their communities. The beauty of these reefs, such as the Buccoo Reef in Tobago, attract tourism. Leisure and tourism activities, including scuba diving, photography, snorkelling and boating, create foreign exchange flows into a country.

Figure 8.8 **A coral reef food web**

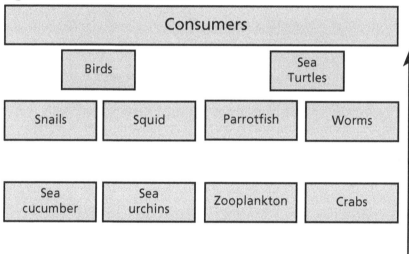

This represents a large number of complex relationships that are not well understood. The fine balance of these is threatened by coastal development, which increases fishing and adds alien nutrients from agricultural runoff (fertilisers) and sewage.

Coastal Protection

The reef front faces the incoming waves and this shallowing of the sea bed forces the waves to break and slow down before they reach the coastline. When destructive waves and storm surges reach the coral reef during storms, the reef acts as a buffer for the shore. Some damage to the reef may occur and, since corals grow slowly, transplantation can help speed up the regeneration process. To protect beaches that are turtle nesting grounds, some governments have constructed artificial reefs.

In Barbados artificial structures using tetrapods are used to protect coastlines at a marina in Port St Charles. These are less reflective than boulders and reduce backwash erosion. Reefs are made using reef balls, which attract coral and fish.

Sustainability of the Fishing Industry

Fishing villages rely on the sea to support their livelihood. Often, inside the calm lagoon is an ideal fish landing harbour. Fish and seafood, including lobster, crab and conch, can be supplied for export, but controls on numbers taken (known as quotas) ensure sustainable fish stocks exist for the future. Governments can pass legislation to protect certain species from extinction, such as the sea urchin, by establishing a closed season for fishing them. They can also ban dynamite and cyanide fishing, both of which are indiscriminate in their impact, and the mining of coral for construction materials or as souvenirs for the tourist trade. This has had some success, but poaching is still a problem in some countries. Protected areas, or marine parks, prohibit fishing and pollution, and allow the ecosystem to thrive.

Threats to and Preservation of Coastal Habitats

The threats to coastal habitats are numerous because these areas are in high demand as marinas, ports, houses and hotels:

*   Coastal development can destroy habitats by draining wetlands and causing soil erosion and siltation of the sea, which blocks sunlight from the corals.
*   Cruise ships and watersports can pollute the sea with oil and can damage corals. Anchors, anchor chains and divers walking on and touching the reef can damage the polyps.
*   Toxic chemicals from industries near the coast leave some coastlines barren.
*   The overuse of agricultural pesticides and fertilisers, along with improper sewage disposal in the sea, can cause the growth of algae over the reef.
*   Global warming has been linked to higher sea temperatures and may cause widespread coral bleaching to occur as polyps die, which restricts its growth.
*   Ocean acidification, where the pH of the ocean interferes with a shellfish's shell formation, has been linked to CO_2 emissions and localised pollution. Using solar and wind energy for heating water and electricity generation, rather than using fossil fuels, has been encouraged by governments as a way to reduce carbon emissions.

Islanders have a special tie to the sea even though today its primary use in many areas has changed from being a natural resource, used mainly as a fishing ground, to a tourist attraction. Local organisations have formed links with large hotels to protect the habitats of turtles and fish. Unspoilt beaches are prized by tourists the world over and every winter tourists arrive, mainly from Europe and North America, to sunbathe and pursue leisure activities. Preserving the sea, the coral reefs and the fishing communities is important as these have become features of the Caribbean's culture and natural beauty known worldwide.

Droughts and Floods

Some experts believe that an El Nino event in the second half of the year brings unpredictable weather patterns, including **droughts** and **floods**.

Drought

A **drought** is a period when there is insufficient rainfall to sustain plant growth. In turn, crop yields decline and there may be a shortage of planting materials, including seedlings or cuttings for grafting. The reduced harvest may lead to food shortages. Droughts can also be a problem for the leisure and tourism sector, which consumes a large amount of water for maintaining golf courses, swimming pools and other uses. Dry conditions can create the danger of bush fires, which may threaten people's lives and property. Additionally, the shortage of water makes fires harder to extinguish.

In response to droughts, governments may have to borrow money or divert capital from other sectors. With reduced water supplies, farmers may have to limit the number of animals kept on farms and water companies may have to spend more money on creating new or additional supplies; for example, desalination plants run on solar energy (in 2013 Ionics began using a solar grid to power desalination of brackish water in Barbados). The government can help by introducing water usage restrictions and creating tax incentives for people to install more water tanks. In Jamaica and Barbados, it has been known for the water supply to households to be restricted to certain days and at certain times, and water trucks are sent to the affected areas so everyone must share the available water. Individuals can reduce water wastage by reporting any burst water mains and generally using water responsibly.

Floods

A **flood** happens when water is unable to permeate the soil or rises above its surface, resulting in overflowing river valleys with blocked roads and flooded buildings. They are usually the result of heavy or persistent rainfall. Normally, residents are warned to expect flooding along a whole river system during a storm, but sometimes heavy showers can create floods in a relatively small area, called localised flooding. The Intertropical Convergence Zone (ITCZ), roughly situated along the equator, is a boundary zone between the north-east trade winds and the south-east trade winds. The ITCZ can experience heavy downpours lasting days and this may be beyond the capacity of the drainage systems. In Guyana, where some coastal areas are below sea level, flooding is possible during periods of instability at the ITCZ.

A flash flood can happen rapidly when the drainage system is blocked. This may occur because of illegal dumping in gullies or rivers. Areas with clay soils (where water does not permeate easily) and steep slopes (where saturated soil makes it prone to landslides that can endanger lives and property) should be avoided for settlements. Land use on these slopes should also maintain the vegetation cover, to aid slope stability. Rural

Key Terms

Drought – a climatic condition where insufficient rainfall occurs over an extended period. This causes a drying up of water supplies and affects people, towns, agriculture, livestock and industry.

Flood – these occur when heavy and continuous rainfall overwhelms the soil or river systems. Water builds up in places where it is normally dry, which affects homes, crops and businesses. Storm surges can result in floods in coastal areas and river valleys.

areas, often with steep slopes, form the source of rivers and these areas are increasingly being cleared for use by agriculture and settlements. These forested areas, along with coastal wetlands, soak up a lot of water and their destruction increases the likelihood of flooding. In paved urban areas, especially, flooding can occur when storm drains are blocked by littering or are unable to cope with the volume of water. A tsunami can cause devastating flooding in coastal regions if an earthquake or volcanic eruption occurs offshore.

Social and Economic Impacts of Drought and Flooding

Droughts and floods can both cause major disruptions to local communities. Agriculture employs many people, and creates food and raw materials for secondary industries. However, a scarcity of water will reduce the cultivable area, which can cause a reduction in agricultural workers needed to plant and harvest crops as well as having a detrimental effect on the income of farmers. Expensive irrigation may be necessary: water tankers can be used, but this is only a temporary measure; the construction of water tanks to collect rainwater is a longer-term solution.

Droughts can have social and health effects, such as poor sanitation, malnutrition and food contamination.

Drought can occur over a number of years due to dry weather patterns. On the leeward side of coastal mountains, in the rain shadow, the effects may be more pronounced. Islands where large areas of limestone are found, such as Jamaica and Barbados, tend to have arid areas here. A lack of rivers and underground water may result in the spread of scrub vegetation in these areas and make them unsuitable to many forms of agriculture.

Did You Know?

In August 2015, Tropical Storm Erika hit Dominica, especially the town of Petite-Savanne, on the south-east coast. Thirteen inches of rainfall caused rivers to overflow, and then flooding. The saturated hillside soils, plus rocks and vegetation, all moved downhill, causing mudslides and landslides. Thirty-four residents lost their lives and 271 homes were destroyed.

Figure 8.9 **Effects of tropical Storm Erika**

People can be swept away and drowned by floodwater. Buildings, furniture and businesses can be ruined. Closure of businesses results in a loss of revenue and lower economic activity overall. Vehicles are damaged; bridges and roads are destroyed; and crops can be lost. Towns may need to be relocated by government, especially squatter settlements.

Flooding also carries health issues. Drinking water can become contaminated, which is especially a threat to vulnerable people because it carries illnesses such as dysentery, and diseases such as those transmitted by mosquitoes can easily spread in areas of dirty or stagnant water.

Did You Know?

During the Zika outbreak in 2015, people were encouraged to be tested in order to pinpoint where the outbreak was occurring. In response, stagnant water was sprayed with oil in order to kill mosquito larvae and a pesticide fog was sprayed to eradicate adult mosquitoes. Residents were advised to use insect repellents, especially pregnant women because of the suspected association of the Zika virus with serious birth defects.

To combat the effects of flooding, trees are planted, surfaces made more permeable, and the installation of concrete or solid paving floors is avoided as these tend to need drains. Any drains need to be cleaned regularly, especially before a storm, and the public needs to be educated on anti-littering through signs in public areas and the media. People also need to be educated on the dangers of illegal dumping and of squatting, which tends to occur in vulnerable areas, and on how to reduce mosquito breeding and protect themselves from being bitten. Residents need to be warned in advance of flood threats through bulletins and know where there is an emergency shelter to which they can evacuate. Vulnerable settlements may need to be relocated and this can be costly to governments. Other, more costly, prevention measures are: installation of underground cables for utilities and improvements to buildings, for instance by using stilts or raising the ground level. Taking out flood insurance can facilitate the recovery process. Fostering a strong community spirit can help people get support and safety from their neighbours.

Quick Facts

Mosquitoes lay their eggs on or around still water, for example, ponds, puddles and water butts. The large number of diseases they transmit, such as Dengue Fever, Yellow Fever and Chikungunya and Zika viruses, makes them the deadliest creature in the world.

Multiple-choice Questions

Scale 1 : 40 000 000

1. Which of the following is the BEST way to reduce the impact of earthquakes?

   A. Hire experts to study seismic waves

   B. Elect government officials to create laws

   C. Follow building codes

   D. Mitigate effects by devising emergency evacuation plans

2. Which symbols correctly match the hazard zones in the Caribbean?

   I. Earthquake hazard

   II. Drought hazard

   III. Hurricane hazard

   IV. Volcanic hazard

   A. I only

   B. I and III only

   C. I, II and IV only

   D. All of the above

3. Which of the following has been the GREATEST danger from recent hurricanes in the Caribbean?

   A. Decline in business activity

   B. Loss of lives

   C. No efficient hurricane warning system in the Atlantic Ocean

   D. Property damage due to poor building materials and locations

4. Which of the following conditions does **NOT** lead to hurricane formation in the Caribbean?

   A. Low ocean heat

   B. Location a few degrees from the equator

   C. Unstable atmosphere (temperature falls as height increases)

   D. Pre-existing thunderstorms and high atmospheric moisture (humidity levels)

5. Soil erosion in the Caribbean can result in:

   I. Crop failure

   II. Starvation of rural communities

   III. A loss of livelihood in farming areas

   A. I only

   B. I and II

   C. II and III

   D. I, II and III

6. What is the MOST suitable soil conservation method that can be practised on agricultural lands?

   A. Educate small farmers on proper drainage

   B. Allow hills to grow natural forests

   C. Contour ploughing

   D. Undertake land tenure reform

7. How are Caribbean coral reefs mainly threatened by human activities?

   I. Coastal development, causing siltation.

   II. Sewage creates eutrophication of the near-shore ecosystem.

   III. The dumping of marine oil or debris and agrochemicals in runoff.

   A. I only

   B. I and II

   C. I and III

   D. I, II and III

8. What social and economic factor should Caribbean governments focus on to protect coral reefs?

   A. Control river dumping

   B. Legislation to ban fishing when scuba diving in national parks

   C. Support the growth of fishing cooperatives to control size and range of species harvested

   D. Require hotels to provide protected habitats on the beachfront of their property

9. In what main social and economic ways does drought affect areas of the Caribbean?

   A. Householders and farmers experience water shortages

   B. Reduction in availability of planting materials such as roots and tubers may then require imports

   C. Low yields for rain-fed crops such as sugarcane

   D. Increase in government spending on pumps to divert water to irrigate crops

10. Complete the following sentence: The main artificial cause of floods in the Caribbean is _____?

    A. Practice of agriculture

    B. Building homes near the flood plains of major rivers

    C. Heavy rainfall associated with tropical weather systems

    D. Poor design and maintenance of drainage channels, which may become blocked by debris

11. What is the most important way to reduce flood dangers in Caribbean countries?

    A. Hazard mapping and building restrictions on risky areas

    B. Adequate design and maintenance of drainage channels

    C. Poverty alleviation schemes, especially in rural areas

    D. Flood basin management, by discouraging sand mining in the river bed

Chapter 9

Societal Institutions

Evaluate the ways in which societal institutions impact on lives in the Caribbean.

Key Term

Social institutions – established or standardised patterns of rule-governed behaviour for individuals with a shared common purpose or clearly defined territorial space. They include family, education, religion and economic and political institutions.

Norms – (social) norms are the rules of behaviour that are considered acceptable in a group or society. People who do not follow these norms may suffer some kind of consequence (such as exclusion from a family/community, isolation, the lack of a sense of belonging). Norms vary according to the environment or situation, and may change or be modified over time.

After revising this topic, you should be able to:
- define and describe different family forms, such as nuclear, extended and visiting, and assess their impact on Caribbean people;
- assess how education in both the pre-colonial and colonial periods has impacted on societal institutions in the region and attitudes to gender;
- analyse how education can influence/engender commonly held attitudes and beliefs;
- assess the role and impact of religion on Caribbean people, and how specifically Caribbean forms have evolved;
- describe the origins and workings of the justice system and assess its impact on Caribbean people;
- identify the challenges facing the judicial system in today's society.

Social institutions are influential societal frameworks that shape our lives. They represent a system of behavioural patterns that each society develops to meet its basic needs. They provide routine patterns for dealing with predictable elements of social life. The main social institutions that influence society and culture in the Caribbean are:
- family
- education
- religion
- political and justice systems.

They are fundamental to the good functioning of society. Society shapes peoples' lives through **norms**, roles and values instituted and reinforced by these social institutions.

Did You Know?

Societal institutions and social organisations

Societal institution is a term used to refer to complex social forms, structures and mechanisms associated with the making and enforcing of rules of cooperative behaviour within a society. They manifest themselves in forms such as government, family, languages and education. A **social organisation** is a tangible social arrangement that pursues collective goals within a specific space and time and usually for a specific purpose within a society. It is administered centrally and controls its own performance. Education, the law, transport and trade are all examples of institutions, while a school, a court, a railway system and a market are organisations.

There are different sociological perspectives on societal institutions and their roles and influences. The two main sociological schools of thought are **functionalism** and **conflict theory** (or **Marxism**).

Functionalists see society as made of a group of societal institutions, such as the family, that exist together and follow basic rules to provide peace, order and stability. If there is disorder, the various institutions will respond to preserve equilibrium. In this view, change is suppressed as it is seen as undesirable. Opposed to this view, conflict theorists see societal institutions, such as the family, as oppressive and reinforcing hierarchy. Marxists also argue that inheritance within the family, usually through the male line, serves to ensure that wealth and high status remain the domain of the elites.

The Family in the Caribbean

The social institution of the **family** is common to all societies and cultures. It represents different ideas and beliefs that people of a certain community have about rearing children and socialising them into the norms of that particular society. The unique experience of Caribbean society, with a myriad of cultural, economic, political and religious influences that, over time, have come to bear on it, has resulted in a variety of types of family structure, none of which can be described as typical.

Functions of a Family

Despite variations in form, 'family', seen mainly from the functionalist perspective, performs four main functions, summarised in Figure 9.1.

Figure 9.1 **The main functions of a family**

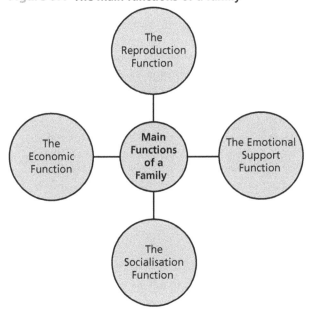

- **The socialisation function** – the family functions, through **socialisation**, to teach the young the norms and values of their culture and society. The family provides the earliest set of concepts, values, knowledge and skills. No society is possible without adequate socialisation of its young. In Caribbean society, the family is the major unit in which socialisation happens. Parents, siblings and extended relatives all help to socialise children from the time they are born.

Did You Know?

Primary socialisation starts during childhood when children look at how the adults in their environment behave and learn which actions make up acceptable behaviour. The family is the main institution engaged in the process of primary socialisation and is in charge of training the child in basic social skills and the use of language to communicate. Interaction with friends and peers also contributes to primary socialisation.

Secondary socialisation is mainly the responsibility of the institution of education, whereby more specific training and skills are learnt. Interaction with teachers and other pupils or students prepares the individual for the world of work. The individual is socialised into skills such as time management as well as how to interact with peers and those in authority.

- **The reproduction or procreation function** – through procreation, the family serves to provide new members for society, and, at a fundamental level, it ensures the continuation of the human species in order for societies to survive. It also provides a framework for and means of regulating sexual activity and gratification within society.
- **The emotional support function** – the family provides its members with love, comfort and help in times of emotional distress. This is important to the mental, intellectual and social well-being of its members. Children need adequate love, care, affection and attention to develop healthy stable personalities.
- **The economic function** – the family provides its members with certain basic needs, such as food, shelter and clothing, and practical support in the shape of finance where possible.

Key Terms

Marriage – a legally sanctioned contract between spouses that changes the legal status of both parties. It establishes rights and obligations between the spouses, between them and their children, and between them and their in-laws. The definition of marriage varies according to different cultures, but it is principally an institution in which interpersonal relationships, usually sexual, are acknowledged.

Hybridisation – the process through which cultures mix to create new forms.

Did You Know?

The role of marriage

Producing offspring is not the only function of the family. **Marriage** helps to establish legal parentage; it also regulates the provision and control of sexual contact, labour and property between spouses, and by extension their families. Marriage creates a joint fund of property for the benefit of children and can establish a relationship between the families of the spouses. None of these functions are universal, but depend on the society in which the marriage takes place and endures. In societies with a gender division of labour, marriage, and the resulting relationship between the spouses, is necessary for the formation of an economically productive household. In modern societies, marriage entails particular rights and privilege that encourage the formation of new families even when there is no intention of having children.

Problems in Defining the Caribbean Family

Due to the complexity of historical factors that have come to bear on Caribbean society and culture, such as slavery, colonialism, emancipation and indentureship, and the **hybridisation** of Caribbean culture, the family in the Caribbean is a complex, fluid concept, sharing multiple creolised features brought by all the communities. These influences have all determined the diversity that exists in the ways Caribbean families are organised, including a multiplicity of family dynamics – extended families, nuclear families, married couples, single parents, co-sharing parents, common-law or consensual unions, visiting unions, matrifocal families, patriarchal families, same-sex families, and so on.

Such complexities make it impossible to define one 'typical' Caribbean family. Instead of trying to define just 'one' Caribbean family, researchers suggest focusing on the shared similarities of Caribbean families with families in other parts of the world. These similarities are the family's function as a provider of love, belonging, care, food, shelter and economic support.

Did You Know?

Creolisation is a term that can be applied to the hybridisation of cultural forms that has occurred in the Caribbean to create a unique 'Creole' form. The term was coined by Edward Kamau Braithwaite in the early 1970s. Colonisation resulted in a mixture among people of indigenous, African, Asian, Middle Eastern and European descent, with which came a cultural mixing, which ultimately led to the formation of new identities, now called Creole. The process of creolisation also brought the mixing of different languages and the creation of new ones, called Creole languages (for example, French Creole, English Creole, Dutch Creole).

Making the Connection

The theory, process and effects of creolisation are investigated in Chapter 7 'Identity and Social Formation'.

Family Forms in the Caribbean and their Characteristics

Functionalism is the dominant view of reality that Caribbean people hold towards the family. However, diversity in family forms existing in the region and the values accepted are not seen in practice and it may be argued that the Marxist perspective of the family provides a clearer and more accurate picture, for example in terms of the division of labour within the family.

The main family 'types' found in the Caribbean are:

- nuclear
- extended
- visiting
- single parent.

The nuclear family, which is not the popular family form of the region, is still held in high esteem. It is argued, however, that this is largely due to the fact that the nuclear family unit represents the values of the rich and powerful in society. The other 'traditional' family form practised in the Caribbean is the extended family, introduced by indentured labourers from East India. On top of these, the unique Caribbean experience has produced variants in traditional family structures common among the majority of the population of the region, the Afro-Caribbean.

Historically, enslaved African people preserved family life through an extended network of community support, though these arrangements did not mirror the extended family in its traditional or classical form, as practised within East Indian communities. These forms were not always based on marriage, as marriage was prohibited to the enslaved community and cohabitation was also banned – men and women lived separately, while children were left in the care of women. Consequently, this has encouraged visiting-type relationships and common-law unions.

Studies have shown that relationships can often start as a visiting union, progress to a common-law union and end up in formal marriage. It has been estimated that 60% of children grow up in two-parent homes, and 30% live in households where they are raised exclusively by their mothers (Powell, D. (1986). 'Caribbean Women and Their Response

to Familial Experiences'. *Social and Economic Studies* 35: 83–130).
Children born to couples in the later stages of family development usually
have two parents in the home.

The Nuclear Family

The nuclear family consists of a mother, father and their unmarried
children living under the same roof. This form was first introduced to
the region by the White Christian colonisers and followed the nuclear
European family.

The nuclear family was viewed by colonial authorities as the norm
or ideal family form. Other family structures, such as single parents or
extended families, were viewed as not 'proper' or even dysfunctional.
This was reinforced by Western Christian teachings, which were highly
ethnocentric and idealised a sense of White European norms and values.
In addition, the nuclear family supported the idea, prevalent among the
colonial authorities, of the supremacy of the male within the household.

Other family forms, such as single parents or visiting partners were
matrifocal and ran against this. Although nowadays it has become more
mainstream, this form is mostly found among the upper and middle
classes. Among the working class, this family form varies according to
ethnicity and culture.

The Extended Family

The traditional extended family consists of members beyond a mother,
father and their children. Several generations may live together in one
household. There may be several married siblings and their children,
together with grandparents and other relatives. Generally, this family form
is predominant among East Indians, particularly Hindus and Muslims.

It is basically patriarchal in authority and is often patrilocal, that is,
upon marriage the couple resides with the parents of the male spouse.
Strong kinship ties exist, and arranged marriages and the practice of
endogamy are customary. Moreover, strict gender socialisation exists.

The Single Parent Family

This occurs when only one parent, either the mother or father, lives with
and takes responsibility for raising children. In the Caribbean, the number
of **matrifocal** households, headed by a mother, far outnumber those
headed by a father. UN figures show that in the early 1980s 44% of all
households in Barbados were headed by a woman while the figure for the
first half of the 1990s in Antigua and Barbuda stood at 42%. Furthermore
54% of all divorced or separated women become heads of households,
most of which have between three and five children depending on the
mother. Again, extended family networks are important in providing child
care and socialisation support. The father may or may not have a role,
financial or otherwise, in child rearing.

The 'Visiting' Family

This is a variation on the single parent family in that it involves the
mother and children living separately from the father, often in her parents'
home, and the father visiting them there. The difference is that the parents
are still in a sexual, and often emotional, relationship.

Key Terms

Endogamy – the choice
of marriage partner is
restricted to a defined
community. The opposite
is **exogamy** where social
norms require marriage
partners to be found from
outside the community.

Matrifocal – coined in
1956, this term refers
strictly to Caribbean
societies, is related to
the working class and is
dominant among those of
African descent. Matrifocal
families are not simply
woman-centred, but rather
mother-centred: women
in their role as mothers
become key to organising
the family group. Men
tend to be marginal to
this organisation and to
the household. Where
matrifocal families are
common, marriage is less
common.

The practice originated in slavery where planters forbade couples to form family units. As a result, the woman took the responsibility for herself and her children. The father of the child may or may not accept responsibility.

Studies carried out in the mid 20th century showed that such relationships were to be found mainly among lower-income Afro-Caribbean families and that women often entered into the relationship for economic support. Thus, for economic survival the woman may have sexual relations with men other than the father. This type of union is not generally approved of in the Caribbean and can be a source of problems in society.

Common-law Unions

Common-law marriage, or *de facto* union, is widespread in the English-speaking Caribbean, especially among the Afro-Caribbean community. It involves a couple committing to each other in a lasting relationship without any form of registration of the 'marriage' (which would make it 'formal').

The term 'common-law marriage' officially has a strict legal definition and, due to their colonial past, territories have statutes concerning common-law marriage similar to those in the UK. However, in the Caribbean, the term is also widely applied to any long-term relationship and there is such a high degree of recognition for this situation that these unions amount to an institution.

The Blended Family

This results from the union of parents with children from previous relationships. It is common among all ethnicities.

Figure 9.2 **Variant family forms that exist in the Caribbean**

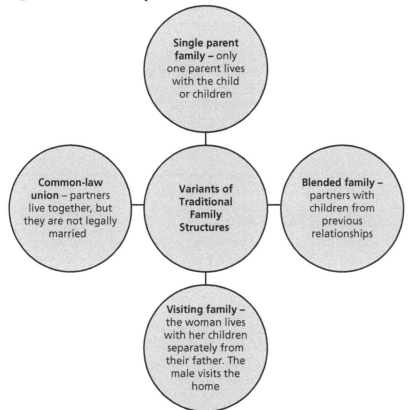

Quick Fact

A study conducted with students from the University of the West Indies suggested that while Caribbean men provide economically for their children, they tend to have poor emotional relationships with them. As a result, boys may view family patterns such as male absenteeism and extramarital relationships as norms and perpetuate them as adults (Sharpe, J. (1996). 'Mental Health Issues and Family Socialization in the Caribbean'. In *Caribbean Families: Diversity among Ethnic Groups*, ed. J.L. Roopnarine and J. Brown. Greenwich, CT: Ablex).

Quick Fact

The sociologist R.T. Smith identified and explained the visiting family type in his study of Guyana.

Making the Connection

The historical narratives that established the constructs of race, colour and ethnicity in plantation societies and the resulting rigid social stratification by caste and class are investigated in Chapter 7 'Identity and Social Formation'.

Quick Fact

The concept of plantation society as a total institution upon which Caribbean society after emancipation was modelled was promoted by economist George Beckford in the 1970s.

Key Terms

Polygamy – the practice of taking multiple wives or husbands. The opposite of this, the situation where a person is faithful to one spouse, is **monogamy**.

Social mobility – the movement of individuals, families, households, and so on, within or between social strata in a society, up or down the social scale. It is a change in social status relative to others' social location within a society (for example, when individuals or a family move from rural Haiti to Miami for better paid jobs and better living conditions).

Historical Factors Influencing the Structure of Caribbean Families

It has been argued that there is a strong link between the current structure of Caribbean families and the plantation system, particularly during slavery. This economic organisation exerted a huge influence on the development of Caribbean society and attitudes. Over time, and particularly with the advent of industrialisation and the modern age, there have been changes from within Caribbean society, brought about by factors such as migration and education in particular. These have had an effect on the occurrence of family types.

Colonisation and the Establishment of the Plantation System

The White planters brought their families to the Caribbean and introduced and promoted the Western European idea of the nuclear family. It became entrenched in Caribbean society under colonial rule; because of the economic and social superiority of White people during this period, the concept of the nuclear family was established as the 'ideal' family structure. This ideal survived into modern times, though in practice it is not the most common form.

Slavery

During slavery, planters did not allow the enslaved people to bond and marriage among the enslaved was banned. The practice of **polygamy**, brought from West Africa, influenced patterns of sexual activity among the enslaved people, with men often fathering children by different women. Planters also often fathered children by enslaved women. Enslaved people could be bought and sold at any time, which also mitigated against the formation of traditional family ties. However, they were allowed to procreate without forming a family unit. These factors all resulted in the formation of matrifocal households, and were later to manifest themselves in visiting-type unions and common-law unions.

Indentureship

East Indians introduced the extended family in the form of a joint household – a strong patriarchal family structure with a stress on early marriage. During and after indentureship, the extended family remained dominant among the East Indians. This family type was deeply established in societies such as Guyana and Trinidad where there were very large numbers of East Indians present. Today this family form is predominant in rural areas. Many Indo-Trinidadians have chosen the nuclear families over the extended form as a result of **social mobility**.

Emancipation and Migration

After the abolition of slavery, freed Black people, especially in the smaller territories, did not have access to land and other economic resources that were vital to their survival. As a result, some migrated to where land was more readily available. Later, the advent of industrialisation created an avenue, mostly for male Afro-Caribbeans, as well as Indo-Caribbeans and Chinese-Caribbeans, to migrate (mostly to North America and Britain) in search of jobs to support their families. This mass migration perpetuated the already matrifocal feature of the Caribbean family. In addition, the efforts exerted by formerly enslaved people and their families to establish themselves as successful small-scale farmers resulted in children working or taking on child-rearing responsibilities for their younger siblings at a relatively young age. Thus, it is plausible to say that the economic hardships after slavery have also greatly influenced the structure of many lower class Caribbean households.

Quick Fact

The construction of the Panama Canal in the early 20th century created numerous employment opportunities for the Caribbean male population. During this period, tens of thousands (mostly fathers) migrated. Unfortunately, some never returned, for varying reasons. In excess of 20 000 workers had died (mostly West Indians) during construction before it was opened in 1914.

Independence

Independence also brought with it changes to family dynamics: as more and more countries became independent in the Caribbean, there were more opportunities for social mobility. Education became the key to attaining upward social mobility for people desirous of improving their socioeconomic lives. Social mobility, together with accepting upper and middle class ideals, is the main reason why more people adopted the nuclear family. Thus, for example, the nuclear family is the ideal type of family practised among the upper and middle classes in Trinidad and Tobago.

Modernisation

Modernising influences have come to bear on the institution of the family. Modernisation has resulted in governments recognising common-law unions in the Caribbean. Legislation has been passed to recognise children and spouses in this union. Children are now legally entitled to inherit family property and so on. Sociologist T.S. Simey argues that common law union in the Caribbean is 'faithful concubinage'. Changes in gendered roles within the family structure have also been brought about by marriages becoming more egalitarian, with more women achieving a higher level of education and acquiring prestigious jobs.

The Influence of Race and Ethnicity

Figure 9.3 **Types of Caribbean families based on race and ethnicity**

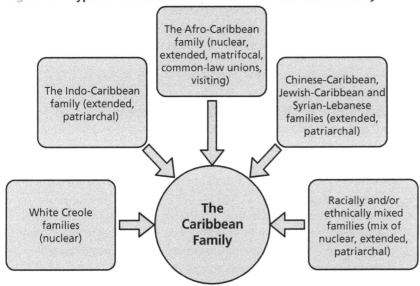

Some features of different Caribbean racial and ethnic communities include the following:

- Indo-Caribbean families are typically **patriarchal**. Fairly strict guidelines govern marriage practices and there are strong kinship ties among communities, making them close-knit. Extended family is the main family structure with several generations and relations living in the same household. Nowadays, global tendencies and equal education opportunities see more equality among the married partners, hence the formation of nuclear type families or at least a moving away from the 'classic' extended family type.
- Afro-Caribbean families are typically matrifocal (care of children either by the mother or grandmother); the male figure is often absent or marginal. These families are usually more affected by poverty than nuclear or extended families. Another common feature in Afro-Caribbean families is child-shifting (care of children by extended family or a close community member). These features have been argued to be the result of the plantation system during slavery. They have persisted post-emancipation, along with the West African culture of polygamy.
- White Creole families usually follow the (colonial) Western family pattern of married partners and a nuclear family.
- Chinese-Caribbeans, Jewish-Caribbeans and Syrian-Lebanese families also generally tend to have extended patriarchal families, though these communities may have family forms that differ in cultural detail from the mainstream forms.

Trends Affecting Caribbean Families Today

Family can determine one's social and economic identity. Children are born into their parents' social class, race and ethnicity, religion and so forth. A financially advantaged or disadvantaged background can determine a child's economic adult life. Some children have advantages throughout life due to the social identity they acquire from their parents (for example, those born into the families of former plantation owners), while others face many financial obstacles because the social class or race and ethnicity into which they are born is at the bottom of the social hierarchy. However, recent academic studies have shown that such stereotypical representations in the Caribbean are decreasing in frequency in today's society mainly because of the increase in global **social mobility**, in which broader educational opportunities have played a large part. Nowadays, two factors that affect families are becoming increasingly important: migration and poverty.

Migration

The Caribbean region has always had a high degree of migration. Most of the Caribbean diaspora lives in the United States or Europe. Research shows such mass migration has major consequences on family life.

- Children and families are uprooted from their local communities and relocated in foreign places (usually in main urban areas such as New York, London or Paris).
- Children are left behind in their Caribbean communities by parents in search of employment in the US or Europe. Although these 'barrel children' are left in the care of the extended family, they can still experience feeling abandoned, lonely or unloved.

- Parents (often mothers) often accept poor work conditions so that they can earn money to support their families left behind.

Poverty

Research has shown that some poor, unemployed Caribbean women are willing to be involved in sexual relationships for financial help, especially if they are mothers. This results in successive relationships, which helps to provide the means for family survival rather than stability. The male partners are often foreign tourists (mainly Americans or Europeans).

The increase of tourism in the Caribbean has given rise to a form of sexual-tourism with holiday companies advertising the 'exotic' beauty of the islands and their women, and foreign men willing to pay for such holidays. This form of tourism is associated with HIV transmission, and other sexually-transmitted diseases, which has catastrophic implications for health outcomes. Often, foreign tourists father children with local women, without providing any emotional or financial support. This has a major impact on both the women left behind and the children, who often grow up lacking a sense of belonging and identity, as well as facing a lifetime of financial and possible health difficulties.

Education in the Caribbean

Education plays an important role in the socialisation process: it transmits norms, values and beliefs that work to underpin a society. It does this openly by teaching and instructing and implicitly through engraining and reinforcing certain attitudes and beliefs. It has also played a key role in the facilitation of social mobility.

The development of education in the Caribbean needs to be viewed within the context of the region's colonialist past. In the English-speaking Caribbean, the education system was established along the lines of the British system and its subsequent development can be analysed as a series of responses to key events such as emancipation and independence.

Key Term

Education – often taken to mean schooling, in its broad sense education can be defined as the wise, hopeful and respectful cultivation of learning undertaken in the belief that all should have the chance to share in life opportunities.

Did You Know?

The functionalist school of thought argues that the education system works with other institutions in society to ensure the smooth working or running of society, while the conflict theorists believe that the dominant ideas of education are those of the elites whose children not only have greater access to education, but are also at an advantage and continue to succeed. They also believe in a hidden curriculum, which is set by the elites to reinforce values and beliefs such as conformity, knowing one's place, waiting one's turn, competitiveness, individual worth and deference to authority.

The Development of Education in the Caribbean

Figure 9.4 Key stages in the development of education in the Caribbean

Pre-colonial Education

- Informal education within Amerindian societies.
- Passing on survival skills from one generation to another, based on gender: women taught girls domestic skills, while men taught boys hunting, fishing, building shelter, fauna and flora.

Pre-emancipation Education

- Formal education provided only for the children of White colonisers; the enslaved population were denied any formal education.
- Plantation owners resisted attempts by missionaries to provide any kind of teaching for the enslaved people they owned, as they believed that any ideas and individual thinking this may encourage would be detrimental to the status quo.
- Informal education occurred, however, within the enslaved household. Women orally passed on songs, poems and religious beliefs as well as different survival skills.
- Spanish colonisers were the only ones interested in building schools for the enslaved; however, they only taught religious education.

Post-emancipation Education

- In 1834 the Emancipation Act (through the Negro Education Grant, which came into force in 1845 and which provided finance for buildings and a basic infrastrucutre) stated that elementary schools should be built throughout the West Indies.
- However, only a few subjects were taught: reading, writing, arithmetic and a little geography, with the Bible as the main text to focus on.
- The taught curriculum followed English Christian values with an emphasis on religious instruction.
- European missionaires and church groups played an important role in the provision of education.
- There were a few fee-paying secondary schools. They followed colonial curricula (French, English, Spanish). Some of their pupils (mostly male) went on to renowed European universities. Some returned home as writers, scholars, lawyers and doctors, and became involved in the process of decolonalisation.

(continued)

Table 9.4 (continued)

Post-independence Education and Caribbean Education Today

- After independence European models continued to be followed in terms of structure (primary, secondary and tertiary), curriculum and an emphasis on certification.
- Traces of **colonial education** are still prevalent in today's Caribbean schools. Until recently, curricula still had a strong colonial influence; however, reforms are being made in order to ensure a more locally inclusive curriculum (one such reform is the recent introduction of Creole as a taught language with grammar, vocabulary and syntax).
- Another new feature of today's education system is more gender equality. However, in higher education women are under-represented in the fields of science and technology, but over represented in the arts and fields related to care of people and children.
- Today the University of the West Indies, established in 1948, is one of the world's renowed educational institutions.

Quick Fact

Missionaries and representatives of the Christian Church were often blamed for inciting rebellions amongst the enslaved people, through their teaching of religious ideals and values that were fundamentally in opposition to the condition of slavery.

Making the Connection

There is more information on the University of the West Indies and the Caribbean Examinations Council in Chapter 15 'The Integration Movement'.

The Impact of Education on Society

Education has affected and still affects different socioeconomic groups. For example, a global trend that is apparent in today's English-speaking Caribbean is that the approach of many schools is biased to the middle classes and to a system that rewards children that have the necessary advantages (also called cultural capital) – such as a higher level of linguistic competence – to succeed in the academic world. For example, the level and type of English required for both school and exam success gives children from the middle classes an educational advantage over those from lower socioeconomic groups who have less exposure to the formal language.

Key Term

Colonial education – a by-product of colonisation whereby colonising nations implement their own form of schooling within their colonies. A main purpose of this is to support the cultural and economic dominance of the colonisers by instilling their value and belief systems among the people of the colonies.

Access

The level of education provided to different groups in society during the colonial period highlighted the perceived needs of the different social groupings according to the colonial authorities. The majority of enslaved peoples did not have any access to education. Even 20 or so years after emancipation, secondary education was only really accessible to White people and some people of colour, with most secondary-level schools being fee-paying and selective. The provision of only, often limited, elementary level education for Black people was still geared towards creating a labour force for the sugar industry, as children were 'freed' from education to enter the workforce at the age of 10. Access to secondary education for the Black and Asian indentured communities through the second half of the 19th century and first half of the 20th century was a slow and gradual process.

As access to both secondary and tertiary education increased for the lower classes, it provided a conduit, mainly for males, to gain upward social mobility through jobs in towns and in professions such as law, medicine, teaching, engineering and accounting. Today, social mobility for individuals is a major expectation of education and it has a direct impact on the lives of many. Students complete primary, secondary and tertiary education in order to secure professional occupations as well as positions in business. Lower qualifications enable others to access technical, industrial and clerical jobs. However, for many other Caribbean people the institution of education has not been enabling. The extreme importance placed on education can create feelings of low self-esteem for those who fail to acquire it. Underachievement may occur for many reasons. These may originate in family circumstances, such as poverty, family trauma or lack of family interest and support, in behaviours such as teenage pregnancy or drug and alcohol use, in learning disabilities, or in poor teaching and a negative experience of schooling that results in disillusionment and disinterest.

The Curriculum and the Importance of Credentials

The curriculum in the colonial period mirrored that of traditional British private schools, out of which many of the teachers originated, with stress placed on teaching students the culture of the former British Empire in all subjects including history, geography and literature. There was also an emphasis on the classics, with Greek, for example, still being taught in some schools in Trinidad and Tobago until the late 1960s. According to Marxist theorists, education served as an agent or tool of socialisation as it was designed to facilitate conformity to the norms and values of the imperial power. In this way, education had a key role in facilitating the colonial agenda.

The importance placed on examinations and certification, based on the British system and administered by British awarding bodies, meant that many white-collar jobs and professions that required these were only open to members of the middle and elite classes. Only they were able to afford the extra lessons and resources to help their children achieve these academic credentials. This system was to break down over time as access for the lower classes gradually improved and the higher levels of education became more inclusive. The establishment of the Caribbean Examinations Council in 1972 finally heralded the advent of exam syllabi specifically geared to the experiences of the candidates.

The Role of Missionaries and the Church

As a main provider of education throughout the colonial period, especially after emancipation, the Church and affiliated groups, such as missionaries, placed stress on the teaching of the Bible, and chose passages that encouraged a sense of duty towards those in authority and the promise of a better life after death once the required colonial labour was carried out on Earth. In much of the English-speaking Caribbean, Church and State worked together to create a joint approach for the advancement of the colonial agenda through education. The Church also set up primary and secondary schools that frequently maintained the status quo and worked closely with the ideals of the colonial powers.

Did You Know?

The social institutions of education and religion are closely linked, even in today's Caribbean, through the existence, popularity and success of denominational schools. These schools are often seen to offer a high standard of education (usually measured by exam success) as well as providing socialisation through an emphasis on the teaching of desirable values. Thus, places tend to be in high demand, which in turn enables the schools to be highly selective, resulting in a form of elitism.

Gender

Gender, in terms of attitudes and opportunities, is another area upon which education has an influence. Post-emancipation and pre-independence, attitudes to the education of girls in the Caribbean mirrored those of society at large, with much more emphasis and importance being placed on access to secondary and tertiary education for boys. Higher education in particular was viewed as a male domain and as a privileged route to becoming leaders in Caribbean society. By the 1960s, however, there was a thrust towards more female inclusiveness and a more equitable curriculum. Today, girls have caught up with their male counterparts in education and have even surpassed them in numbers of scholarships and university enrolments. They have also acquired key leadership positions in politics, business and the professions.

Even today, however, there is still an implicit assumption that girls prefer and are better suited to 'softer' subjects connected to the arts and the care industry, while boys study subjects such as the sciences and various forms of technology. Although opportunities are open to girls to pursue these subjects, socialisation, reinforced by the education system, tends to dictate that these gendered choices are perpetuated.

Quick Fact

Research shows that very little is being done to reintroduce students without any educational credentials back into the education system. Thus, for those who fail to achieve educational credentials, there are few options in the Caribbean that can enable a comfortable adult life. This constitutes a strong reason for looking to migration as an alternative means to upward social mobility.

Religion in the Caribbean

Religion affects lives as a conservative force linked largely with positive values, as Christian worship in the region has historically been associated with preserving social life in keeping with accepted norms and values. However, the existence of syncretism of religious forms, such as Rastafarianism, exhibits aspects of resistance and independence. They therefore assist in comforting the worshipper, but at the same time oppose mainstream values and so seek to undermine the status quo. Overall, however, the functionalist perspective of religion as a stabilising force can be said to be most dominant in the Caribbean.

The Main Caribbean Religions

The religious history of the Caribbean is closely tied to the process of conquest, colonisation and immigration, leading to assimilation, acculturation and syncretism. The arrival and development of the main religions in the region are discussed below.

Christianity

Post-conquest, religion was used as a tool for colonisation. European colonisers brought with them Christianity – together with their Western education and justice systems – and imposed it on the other peoples in the region as the only permitted religious system. In order to survive, the rest of the population, Amerindians and enslaved Africans, had no choice but to adopt Christianity and with it acceptance of the social values it entailed as well as an implicit recognition of the superiority of European culture over their own. There was a strong religious element to the Encomienda system enforced upon the indigenous population in early Spanish colonies, with forced conversion and acceptance of religious instruction forming part of the Amerindian side of the 'contract'.

Colonial authorities established 'official' Christianity in the form of Roman Catholicism in French and Spanish colonies, and Anglicanism and the Dutch Reform Church in British and Dutch colonies, respectively. However, after emancipation in 1838, in the British West Indies, many formerly enslaved people turned to alternative non-Conformist forms such as Moravian, Methodist, Baptist and so on. This was both as a form of protest against the authorities and because these non-Conformist groups were significant in helping to ease the transition of many Black people from enslaved to free members of society, for example through the establishment of free villages and schools.

African Religions

Despite outwardly adhering to Christianity, within their household and close communities the enslaved still kept some of their own African religious beliefs. These beliefs themselves had diverse features because of the different geographical and tribal origins of the enslaved people within West Africa. Examples are Vodou in Haiti, Orisha in Trinidad and Tobago, Obeah throughout much of the region.

Did You Know?

The French closely regulated their slave trade, and because France had close links with the Guinea Coast of West Africa, mainly the kingdom of Dahomey (today's Benin), the majority of the enslaved people who were brought to St Domingue (modern Haiti) were from there. These African populations were the primary practitioners of Vodou (or Vodun), and so they brought their religious beliefs with them. Throughout French colonial rule and up until today Vodou has been a predominant religion in Haiti and its diaspora.

Creolised or Syncretic Religions

After emancipation, the region witnessed a flowering of Creole (or syncretic) religions. These all had their roots in West African religions, which were then blended with aspects of Christianity. Examples include Santeria in Cuba, Shango in Grenada and Trinidad, Kumina (or Cumina) and Revival (or Myal or Pocomania) in Jamaica. Rastafari, developed in Jamaica in the 1930s, was a later addition to this group of religious beliefs, all of which are unique to the Caribbean.

These religions all represent a resistance to, or subversion of, dominant Western religious beliefs and structures, and with them mainstream values and European power and authority over the colonies, while still providing the traditional 'comfort' and 'safety' functions of religion by combining traditional beliefs and practices with more recently acquired Christian ones.

Hinduism and Islam

These religions were brought to the Caribbean from Asia by indentured East Indians and Javanese. These groups for the most part have retained their religion and still practise them among their communities, though in Trinidad and Tobago there is a relatively large Presbyterian (Christian) following among the East Indian community. The Muslim community in the Caribbean has been added to over the years by immigration from areas of the Middle East such as Syria.

Both of these religions involve cultural practices that affect the everyday life of their adherents. Muslims should pray five times a day, only eat halal meat and refrain from alcohol, while Hindus are forbidden to eat beef (many are vegetarians) and many perform regular rituals either at home or in the temple. Hindu society is dictated by a rigid caste system that regulates social interaction between the various levels, prohibiting marriage between castes and even within other relationships such as in work or business.

Quick Fact

Advances in broadcast technology in the late 20th century resulted in an influx of fundamentalist Christian beliefs into the region, mainly from the US, and a huge increase in their popularity.

Making the Connection

Chapter 5 'The Historical Process' discusses the Encomienda system and the post-emancipation experience of formerly enslaved people in detail.

Making the Connection

The beliefs of Rastafari and its impact in the Caribbean are described in more detail in Chapter 17 'Intellectual Traditions'.

The Impact of Religion on Caribbean Society and Culture

The main contributions of various religions to society and culture as viewed from the functionalist perspective can be summarised as:

*   Religion can provide or add to a sense of heritage while also serving as an expression of cultural diversity.
*   Religion spiritually grounds Caribbean people and allows them to have an identity. Their daily lives can be guided by the decisions and teachings of their leaders and those included in religious books.
*   The recognition and celebration of religious festivals and national holidays promotes cultural diversity, and understanding and tolerance between communities.
*   Religion exerts an influence on different aspects of culture such as literature, art and music by providing both an avenue and subject matter for artists, performers and writers.

Conflict theory sees religion as a tool used by elites to maintain the status quo.

Along with education and the justice system, religion within today's Caribbean needs to be analysed in terms of the legacy of the relationship between the colonisers and the peoples they governed.

The Relationship Between Christianity and Syncretic Forms

Despite the development of syncretised religions and the arrival of Hinduism and Islam, the strong presence of Christianity with all its branches and denominations – Roman Catholic, Protestant, Quakers and so on – still continues to have a strong influence upon Caribbean society. Indeed, Christianity (both Roman Catholicism and Protestantism) is the most influential and dominant religious body in Caribbean society and it influences laws, values and beliefs.

Christian religion in the Caribbean, as with family structure, tends to be socially stratified, with the reasons for this rooted in the colonial past. Elites are usually members of the mainstream Christian churches while the lower socioeconomic classes follow more of the Creole (syncretic) religions or belong to non-Conformist churches or to newer fundamentalist Christian denominations to the region such as the Seventh-Day Adventists.

During the colonial period, these non-Conformist churches were for the most part sanctioned by the authorities as, despite existing outside the 'establishment', they still served to promote law and order and preached anti-violence. However, some forms took on syncretic aspects, such as loud expressive singing, drumming and dancing, of which the European authorities did not approve as they were viewed as being too close to African traditions and therefore potentially subversive. Many joined these churches, and the more African-influenced syncretic religions, as a form of protest against the colonial establishment and in attempt to shape their own alternative value systems. Others outwardly conformed by attending mainstream Christian churches while at home still celebrating African-based rituals.

Making the Connection

The Hindu caste system is explained in more detail in Chapter 7, 'Identity and Social Formation'.

Quick Fact

Functionalists see religion as a conservative force in society that preserves and promotes basic shared values and social coherence. Conflict theorists see it as a smokescreen imposed and controlled by elites as a means to blind the lower socioeconomic classes to their oppressed state.

Other Religious Forms

Similar to the Afro-Caribbean community, Chinese, East Indian and Jewish immigrants to the English-speaking Caribbean have continued over time to both celebrate their 'home' beliefs and also to mix these with other religions. For example, members of the Chinese community combine Catholicism with beliefs drawn from Chinese religions such as Taoism and Confucianism. This process of mixing thus created a multiplicity of creolised religious beliefs, started during slavery and continued to the present day.

Through this interaction over a period of time, cultural diversity exists in each country in its own unique way. This is also influenced by the ethnic make-up of different countries. Suriname, for example, is home to 25% of Muslims in the Western hemisphere. This naturally has resulted in a strong social and cultural Islamic presence. Many food outlets advertise halal food and both major Islamic festivals of Eid al-Fitr and Eid al-Adha are recognised as official public holidays.

Figure 9.5 shows the main Caribbean religious groups, along with their most prevalent cultural characteristics.

Figure 9.5 The main religious groups in the Caribbean

	African (heavily influenced)	Asian (East Indian and Javanese)		European and USA derived	Syncretic
Religions	Examples: Vodou; Shango; Kumina; Obeah	Hindus	Muslims	Christianity	Examples: Rastafari; Santeria
Examples of groups	Vodou (Haiti); Shango (Trinidad and Grenada); Kumina (Jamaica); Obeah (much of the Caribbean)	Members of different castes	Sunni Shia	Roman Catholics; Anglicans/ Protestants; Methodists; Pentecostals; Seventh-Day Adventists; Jehovah's Witnesses; Latter-day Saints (Mormons)	
Typical/ traditional Dress	Wearing of purple and white	Women wear saris and the bindi, a black dot on the forehead; gold jewellery	Some men wear a white loose garment and grow beards; women wear modest clothing and many cover their hair, and some cover the majority of their body except hands, feet and eyes		Rastafarians: hair in dreadlocks; wearing of red, gold and green
Food preparation		Eat no beef; often vegetarian Food such as curry and roti have become part of Caribbean culture	Eat no pork; no alcohol; meat must be halal	Many Christian groups, such as Madeiran Portuguese, have their own culinary culture especially for major feasts such as Christmas	Rastafarians: little or no salt; vegan diet; use of ground provisions
Burial practices	Mourning ground ceremony, nine nights, wakes		Bury, preferably on same day		
Religious practices, festivals and special characteristics	Baptism by immersion in water, pouring water or rum as libation; spirits of ancestors (duppies)	Diwali; Phagwa; flying jhandi flags (bamboo flags) outside the home	Calling to prayers in Arabic (Friday is an important day); Ramadan (fasting period); Eid al-Fitr (the end of Ramadan) and Eid al-Adha (commemoration of Abraham's sacrifice of the lamb), one or both of these are public holidays in Guyana, Trinidad and Suriname	Christmas and Easter holidays In most Caribbean schools assembly incorporates Christian themes and Christian religious lessons are taught. Attend church on Sundays or Saturday	Rastafarian: Smoking of ganja. Belief in Haile Selassie of Ethiopia. Santeria: Initiation rituals; traditional healing practices
Music and popular culture	Goat skin drum	Chutney music; sitar; films		Gospel music; festivals	Rastafarian: Reggae and dancehall music; Bob Marley is a popular cultural icon

The Justice System in the Caribbean

The **justice system** is an integral part of the political, legal and judicial framework in a country:

- **Political** – citizens entrust to their government the power to make decisions on their behalf that protect and uphold their freedom, rights and interests, which are often laid out in the **constitution** of a country.
- **Legal** – a system of laws derived from the principles embodied in the constitution that treat all citizens equally and fairly.
- **Judicial** – the implementation of laws by ruling on conflicts over rights, fairness and justice.

Key Terms

Justice system – the interaction of societal institutions that are identified with social control and regulation; the system through which laws are set and enforced and punishments are administered by state institutions such as courts, protective services, police, judges and prisons, and therefore concerned with maintaining a society in which citizens are treated justly and fairly.

Constitution – the overall rules and principles for government in a country, including the rights, freedoms, and responsibilities of that country's citizens.

Did You Know?

Social justice is a concept and underlying principle that promotes a just society by challenging injustice and valuing diversity. Social justice is generally equated with the notion of equality or equal opportunity in society. The justice system, on the other hand, is an institution that channels the implementation of justice as embodied in the law through enforcement (the police), judgement (the courts) and rehabilitation/ punishment (the correction system). Institutional justice or fairness refers to the idea that an institution is morally right, an institution that may be defined according to ethics, religion, fairness, equality and law.

As with other societal institutions, there are different perspectives on the justice system. The functionalist and conflict perspectives are as follows:

- Functionalist perspective:
  - The justice system is a means to safeguard social stability and shared values by creating just ways to deal with deviance (law breaking).
  - Deviant behaviour can be understood in terms of a breakdown in socialisation within the family or how individuals respond to changes in society.
  - Society must deal with deviants and deviancy, as they lead to disorder, chaos and confusion.
  - The justice system has been shaped to take care of deviants by punishment, deterrence or rehabilitation through the police, the courts and methods of correction.

Making the Connection

The ideological ideas of Rastafari are investigated in Chapter 17 'Intellectual Traditions', while Chapter 11 'Caribbean–Global Interactions' looks at the global impact of Rastafari communities.

Making the Connection

Concepts and issues of social justice in the Caribbean are dealt with in more detail in Chapter 19 'Social Justice'.

- Conflict perspective:
  - The justice system is oppressive and exploitative of the lower class; it props up the status of the elites through legislation and enforcement systems that serve their interests to the detriment of the poorer classes, who tend to be on the receiving end of law enforcement and correction.
  - Fairness is not extended to members of the lower class, who are generally targeted as criminals. Those who commit white-collar crimes are from the upper classes and are hardly ever pursued by the police or convicted in the court. This makes it appear that crime is mainly a lower class activity, which may not actually be the case.
  - Criminal acts committed by poorer groups are a form of rebellion against structural inequalities in society rather than deviancy.
  - Crime is used by elites as justification to enact legislation to control the poor.

How the Justice System Works

The Police

The police force is the part of the justice system that affects citizens most directly. Its role is to both control and protect the population through enforcement of laws and protection of life and property. The modern perception of the role of the police includes the promotion of the well-being of a community, free from crime and the fear of crime. This approach, through **community policing**, entails a much more personal, cooperative, communicative and mutually beneficial approach to policing than has traditionally occurred.

The maintenance of security is tied to development. CARICOM decided in 2010 to elevate security as a priority in order for development to occur in the Caribbean, because high levels of crime have been shown to hamper local development (small businesses as well as tourism and the banking sectors).

Police brutality can erode public trust in the force, and the judicial system in general, by members overstepping their authority. Despite police organisations voicing their commitment to reform and community policing, many citizens remain wary and can be reluctant to cooperate with investigations. This creates a challenge for the police in the face of generally rising crime rates.

Did You Know?

As with education, the policies of the region's colonial rulers have directly affected the development of the police system. Many top officers in the colonial police force throughout the Caribbean were either from or trained in the colonising countries. Their remit was to preserve the status quo – by coercion if necessary. As a consequence, in a country like Jamaica – with a rigid racial hierarchy – the police developed into a coercive force operating with a significant lack of accountability, towards the Afro-Caribbean population in particular, and this was approved by those in authority, who were mostly White Creole descendants of former colonisers. This basic mistrust of the police endures to this day.

The Courts

Most English-speaking Caribbean countries have both a higher and a lower judiciary, based on the judiciary of the United Kingdom, although this system varies to a certain degree from one country to another. The judiciary structure of Jamaica is shown in Figure 9.6.

Figure 9.6 The Jamaican court system as an example of a typical Caribbean judiciary system

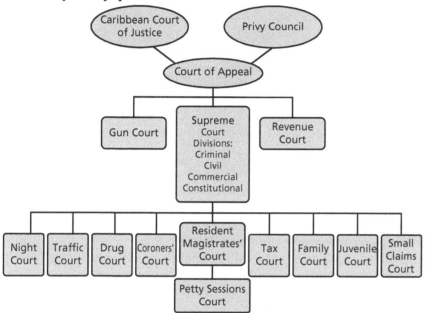

In most Caribbean countries the **lower judiciary** is formed by magistrates – collectively known as the **magistracy**. They preside over the Magistrates' Court (or Petty Sessions Court, which in Jamaica, for example, is presided over by Justices of the Peace) where they decide which cases should be sent for trial in the High, or Supreme, Court. They usually deal with minor cases themselves and send the more serious ones to the High Court.

The **higher judiciary** consists of judges sitting in the High Court. Some countries' systems combine the High Court and the Court of Appeal, others keep them separate. The High Court holds trials by jury in criminal and serious civil cases. The Court of Appeal decides whether the law has been interpreted correctly in disputed cases. The highest Court of Appeal for English-speaking Caribbean countries is still the Privy Council in Westminster, in the UK.

Did You Know?

Efforts are being made for the highest Court of Appeal to move from Westminster, UK, to the Caribbean Court of Justice established by CARICOM. The Caribbean Court of Justice (CCJ) was first proposed in 1970 by Jamaica, but established only in 2001, when an agreement was signed by most CARICOM countries. Its headquarters today are in Trinidad. At present it deals only with cases related to regional integration, and to CARICOM in particular. In the future it is hoped that it will be able to judge appeals in both civil and criminal cases.

The Caribbean justice system also comprises specialist courts, such as the Family Court, dealing with divorce and domestic violence, and the Traffic Court, dealing with traffic infringements.

The Correction System

The role of the judiciary is to form a judgement on whether a crime has been committed and to hand down punishment according to the crime. Minor crimes are usually punishable with a fine or community service. More serious crimes result in the offender being sent to prison for a set period of time.

The concept of correction, rather than purely punishment, is the new paradigm when discussing prisons, their management and the treatment of offenders. It involves not only punishing people through imprisonment, but also addressing their offending behaviour and **rehabilitating** them at the end of their sentence.

Correction works in the following ways:

- Securing the imprisoned person – this serves as a form of punishment, a deterrence, as protection to individuals or society in general, especially in cases of serious crime, and a means to rehabilitate.
- Identifying the needs of the imprisoned person and devising an intervention programme in order to correct their behaviour. These may include: group sessions, conflict resolution, anger management, addiction treatments, reading, writing, art, music and vocational skills. These also serve to keep them busy and establish a sense of self-esteem.
- Establishing a reintegration programme to assist them to return to their lives. In this, there are a number of challenges, not least persuading the community to accept them and give them another chance.

The reality in many Caribbean countries, however, is far from the ideal. Overcrowding in prisons combined with the need to find ways to survive in a harsh and violent environment tends to engender a high rate of **recidivism**.

The Impact of the Justice System on Caribbean People

As in the case of other societal institutions, the Caribbean justice system has inherited ideas from European justice systems and has merged them with local ideas, in this case about rights and cultural diversity. Caribbean constitutions thus reflect the ideals local people have about justice. The ways these ideals are put into practice, however, impact upon people in different ways, for example according to their race or ethnicity, their gender, their social status and their degree of wealth.

Common across societies is the idea of reciprocity: the government establishes and maintains the justice system to ensure everyone enjoys their civil and human rights while in return citizens are expected to be law-abiding. In theory, it is when this basic contract breaks down that the other arms of the justice system, which provide punishment and deterrents, come into play. In practice, however, it is not so simple. Policy-makers do not always have the interest of the whole of society in mind when legislation is created. Even after emancipation, colonial legislative bodies did not represent the majority of the population – the Afro-Caribbeans. Acts of discrimination based on race, gender, colour and age continue to be perpetrated even in today's modern society, both

Key Term

Rehabilitate – to provide the encouragement and the means to reform.

Key Term

Recidivism – the tendency to continue to offend after release from prison.

in legislation and in the application of the system by the police and courts, with accusations of false, or trumped up, charges and unfair trials.

The justice system can be viewed as restrictive of individuals' freedom of choice in personal matters such as abortion or same-sex marriage, both of which are illegal in most Caribbean countries. In the case of abortion, the law is acting as guardian of the unborn child, but this then begs the question of where the woman's right to a personal choice in such matters lies.

Caribbean justice systems also impose certain legal age restrictions that could be viewed as arbitrary and even discriminatory: compulsory retirement at age 65, for example, is seen by some as a way to legally discriminate between different groups according to age. Likewise, people aged under 18 are considered minors and the responsibility of an adult. A minor cannot vote, and in some Caribbean jurisdictions neither are they permitted to drive a motor vehicle. There are also laws that protect the rights of minors and set the age of sexual consent.

Challenges Faced by the Justice System Today

The challenges faced by the justice system in response to today's changing society are many, but the most important are rooted in a basic mistrust of the system among the majority of the largest population group in the region, which has its origins in colonial attitudes.

- The legacy of the early history of the police as a force to oppress and coerce the majority, rather than to protect all members of society, has lived on and is reinforced by instances of heavy-handedness and brutality, usually directed at the Afro-Caribbean community.
- This is coupled with laws and a judiciary that would appear to favour elites with lenient punishments for white-collar crimes, usually committed by members of the middle and upper classes, and imprisonment for petty crimes, such as loitering, with which many Afro-Caribbean males are charged.
- Alleged cases of police and judges accepting bribes have done nothing to increase people's confidence in the system.
- An increase in poverty coupled with pressure to acquire the means to achieve social capital through brand-name material possessions has resulted in young people who have no other avenue to achieve this entering a life of crime.
- The predominance of Afro-Caribbean males among the prison population is witness to the social and economic conditions they live under, but is also partly due to the inequities of the judicial system.
- The police also need to tackle high and increasing crime rates, which are in comparison to low apprehending rates. This is due to a number of factors, including mistrust among potential sources and the application of outdated methods and attitudes. The surge in crime connected to the narcotics trade and distribution has resulted in many arrests, but most of these have been of members of the lower echelons of the gangs (again, mostly Afro-Caribbean males), not the kingpins.
- Many laws need updating and revising to deal with the relative severity and types of crime predominant in today's Caribbean in light of increases in violent crimes against women, narcotics trafficking and drugs-related violence, and crime involving the use of weapons, for example.

Making the Connection

The reasons for the slow uptake of the appellate function of the CCJ among CARICOM members are reviewed in Chapter 15 'The Integration Movement'.

- Despite its establishment in 2001 as a court dealing with internal CARICOM issues such as the right of entry of CARICOM nationals, land issues involving indigenous people and state liabilities, the other main function of the Caribbean Court of Justice (CCJ) as a final appellate court for the region has been slow in coming. As of March 2015, only Barbados, Belize, Dominica and Guyana had replaced the Judicial Committee of the Privy Council with the CCJ.

Making the Connection

Chapter 6 'Characteristics of Society and Culture'

Chapter 7 'Identity and Social Formation'

Exam Tip

'**Discuss**' requires an extended response defining key concepts, giving the facts, exploring related concepts and issues and presenting reasoned arguments. You must use detailed examples but **not** necessarily draw a conclusion.

Check Your Knowledge

Discuss the various ways in which societal institutions have formed present-day Caribbean society.

Demonstrate an understanding of the following concepts:

- Societal institutions (know each type)
- Society
- Culture
- Syncretism
- Creole
- Hybrid

First, define the concepts: society, societal institutions.

List the institutions to be discussed: Educational institutions, religious institutions, judicial and family institutions.

State that these institutions have created a society unique in its own way.

For each societal institution, show how it has contributed to the formation of today's Caribbean society:

- The family:
  - Present-day Caribbean society has been shaped with various types of families – all a result of colonialism. Pre-independence, such as during the days of slavery/indentureship (plantation society), the nuclear style of family was viewed as more socially acceptable as this was the form more practised by the colonial masters. For enslaved people, family life was discouraged, though procreation was permitted. The visiting-type style of relationships was therefore established between the enslaved – a trend that continues today within West Indian society (a feature). This is where the matrifocal families come into play (single parent type).
  - The East Indians brought the notion of the extended family type where grandparents, aunts, uncles, and so on all live together – a feature now quite common to all West Indian ethnicities and no longer defined to East Indians alone.
    Nuclear families still exist – a feature of the lives of former colonial masters and part of West Indian society today where marriage plays a prominent role.
  - The family continues to socialise their young into the acceptable norms, morals, values and folkways practised in West Indian society, which have become a way of life for West Indians, shaping a society built on a colonial culture, yet creolised to match the West Indian environment.
- Educational institutions:
  - These, too, have shaped West Indian society, seen in the evolution of education in the West Indies away from colonial-style education (where the affluent White/mixed race people were educated following a colonial-style syllabus). This left the poor non-White people at a disadvantage as most learnt only the rudiments of education, which involved mostly agriculture and subjects that did not suit the West Indian environment. This supported the rigid social strata, with the White affluent citizens at the top and little to no opportunity for Black people to reach the apex.

- This changed post-independence where West Indians wanted to learn, improve themselves and become more knowledgeable about their environment. The Caribbean Examinations Council (CXC®) of the 1970s aided this process. The new syllabus (no longer British style and containing a 'hidden curriculum' inculcating good colonial attitudes to maintain the status quo) contributed to a West Indian society no longer reduced to merely agriculture but knowledgeable in every aspect of education; reflected in the courses offered at the University of the West Indies, which has expanded hugely from offering education only in agriculture in the 1940s.

- Education has a created a West Indian society where females outdo males in the field – this shows equal opportunities that did not occur pre-independence when emphasis rested on males in education. Education has allowed West Indian women key leadership positions in previously male domains – politics, business and the professions – seen especially with recent female prime ministers in Jamaica and Trinidad.

- Religion:
  - Functionalists believe religion provides spirituality and identity to members. In so doing, it has shaped the outlook of Caribbean society, especially as it is filled with a plethora of religions brought in by immigrants. The colonial masters brought Christianity (both Protestantism and Roman Catholicism) and the East Indians brought Hinduism and Islam – which all preach ideas of spirituality and peace within society.

  - The diversity continues in the religions that have mixed Christian and African beliefs – Santeria in Cuba, Shango in Grenada and Trinidad, Kumina (or Cumina) and Revival (or Myal or Pocomania) in Jamaica (notion of syncretism). These religions serve a major purpose: to provide the 'comfort' and 'safety' all members search for.

  - Though conflict theorists see religion as a tool used by elites to maintain the status quo, functionalists see religion as providing a sense of heritage while also serving as an expression of cultural diversity.

  - Providing spirituality and an identity as a Caribbean people, guided by the teachings of their religious leaders and those included in religious books.

  - Promoting cultural diversity, and understanding and tolerance between communities through recognition and celebration of religious festivals and national holidays.

- Justice System:
  - According to functionalists, all societies have various forms of justice system, which is meant to ensure peace in society and create ways to deal with those who disturb it. The justice system is now in the hands of West Indians who look to it for stability, equity and peace, social control and regulation.

  - Laws are set and enforced in the various constitutions, which represent all in Caribbean societies and not a minority as during the days of colonialism.

- Punishments are administered by state institutions such as courts, protective services, police, judges and prisons, and are therefore concerned with maintaining a society in which citizens are treated justly and fairly. West Indian society is riddled with crime, which has resulted in national institutional arms, such as constitutions to protect citizens, the community police, high courts, magistrate courts and family courts, as well as the CCJ to deal with regional West Indian matters.

- Most Caribbean islands are independent and can no longer rely on their mother country in this department.

You could make brief mention of different theories of Caribbean society and the role of these institutions in forming them (for example, the role of the family and religion in plantation society; the maintenance of separate key institutions, such as the family and religion and language by ethnic groups, within the plural society thesis; creolisation of the family and religion, and so on).

The conclusion must entail a very brief synopsis of the essay, stating that the four institutions mentioned have shaped the Caribbean society into one that is unique as having to adapt to the West Indian environment.

Multiple-choice Questions

1. Wearing conservative clothes and displaying proper etiquette in a restaurant represent

   A. Norms

   B. Morals

   C. Values

   D. Beliefs

2. One of the NATURAL functions of the family is to

   A. Procreate

   B. Impart ethics

   C. Provide religious education

   D. Impart values and norms to the offspring

3. Identify the institution that contributes to secondary education of an individual

   A. The family

   B. The school

   C. The church

   D. The justice system

4. The establishment of the CXC® in 1972 was aimed at

   A. Continuing the colonial agenda

   B. Introducing exam syllabi specifically geared to the experiences of Caribbean candidates

   C. Introducing Caribbean nationals to British style education

   D. Introducing A Level subjects to the curriculum

5. Functionalists believe in all of the following except

   A. That the aim of social institutions is peaceful co-existence

   B. That institutions socialise people with basic rules to provide peace

   C. That institutions exist to ensure stability in society

   D. That societal institutions, such as the family, are oppressive

6. The term 'creolisation' was a term coined by

   A. Edward Kamau Braithwaite

   B. Aubrey Cummings

   C. Marxist theorists

   D. Functionalist theorists

7. Which of the following can be deemed a syncretic religion?

   A. Protestantism and the Kumina

   B. Myal and the Shango

   C. Kumina and Moravian

   D. Rastafari and Lutheranism

8. One of the aims of the Caribbean Court of Justice is to

   A. Accommodate appeals of verdicts

   B. Transfer all appeals to the Court of Appeal in the UK

   C. Assist the RSS in policing the Caribbean against the drug trade

   D. Uphold all laws of CARICOM

9. Conflict theorists see education as

   A. Part of the socialisation process

   B. Providing a productive workforce

   C. Providing a skilled workforce

   D. A system for the maintenance of social stratification

10. Which of the following islands can boast having two Nobel Prize winners?

   A. St Lucia

   B. Trinidad

   C. Barbados

   D. Dominica

Chapter 10

Arts and Popular Culture

Syllabus Objective

Evaluate the ways in which the Arts and popular culture impact Caribbean society.

Making the Connection

Different cultural definitions, characteristics and forms are looked at in Chapter 6 'Characteristics of Society and Culture'.

After revising this topic, you should be able to:

* identify and describe various art forms of the Caribbean (popular music, culinary arts and festivals);
* discuss how various art forms (popular music, culinary practices and festivals) have been influenced by different ethnic groups and how they contribute to a unique Caribbean identity;
* explain and assess how the Arts contribute to human and cultural development in the region;
* discuss contributions made by individuals to the development of culture in the region, for example Rex Nettleford, Louise Bennet, Beryl McBurnie, Paule Marshal, Aubrey Cummings, Martin Carter;
* identify how Caribbean art forms have crossed international borders via the diaspora, including carnivals such as Notting Hill, Caribana and the West Indian Day Parade;
* assess how these diasporic art forms contribute to the economic, cultural and social aspects of the region and its diaspora.

Cultural expression in the Caribbean is key to identity in the region and to its human and cultural development. It can take many forms, ranging from painting and drawing to the culinary arts, folk crafts to performance art and festivals. There are many discussions surrounding what exactly are 'the Arts' and whether they include some or all forms of 'popular culture'. For the purposes of this chapter a broad definition is used.

Key Terms

The Arts – vehicles for cultural expression, which can be taken to only include 'high art' forms such as classical approaches to painting, sculpture and music, or can be interpreted more widely to include various forms of popular and folk culture. The Arts comprise three main categories: literary (such as literature and poetry), performing (such as music, dance, drama) and visual (such as painting and sculpture).

Popular culture – mainstream culture based on the tastes of ordinary people, or the masses, rather than *elite* culture or *high* culture (for instance, popular music forms rather than Classical music).

Making the Connection

The processes of hybridisation/syncretism and creolisation are addressed in more detail in Chapter 7 'Identity and Social Formation'.

Caribbean Art Forms

As with many features of the Caribbean and its societal institutions, hybridisation, syncretism and creolisation have played a large part in the creation of rich and diverse cultural forms that are unique to the region.

In more recent times, computer technologies and the mass media have contributed to the growth, acceptance and appreciation of Caribbean music, cuisine and festivals across international borders.

Music

The music of the Caribbean has helped to define the region as a whole and has placed it on the world map. Most kinds of music in the region can be traced back to its migratory history, with different peoples importing their traditional forms that then went through a process of syncretism to produce many of the forms of today. Whether it is Reggae, Soca, Punta or Zouk, Caribbean music gives Caribbean people their identity, whether they reside at home or are part of the diaspora. Just a few of the many Caribbean music and dance forms are discussed below.

Reggae

Reggae is the most internationally famous style of Caribbean music. It has its origins in Jamaica in the late 1960s. It is widely identified as the music of Jamaica and its diaspora and has gained international prominence, for example in the United States of America, Africa, Japan and Germany, because of its infectious rhythms and dynamic performers.

In the view of Professor Peter Manuel (1998), "Reggae can be considered to be a reinterpretation of American rhythm and blues". It also has evidence of Jazz, Calypso and African music and is sung in Jamaican Patois and Jamaican English.

Reggae was popularised in the 1970s by Bob Marley with his Rastafari lifestyle. His album *Exodus* was listed by *Time* magazine as the album of the century. The music has become popular among young people because of the message it carries – a message of peace and love that they can identify with. It is also an outlet for documenting social and political criticism.

In Jamaica it is one of the largest sources of income as it is a major earner of foreign exchange. For example, the Reggae Sumfest held in Jamaica annually has attracted an international audience. Bob Marley and the band Third World have placed Jamaican Reggae music on the European, American and Asian music charts.

Calypso

Calypso had its origins in Western African music and singing, and resistance by the lower socioeconomic classes to the colonial powers. It was a means to poke fun at important people and institutions, such as the Roman Catholic Church, and today this music form provides a social and political commentary of events, mainly in Trinidad and Tobago. Apart from entertaining, Calypsonians such as The Mighty Sparrow act as voices for their people, expressing their views and protesting government actions, for example. However, Calypso has not gained as large an international audience as Reggae. Exceptions are Arrow's "Ah feeling hot, hot, hot" (which could be defined as Soca, a development of Calypso, see below), which has gained international recognition, and Calypso Rose's "Fire in meh wire", which has been sung in nine different languages. Rose and others have helped to open the doors of Calypso to the rest of the world and these doors can help foster development in the region, bringing in tourists and much needed foreign exchange.

Making the Connection

Rastafari and its beliefs are examined in Chapter 17 'Intellectual Traditions'.

Quick Facts

Other internationally renowned Jamaican music artistes include dancehall musician Shabba Ranks. Dancehall is often viewed as 'youth' music and has connections with US Hip Hop and Rap music.

Quick Facts

Other songs by Calypso Rose include "Tempo", "Leave meh alone" and "Do them back", while some other famous Calypsonians are The Mighty Sparrow, Lord Kitchener and Chalk Dust.

Did You Know?

Popular arts have great significance in social analysis as they are a means to express the views of the masses. Calypso provides many examples of this. For example, Dr Leroy Calliste's (Black Stalin) "Caribbean Unity" (1979) and David Rudder's "Haiti I'm Sorry" (2010) both express a unity plea or a longing of Caribbean people for a collective regional identity and regional solidarity.

Rudder has been recognised internationally for his quest for national and regional integration as well as capturing the essence of Trinidad and Tobago's multi-cultural society via his music. Black Stalin's Calypso "Caribbean Unity" asked some pertinent questions of politicians on issues such as CARICOM and CARIFTA and on integration attempts from the top down that ignore a popular groundswell of opinion yearning for unity.

Both men have been conferred with an honorary doctorate from the UWI for their sterling contributions to Caribbean development in music.

Calypso has a special connection to Carnival, and Calypso competitions have been held at Carnival since shortly after Emancipation in the British Caribbean in the 1830s.

Steel Band

The steel band is the only musical instrument to have been invented in the 20th century. It has its origins in Trinidadian Carnival musical traditions and developed in the middle of the century out of experimentation with readily available materials and objects that could be used and tuned for percussion. Today the steel band is mass produced and referred to as an 'orchestra'. It is also electronically tuned from soprano to bass to produce different sounds.

Quick Fact

The Steel Pan European (European Steelband) Association has been formed to promote pan music appreciation in Europe.

The steel pan as an instrument was associated with grassroots people such as those from poor communities on the outskirts of Port-of-Spain. The names selected for the bands, such as Tokyo, Invaders and Red Army, reflected the current situation of the war years, elements of resistance to domination and the desire to project a tough image. The steel pan is widely used throughout the Caribbean region as well as in the diaspora. Local pan players went abroad to play pan, then settled and have now become involved in teaching young people there, not only to play the pans but also to tune them. This has resulted in steel pan music becoming part of some schools' curriculums in Europe and North America. Its popularity is partly because all kinds of music are played: Reggae, Rhythm and Blues, Calypso, Soca and Classical music; which means, therefore, that it can be internationally accepted and appreciated. Steel pan music has been syncretised with Indian music, and Hip Hop and Pop have also embraced this musical form.

Quick Fact

The making of the steel pan is a growing skill that can contribute to national income and the growth of economies, both locally and abroad.

Punta Rock

This music form originated in Belize in the 1970s out of traditional Garifuna Punta percussion music and dance, and has become popular in Central America. It was taken abroad, significantly to the Belize community of New York, where it grew in popularity and developed to take on new elements of more percussion, musical accompaniment and sophisticated arrangements. The songs are mainly in the form of call and response with drums. While originally in the Garifuna language, the music is now translated into English and Spanish.

Other Examples of Caribbean Music Forms

Over time, various forms of music have evolved to cater to the tastes of the younger generations, as in the case of the development of Punta Rock out of traditional Punta forms. Other examples of this development are the many forms of Reggae (such as Roots Reggae, Ragamuffin) and of Calypso (such as Chutney, Soca, Rapso, Reggae Soca).

Soca music is the music that is in most demand at Carnival. Its international popularity is growing and iTunes has its own Soca category. It developed out of Calypso in the 1970s and 1980s, introducing Indian rhythms, and is essentially dance music. Soca has always incorporated Indo-Caribbean influences, but Soca Chutney is more Chutney in style.

Did You Know?

A feature of many Caribbean musical forms is drumming. This has a direct connection to the traditions of West Africa and came to be a form of opposition to the colonial powers. Drumming was strongly discouraged and even forbidden among enslaved communities, and still in the post-Emancipation era was frowned upon as potentially subversive.

Culinary Practices

The **culinary practices** of the Caribbean are wide and varied and are based on those brought here mainly by the Amerindians, Europeans, Africans, East Indians and Chinese. Generally, Caribbean cooking is hot and spicy, which is a feature of both Indian and African cooking. Many dishes are common across the region, but preparation may differ from place to place.

- Some culinary practices and foods inherited from the indigenous peoples are: corn beer, the art of cooking wild meat (barbecued and jerked), pepperpot soup (today, hot sauce is used in many dishes), the use of roots and tubers and the making of bread from cassava.
- A staple item in the diet across the Caribbean is salt fish. It was imported by the British to feed the enslaved people. Today, this has developed into regional variations such as: fried fish cakes (Barbados); saltfish and dumpling, saltfish pelau, saltfish accra (Trinidad); saltfish and roast breadfruit (St Vincent); and ackee and saltfish (Jamaica).
- Dishes such as peas and rice, salted meat, smoked herring, black pudding and souse (made from discarded animal parts – chicken feet, pig feet, pig snout, fish head, cow heel or goat belly – and fed to the enslaved) all have a long regional heritage.
- Various root crops (such as cassava, yams, dasheen or eddoes) that were part of the enslaved's diet are still very popular. So, too, is breadfruit, which can be steamed, roasted, stuffed or baked into chips.
- From the East Indians came the curries, pepper, lentil peas and various herbs and spices that are widely used in cooking, while pholourie, doubles and dhalpourie roti are generally consumed by all.
- The Chinese brought their ever popular Chinese-style fry rice, fry chicken and vegetables.
- The English/Irish potato is linked to the British presence and is still a staple in the diet (though often cooked in a distinctly Indo-Caribbean way as Aloo). The fact that tea is still widely consumed is part of the link to the British. Also, the British influence of eating porridge for breakfast is still seen today.

Quick Fact

Chutney and Chutney Soca are hybridised forms of music combining East Indian folk rhythms and instruments with African-based music traditions such as Calypso. An important element of Chutney is the dancing that accompanies it, which has evolved from traditional East Indian movements.

Quick Fact

In Trinidad and Tobago, Parang is the traditional music at Christmas. It combines elements of Spanish, Amerindian and African heritage and is sung in Spanish. This, too, has been hybridised into what has become known as Parang Soca.

Quick Fact

Dance forms originating in the Caribbean include Beguine, Mamba, Zouk and Meringue. Popular formal dance forms are ballet, often infused with local culture, and folk dances such as Jamaican Jonkonnu.

Key Term

Culinary practices – the methods used in the preparation and consumption of different foods that are distinct or unique to cultural or ethnic groups.

Quick Fact

Many foods originally deemed only fit for consumption by enslaved people (root crops and animal feet, heads and intestines, for example), have become over time staple, tasty and popular parts of the Caribbean diet.

Quick Fact

The East Indian culinary tradition that the Caribbean now enjoys has enriched Caribbean culture by making it more diverse and has even come to dominate some territories; for example, Trinidad and Tobago. Certain dishes, such as doubles, originated in the region.

Key Term

Multiplier effect – when money is spent in an economy, this spending impacts on different associated areas and results in a knock-on and multiplied effect on economic output, employment, etc.

Quick Fact

Carnival is no longer just a national celebration; it has been influenced by extra-regional countries with regard to: how individual events and overall presentation reflect the global rather than the local market; how it is packaged for tourists; an increase in commercialisation due to technology; the export of associated music throughout the globe.

The Caribbean has caught up with modern trends in food preparation, especially from North America. As more people are working, there is increased demand for fast food. For the same reasons, demand for pre-cooked foods has also grown, as has the incidence of households cooking and freezing their food for future consumption.

West Indians who have migrated to metropolitan countries have been responsible for the expansion of the local cuisine and the creation of West Indian markets and restaurants in those areas. Rum, Angostura bitters and jerk seasoning have all become lucrative export products.

Festivals

The influence of early settlers on the economic, cultural and social life in the Caribbean is very evident in the festivals of the region. These reflect the region's history, connecting present-day society to the past and, at the same time, including contemporary elements. Caribbean festivals are distinctive in their use of costumes, the importance of music and dance and a high level of audience interaction. Caribbean society is culturally diverse and the festivals in the various islands bring all ethnic groups together.

Secular Festivals

Carnival (Trinidad, but has spread to other parts of the region):
- This has contributed to the growth and development of the Caribbean and is the single festival that has defined the Caribbean. It is a street festival, combining steel band music, dance and costumes. It has contributed to the region in the following ways:
  - Local music is given a place on the world stage.
  - It brings all classes of people together.
  - It fosters the growth and development of the entrepreneurial spirit, in particular the creation of small businesses.
  - There is the transfer of technologies as band leaders incorporate these technologies.
  - It brings in foreign exchange, particularly by attracting tourism.
  - It provides tax revenue for the government.
  - Employment generation is a direct and indirect result through the **multiplier effect**.
  - There is an increase in gross domestic product (GDP) leading to growth and development of the region.

Did You Know?

Caribbean Carnival emerged out of the Christian festival that marks the day before the beginning of Lent. It was traditionally the day when households used up their supplies of meat and rich food (carne vale = 'farewell meat' in Latin) and people were able to indulge in merriment and past-times before the onset of the austerity of Lent. The French in particular brought these traditions and, along with other European traditions, such as masquerade and street theatre, they merged with traditions brought from Africa to create the Caribbean celebration of Carnival.

Carnival is still often held just before Lent in countries with a strong Roman Catholic influence, such as Trinidad and Haiti, while other countries celebrate at other times of the year. In Antigua and Barbuda and Barbados, Carnival celebrated Emancipation.

Crop Over Festival (Barbados):
- This festival has its origin in the 1780s when Barbados was the world's largest producer of sugar. The festival lasts for five weeks and highlights the history, art and culture of Barbados. Cohobblopot is a large Carnival style show with various bands showcasing costumes. There is a Calypso contest where Calypsonians compete for prizes as well as a title. The festival ends with a parade – The Grand Kadooment.

Junkanoo (The Bahamas):
- It is usually celebrated at Christmas-time and started during slavery as a day when the enslaved were allowed to leave the plantation and celebrate with their community; with dance, music and costume.

Reggae Festival (Jamaica):
- This started in 1978 and takes place in early August. The celebrations last for one week. Different types of Reggae music are played each night. It has evolved into what is now called Reggae Sumfest.

Tobago Heritage Festival:
- A re-enactment of the history of the island that includes the Old Time Wedding, music and dance, and a crab and goat race, which is the highlight for the many tourists who visit the island specially to witness this event.

Tobago Jazz Festival:
- A yearly event that attracts artistes and patrons from the United States of America, Canada and the United Kingdom.

Religious Festivals

Christian festivals were brought to the region by the European colonisers and imposed upon both the Amerindian and later African populations, while Muslim and Hindu festivals arrived with the East Indian indentures. Carnival has its origins in a Christian festival that became creolised and transformed into a uniquely Caribbean celebration.

The religious festivals listed below impact on or are celebrated across the region, and in many places are given national prominence as they are usually designated public holidays. It is important to note that they have become quite commercialised.

Muslim festivals:
- Eid al-Fitr – a religious celebration that marks the end of the period of Ramadan fasting for Muslims. It is a national holiday in Trinidad and Tobago.
- Eid al-Adha – a holy festival known as the festival of sacrifice.

Hindu festivals:
- Diwali – connects the East Indians to Mother India and is the festival of light over darkness. It is a national holiday in Trinidad and Tobago.
- Phagwa – also called Holi, a spring festival of colours.

Christian festivals:
- Easter – the Christian festival symbolic of the death and resurrection of Christ, celebrated with an Easter parade.
- Christmas – represents the birth of Christ. It is celebrated by all nationalities and is highly commercialised and to some extent has lost its religious significance.

Making the Connection

Major Christian festivals in particular have been commercialised, mainly through globalisation with the import of foreign goods and the spread of especially US and European influences, while other festivals, such as Ash Wednesday and Corpus Christi, have retained their local character. Impacts of globalisation on the region are assessed in Chapter 14 'Globalisation and Development'.

How the Arts have Contributed to Caribbean Human and Cultural Development

Human Development

Development is a holistic term, with people as the mechanism to create both economic and sustainable development. The Arts foster human development. They:

- empower and unite the people
- increase people's productivity
- create greater equity in society
- create sustainability.

Empowerment

The Arts:

- allow people the stage to develop and display their talents and allow them to develop their human potential;
- provide people with an important means of creative self-expression and intellectual growth and act as therapy;
- develop and establish group and community cohesion and unity via street festivals;
- can also help engender a sense of pride and identity in the heritage of the Caribbean, which in turn aids resistance to cultural imperialism. Individuals such as Rex Nettleford, Louise Bennett and Aubrey Cummings help us to comprehend ourselves and our place in the world by shaping the Caribbean identity and sense of self.

Productivity

The Arts create opportunities for people to be gainfully employed and they also create a multiplier effect, increasing the overall level of employment in the economy. Increased trade and foreign exchange can also result as artistes travel and the works of artists are bought and sold internationally as well as locally. Along with popular culture, they also provide a form of relaxation and recreation, which contribute to promoting a sense of well-being which then heightens people's productivity.

Greater Equity in Society

Arts and popular culture represent a valuable aspect of Caribbean heritage. They are the tool used to express both the Caribbean people's struggles for justice and against oppression, by various forces both within and outside the region, and a celebration of their culture.

A sense of self-worth can be fostered through the Arts as individuals achieve recognition on the international stage or in their area of accomplishment or expertise. This can be liberating in a society that tends to still be tied to its colonial past and the legacy of attitudes towards gender, race, colour and wealth associated with this.

Sustainability

People are agents through which development can take place and be sustained. It is through the Arts that language, customs, dress and way of life can pass from one generation to another. **Human capital** can therefore be developed through the Arts.

Many Caribbean governments are making an effort to keep cultural traditions alive by promoting folk festivals. This is a form of cultural retention and can be marketed to promote economic and sustainable development via tourism.

Cultural Development

Art forms in their widest sense contribute to the formation of culture and society. The Arts can provide a means of socialisation as, through them, people learn about their culture's values, beliefs and identity. This acquisition of knowledge and an understanding of the basis of one's society enable its continued growth, evolution and development. Many government and non-government agencies support the Arts because they promote and help define cultural pride and identity.

Contributions made by Individuals to Caribbean Development

The people presented in this section, through their art, music, dance, painting, teaching and travels, have contributed to the development and promotion of Caribbean identity, particularly after independence. They have made Caribbean people aware of their history and have created and established an appreciation of their heritage. More importantly, they have presented Caribbean culture in a manner that has been widely appreciated by international audiences. They have been the real ambassadors of Caribbean Arts and popular culture on the international stage.

Rex Nettleford (1933–2010)

- Was a Jamaican scholar, historian, social critic, choreographer and poet.
- Was a co-author of a seminal study of the Rastafarian movement in 1961.
- His artistic work, particularly his choreography, was based on the concept of 'cultural marronage', which represented the spirit of resistance to the colonial rulers shown by the maroons.

Louise Bennett (1919–2006)

- Was a Jamaican educator, poet, writer and folklorist.
- Travelled throughout the world publicising areas of Jamaican culture. This was done through her performances and lectures, and her work has been translated into foreign languages.
- Through her work, she gained international popularity and recognition for herself and, most importantly, Jamaican culture.

Key Term

Human capital – the skills, knowledge, productivity or other intangible assets that individuals use to the benefit of themselves, their employers or their community.

Making the Connection

Cultural retention is discussed in Chapter 7 'Identity and Social Formation'.

Quick Fact

While tourism and the dissemination of culture via agencies such as the media may be a tool for preserving and promoting traditional arts, there is the inherent danger that the original forms may be diluted or adapted as part of the broadening process.

Making the Connection

Definitions and characteristics of culture are investigated in Chapter 6 'Characteristics of Society and Culture'.

- Her work provided a perspective on the lives of working-class women in the colonial and post-colonial world.
- Wrote her poems in Jamaican Patios and enabled Patois to be regarded as a national language.

Beryl McBurnie (1914–2000)

- A Trinidadian dancer and teacher.
- Was responsible for the promotion of the culture and arts of Trinidad and Tobago.
- Articulated Trinidadian culture and heritage through her dance and was the first person to promote primitive and Caribbean dance.
- Taught West Indian dance in New York and performed at the Brooklyn Academy of Music.
- Formed the Little Carib Dance Company, which gained an international reputation and was instrumental in spreading Caribbean culture to Canada, paving the way for Caribana.

Paule Marshall (1929–)

- An American author who has her roots in Barbados.
- Her writings are an attempt for Black Americans to reclaim their African heritage.
- Many of her books have a Caribbean context or themes running through them.
- Her works feature strong, Black, working-class women.

Aubrey Cummings (1947–2010)

- Was a famous Guyanese musician, artist and singer.
- Believed popular music contributed to 'the healing' of Guyana during the 1960s and 1970s, around the time of independence and general political upheaval.
- The influence of race, class and colour in Guyana during the 20th century can be found in his music.

Martin Carter (1927–1997)

- Has been widely regarded as the greatest Guyanese poet.
- Is best known for his poems, which were based essentially on the themes of protest, revolution and resistance.
- Played an active role in Guyanese politics, being detained for a time because of his support for the People's Progressive Party, which the British viewed as communist. He later briefly became Minister for Information.

Quick Fact

The Caribbean can boast of three writers awarded the Nobel Prize for Literature: Derek Walcott (from St Lucia), V.S. Naipaul (from Trinidad and Tobago) and Saint-John Perse (from Guadeloupe).

Caribbean Arts and Popular Culture in the Diaspora

Wherever Caribbean nationals have settled they have influenced the economic, social and cultural life of that society. The mass media has contributed to this. Music in particular is an art form that has reached across the huge distances that exist between the diaspora and their homelands, and has helped ease the settlement of Caribbean people in their new homes as well as cement their sense of identity in new societies. In this way, music has contributed to the phenomena of **transnationalism**.

Major expressions of Caribbean art forms in the diaspora are carnivals:

- The Notting Hill Carnival (London, UK) – the largest street festival in Europe, it began in the mid 1960s. It allows cultural expression for the London West Indian community and makes the people of London, and more generally the UK and even the world, aware and appreciative of the cultures and traditions of Afro-Caribbean communities.
- West Indian Day Parade (Brooklyn, New York) – also called Labour Day Parade, held since 1969 in Brooklyn (but the earliest known carnival parade was in Harlem in 1947), it celebrates Caribbean culture with dance, dress, music and culinary delights as the focal points of the parade.
- Caribana (Toronto, Canada) – a musical street festival that depicts Caribbean culture. It began in 1967 and has developed into the largest cultural festival in North America.

These events have impressed Caribbean culture upon metropolitan countries and create a link with the various carnivals and art forms of the Caribbean. Artistes from the Caribbean travel to take part in all these celebrations.

Did You Know?

The early period of both the West Indian Day Parade and the Notting Hill Carnival was met with resistance from the authorities because of concerns about associated violence and the cost of policing such events. Indeed, the early years of the Notting Hill Carnival were accompanied by some violent incidents caused by the racial tensions that were current at the time. Since then it has been a relatively peaceful event and has brought in large amounts of revenue to the local community.

Diasporic carnivals serve to bring different elements of the community together, create links between Caribbean culture, society and economies and the metropole or host country, expose people of different countries to the lifestyle of the Caribbean in terms of food, music, dance and creativity and generate income for those involved and the surrounding areas.

Check Your Knowledge

Explain FOUR ways in which Caribbean art forms and popular culture can enhance regional development.

Demonstrate an understanding of the following terms and concepts:

- Caribbean
- Art forms
- Popular culture
- Regional development
- Economic development
- Human development
- Cultural development
- Sustainable development
- Human capital
- Culture
- Society

Cover in detail FOUR of the following points under the particular sub-headings, using examples to illustrate your points.

Quick Fact

Caribbeans in the diaspora have taken their unique dance culture with them. In Canada, for example, Toronto's Ballet Creole combines Caribbean and African styles to create a distinctive dance form.

Key Term

Transnationalism – a social phenomenon involving the heightened interconnectivity between people across geographic and political boundaries.

Quick Facts

Writers and poets who are, or have been, part of the Caribbean diaspora include: V.S. Naipaul, Linton Kwesi Johnson, Paule Marshall, Derek Walcott, Rosa Guy, Jean Rhys, Caryl Phillips and Jamaica Kinkaid.

Making the Connection

Chapter 6 'Characteristics of Society and Culture'

Chapter 12 'Concepts and Indicators of Development'

Chapter 13 'Factors that Affect Development'

Exam Tip

'**Explain**' requires statements on what happened, how and why. Terms, concepts and approaches need to be elaborated on.

- **Economic development:**
  - Art forms and popular culture (food, music, crafts) create jobs and income for those directly involved in the industry (such as musicians or young entrepreneurs) and through the multiplier effect (for instance, through tourism and so indirectly construction, food supplies, or transport), both within the region and via remittances from members of the diaspora.
  - There is a successful export market in many forms of popular culture (especially music, dance, crafts and food).
  - Secular festivals attract both Caribbean citizens and foreign tourists, resulting in an increase in foreign exchange, thus enhancing GDP.
  - Elements of popular culture (food, crafts, music, dance) contribute to the overall tourist 'package' offered by the Caribbean region. Similarities in history and culture across the region enable it to be marketed to as a whole, thus allowing for economies of scale.
  - The Arts and popular culture provide a form of relaxation and recreation, which contributes both to promoting well-being and increasing productivity.
  - All generated income can be used to develop infrastructure, and so on.
- **Sustainable, human and cultural development:**
  - People are the agents through which development occurs and is sustained. Human capital can be developed via arts forms and popular culture as they are a means of transmitting a society's material and non-material culture. In turn, human and sustainable development are fostered.
  - Many government and non-government agencies support the Arts because they promote and help define cultural pride and identity, thus fostering cultural development as well as enhancing economic benefits through tourism, for example.
  - The lower class or grass roots in society are given an opportunity to exhibit their culture and take pride in it. This cultural confidence can give rise to or augment a general confidence in society, which can help withstand the impact of cultural imperialism across the region, especially as many elements of Caribbean culture are shared between the various Caribbean societies.
  - The Arts allow people to develop their human potential and provides them with an important means of intellectual growth. They can provide a form of therapy for people.
  - Social cohesion and unity are promoted through events such as festivals.
  - Greater equity is promoted through providing a means of expression (both individual and social) and a channel for experiencing self-worth and achievement.
  - Individuals such as Rex Nettleford and Martin Carter help to shape the Caribbean identity and sense of self through their work.
  - The sharing of forms of popular culture with the diaspora provides members of the diaspora with a connection to the Caribbean, which can help them with settling into their new environment as well as a continued sense of identity.

- These all assist with productivity, and therefore with the ability to support the development of the region in general.

Summarise the main points in your conclusion. It could state something along the lines of:

- *Caribbean art forms and popular culture can be mechanisms that foster regional development as they can promote the Caribbean in many areas (economic, sustainable, cultural, human) as well as create a global identity for the region.*

Multiple-choice Questions

1. Caribbean people who are dispersed throughout the world from their original homeland form part of the

    A. Diaspora

    B. Popular culture

    C. West Indian migrants

    D. Caribbean society abroad

2. Which of the following individuals was known for poems that were based essentially on protests, revolution and resistance?

    A. Martin Carter

    B. Aubrey Cummings

    C. Beryl McBurnie

    D. Louise Bennett

3. Cassava, yams, dasheen and eddoes represent

    A. Part of the diet of the enslaved people

    B. Root crops from the Amerindians

    C. Food brought by the Syrians

    D. Root crops planted by Europeans

4. West Indians who migrated abroad are responsible for

    A. Introducing the culinary arts to the countries they settled in

    B. Introducing spices to the Caribbean diet

    C. Using cod fish as the base of most Caribbean cuisines

    D. Introducing English tea to Caribbean

5. Which of the following can be considered to be a reinterpretation of American rhythm and blues?

    A. Reggae

    B. Calypso

    C. Punta

    D. Zouk

6. The instrument of the Caribbean transported to North America, where it now forms part of the curriculum in some schools, is

    A. The steel pan

    B. The chac chac

    C. The East Indian tassa drum

    D. The guitar

7. The West Indian Day Parade represents

    A. The art form of the diaspora

    B. A Caribbean street festival in Europe depicting Caribbean culture

    C. A Canadian festival depicting Caribbean culture

    D. A Caribbean festival meant to showcase Caribbean culture in Notting Hill

8. Which of the following festivals can be declared secular, hybrid festivals?

    A. Carnival, Crop Over

    B. Carnival, Diwali

    C. Eid al-Fitr, Tobago Jazz Festival

    D. Christmas, San Fest

Chapter 11   Caribbean–Global Interactions

Analyse how the global community and Caribbean society impact each other.

After revising this topic, you should be able to:
- describe and assess Caribbean influences on extra-regional countries:
  - political issues created in Europe and North America by the presence of large numbers of Caribbean people
  - the impact of Caribbean festivals on metropolitan countries
  - the impact of migrant labour on metropolitan countries
  - the impact of Rastafari throughout the world;
- describe and assess the influences of extra-regional societies on the Caribbean:
  - consumption patterns (remittances, goods and services)
  - the impact of colonialism on art forms (music, theatre arts, visual arts)
  - the impact of colonialism and the information age on education, including language and curriculum reforms
  - political influences (the Westminster System, rule of law, electoral processes, migratory labour)
  - sport (cricket, soccer, basketball, track and field)
  - religion (traditional and non-traditional religious practices).

The formation of Caribbean society was based on migration, and its people have adopted a culture of continued migration since the abolition of slavery in the 19th century. This migration only intensified with the advent of industrialisation, which gave rise to more advanced means of transportation being used to get to other parts of the Caribbean, Central and North America, Europe and even to parts of Africa and Asia. This migration has inevitably led to Caribbean people adopting many aspects of the culture of these places while at the same time imparting aspects of Caribbean culture on their societies.

Making the Connection

The migratory movements that have established Caribbean society are described in Chapter 5 'The Historical Process'.

Caribbean Influences on Extra-regional Countries

Due to extensive migration, especially since the beginning of the 20th century, it is true to say that the Caribbean has influenced and contributed to the societies and cultures of North America and Europe. However, many argue that the 'outward' influence of the region is more limited than the 'inward' impacts created by the legacy of colonialism and the current hegemony of globalisation.

Political Issues

Since the mid-19th century, Caribbean migrants have mostly travelled and settled outside the region in North America (Canada and the USA) and Europe (Britain, France and Spain). The reasons for migration have varied from travelling to seek job and employment opportunities and access to better health, education and recreation amenities, to seeking political asylum, and, of late, in the cases of Cuba and Haiti, asylum from discrimination and prejudice.

As a result of this migration, Caribbean nationals have helped to shape and form the policies and politics of extra-regional societies directly through lobbying, voting and being policy makers, and indirectly by forcing the hand of policy makers to implement policies to facilitate, regulate and monitor the flow and impact of these Caribbean immigrants.

- Visa and citizenship related policies and laws are usually implemented in host countries to regulate the number and nature of the immigrants flowing in. Host countries are careful not to facilitate more immigrants than their resources can manage, added to the fact that they need to ensure that immigrants are not fugitives or criminals who intend to expand their activities.

- Labour laws relating to the documentation and treatment of immigrants are also implemented to protect them from exploitation. These laws also ensure that immigrants are absorbed into industries that need their labour, and that they are not competing for spaces in industries that are already heavily subscribed.

- Host countries also need to ensure that the study intentions of migrants are legitimate. Most countries are willing to facilitate overseas students on the condition that they return to their native countries after the duration of their study, unless they become a resident or naturalised citizen of the host country.

- Human trafficking laws are implemented to ensure that adults are not forced into other countries as workers, enslaved workers or to be part of the illicit sex trade. Laws are also implemented to restrict the movement of children to ensure that they are not sold and smuggled into host countries. These policies on human trafficking have even been embedded in the constitutions and laws of most countries as part of the United Nations bid to stop the forced movement of people from their homelands.

- Most host countries have also put in place laws restricting the movement of cash accompanying the movement of people from one country to another. Money laundering laws are enforced at the port of entry in host countries, starting with the requirement that all immigrants declare the cash they are travelling with to ensure it does not exceed the limit allowed per migrant.

- The arrival of immigrants, and especially the establishment of immigrant communities, can lead to racial tensions. In the UK, this surfaced in the Notting Hill riots in 1958 and was dealt with politically and judicially by a series of Race Relations Acts in the 1960s and 1970s, which have since been replaced by the Equality Act of 2010.

Quick Facts

Early 20th century immigration in the US was curbed by the Immigration Act of 1924, while later, in 1962, the Commonwealth Immigration Act in the UK introduced restrictions on Commonwealth migration.

Did You Know?

Members of the Caribbean diaspora who have made an impact on the politics of extra-regional countries include: in the UK, the first MPs of Caribbean origin, Diane Abbott (of Jamaican descent) and Bernie Grant (born in Guyana), and trade union leader Bill Morris (born in Jamaica); in the US, former Secretary of State Colin Powell (of Jamaican descent), Texas Senator Ted Cruz (of Cuban descent).

Making the Connection

The ideological background to the Cold War in the mid to late 20th century is reviewed in Chapter 14 'Globalisation and Development'.

Quick Fact

The 1980 Mariel boatlift brought an additional 150 000 Cubans to Miami.

The Political Impact of Cubans and Haitians on US Politics

Cubans have been migrating to the USA in numbers since the late 1800s and early 1900s – well before the revolution of 1959. At the time, many American companies had interests in Cuban banks, the railway system, plantations, hotels and casinos and newly developing industries, while Cubans went to the US to help establish tobacco cultivation and a cigar-making industry. In 1910, the number of Cubans living in the US was estimated at a little more than 15 000.

Fidel Castro's accession to power in 1959 was followed by signs of his intention to ease the country into communism and, as a result, the Cuban population in the US exploded over the years immediately following. Many of those migrating were wealthy plantation owners, merchants and manufacturers who had lost their interests in property as a result of the state taking over all resources under the newly established communist regime. Many educated professionals also fled, thinking that the country would spiral down into a system of state control and regulations that would devalue their position and worth.

Ideologically, the US and Cuba were in opposition, resulting in a propaganda war. Some of this propaganda encouraged Cubans to flee Cuba and leave behind what they considered to be an oppressive regime. In 1966 the US government passed the Cuban Adjustment Act giving Cuban exiles a chance at permanent residency, essentially providing immediate naturalisation regardless of quotas and visa procedures.

The fall of the Soviet Union in 1991 saw increased intensity in attempts to reach the US, so much so that, in 1994 alone, the US Coast Guard intercepted 33 000 Cubans trying to infiltrate their borders. Cubans used unseaworthy make-shift boats to transport hundreds of people at once. Due to the huge numbers, the US government legislated the 'wet foot, dry foot' policy in 1995, which remains in effect today: any Cuban who successfully arrives on US soil is accepted and naturalised; however, those who are intercepted at sea are repatriated. Since President Obama announced renewed ties with Cuba in December 2014, the number of Cubans entering the US has increased by 78%. In 2015 alone, more than 43 000 Cubans entered the US legally, compared to approximately 15,000–20,000 per year in previous years.

In 2013 approximately two million people of Cuban origin were living in the US. Of all the Latino groups, Cubans are the most regionally concentrated, with nearly 70% of the population in Florida. A 2010 US census showed that about 35% of the population of Miami was of Cuban origin. This is because Florida is the closest geographical American state to Cuba and so is easiest to get to, particularly in the often make-shift vessels used by Cubans to reach the US, and is a well-positioned site from which to launch opposition to the communist regime.

Nearly 60% of US Cubans were born outside of the US and more than half are US citizens. This has given the Cuban diaspora in Miami immense political clout because many US politicians see these voters as a group that can determine elections. As a result, many campaigns target immigrants with the promise of immigration reform, job opportunities and anti-discrimination laws. Cubans of Florida have also created one of the nation's strongest ethnic lobby groups in the Cuban American National Foundation.

Cubans, more than any other Latin American group of immigrants living in the US, are highly politically active. Statistics show that while 48% of all eligible Hispanics voted in the 2012 election, the rate was approximately 67% for Latinos of Cuban descent. They tend to be the most conservative of all Latinos living in the US: in the 2012 presidential election, 70% of Latino voters supported Democrat Barack Obama, but Florida's Cuban-American voters split, with 49% supporting Obama and 47% in favour of Republican Mitt Romney.

Immigration to the US from Haiti has occurred since the Haitian Revolution, but the decades of the late 20th century and early 21st century saw a large increase in the wake of successive failed governments and ensuing political violence and social unrest in this country. The disastrous earthquake of 2010 drastically increased the numbers as many sought refuge from the ensuing food and water shortages and economic hardships. By 2012 there were almost a million Haitians in the US, triple the number in 1990, with half of that figure living in Florida.

The number of elected local officials coming from the Haitian-American community is on the increase and includes State Representative Daphne D. Campbell. These politicians have pushed for improved immigration policies to help Haitians secure US residency or citizenship status, and for policies to help integrate Haitians into American society. Organisations such as the Haitian-American Democratic Club and the Haitian-American Nurses Association of Florida are active in recruiting candidates, hosting voter drives and forming alliances with the aim of getting more Haitian-Americans elected. Thus, Haitians are trying to make a direct impact on policy making in Florida to amalgamate and strengthen their presence in the US.

In recognition of the increased presence and the lobbying powers of Haitian-Americans, the government implemented the Haitian Family Reunification Parole (HFRP) policy in 2014, which allowed Haitian families in the US with green cards or residency status to file for their immediate family members living in Haiti to come to America. This policy strengthens the Haitian presence and culture in the US and aids those suffering in Haiti because family breadwinners have relocated to the US to seek better opportunities. The programme also allows Haitians who have applied for US residency and citizenship to acquire temporary work permits until their applications are approved.

The Impact of Caribbean Festivals

The migration of Caribbean nationals to North America, Canada and the United Kingdom has led to the spread of Caribbean culture to these extra-regional societies. One of the main cultural forms to be transplanted is the Caribbean manner of celebrating special occasions, especially carnival. This has become contagious in other parts of the world, especially London (Notting Hill), Toronto (Carabina) and New York (Labour Day Parade), but it is also popular in the form of smaller festivals in other parts of the UK and North America that have sizeable Caribbean communities, because Caribbean festivities are imbued with popular cultural forms such as music (reggae, dancehall, calypso and soca), dress (use of brightly coloured and highly reflective costumes), dance (usually modern Caribbean erotic dances) and cuisine.

> **Quick Fact**
>
> The US Coast Guard has come under criticism for its treatment of Haitians attempting illegal entry to the US and many critics have pointed out the contrast with US treatment of Cuban refugees.

Positive Impact of Festivals

- Strengthens the presence and impact of a Caribbean community in the host country and informs and educates local people about Caribbean history and culture.
- Provides an introduction to and promotion of Caribbean music, dance and food, potentially leading to increased demand for these goods, products and services.
- An economic earner for host countries (employment – though seasonal and short-term – networking, sale of goods and provision of services). Caribbean businesses can also develop out of these festivals as their presence can be a productive marketing tool.
- Provides a showcase for the talents and creativity of Caribbean nationals, which can lead to a heightened interest in Caribbean craftsmanship in the host countries and the potential for forging links to develop products for markets in the host countries.

Negative Impact of Festivals

- Host country nationals may look down on Caribbean cultural symbols and identity (ethnocentrism) because they are not familiar with them, in particular there may be negative views of the nature of the sometimes erotic dancing and suggestive lyrics of many songs played at festivals.
- The festivals may be seen as an inconvenience for many locals who have no interest in taking part, as roads are closed and public spaces are dedicated to the festivities and celebrations.
- They may incite feelings of xenophobia among the nationals of host countries, who may feel that the influence of Caribbean people is too strong in their country or locality because of the sheer size of the Caribbean festivities. In the early years of the Notting Hill carnival, for example, there were incidents of racially incited violence.

The Impact of Migrant Labour on Metropolitan Countries

Much of the historic migration from the Caribbean to metropolitan countries, especially since the early 20th century, has been for the purposes of work: more opportunities, better jobs, better conditions and higher wages have been major pull factors. After the Second World War, many migrants left the Caribbean for Europe to support the post-war rebuilding efforts, fill gaps in the labour market and provide essential services.

Migrant labour from the Caribbean, whether temporary and seasonal or more permanent, has had an impact on the societies and economies of the host countries. For example, a shortage of nurses in post-war Britain resulted in many young Caribbean women being recruited to go to the UK to train as nurses in the newly established National Health Service, which they helped build. Many stayed on in the UK, continuing their careers and raising families. A large number of Caribbean male migrants worked in the transport industry as bus and train drivers or conductors and guards. Later, migrants were recruited to counter a shortage of teachers.

Today, seasonal labour from the Caribbean is critical to the agricultural sector in parts of Canada and the US, such as fruit growing in Ontario, Canada, and sugar cane cultivation in Florida. The work of the labourers supports the local economies and helps keep the local farming sector profitable, because local labour in the quantities required would be too expensive. The wages are low by local standards, but relatively high for the Caribbean. Not all the money earned comes back to Caribbean, however, as much is spent on small appliances, clothes and gifts before the workers return.

Key Term

Migrant labour – paid work carried out in a country where the worker is not a citizen.

Making the Connection

The historic context of extra-regional migration is provided in Chapter 5 'The Historical Process'.

Did You Know?

Since the 1960s, the Canadian Seasonal Agricultural Workers Program (CSAWP) has allowed for the organised entry into Canada of low- to mid-level skilled farm workers from participating Caribbean countries and Mexico for up to eight months a year to fill labour shortages on farms during peak periods of planting, cultivating and harvesting of specified commodities. The programme is run jointly with the governments of Mexico and the participating Caribbean states, which recruit the workers and appoint representatives in Canada to assist in the programme's operations. Airfares are paid by the farmers, who also provide accommodation for the period of the contracts.

Quick Fact

The British Nationality Act of 1948, allowing free entry to Britain for all Commonwealth citizens, encouraged many Caribbean workers to look for employment and new opportunities there.

The Impact of Rastafari

There are more than one million practising Rastafari in the world and it has become a transnational movement with adherents spread globally from Japan to Botswana to the US. The movement grew out of 1930s Pan-Africanism in Jamaica and promoted its ideals of 'back to Africa'. The movement heavily promoted many doctrines advocated by Marcus Garvey and often preached the unification of the Black race, black militancy against White oppressors and colonisers, Black leadership in Black states, and the promotion of Black-owned businesses and enterprises that would lessen dependence on White employers.

The spiritual side of Rastafari developed with the coronation of Hailie Selassie as Emperor of Ethiopia, which was seen as the fulfilment of a Biblical prophecy. At the time, Ethiopia and Liberia were the only independent Black African states.

The popularity of the movement spread to the rest of the world in the 1960s and 1970s through the reggae music of musicians such as Robert Nesta Marley, otherwise known as Bob Marley, and Burning Spear. Through his hit songs and charismatic stage performances, often advocating peace and brotherhood, Marley appealed to many across the world who were against colonialism in the Caribbean and Africa, and the heavy influence of the authorities (often called Babylon) in people's lives.

Making the Connection

The beliefs of Rastafari and the movement's impact on the Caribbean are summarised in Chapter 17 'Intellectual Traditions'.

Rastafari has affected elements of societies and culture throughout the world:

- The Rastafarian dress code has become popular globally and is instantly recognisable. The wearing of locks, for instance, has become a mainstay in the fashion world and is embraced by people of all races.
- Rastafarians use the colours of red, gold and green (the colours of the original Ethiopian flag) as their symbol of resistance to colonialism (Ethiopia was the last African country to come under European control). These colour combinations are used in clothing and accessories as a fashion statement, embraced by many who are not practising Rastafari.
- Rastafari is a religion that promotes peaceful protest against racism and colonial ideals and, as such, is used as a medium to enlighten people around the world about how colonialism erodes native cultures while replacing it with Eurocentric or North American ideals, which Rastafaris reject.
- Rastafari is a vehicle for the promotion of Caribbean music and language throughout the world, which draws people from different countries to learn more about Caribbean culture generally.
- Rastafari culture has contributed to economies throughout the world via Rastafari musical acts headlining international music festivals.
- The ceremonial and spiritual use of marijuana has led to its widespread use around the world. Rastafari has long promoted the usefulness of marijuana as a herbal remedy for many illnesses. Despite the plant being considered an illegal drug in most countries, it is used by many pharmaceutical companies as a main ingredient in pain-relief drugs and has now been decriminalised, made legal and even promoted in some US states.

The Rastafari diet, 'ital', is vegetarian, excludes preserved foods, and often dairy, and focuses on food preparation applying as little heat as possible. It has become popular worldwide as part of a general trend in vegetarian and health food, especially in North America and Europe where ital restaurants have been established.

Quick Fact

Caribbean nations have been branded over the years as spaces that promote the illegal use of marijuana, and Caribbean governments have had to respond to international criticism of their containment of the drug as there have been instances of it being exported in large quantities to extra-regional states.

Did You Know?

The popularity of Rastafari has created many stereotypes about Caribbean people among the international community. These range from a belief that all or most Caribbeans are practising Rastafari (it is one of the least practised religions of the region), and that many Caribbeans are users of marijuana (which is still illegal in most Caribbean states). Another unfortunate stereotype that can be attributed to the popularity of Rastafari is that all Caribbean people, especially Jamaicans, speak the Rastafari 'language' and use certain expressions such as 'No problem'.

Despite such stereotypes being used in tourism marketing campaigns to attract visitors to the region, they are viewed as negative by many Jamaicans. They have also limited diversification of the Caribbean's tourism product because many tourist-focused businesses subscribe to the stereotypes while ignoring many other aspects of the region's rich cultural heritage.

Check Your Knowledge

Describe FOUR ways in which migrant labour has impacted on the politics/policies of extra-regional societies.

Demonstrate an understanding of the following terms and concepts by defining and using them correctly:

- migrant
- labour
- extra-regional societies
- politics
- policies

You are expected to clearly describe any FOUR of the following points and demonstrate understanding by giving specific examples:

- Examples of direct influences via lobbying, voting and being policy makers:
  - Florida, where there is a large Hispanic-Caribbean community (largely of Cuban, Puerto Rican and Haitian origin), is generally recognised as an important 'swing state', the political alignment of which cannot be easily predicted and which can therefore play a key role in determining the outcome of elections, particularly presidential elections.
  - The powerful Cuban lobby in Florida and other southern states of the USA has had a direct impact on legislation regulating legal and illegal migration from Cuba to the US. It is also a powerful pressure group that has affected governance and voting in the US as well as influencing policy to persuade Washington to continue to enforce the economic blockade against Cuba. They enthusiastically supported the Helms Burton Act of 1996, which seeks to institute and maintain international sanctions against the Castro government, and plan for a transitional government resulting in a democratically elected government.
  - The Haitian-American community is increasing its political influence through a growing number of elected local officials, active recruitment of candidates and organisation of electoral support for them. Politicians have supported improved immigration policies to assist Haitians to obtain US residency or citizenship status, and for policies to assist in integrating Haitians into American society. These include the Haitian Family Reunification Parole (HFRP) policy of 2014.
  - In the UK, migrants who arrived to work in the second half of the 20th century, and who subsequently forged careers in politics, include Bernie Grant and trade union leader Bill Morris. Diane Abbott, born of migrants from Jamaica, became the first Black MP in the UK. Darcus Howe, originally from Trinidad, is a prominent civil liberties campaigner and broadcaster on social and political issues.
- Examples of indirect influence through forcing the hand of policy makers to implement policies to facilitate, regulate and monitor the flow and impact of immigrants and to respond to their presence:
  - Visa and citizenship related policies and laws are normally implemented in host countries to control the number and nature of the immigrants flowing in. The British Nationality Act of 1948, along with UK government promotion of migration to the UK, encouraged many from the Caribbean to go to the UK for work.

Making the Connection

Chapter 5 'The Historical Process'

Chapter 7 'Identity and Social Formation'

Exam Tip

'**Describe**' requires a lengthy answer in which you explain key concepts and issues and give logical arguments. You must use detailed examples, but not necessarily draw a conclusion.

This inflow was subsequently curbed by the 1962 Commonwealth Immigration Act, which introduced restrictions on Commonwealth migration. Earlier, immigration in the US had been restricted by the Immigration Act of 1924.

- Other legislation is concerned with the treatment of immigrants:

  - Labour laws are implemented to protect migrant workers from labour exploitation and to ensure that immigrants are absorbed into industries that require their labour, and are not competing for spaces in industries that are already heavily subscribed.

  - Human trafficking laws are implemented to guarantee that adults are not coerced into migrating and to limit the movement of children. These policies on human trafficking have even been entrenched in the constitutions and laws of most countries as part of the United Nations bid to end the forced movement of people from their homelands.

  - Certain laws and immigration rules are implemented to make certain that the study intentions of immigrants are legal and to limit the movement of cash through money laundering laws that require all immigrants to publicly state the cash they are travelling with.

- It could be argued that one of the political and social successes of the post-war restructuring of Britain, the establishment of the National Health Service, was largely boosted by the arrival of young women from the Caribbean to train as nurses. These women then helped to establish the fledgling institution.

- The arrival of immigrants and the establishment of immigrant communities can result in racial tensions. In the UK, this erupted in the Notting Hill riots in 1958 and was addressed politically and judicially by Race Relations Acts in the 1960s and 1970s, which were subsequently replaced by the Equality Act of 2010.

- Political, social and economic issues, such as racial discrimination, especially by the police, and high unemployment and poverty, can have a strongly negative impact on immigrant communities, and these factors are considered to be behind the riots in the 1980s and 1990s in Brixton, London, and other parts of the UK. In response, political measures were taken to control police behaviour through the Police and Criminal Evidence Act 1984 and the creation of an independent Police Complaints Authority, though critics would argue that these have been generally ineffective.

A possible conclusion can be a summary of the main points provided in this essay.

Key Terms

Homogeneity – uniform, or **homogeneous**, in composition or character.

Neocolonialism – the use of economic, political, cultural or other pressures, through capitalism, globalisation and cultural imperialism, to control or influence developing countries, especially former dependencies, in the place of direct military or indirect political control.

Dependency syndrome – an attitude and belief leading to an expectation that a society cannot manage its affairs or solve its problems without external input such as ideology and approaches, finance and organisations. It is in opposition to concepts of empowerment and the assumption of responsibility.

Influences of Extra-regional Societies on the Caribbean

Caribbean society carries heavy metropolitan influences in many areas, especially in main institutions such as family, religion and the justice system, as part of the colonial legacy. Since the mid-20th century, and the achievement of independence, other external forces have come to bear on the region in the form of globalisation, which fosters, and even imposes, **homogeneity** in aspects such as culture, norms and values, economics, politics and so on. This homogeneity is ruled by the cultural forms and policies of powerful industrialised states such as the US and western Europe and its promotion is referred to as cultural imperialism or **neocolonialism**. The US, in particular, wields global financial and economic sway as the dominant power behind international institutions such as the World Bank, the International Monetary Fund and the World Trade Organization. Thus, the **dependency syndrome** of the colonial period is effectively being perpetuated by the onset of globalisation.

Consumption Patterns

Remittances

The importance of remittances, from Caribbeans who either work or are permanently settled abroad, to the economy of the region cannot be understated. In 2015, for example, estimates based on US Central Bank data give a US-based remittance total for Haiti as $2 198 million (22.7% of GDP) and for Guyana as $317 million (10.6% of GDP). Not only do they provide financial support for family members still located in the home country, but they are also an important source of foreign exchange.

Goods and Services

Historically, the colonies were designated as a source of raw materials for the metropole and so plantations were dependent on metropolitan imports, and a surviving legacy of this reliance is a general taste in the region for foreign goods, with the kudos they carry and their perceived superiority over local production, for which there is no long-established tradition. Before independence, production in the colonies was limited and dominated by external decision-makers based in the metropole, and this pattern of power continues today, even post-independence, in the dominance of multinational corporations headquartered in the developed world.

Art Forms

The Impact of Colonialism

As with other aspects of Caribbean culture, colonial influences come into play, but are often diluted or adapted with local elements and traditions. Often 'high art' is the form that most reflects that of the colonial powers, while more popular or grassroots cultural forms have uniquely Caribbean characteristics. Many of the religious festivals celebrated across the region are Christian and were originally imported with the colonists, and even the archetypal Caribbean festival – carnival – derives from Christianity.

Music, Theatre Arts, Visual Arts

The more internationally popular Caribbean music types, such as reggae and calypso, as well as the steelpan bands all originated at a popular and grassroots level as a response to colonialism and the restrictions imposed by authority. At the other end of the cultural scale, 'high culture', represented by classical music, fine art and so on, was and still is strongly identified with colonial traditions and the upper classes. Both ends of this scale have experienced a form of ongoing evolution, with traditional or grassroots music, such as Punta, undergoing changes to make them more accessible and palatable to those outside their place of origin, and

Making the Connection

Chapters 7, 8 and 9 look in detail at how Caribbean culture and society have been influenced by the colonial experience; global institutions and aspects of globalisation are analysed in Chapter 14 'Globalisation and Development', while the role of the media in promoting cultural imperialism is discussed in Chapter 18 'Roles and Functions of the Mass Media'.

Quick Fact

The downsides of migration include 'brain drain' and 'barrel children' who are left behind by their parents and who can suffer emotional damage as a result.

Making the Connection

Chapter 14 'Globalisation and Development' looks in more detail at the impact of foreign goods, services, companies and technology on Caribbean society, policies and the economy.

Making the Connection

The colonial and global influences on Caribbean food and festivals is discussed in Chapter 10 'Arts and Popular Culture'.

'high' cultural forms being given a local flavour, often a conscious post-independence statement of a separate Caribbean identity.

Typically of the Caribbean, many of those involved in 'high' cultural and art forms add a local twist to their work. The Jamaican composer Peter Ashbourne has written and performed classical works and jazz as well as working with popular musicians such as Burning Spear. Jamaican pianist Oswald Russell arranged *Three Jamaican Dances*, an example of a classical work that incorporates folk music. Theatrical or modern dance is also an art form originating in the West, but adapted in the Caribbean to express the region's own culture and traditions; as through the National Dance Theatre Company of Jamaica, co-founded by Rex Nettleford.

In the visual arts, there is a discernible division between mainstream artist movements related to Western stylistic trends, and often rooted in national development, and self-taught artists whose works reflect folk culture and show less exposure to foreign influences. Even so, artists have recently found ways to fuse both forms, giving rise to art that is unique to the Caribbean identity and experience.

Poet and dramatist Derek Walcott gives expression to the Caribbean situation and search for identity through his work; in particular, addressing the post-colonial liminal status of the region. He uses aspects of Caribbean culture and motifs within traditional Western art forms.

Education

The Impact of Colonialism

Throughout the colonial period, education reflected and served the needs of the metropole and the plantation elite over and above the majority of the population. Access was restricted and only after emancipation was it progressively granted to the children of formerly enslaved parents, with universal secondary education only achieved post-independence. Since independence, efforts have been made to bring the education system and its curriculum more into line with the needs of the people, but, as with other societal institutions, vestiges of the colonial legacy remain, not least in people's perceptions of what a 'good' education actually is.

The Information Age

Increased use and penetration of information technology, particularly the Internet, has both contributed to and been a result of the general and ongoing process of globalisation. For the Caribbean, this has meant more open exposure to external cultural influences, but also, for a scattered island region, it has facilitated communications, the sharing of information and distance learning, especially at tertiary level. A challenge for educational organisations is increased competition from extra-regional bodies in the provision and delivery of self-study and distance-learning programmes.

Language

Standard English, as used in formal situations and official documents, is the form of English used and taught in schools and other educational institutions. There is a belief and an expectation that this should be the form of English in which education is delivered. However, this does not reflect the complex and diverse situation in language that exists across the region, with the 'European' form rarely spoken in informal situations.

Quick Fact

The steelpan orchestra repertoire today includes classical, jazz and reggae music among many others.

Quick Fact

Composer Peter Asbourne has fused elements of high and popular culture in his reggae opera based on the life of dub poet Mikey Smith.

Making the Connection

Rex Nettleford's contribution to the formation of an independent Caribbean identity through the arts is looked at in Chapter 10 'Arts and Popular Culture'.

Quick Fact

Derek Walcott's epic poem, *Omeros*, and his play, *Odyssey*, are both rewrites of classical Greek works set in the modern-day Caribbean.

Making the Connection

The institution of education, its evolution from colonial to modern times and its impact on Caribbean society are analysed in Chapter 9 'Societal Institutions'.

Many educationalists believe this should be reflected and represented within education, which has sparked a huge debate on the relative values of the various forms.

Curriculum Reforms

Until quite recently, the curricula still had a strong colonial influence, mirroring that of traditional British private schools, with stress on academic subjects such as history, geography and literature. As most of the materials were written by British educationalists, there was a predominant British-centric flavour, which augmented the hidden curriculum of upholding the overriding superiority of British culture, its attitudes and beliefs. The introduction of more practical studies was met with some resistance as these were viewed as being of less value, especially in terms of social mobility prospects.

There was a huge emphasis on academic attainment, especially to gain access to prestigious secondary schools, many of which were administered by Church bodies, which served to further reinforce the Western values and attitudes they imparted. The British system of examinations, administered by British awarding bodies, also continued beyond independence. Although, post-independence, governments worked to make education more Caribbean-focused, it was only with the establishment of the Caribbean Examinations Council in 1972 that there were exam syllabi specifically geared to the experiences of the candidates and a curriculum designed around their own needs and perspectives.

Political Influences

Nowadays, by dint of location if nothing else, the US is the main power to exert political influence over the region. It controls much of the financial aid received by countries through institutions such as the IMF and until the end of the Cold War had a vested interest in keeping the Caribbean nations 'on side' and away from communist influence, which had already taken hold of Cuba. To this end, it launched the invasion of Grenada in 1983, after internal affairs there reached crisis point with the overthrow and execution of Maurice Bishop, ostensibly to restore democracy. However, in terms of systems of government, the Caribbean still follows European models.

The Parliamentary Process in the English-speaking Caribbean: The Westminster System/Model

This **parliamentary** system of government, named after the Palace of Westminster, the home of the British Parliament, is in use today in many former British colonies in the Caribbean. Like the judicial system, it is part of the legacy of British colonial rule, though it is important to note that there are many variants on the basic system, in structure and where specific powers lie worldwide – and even within the Caribbean region itself.

Many Caribbean states are constitutional monarchies that still recognise the British sovereign as head of state, represented by a governor-general. In fact, many British ex-colonies around the world adopted, and adapted, the Westminster System and together make up the British Commonwealth with the British monarch as its head.

Making the Connection

Some of the challenges posed to educational providers by the information age are discussed in Chapter 15 'The Integration Movement'.

Making the Connection

The implications of the use of 'Standard' English in formal education for Caribbean society are discussed in Chapter 9 'Societal Institutions'.

Making the Connection

Chapter 14 'Globalisation and Development' looks at the impact of global politics and ideologies on the region, especially during the Cold War and after.

There are four main parts to a Westminster type system of government:

1. The head of state – the monarch (king or queen), represented in the British Commonwealth by a governor general, or a president, the role of whom is mainly ceremonial. They also form part of the executive.

2. The executive arm – the government, responsible for administering laws and mainly consisting of key members of the legislature in ministerial positions, who form the cabinet (or executive council) led by the head of government, usually called the prime minister, premier or first minister.

3. The legislative arm – the elected parliament who make laws, approve budgets and to whom the executive is accountable.

4. The judiciary – the judges, responsible for the application and interpretation of laws. They are independent of the executive and the legislature.

The government is supported by a permanent and politically unaffiliated civil service.

Making the Connection

Prior to independence, British colonies were under Crown Colony rule, which in many places had replaced the Old Representative System. These systems of government, and the process by which one replaced the other, are explained in Chapter 5 'The Historical Process'.

Key Term

Parliament – a legislative elected body of government. A parliament generally has three functions: representing the electorate, making laws and overseeing the government.

Did You Know?

The constitutions of the independent Caribbean states reflected British common law through a legal principle called the savings law clause, which allows for the principles of British common law that protect the fundamental rights of citizens to be transferred to the new constitutions without changes to their interpretation and meaning.

Figure 11.1 The branches of government in the Westminster System of government

The Legislature	The Executive	The Judiciary
	The Head of State – the monarch (governor general) or president	
The Upper House The Lower House	The Head of Government The Cabinet/Executive Council	The Courts
Consists of government appointees (upper house) and elected members of parliament (lower house). (Not all legislatures have an upper house.)	Consists of ministers and other members of the executive who are usually selected from the legislature.	Comprises different kinds and levels of judges and courts.

Quick Fact

The Westminster System is different from other forms of democracies in that the *head of state* is usually a monarch (in the case of constitutional monarchies) and differs from the *head of government*.

The real power lies with the head of government, usually called the prime minister, who has full executive and constitutional powers as outlined by the constitution and heads the main policy-making body of government known as the cabinet. The cabinet is usually drawn from the lower house of parliament and is chosen by the prime minister to head the various government ministries/departments. Appointments from the upper house are often limited to two.

Parliaments can be bicameral, consisting of two assemblies (the lower house, usually called the House of Representatives or House of Assembly, and the upper house, usually called the Senate) or unicameral comprising just one assembly. Members of the lower house are elected in general

Making the Connection

The achievement of political independence in the Caribbean is described in Chapter 5 'The Historical Process'.

elections to represent various areas, called constituencies, or sections of the population. Members of the upper house in the Caribbean are usually nominated by the head of government, the parliamentary opposition and/or the governor-general and appointed by the executive. The upper house is the smaller of the two legislative bodies and while in theory both houses have similar levels of authority, apart from on financial matters, actual power usually lies predominantly with the lower house, as in the UK. The role of the upper house is therefore usually to review legislation approved by the lower house.

Typically, politics in the Westminster System are multi-party, usually involving two main parties in opposition to each other. The party that wins most votes forms the government and its leader usually becomes the head of government. The opposition party forms what is known as a shadow cabinet, or shadow government, to mirror, scrutinise and respond to the various departments of the executive and their activities. Those members of the ruling party who are not appointed to governmental positions form the 'back benches'. Traditionally, these back-bench MPs provide another check on the government as, in principle, they are free to vote as they choose.

The third arm of government is the judiciary. This group is the only arm that is in no way aligned to the elected members of parliament in their constitutionally defined roles and obligations. It is the job of the courts, through judges, to interpret the law (which may sometimes differ from what the legislators intended) and influence the law-making process through judicial reviews and setting judicial precedents via rulings. The principle that divides the role of judges from the parliament, and shields them from parliamentary influence, is known as **separation of powers**.

Did You Know?

There are some fundamental differences between the Westminster System as it exists in the UK and how it has been implemented in the Caribbean. These include:

- The role of governor-general in the Caribbean has no equivalent in the UK, where the monarch is the direct head of state.

- The UK has no written constitution and so the rules governing parliament are conventions. In the Caribbean, they are codified in the form of constitutions.

- The existence of a written constitution means that the concept of 'parliamentary supremacy' in the UK is replaced by that of 'constitutional supremacy' in the Caribbean.

- The relatively small size of Caribbean parliaments can mean that the in-built systems of formal opposition to the government in parliament (the parliamentary opposition and back-bench MPs) are so small in number as to be negligible.

The Rule of Law

The **rule of law** is a principle emanating from the constitution. The concept can be dated back to Ancient Greece and its principles lie behind such formative political statements as Magna Carta in the UK

Making the Connection

The role of the constitution in the creation of a legal basis for government and society is discussed in the section on the Judicial System in Chapter 9 'Societal Institutions'.

Quick Facts

Within the English-speaking Caribbean, heads of government carry different titles. Antigua and Barbuda, The Bahamas, Barbados, Belize, Dominica, Grenada, Jamaica, St Kitts and Nevis, St Lucia, St Vincent and the Grenadines, and Trinidad and Tobago all have a 'prime minister', while Bermuda, the British Virgin Islands, the Cayman Islands, Montserrat, and Turks and Caicos Islands have a 'premier'. The Republic of Guyana has a 'president' and Anguilla has a 'chief minister'.

Quick Facts

Most Caribbean parliaments are bicameral, while those of Dominica, St Kitts and Nevis and St Vincent and the Grenadines are unicameral. The British parliament at Westminster is bicameral.

Separation of powers – a principle central to modern democracies whereby the powers and responsibilities of a government are divided among the legislative, executive and judicial branches. This is done as a means of limiting corruption and ensuring that each arm of government holds the others accountable for their actions.

Rule of law – the legal principle that all citizens are subject to well-defined and established laws. It is the role of the judiciary to ensure that these laws are upheld in an equitable and fair way. In a political context, this is the principle that a nation should be governed by, and not be subject to arbitrary exercise of power.

Under the Westminster System, the highest court of appeal for the Caribbean was traditionally the Privy Council in the UK. CARICOM's establishment of the Caribbean Court of Justice (CCJ) has effectively cut this direct link back to the British legal system.

and the American Constitution. This principle is also entrenched in the structure of governments and is evident in the way these systems restrict or limit the arbitrary exercise of power of any elected or nominated member of parliament, member of the judiciary or their bureaucrats and technocrats.

There are criticisms that the separation of powers in the Westminster System has not always worked in the Caribbean because the legislature and executive are not sufficiently separate, which allows party leaders, as heads of government, too many powers that are open to abuse.

However, it cannot be denied that the often almost instant change from colonial rule to full-blown democracy in the region has gone relatively smoothly, with only few serious incidents where the rule of law has been infringed; for example, the takeover and subsequent overthrow of Maurice Bishop in Grenada and the attempted coups in Trinidad and Tobago in the 1970s and 1990s.

Electoral Processes

General elections are usually held in Caribbean countries every five years. The 'first past the post' electoral system that is used in most of the English-speaking Caribbean was adopted by the colonies even before they gained independence. This system divides the electorate into constituencies. These constituencies are contested in a general election by a representative from each of the major political parties vying to lead the country. Independent candidates may also contest constituencies in general elections.

This first past the post electoral system does not rely on the total popular vote to determine the party that will form the government, as does the **system of proportional representation (PR)**. The government is determined instead by the party that wins the most constituencies throughout the country, and therefore seats in parliament.

Criticisms of this system include the following:

- The fact that Members of Parliament, once elected, focus on voting along party lines, rather than truly representing the needs and rights of their constituents, so that the policies and laws desired by their party can be passed.
- It may lead to gerrymandering where the sitting government manipulates constituency boundaries to ensure continuous general election wins.
- The fact that elections are held every five years, and that the winning party gains almost complete control of the legislature and the executive, can result in complete exclusion of others from participation in government.

The Influence of Migratory Labour

The influence of migratory labour on the Caribbean is two-fold:

1. The Caribbean is influenced by those who come to work in the region from other countries, who may dwell in the Caribbean for long periods at a time depending on their contractual arrangements. In order to facilitate use of these foreign workers, Caribbean governments need to legislate for aspects such as work permits, residency and tax.
2. There are those Caribbean nationals who migrate to other countries in North America and Europe for work and live there for extended periods at a time. They may not only have developed a taste for foreign goods and services, but also become politicised. Thus, on their return, they may add new ideas to the political mix.

Sport

The Caribbean is internationally famous for its sports and sportsmen and women, particularly within cricket and track and field, though the region's teams have enjoyed success in other sports also. All major international sports came to the region through the colonial powers, or later through the influence of neocolonial powers such as the US.

Cricket

Cricket was introduced by the British in the 19th century and was at first played only by the White elites. Even today, it is a game mostly associated with Britain and her ex-colonies. Over time, its popularity spread and the first combined 'West Indies' team toured Canada and the US in the 1880s. From there, the game spread to eventually embrace Caribbean people from all walks of life and many Caribbean players play for foreign-based clubs around the world (such as India, the UK and Australia). In the UK, until recently, it was traditionally viewed as a 'gentleman's game' and it would be true to say that it was in the West Indies that it first became more of a sport of the masses, with flamboyant personalities and styles of play, and spectator involvement through various rituals and music. In fact, it could be argued to have become a Caribbean institution.

Soccer

Soccer is known simply as 'football' in the UK, where it originated, and throughout most of the world and it is probably the most popular game today. Internationally, Caribbean countries are represented individually and not regionally, as with cricket. Local nations have enjoyed only limited success at the international level, with only Haiti, Jamaica and Trinidad and Tobago reaching the World Cup finals. The region is achieving more recognition at international level, however, as shown by Jamaica being invited to participate in the 2016 Copa America.

Basketball

This is a recent and fast-growing addition to the Caribbean sports repertoire thanks to the influence of the US and its media. The game is relatively short and fast-paced and so appeals to the youth. The fact that successful players can also earn vast amounts from contracts and sponsorship adds to its appeal. Many young Caribbean players are therefore inspired to apply for sports scholarships to the US.

Track and Field

This is probably the sport the region is most famous for internationally. The phenomenal achievements of Caribbean athletes have even inspired a form of sports tourism, attracting visitors to watch athletes training and to view the training regime and facilities that have created so much success. World-leading athletes include Kirani James of Grenada, Usain Bolt and Shelly-Ann Fraser-Pryce of Jamaica and Keshorn Walcott of Trinidad and Tobago.

Religion: Traditional and Non-traditional Religious Practices

Extra-regional religious influences include both directly imported religions, such as Christianity, Hinduism and Islam, and the many syncretic religions that exist across the region.

Syncretic religions in the Caribbean have resulted from the merging of European Christian beliefs with traditional African, mainly animist, beliefs. Different religions have merged these components in differing ways and to different degrees. For example, Shouter Baptists view themselves as Christians with elements of African traditional worship, while Orisha, Obeah and Vodou are more strongly based within the African tradition and have taken on aspects of Christianity, such as the merging of Roman Catholic saints with African ancestral spirits and deities in Orisha.

Christianity was the religion imposed on the enslaved Africans by their masters and which, post-emancipation, continued to carry a sense of social acceptance and superiority. Thus, for many in the Caribbean, there emerged a religious duality: outward conformation to one of the established forms of Christianity coupled with more private adherence to African-based traditions. Even today, adherence to a mainstream religion, mostly Christianity, does not exclude following or, on particular occasions and for particular needs, resorting to other forms, syncretic or more traditionally African.

Making the Connection

Religion in the Caribbean, its different forms and their influences and impact, is discussed in detail in Chapter 9 'Societal Institutions'.

Making the Connection

Sports tourism is discussed in Chapter 16 'Contributions of Sport to Development'.

Quick Fact

In the late-19th and 20th centuries, newer forms of Christianity, mainly from North America, took hold in the Caribbean, especially among the lower social classes. The popularity of non-conformist churches, such as the Seventh Day Adventists and the Baptists, grew as a result of missionary activity and the return of converts to the Caribbean from the US.

Multiple-choice Questions

1. The 'wet foot, dry foot' policy of 1995 allowed

    A. Cuban refugees who successfully arrived on US soil to become naturalised citizens

    B. President Obama to renew ties with Fidel Castro

    C. All displaced Cubans to return to their homeland from Miami

    D. President Obama to deport all illegal Cubans from Miami

2. Which of the following aspects of Rastafarianism has negatively affected extra-regional countries?

    A. Their vegetarian style diet

    B. The Rastafarian dress code of sandals and green, yellow and black colours

    C. The dreadlock hairstyle

    D. The ceremonial use of marijuana

3. Which of the following was a consequence of xenophobia in Great Britain in the 1960s?

    A. The outcry against the introduction of visitors' visas for Caribbean tourists

    B. The outcry against the introduction of temporary work visas for Caribbean workers in Britain

    C. The Notting Hill riots

    D. The trade union riots

4. The enactment of a series of acts culminating in the Equality Act of 2010 was the British government's response to

    A. The Notting Hill riots of the 1960s and subsequent racially based disturbances and instances of discrimination

    B. Money laundering issues at the UK borders

    C. The 'sacking' of the first Afro-Caribbean female in the British Parliament

    D. The deportation of Caribbean Black people who illegally lived in Britain

5. The islands of the Caribbean whose parliaments are bicameral in nature adopted this sytem from which of the following former colonial masters?

    A. Britain

    B. France

    C. Spain

    D. Holland

6. Which of the following can be viewed as syncretic religions?

    A. Roman Catholicism, Presbyterian, Moravian

    B. English Catholic, Shouter Baptist, Vodou

    C. Orisha, Vodou, Obeah

    D. Baptists, Lutheran, Orisha

Issues in Caribbean Development

Chapter 12

Concepts and Indicators of Development

After revising this topic, you should be able to:
- correctly describe the concepts of development:
  - sustainable development
  - economic development
  - human development;
- identify, describe and explain the indicators used to measure development:
  - Gross Domestic Product (GDP), Gross National Product (GNP), per capita, Gini coefficient, Human Development Index (HDI), productivity, internet penetration, modern technology, good governance and responsible environmental factors.

Concepts of Development

The definition of development is complex, but it is generally accepted to mean improving the standard of living and quality of life of a country's people. It is related to economic, political, environmental and social factors and there are many variables that affect a country's level of development. Government development policies aim to increase prosperity, lower the level of poverty and improve the economic and social situation of its people. It is a reflection of how a country's resources can be used to meet basic needs.

All people have basic needs and these can be met either by themselves or by the state. If there is available employment, people can earn an income and so are able to support themselves: they can consume a healthy diet, pay for medical care, acquire an education, save for emergencies and provide themselves with a safe home. In such cases, the government can spend more on a country's infrastructure and a wide range of development projects. Development can bring about economic growth, increased specialisation and an increase in employment options.

There is a wide difference in levels of development in different regions of the world, and within regions. Less economically developed countries (LEDCs) have a lower standard of living and their people have a lower life expectancy, less education and lower incomes. Many LEDCs, such as countries in the Caribbean, are of a small size with a large population, the majority of which live in a capital city. The economy of most Caribbean countries is service-sector driven, for example by tourism and wholesaling, except for Trinidad where oil and gas production is the primary income earner.

Key Term

Economic development – development that improves the standard of living of people in a country by increasing economic activity.

Quick Facts

An economic 'boom' or expansion is when an economy has sustained GDP growth over several consecutive economic quarters.

A recession means that a country's production/ services has fallen and it is signalled by a falling GDP or growth below 2% for two consecutive quarters (six months).

In more economically developed countries (MEDCs) there are more varied and complex business, service and industrial activities, which generate larger amounts of capital. Profits can then be used to invest in or expand business.

Economic Development

Economic development focuses on the economic growth of a country. An economy is healthy when there is an increase in the value of goods and services produced by that country. The focus is on capital investment with jobs and technology improving production and productivity. This leads to wealth and savings. The main measure of economic health is the GDP per capita (per capita income). Per capita income is the total income earned from goods and services produced by a country in one year divided by the total population for that country in that year. It can be used to compare the wealth of countries and to give an idea of the average income of its inhabitants.

Per capita income is criticised because it represents the average income of the population and does not take into consideration the unemployed, old and retired individuals or children, who, in most cases, earn no income but are included in per capita income calculations.

The Caribbean's Place in the World Market Economy

There is an argument that industrial development by MEDCs, such as the USA, Japan and those in Europe, has led to LEDCs, such as countries in the Caribbean, becoming weaker members of the world market economy. This is because over time the Caribbean has been able to purchase fewer manufactured goods due to the lower relative value of its exports compared to those of the developed world. In response to this, there has been the relatively successful establishment of import substitution industries by small local and regional markets within the Caribbean – for example, salad vegetable farming, chicken processing, ice-cream manufacturing, milk and juice manufacturing. However, for development to occur there must be a surplus of goods for export, and this is a challenge with a small land area and population. Economic growth has become centred on a few favourable locations, leaving other places underdeveloped in comparison.

Figure 12.1 **Some exports from Caribbean countries**

Caribbean country	Main exports
Jamaica	mining of bauxite, garment industry
Trinidad and Tobago	oil and gas production, financial centre, chemicals, steel products, beverages, cereal, cocoa, coffee, citrus fruits, vegetables, flowers
Antigua and Barbuda	financial services, offshore education, agroprocessing
The Bahamas	offshore banking
St Kitts and Nevis	rum
St Martin	salt, sugar

A Growth Sector: Tourism

Since 2009 the Caribbean region tourism sector has been recording measurable growth. For example, flights have been increasing to the Dominican Republic and Jamaica. Outstanding quality in tourism products, as well as health and hygiene improvements, a good safety and security record, a favourable business environment, quality human resources and tourism-related infrastructure, have attracted growth. The expansion of seaports and increases in tourist flights and hotel room capacity have been successful in promoting tourism growth in these countries. However, overdependence on tourism is also a weakness.

Much of the profit from Caribbean tourism is earned by corporations outside the Caribbean (mostly from the US or Europe – the region's former coloniser). As a consequence, researchers describe this phenomenon as **neo-colonialism**. Specifically, during the current neo-colonial era, roughly two-thirds of the hotel rooms in the Caribbean are foreign owned. Tour companies who arrange visitors' activities are also often foreign owned. The more luxurious the accommodations, the more likely that profits are made by foreign firms. Furthermore, many resorts are all-inclusive and vacationers in these resorts rarely eat out at locally owned restaurants, rent water sports gear from local entrepreneurs or arrange island tours with local taxis. Most of the food served at hotels is imported; locally grown fruit – such as breadfruit, bananas and mangoes – is rarely served. Only about 30% of money spent by foreign visitors remains in the Caribbean, the rest is retained by overseas firms.

The Impact of Recession

The most recent worldwide **recession** was 2008–2009 and this had a big effect on most Caribbean countries as a result of close ties with, especially, the US and UK, for tourism, investment and remittances. Recession is characterised by the following:

- A rise in unemployment rates as companies try to cut costs.
- Anti-competitive mergers and bankruptcies.
- A credit crunch, or a shortage of money for banks to lend people.

This then results in low investment, business profits and sales. Workers have a wage freeze and there is no new hiring or promotions. With lay-offs, there is a reduction in household income and savings and extravagant spending is limited. Labour markets most at risk in the Caribbean in 2008–2009 were construction, tourism, energy (electricity), finance, retail, manufacturing, wholesaling, insurance and property maintenance.

Possible Causes of a Recession in the Caribbean

- Problems that have an impact on tourism, business services and wholesaling: in the 1980s the Barbados dollar was strong and this reduced the number of tourists from the UK. In 2000 The Bahamas was blacklisted in order to combat money laundering, hampering its offshore banking sector. The 2008 world economic downturn affected everyone.
- Inflation: this occurs when there is a gradual increase in the price of goods and services due to increased production costs, higher energy costs or national debt. Consumers may seek government control on the increase of food prices.

> ### Key Terms
>
> **Neo-colonialism** – the geopolitical practice of using capitalism and business globalisation by countries from the developed world in order to influence the internal affairs of the countries of the developing world. This term is usually used in the context of the (former) colonial powers who continue to apply existing and past international economic arrangements to their former colonies.
>
> **Recession** – a period of time during which there is negative economic growth.

- Falling consumer demand or consumer confidence so that only necessary items are bought: in the 1980s in Guyana and Jamaica, a fall in the price of their export commodities, sugar and bauxite – because of reduced demand – resulted in monetary losses.
- Rising exchange rate: this makes exports expensive and reduces demand for them.
- Disastrous floods or other natural disasters: an example is the flood in Guyana in 2005.
- Political unrest: this can cause a drop in foreign investment.

Ways to Stimulate Growth and Economic Recovery

Governments can take many, sometimes controversial, measures to turn around growth:

- Examine the sources of reduction in output and implement counter measures. Examples of this would be to identify which sector is involved, such as tourism, and explore remedies, such as alternative tourist markets, or to diversify from main exports to higher value goods.
- Implement lower interest rates to increase the money supply so that consumers can have money to spend on goods and services.
- Increase government spending on poverty reduction, thus creating a **multiplier effect** and reducing extreme poverty.
- Seek loans from international capital markets, but loans may come with strict **structural adjustment programmes** (**SAPs**) because of high levels of debt in some countries. The Jamaican government received a support package from the IMF, World Bank and IDB to stabilise the economy in 2013, which was only granted on the basis of strict controls on government spending to tackle the crime problem. This itself threatens economic growth.
- Enforce wage freezes, and other measures that affect higher earners. In Barbados in 2013 there were lay-offs and a wage freeze for civil servants. There was also the scaling back of some universal government programmes to leave out higher income groups.
- Decreasing taxes, which has a quick effect but reduces revenue.
- Bail out financial and other companies to protect employment or, alternatively, force a change in company ownership or management. For example, in 1987 some Jamaican tourism and agriculture state-owned enterprises were denationalised – made into privately run companies.
- Support mortgages so that homeowners are not forced to sell.
- Strengthen regulatory bodies and government policies to revive the economy, such as creating industrial parks and selling government bonds and securities to raise revenue.
- Protect local industry with a 'buy local' campaign and increase funding for small businesses.
- Devaluation, or decline in the value, of the currency of a country. This makes imports more expensive and so locals are forced to do without, or buy substitutes or local alternatives. As a result of devaluation, exports are cheaper for foreign countries to buy. The Jamaican dollar was devalued several times in the 1980s, causing imports to fall.

Key Terms

Multiplier effect – when an increase in spending produces an increase in national income and consumption greater than the initial amount spent.

SAPs – structural adjustment programmes are economic policies prescribed by the World Bank and the International Monetary Fund in order for countries to access loans or repay debts.

The signals that a country is coming out of its recession are an improvement in its GDP and employment rates. Stable house values and a strong stock market are also signs of a recovery. In addition, people saving more, high retail sales – especially in the purchase of luxury items like cars, furniture and appliances – and increased demand for building materials are all positive indicators.

Did You Know?

Major economic institutions in the Caribbean:

- CARICOM (Caribbean Community) is the most important regional institution guiding regional integration. As a body it has created the CARICOM Single Market and Economy (CSME).
- The ACS (Association of Caribbean States) consists of the members of CARICOM along with some South American countries. Its purpose is to assist in trade, travel and tourism in the region.
- The Cariforum organisation groups CARICOM members with Dominican Republic and Cuba to extend regional integration. It also serves as a base for economic dialogue with the European Union.
- All CARICOM members can access loans through the CDB (Caribbean Development Bank) to use for education or infrastructure.
- The OECS (Organisation of Eastern Caribbean States) is a group of nine islands in the Lesser Antilles, Eastern Caribbean, which have established a shared currency, the Eastern Caribbean Dollar.

Sustainable Development

Sustainable development is the planned and balanced development of a society's resources to provide for itself without compromising the ability of future generations to meet their needs. This is important because as resource consumption increases it puts pressure on the Earth's environment. Healthy air quality and safe drinking water are essential resources, but if accelerated production contaminates a country's water, erodes the soil or destroys the coral ecosystem then the future economic prosperity of that country may be damaged. Any gains will be lost in the long term.

Sustainable development means not doing anything today which will adversely affect the future. In the Caribbean, in terms of development, particular areas of concern include:

- town planning – clean air and landfills to dispose of waste and not contaminate water supply or soil;
- health – well-staffed and equipped hospitals, available drinking water and reliable food supply;
- energy sources – sustainable supply of electricity, fuel for vehicles, and so on;
- education – adult literacy, knowledge skills, research to advance science, positive social behaviour, provision for social mobility, reduction in social inequality, increase in gender awareness, higher levels of employment;
- environmental conservation – a green economy, no careless use of resources, safe disposal of waste products, slower rates of resource consumption, agricultural practices such as compost and manure use, limits on mining and afterwards returning land to former use, recycling solid waste, cutting pollution, protecting marine life and forests;
- global warming – cut carbon emissions to reduce climate change.

Quick Facts

Some of the major international financial institutions:

IDB – the Inter-American Development Bank, the main source of development financing for the Caribbean and Latin America.

World Bank – an international financial institution that provides loans to LEDCs.

IMF – the International Monetary Fund, an international financial institution which promotes economic and monetary cooperation and can make resources available to countries in financial difficulty.

Making the Connection

These institutions are examined in more detail in Chapter 15 'The Integration Movement'.

Key Term

Sustainable development – a comprehensive approach to development that takes account of social and economic as well as environmental aspects. It is a long-term process.

Quick Fact

In 1987 the Brundtland Commission put forward a plan titled 'Our Common Future', also known as the Brundtland Report, to achieve a healthy society. It addressed social, economic and environmental issues together and so introduced the concept of 'sustainable development'.

Making the Connection

Chapter 15 'The Integration Movement'

Exam Tip

'**Describe**' requires a lengthy answer in which you explain key concepts and issues and give logical arguments. You must use examples but **not** necessarily draw a conclusion.

Check Your Knowledge

Describe THREE similarities and THREE differences between sustainable development and economic development.

Demonstrate an understanding of the following terms and concepts by defining and using them correctly:

- Development
- Sustainable development
- Economic development
- Gross Domestic product (GDP)
- Gross National Product (GNI)

- Per capita
- Linkages
- Income/wealth
- Standard of living
- Quality of life

Explain the terms 'sustainable development' and 'economic development'.

Show that you understand and can argue any THREE of the following similarities and differences between the two concepts:

- **Similarities**:
  - Increasing income/wealth is the aim of both. CARICOM and ACS each have a combination of objectives concerning both economic and sustainable development for the region.
  - Both invest in the economic and the social sectors – sustainable development is not just about the environment.
  - Both involve the pursuit of productivity, but in different ways (see differences below).
  - Both see improvement in the standard of living as their main goal.

- **Differences**:
  - Sustainable development focuses on consultation about the best ways to proceed to both exploit the environment and provide a continuing resource for the future, while economic development monitors progress through measurements using indices of economic growth.
  - Economic development is measured by GDP/GNI per capita, while measurements for sustainable development are more complex and include measurements of environmental factors such as recycling rates and fish yields.
  - Economic development is marked by a higher income for citizens, whereas sustainable development is a longer term process that aims for a better standard of living for both present and future generations. This may also result in higher income for citizens, but is concerned with non-economic quality of life.
  - Sustainable development takes a grassroots approach to issues and directly involves people in a process of dialogue, while economic development takes a macro perspective and usually comes in the form of policies and programmes imposed from above.
  - Sustainable development incorporates a holistic approach to the question of development, involving all sectors of society, and is concerned with a combination of factors, for example, educational, environmental, governmental, health. However, economic development places emphasis on economic growth and uneven development for capital gain.

- Sustainable development creates links between sectors, for example the agricultural, manufacturing, construction and commerce sectors. This results in a trickle-down effect that involves the various sectors in sustaining one another, thus maintaining a cycle of development. Economic development does not rely on such links.

A possible conclusion is to summarise comprehensively the main points in your essay.

Human Development

From the 1990s there was a shift away from thinking about development purely in terms of economic growth, and towards new ways of describing development. The Human Development Paradigm was a new approach that looked at economic and sustainable development together and, importantly, put people at the centre of the discussion. It drew on ideas of social justice and identified four essential components, or pillars, required for **human development**: **Equity**, **Productivity**, **Empowerment** and **Sustainability**. By adopting these principles, economic growth would be reflected in improved living conditions, education and healthcare.

What is Poverty?

Poverty is when individuals do not have the basic requirements necessary for a good quality of life. Combating poverty is therefore necessary for human development to be achieved. These requirements would include food, clothing, water, shelter, employment, health, education, social services. In Barbados, for example, the government housing areas and some rural communities are isolated communities of poverty. The 'poverty line' is the minimum level of income deemed adequate for a person to live on in a particular country. The threshold of the international poverty line has varied over time, but in 2015 the World Bank defined it as anyone living on less than US$1.90 per day. People living below this line are not getting enough calories of food to sustain a healthy existence. This contributes to family and gender conflicts, human trafficking, security risks, crime, deplorable living conditions, hunger and urban migration.

Figure 12.2 illustrates the poverty trap and the interrelation between low income and low levels of development.

Figure 12.2 The poverty trap

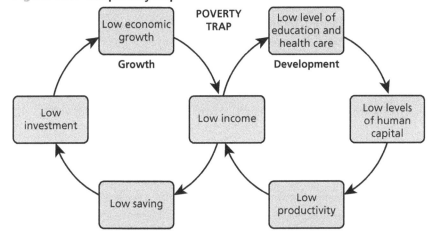

Key Term

Human development – development concerned with improving people's well-being through better opportunities and freedoms and trying to ensure an individual's basic needs are met for food, water and housing.

Quick Facts

The four pillars of the Human Development Paradigm:

- **Equity** – people must have access to equal opportunities.

- **Productivity** – people must be enabled to increase their productivity and participate fully in the process of income generation and remunerative employment.

- **Empowerment** – development must be by the people, not just for them.

- **Sustainability** – access to opportunities must be ensured not only for the present generations but for future generations as well.

Making the Connection

The relationship between development and social justice is discussed in more detail in Chapter 19 'Social Justice'.

Making the Connection

See Chapter 16 'Contributions of Sport to Development' for more on how sports and access to facilities can aid human development.

Ways of Combating Poverty

Examples of measures that could be taken include:

- creating more licenced vendors in the tourism sector, allowing them to sell directly to tourists in order to earn income. This also enables more people to share in the direct profits of one of the main economic activities of the region;
- obtaining aid from aid agencies;
- positive government action, such as providing subsidised housing and reducing taxation on low-income earners;
- reviewing land ownership and implementing reforms as necessary;
- establishing a government employment scheme, with the uneducated poor benefiting;
- universal education and scholarships where students can access free transport, books, internet and school meals;
- promoting agencies that help the poor and disabled, including the churches, NGOs (non-governmental organisations) and charities.

Poverty as a Global Issue

The United Nation's Human Development Report of 2014 speaks of the progress towards alleviating poverty as limited. It can be argued that this is mainly because local leaders have not redirected enough funds to address the issues surrounding poverty and lack the will to do so. In addition, the richer MEDCs, who can afford to, are not willing to share enough of their wealth with the poorer nations, including the Caribbean. The proponents of this point of view would argue that, rather than place tariffs on imports from the Caribbean to protect their own industries, the MEDCs could help by buying more Caribbean products.

Other Factors Affecting Human Development

- **Education and adult literacy** – the adult literacy rate is the percentage of adults who can read and write. Literacy affects a person's independence and therefore their empowerment. A well-educated population tends to result in higher entrepreneurship activity. High rates of illiteracy reflect a shortage of schools and trained teachers. Uneducated parents are more likely to not vaccinate their family against diseases or provide sanitation, basic healthcare and nutritious food preparation. Education has also been linked to higher life expectancy due to better employment, income and quality of life.
- **Life expectancy at birth** (**LEB**) refers to the average number of years that a new-born baby can expect to live. It is a reflection of the level of development and affluence of a place, and is directly affected by the quality of maternal health. It will also depend on the health facilities available, personal health habits, occupation and nutritional levels. For example, universal access to sports and recreation facilities would tend to increase life expectancy, while the occurrence of war or life threatening illnesses such as HIV/AIDS would decrease it. Women biologically live longer than men, they also tend to take fewer risks and have less dangerous jobs.
- **Self-esteem** of a people and society is attached to how they view their value and role in the world. Others' views of a society can also shape this, but it should not be the only measure. Honesty and integrity within a society is important for the preservation of dignity, a pride

in local culture and respect for and tolerance of others. Freedom to make dreams into tangible goals is also an important societal trait to cultivate.

Check Your Knowledge

Discuss FOUR indicators of human development and the challenges associated with them faced by Caribbean countries.

Demonstrate an understanding of any FOUR of the following concepts by defining and using them correctly:

- Human Development
- Poverty
- Education
- Gender equality (Male/female equality)
- Infant mortality rate
- Maternal health
- Access to basic services
- Access to healthcare
- Risk of disease: HIV/AIDS, malaria and other diseases
- Productivity
- Modern technology
- Literacy rate
- Life expectancy
- Government spending priorities

Explain 'human development' and FOUR of the above indicators.

Discuss the challenges associated with the FOUR indicators faced by Caribbean countries. Some examples are as follows:

- **Education** – the challenge of making education relevant to the Caribbean as well as attaining and maintaining a high quality of education. To some extent the education system is still gender biased to males. It is also Eurocentric, following the colonial legacy aimed at producing an elite class. This has failed to empower the masses and prepare them for the existing competitive labour market.

- **Modern technology** – for example in Trinidad and Tobago, and other Caribbean countries, there is heavy dependence on imports of technology that can cause citizens not to be as inventive and innovative as they could be. This develops a culture of dependency and the belief that everything that is foreign is better than that which is local.

- **Gender equality (male/female equality)** is a factor hindering human development in the Caribbean. Many households are headed by women, but gender inequality is reflected in the position of women in the labour force and their empowerment in political life as well as their reproductive health. Women who lack equal access to the workforce deprive society of important skills and knowledge that would enable it to fully benefit from the contribution of all its members. They experience a glass ceiling: selective access to jobs has stifled the ambitions and potential of professional women and their contributions to development. Women tend to be in lower paid occupations and experience a gender wage disparity. The marginalisation of pregnant females in schools and in society causes them to lose out on education, training and work experience. Women also continue to face disadvantages with regard to their human rights. Gender-based violence persists and they are subjected to sexual harassment and human trafficking. Leadership is viewed as natural for males and this is a gender stereotype. Moreover, there is lack of enforcement of laws such as the Equal Opportunities Act, of the implementation of policies and of public dialogue towards gender equality.

Making the Connection

Chapter 13 'Factors that Affect Development'

Exam Tip

'**Discuss**' requires an extended response defining key concepts, giving the facts, exploring related concepts and issues and presenting reasoned arguments. You must use detailed examples but **not** necessarily draw a conclusion.

- **Poverty** – the challenge of breaking the cycle of poverty exists in the Caribbean because people are unable to find the means of education or wealth to break it. This cycle of poverty results in isolated communities that experience poverty, for example housing areas separated from gated communities. There are few opportunities for social mobility. In Haiti, food security is a challenge. The economy is very dependent on a declining agricultural sector for most of its GDP. Adverse climatic conditions have led to food shortages and hunger. Environmental vulnerability is also a challenge for Caribbean countries. Since the 2010 earthquake in Haiti, which killed about 250 000 people, most of the population live in abject poverty and little or no development can occur.

- **Health** –there has been an increase in nutritional deficiencies in childhood and early childhood, which has led to cognitive underdevelopment, and this contributes to an increase in the mortality rate and a drop in productivity. In later adulthood and the aging population, the life expectancy for both men and women has increased because of improved health facilities. However, there has been an increase in deaths caused by diabetes, homicide and suicide, HIV/Aids, violence and injuries. Chronic non-communicable diseases, such as strokes, heart diseases, diabetes, cancer and injuries, are the main causes of death for the elderly. The challenge is to ensure proper nutrition and increased levels of physical activity, which can solve these problems.

- The ageing population presents other challenges, such as pension payments for more people, a rise in demand for services and facilities to care for the aged, an increase in the levels of non-communicable disease and a lack of job opportunities for an increased workforce over 60 years of age.

- Regular medical checks, vaccinations and public health campaigns, beginning in the primary schools, will result in greater awareness among society.

The essay can end with a conclusion that summarises the main ideas.

Indicators and Measurements of Development

Gross Domestic Product (GDP)

GDP is a measurement of a country's total national income, or the value of its goods in production and the services provided by it for a year, no matter the ownership. It is calculated from government figures, although these cannot report certain areas of income, such as income from the informal sector (cash only transactions) or the black market. It does not take into account taxes or subsidies and can hide inequalities in income. It excludes overseas earnings and so tends to undervalue countries that are heavily involved in offshore activities. It also does not reflect any losses in human or natural resources. To make it easier to compare across countries, GDP is given in US dollars (US$). Usually, GDP is a good indicator of the economy and standard of living in a country.

Key Term

GDP – the total value of all the goods and services produced by a country over a year.

Figure 12.3 The GDP per capita, GNI per capita and unemployment rates for five Caribbean countries over various periods of time

	GDP per capita $US (2012–2013)	GNI per capita $US (2005–2015)	Unemployment rate % (2007–2015)
The Bahamas	22 312	20 980	14.2
Trinidad and Tobago	18 372	20 070	6.3
Barbados	14 917	15 310	11.9
Jamaica	5 289	5 150	13.1
Guyana	3 739	3 940	11

Gross National Product (GNP)

Included in **GNP** is money in the form of investments or remittances from overseas. Remittances to Caribbean countries from friends and family abroad have been on the rise from 2000, but they can be difficult to measure. Also included in GNP is money sent back from companies or properties that are located overseas but owned by locals. It includes the money made in the country by foreign people and businesses.

The GNP does not account for sources of income such as the shadow economy (the black market and undeclared earnings, such as from domestic work). Wealthy citizens have been known to lodge their profits abroad and so their income is not fully captured in the GNP. It is a measure of *economic* growth only, and does not include factors such as non-market activities, pollution, resource depletion and environmental degradation. GNP does not show how equitably a country's income is distributed and so an increase in GNP does not necessarily mean an improvement in standard of living for all.

GNP is a less commonly used measure than GDP, but, if compared with it, can indicate if the country has many important investments overseas. Since 2000, the term **GNI (Gross National Income)** has largely replaced the term GNP – it too measures income received by a country both domestically and from overseas.

Per Capita

Per capita is used to provide average measurements of development across a total population. For example, the amount of wealth in a country is measured by the GNP per capita, meaning the calculation of a country's GNP (total value of goods and services) divided by the number of people living in the country. For instance, a GNP per capita figure of US$15 366 means the amount each person's income would be if the total GNP was shared out evenly among the population. However, per capita measures show averages and therefore hide extremes and the gap between the rich and the poor. There are other problems with this as a measure, as it cannot be totally precise due to difficulties in accurately counting population and the fact that the birth rate can affect the statistics (because babies and children are included in the numbers but cannot earn an income).

Gini Coefficient

The **Gini coefficient** compares the ideal situation, in which everyone in a country would have equal income, to who actually receives the income. Values range from perfect equality at 0 to inequality at 1. World averages

Key Terms

GNP – the total value of goods and services produced by a country each year, including earnings from citizens or businesses located overseas.

GNI (Gross National Income) has largely replaced the term GNP.

Key Term

Per capita – this literally means 'for each person'.

Key Term

GINI coefficient – a measure of wealth inequality between socio-economic groups in a country.

are between 0.2 and 0.6. Most Caribbean countries have Gini coefficients of 0.43 to 0.46.

It is a simple ratio and the most common way of measuring inequality, but there are some limitations in what it can show. If GDP is rising and Gini is also increasing, then it may mean that the majority are not benefiting from a rising income. When this gap becomes large, social stratification is permanent and the poorer groups can find it hard to get high-paying jobs, bank credit, training, healthcare or housing. A small gap means social mobility is possible through education and job rewards. Governments can try to redistribute income through social programmes and taxation policies.

Human Development Index (HDI)

In 1990 the United Nations produced the Human Development Index (HDI) as the main indicator of development. For example, 0.937 means high economic, education and healthcare status, suggesting that the government of a country with this number clearly allocates funds to health and education schemes. The index does not measure human rights in a country. Some examples of HDI indicators in Caribbean countries for 2014 are shown in the table in figure 12.4, which also shows world ranking of 16 Caribbean countries in 2014.

> **Key Term**
>
> **HDI** – the Human Development Index combines GNI per capita, life expectancy and the adult literacy rate into a score from 0 to 1 that indicates a country's social and economic development.

Figure 12.4 **HDI and global ranking of 16 Caribbean countries in 2014**

Caribbean country	Global ranking 2014	HDI 2014
1. The Bahamas	55	0.790
2. Barbados	57	0.785
3. Antigua and Barbuda	58	0.783
4. Trinidad and Tobago	64	0.772
5. Cuba	67	0.769
6. St Kitts and Nevis	77	0.752
7. Grenada	79	0.750
8. St Lucia	89	0.729
9. Dominica	94	0.724
10. St Vincent and the Grenadines	97	0.720
11. Jamaica	99	0.719
12. Belize	101	0.715
13. Dominican Republic	101	0.715
14. Suriname	103	0.714
15. Guyana	124	0.636
16. Haiti	163	0.483

Source: UNDP report on HDI, 2014

Productivity

> **Key Term**
>
> **Productivity** – a measure of the efficiency of production or the rate of output. This rate can be increased by the use of advanced or appropriate technology.

Productivity is the level of output produced for each unit of input. Labour productivity is measured by dividing the total output in a given time by the number of workers employed for that time. For example, 10 bags of cement per worker per week. This indicator emphasises the output of a society, or how industrious or efficient they are.

Efficiency can be increased by:

- management that is worker-friendly. If people are happy at work, they look forward to their work the next day and this helps to ensure the business is successful and is able to expand. This also can be beneficial to each person as they can obtain job satisfaction and professional development through promotion;
- rewarding productivity, because companies can tie a worker's output to their income and this means that more productive employees would receive more pay;
- employing skilled workers and training staff in efficiency;
- reducing the time and resources used to produce items;
- using advanced and appropriate technology to increase output per person.

In contrast, constant strikes or civil unrest point to social problems and these need to be addressed by management before too much time is wasted and too much money lost.

Internet Penetration

This indicates how many people have access to the internet as a percentage of the total population. A user is defined as someone over two years old who went online in the past 30 days. People access the internet through computers, smartphones, digital TV or other devices via fibre optic cables, cellular masts and Wi-Fi. The internet provides access to information, news, social media and online services such as shopping and banking. In 2009, the World Bank announced that broadband and mobile phone technology would lead to economic development and job creation. ICT (information and communication technology), including the internet, world wide web and mobile phone technology, can make shopping, banking and accessing information from far-away places easier, and can boost commerce and employment in sales, retail and support services such as shipping. Internet penetration in Caribbean countries typically ranges between 50% and 80%. According to one source, in 2016 internet penetration in Jamaica was 43% while in Barbados it was 80%.

Modern Technology

Modern technology (technology developed in the last 20 years) and infrastructure can affect many sectors of the country. Technology can be used to design, manufacture or use goods and services and can also be useful in organising human activities. Some Caribbean countries do not have a fully functioning telephone system, efficient public transport, water or electricity supply, telecommunications or port facilities. There is often a slow response to adopting new technology because of the high cost associated with machines, maintenance and human resource training. Bureaucratic procedures can also cause complications or delays in updating infrastructure.

Good Governance

Good governance has a direct, positive effect on a country's development. One of a number of essentials for good governance is participation by the people in democratic elections. Steps are taken to ensure social and cultural harmony and economic and political fair play.

Key Term

Good governance – when public resources and problems are managed effectively, efficiently and in response to the critical needs of society. Effective democratic forms of governance rely on public participation, accountability and transparency.

The indicators and interpretation of good governance are subjective, but it is generally agreed that government should:

- be responsive to all citizens' needs and rights, including the poorest and most vulnerable;
- have transparency in money matters;
- allow for access to information and a free press;
- have accountability for spending and earnings as this can affect credit rating;
- allow independence of the judiciary so that there is less possibility for corruption;
- ensure prudent use of natural resources;
- have an efficient civil service;
- allow freedom of expression and assembly.

Government should ensure efficient policy making, and have an established administrative system. Its representative bodies should meet to decide on how to raise revenue, determine how public money should be spent and continue to guide and implement sound social and economic development. By contrast, undemocratic political systems can have an adverse impact on development.

Responsible Environmental Factors

Human development emphasises the importance of environmental factors in a country's development. Government is responsible for managing the area within its international borders, including land, sea and air. Importance is given to conservation and preservation of the ecology, and the study of habitats. Habitat is affected by temperature, sunlight, carbon dioxide, rocks, nutrients and water. Humans can protect wetlands, coral reefs, woodlands and fragile ecosystems by creating protected parks, nature trails or reserves. In turn they benefit from clean air to breathe and beaches and parks to relax in. The natural environment for parts of the Caribbean is also a major tourist attraction.

Examples of responsible environmental governance include the following:

- Acting against pollution:
  - Pollution of air or water should be kept to a minimum and penalties for polluters enforced.
  - Solid and liquid waste should be disposed of properly and not dumped on unused land or at sea.
  - Industrial accidents, spills or fires can pollute, as can noise and congestion, and all should be investigated and penalised appropriately.
- Education in the agricultural sector
  - Farmers should be educated on using the least amounts of fertilisers and pesticides needed so that water does not become contaminated.
  - Over cropping and overgrazing should be discouraged.
  - There should be continued support for organic farming, including crop rotation and the use of fallow land (a field left for a period for the soil to regain its organic content). Organic farm production can be labour-intensive, have low yields and result in higher priced fruits and vegetables, but it is better for the environment than using chemical fertilisers and pesticides.

Quick Fact

The habitat of an organism (living thing) is where it lives. Protection of habitats is a key feature of responsible environmental management

Multiple-choice Questions

1. The best definition for Gini coefficient is
   A. The rate at which imports flow into a country
   B. An aggregate score of a county's growth
   C. The ranking of disparity in income between socio-economic groups
   D. A score calculated by measuring real GDP, life expectancy and literacy

2. One major problem of using GDP per capita as an indicator of development is
   A. GDP is used to describe living standards
   B. GDP can hide large inequalities in wealth of different socio-economic groups
   C. GDP is calculated per capita, which means it is an average not a percentage
   D. GDP uses $US as its currency and its exchange rate is subject to fluctuation

3. One of the advantages of using HDI to define development is that
   A. Health and education are factored in
   B. HDI can signal that a country has a trade imbalance
   C. Human development is calculated by population size
   D. The HDI is proportional to the size of disparities in wealth

4. Which of the following conditions does NOT exist in a country that is environmentally responsible?
   A. Incentives to recycle plastic bottles
   B. Clearing of wetlands to build tourism developments
   C. Cleaning and clearing of empty lots, thus reducing mosquito breeding sites
   D. Farmer education on water conservation technology and organic farming

5. Which of the following measures is BEST taken by government during a recession?
   A. Devalue the currency
   B. Deregulate the mortgage market
   C. Spend more on security and defence
   D. Lower interest rates for accounts at financial institutions

6. To avoid borrowing from international lenders, a government can best seek finances by
   A. Raising taxes
   B. Curbing government spending
   C. Raising the prices of goods and services
   D. Selling government savings bonds and securities

7. "Vote for us and we promise that you, your children and generations to come will reap more crops, catch more fish than you do now and a still live to be wealthy."

   This statement relates BEST to which of the following concepts?
   A. Human Development
   B. Economic Development
   C. Sustainable Development
   D. Cooperative Development

8. The main difference between GDP and GNP is
   A. GDP includes overseas earnings
   B. GNP includes overseas earnings
   C. GDP is calculated per capita and GNP is not
   D. GNP is a social indicator and GDP is an economic indicator

Chapter 13

Factors That Affect Development

Evaluate how development in the Caribbean region is shaped by political, economic, social, cultural, environmental and technological factors.

After revising this topic, you should be able to:
- define and explain related terms and concepts;
- evaluate how the following can promote or hinder development:
  - gender inequality
  - political ideologies and popular movement
  - distribution of wealth and resources
  - changing class boundaries
  - entrepreneurial drive and activity
  - natural and human-made disasters
  - government policies
  - use of technology
  - global conditions
  - quality and relevance of education
  - tourism
  - culture.

The factors that influence development in the Caribbean are multi-faceted and can be categorised as social, political, economic, environmental, technological or cultural. It is, however, very difficult to separate any one factor that accounts for the level of development in any one society. Like many issues, none of these factors stands in isolation; they are strongly interconnected or interact with each other. However, the nature of each factor and the subsequent level of development that follows vary from one country to another. Additionally, one factor can have both positive and/or negative effects on the development of a country.

Key Terms

Gender inequality – an imbalance in treatment and quality of life of men and women in terms of human development, reproductive health, empowerment and economic status.

Social Factors

Gender Inequality

Gender inequality hinders Caribbean development in the following ways:
- Lack of equal access to the workforce deprives society of important skills and knowledge that would enable it to fully benefit from the contribution to be made by all of its members, and prevents the economy getting the full benefit of its human potential. While men take the higher status scientific, technical, administrative and managerial jobs, women are employed in lower status positions in the health and education sectors and lower level administrative office and commercial positions.

- Even if women gain access to professional and managerial positions, they experience a **glass ceiling**. This selective access to jobs has stifled the ambitions and potential of professional women.
- Women tend to be in lower paid occupations and experience a gender wage gap. Employers justify giving them lower incomes compared to men by arguing they are 'the weaker sex'.
- The marginalisation of pregnant female students in schools and in society causes them to lose out on education, training and work experience. Consequently, there is also an increased demand for services for reproductive health, sex education and birth control.
- Women continue to face disadvantages with regard to their human rights. Examples are:
  - the persistence of gender-based violence, usually by a man in the family against a female partner or female children;
  - sexual harassment against women (which is more about power than violence) includes stalking and sending unwanted emails and text messages. It is usually inflicted on women in junior positions and can restrict chances of promotion and financial advancement;
  - the human trafficking of people, often women, who are vulnerable and unemployed. They are coerced into travelling to another country where the promised job is a hoax and they end up in sex work or domestic servitude.
- Leadership is viewed as 'naturally' male and this is a gender stereotype in a patriarchal society. The results are women being limited in their democratic participation and low female representation in the political parties.

The negative effects of gender inequality are perpetuated by a lack of will in the enforcement of laws such as the Equal Opportunities Act and the implementation of anti-discrimination policies, by an unwillingness to open up public dialogue towards gender equality and the failure to educate society to overcome the disadvantages faced by women.

However, progress has been made and the work of feminist and women's groups have advanced the cause of women in society by facilitating, for example, public discussions for women's voices to be heard and the dissemination of research. They have influenced, often directly, a change in state policy with laws being enacted such as the Domestic Violence Act, Sexual Offences Act and Equal Opportunities Act to protect women's rights. Women have made other gains; for example, they can seek a divorce and hold a bank account – rights that were once denied to them.

Gender equality can promote Caribbean human and economic development in several ways:

- Increased educational opportunities result in an increase in both the knowledge and skills bases, as women have the opportunity to realise their full potential by increasing productivity and becoming fully empowered in society. Already, many women have advanced themselves academically and at present dominate all faculties at the University of the West Indies.
- An increase in the knowledge base would help women challenge and remove the glass ceiling and allow more to achieve leadership and managerial positions. The Regional Action Plan of CARICOM not only addresses the need for more inclusive politics and styles of

Key Terms

Glass ceiling – climbing the career ladder up to a certain point where people reach an invisible social barrier and cannot climb further.

Making the Connection

The role of women's groups such as Caribbean Association for Feminist Research Action (CAFRA) and Women's Association for African Networking and Development (WAND) in promoting human and social development is outlined in Chapter 14 'Globalisation and Development'.

governance, but also for the participation of young women in making public policy. Today, women such as Kamla Persad-Bissessar, in Trinidad and Tobago, and Portia Simpson, in Jamaica, have made vital contributions to the social and political landscapes of the Caribbean.

- Certain international lending agencies insist on gender equity as a stipulation for aid. As a result of empowering women, many Caribbean countries would thus obtain the funding for national projects to allow them to actively develop their societies.
- Empowering women to take charge of their reproductive health has served to reduce health issues such as HIV/Aids, which in turn increases productivity.
- Empowering women can assist them in being able to equally access and contribute to the labour force and productivity. This is particularly true for the Caribbean, with its tradition of women- and grandmother-dominated households.

Quick Fact

The UN Gender Inequality Index (GII) measures inequality in three important aspects of human development – reproductive health, empowerment and economic status. It is designed to expose differences in the achievements between men and women and so measure the human development costs of gender inequality (the higher the GII, the greater the cost).

Making the Connection

Chapter 6 'Characteristics of Society and Culture'

Chapter 7 'Identity and Social Formation'

Chapter 12 'Concepts and Indicators of Development'

Chapter 14 'Globalisation and Development'

Chapter 19 'Social Justice'

Check Your Knowledge

Describe FOUR ways in which women have experienced discrimination and how these have inhibited Caribbean development.

Demonstrate an understanding of the following terms and concepts by defining and using them correctly:

- Discrimination
- Caribbean
- Development
- Gender discrimination
- Glass ceiling

- Wage disparity
- Sexual harassment
- Gender-based violence
- Human trafficking
- Occupational segregation

You must **describe** any FOUR of the following examples and demonstrate understanding by giving specific examples. You must also show the link between discrimination and development:

- Development is tied to social and economic equity. Discrimination against women works contrary to this in many ways.
- Women lack equal access to the workforce, which denies society vital skills and knowledge that enables everyone to reap the benefits of the contributions of all members.
- Women are usually in lower paid occupations and experience a gender wage disparity. This has a direct impact on the economy (GDP), which further increases the gender wage gap.
- Women experience a glass ceiling, which stifles their ambitions and potential and the contributions they can make to development.
- Tradition views of leadership as 'naturally' male restrict women in their democratic participation. Gender discrimination in social institutions, especially education, contributes to a lack of leadership skills among women, which in turn hinders development.
- Gender discrimination leads to lack of knowledge and awareness that can hinder the advancement of society generally. This is exacerbated by a lack of implementation of laws such as the Equal Opportunities Act, public dialogue towards gender equality and the education of society to overcome the discrimination faced by women.

- Marginalised pregnant students in schools and society lose out on education, training and work experience. There is a resulting increase in demand for services for reproductive health, sex education and birth control, as well as a decrease in productivity.
- Women experience discrimination in terms of human rights with high incidences of gender-based violence, sexual harassment and human trafficking.

A possible conclusion can be a summary of the main points addressed in this essay.

Exam Tip

'**Describe**' requires a lengthy answer in which you explain key concepts and issues and give logical arguments. You must use detailed examples, but **not** necessarily draw a conclusion.

Changing Class Boundaries

In plantation society, a closed system existed where status was ascribed on the basis of race, colour and ethnicity. This resulted in a rigid social stratification in which people were not socially mobile. After emancipation, World War II and independence, a more open system evolved and to some extent social change meant people of European descent were no longer viewed as superior and so no longer feared. However, social stratification based on race, colour and ethnicity largely remained.

The provision of education also facilitated social mobility as, by attaining it, the poor and peasant classes challenged traditional structures and experienced upward mobility. This led to a new class of educated descendants of formerly enslaved people and indentured Asians who could aspire to white-collar jobs, set themselves up in small businesses and train for professions such as law, medicine, engineering and accounting.

Changing class boundaries have promoted development:
- There has been an improvement in the standard of living of members of the working class as they became more socially mobile. For example, the formerly enslaved engaged in non-farming activities to improve their socio-economic status and in Trinidad a minority of East Indians became wealthy through business.
- The new peasantry, swelled by ex-indentures, introduced economic and agricultural diversity with crops such as rice, cocoa, coffee and bananas.
- Chinese and Portuguese immigrants also went on to start successful retail businesses.
- Society has been able to harness the potential of more of its members through the provision of universal education, which has enabled more people from the working classes to aspire to higher education and the higher echelons of business, commerce and public life.

However, development has also been inhibited.
- Equal opportunities did not, and, it can be argued, still do not, exist for all groups in society. The underclass has suffered from the cycle of poverty. Matrifocal households and visiting-type unions have been viewed by some as the cause of such socio-economic circumstances, with the poor becoming heavily dependent on the state for welfare assistance. This can be very costly to Caribbean states.
- To some extent, the plantation model of stratification is still adhered to, thus limiting social mobility to mainly the privileged few.
- The fact that ethnic tensions and discrimination continue to exist in some Caribbean territories demonstrates that factors such as race, colour and ethnicity still play a role in contemporary societies.

Making the Connection

Social stratification in plantation society both before and after emancipation, and subsequent increased social mobility, are assessed in Chapter 7 'Identity and Social Formation'.

Even so, social class boundaries are slowly changing for the working classes. There have been several welfare programmes established by Caribbean governments designed to break the cycle of poverty and to make people less dependent on the state for welfare assistance.

Making the Connection

The concept of welfare is discussed in Chapter 19 'Social Justice'.

Quality and Relevance of Education

Education, or lack thereof, is a key indicator of the level of development. There is evidence that education has unmatched power to develop human resources by improving lives, particularly for girls and women. Many organisations, including the UN and its agencies UNESCO, UNICEF, UNDP and the World Bank, agree on the huge importance of education to sustainable development. The 2016 UN Sustainable Development Goal 4 (Quality Education) states: 'This goal ensures that all girls and boys complete free primary and secondary schooling by 2030. It also aims to provide equal access to affordable vocational training to eliminate gender and wealth disparities, and achieve universal access to a quality higher education.'

The quality and relevance of education promote Caribbean development in the following ways:

- Facilitates the continuous development of literacy, numeracy and technical skills. These then aid further learning of higher-order skills such as problem solving.
- Inculcates life skills in members of society.
- Helps people in the Caribbean to improve their quality of life and standard of living by assisting them to obtain decent work, raising their incomes, increasing productivity and facilitating upward social mobility, which in turn all fuel economic development.
- Can lead to a healthy lifestyle, reduce malnutrition and help prevent or stop the spread of diseases.
- Responds to rapidly changing job markets and opportunities to develop human resources. In the Caribbean, strides have been made in the use of distance learning in areas of work such as hospitality, accounting, business studies, light-manufacturing (furniture) and agriculture. Technical Vocational Educational Training (TVET) schemes, which provide practical life and technological skills as well as general education, are being financed by the CDB in places such as Belize, Haiti, Grenada and St Kitts and Nevis.
- Physical/sports education also develops the region's human resources. The Caribbean is becoming a popular destination for sports tourism and people who are trained in this area can enhance this.
- Cultural education improves the understanding of cultural diversity in the Caribbean and reflects and transmits the various norms, values and cultures of Caribbean society. This not only prepares individuals for different roles in society, but can also promote appreciation of various cultural forms and attract tourists to the Caribbean. In turn, this creates not only a national, but also a regional identity.

The delivery of quality and relevant education poses financial and logistical challenges in some parts of the region. Urbanisation, or where towns tend to grow in size at the expense of surrounding rural areas, and persistent poverty have made the provision of education challenging, while financial support for education at all levels can be difficult to secure. Region-wide cooperation is therefore needed to offer suitable education facilities.

Caribbean development is hindered by the following education and training issues:

- Generally, high rates of illiteracy exist in some Caribbean countries. People lack basic skills that will enhance their employment opportunities and result in greater productivity.
- Although literacy rates are high in some Caribbean countries, illegal activities and domestic violence show uneducated choices and suggest that what people are being taught may be irrelevant to their lives.
- At times there are inadequate skilled labourers in the local population, and Caribbean governments or businesses need to seek external labour. There are also cases of skilled workers, who have problems finding local employment, seeking jobs elsewhere, even outside the region.
- The inherited colonial-style education system aimed at creating an elite class has not empowered the masses for a competitive labour market.
- A few Caribbean countries are not fully ready for ICT technology in terms of infrastructure and levels of internet connectivity; for example, electricity supply is interrupted to some schools.

Political Factors

Some political factors that promote and hinder Caribbean development include **political ideologies** and **popular movements**, and government policies.

Political Ideologies and Popular Movements

Political Ideologies

Key Terms

The world is divided into different ideologies on economic and political issues:

- **Market economy or capitalism** – a right-wing political and economic ideology where the principle means of production and distribution are in private hands, not the state. Prevalent in Western countries including the USA, Spain, France, Canada, Japan, Britain, West Germany and other allies that believe in political democracy and the economic system called the 'market system'.

- **Marxism/communism or centrally planned economy** – extreme left-wing ideology based on the revolutionary socialist teachings of Marx involving collective ownership and a planned economy based on the principle that each should work to their capability and receive according to their needs. Mostly prevalent in the 20th century in the East, where people believed in the communist philosophy of a centrally planned economy and the political control of a one-party state. The main centre of the communist ideology was the Soviet Union. The economies of these countries were closed and they traded only among themselves, with the absence of global trade which exists today.

Quick Fact

There have been changes in the education system to better reflect people's history and experiences in the Caribbean. Until the 1960s and independence, the education children received reflected the ideals of the metropole. In Trinidad and Tobago, for example, the school of education opened in 1973, and in 1979 CXC® CSEC® examinations in mathematics, geography and English were piloted.

Making the Connection

The role and development of the institution of education in the Caribbean are discussed in Chapter 9 'Societal Institutions' and Chapter 11 'Caribbean-Global Interactions'.

Quick Fact

Emphasis is being placed on ICT in schools, which, when combined with effective teaching, facilitates learning (for example, the Laptop Initiative in secondary schools in Trinidad and Tobago from 2010). However, this varies considerably across the region.

Key Terms

Ideology – a set of basic beliefs and ideas about political, economic, social and cultural affairs. It refers to certain ideas about what is considered to be the best form of government and the best economic system, (such as capitalism or socialism).
Political ideology refers to allocation of power and to what ends it should be used.

Popular movement – a body of thought and action initiated by ideas from the masses, or developed for the masses. It can have local and/or international appeal, such as Garveyism and Rastafari.

Quick Fact

The Communist Eastern Bloc, headed by the Soviet Union, collapsed for several complex economic, political and social reasons (both internal and external) in the late 1980s and 1990s.

Quick Fact

Black Power was a civil rights issue with African-Americans responding to racism, predominantly in the 1960s and 70s, in some peaceful but many violent ways. There were also advocates of Black Power in the Caribbean, such as Walter Rodney (see Chapter 17).

- **Capitalist or free state/enterprise** – the dominant political ideology of the Caribbean. However, there were Marxist-type revolutions – attempts at increasing human equity – in Cuba (1959), Guyana (1960s–1970s) and Grenada (1979). Today, Cuba still follows communist ideology.

On the one hand, political ideologies can promote development in the Caribbean by:
- producing cadres of informed leaders with well-defined goals;
- offering clear guidelines for social and economic development;
- sensitising the youth about political issues because these youths become the next generation of leaders;
- involvement in the extra-regional dimension, such as supporting the liberation of African colonies.

On the other hand, political ideologies can hinder development in that they can:
- be viewed as too Afro-centric; for instance, Black Power can create ethnic tensions or barriers within multi-ethnic populations such as Guyana and Trinidad and Tobago;
- be viewed as too Eurocentric and as such perpetuate a colonial mentality;
- foster fragmentation and make countries vulnerable to external interference in domestic affairs;
- exclude women as an essential group;
- lead to and inflame political social conflict, such as coups, plots, revolutions and ethnic clashes;
- fail to deal with issues of difference: that is, race, colour, ethnicity.

Popular Movements

Some examples include:
- Rastafari
- Garveyism
- Black Power Movement
- Universal Negro Improvement Association (UNIA) and African Communities League
- Women's movements such as WAND
- CAFRA
- Sistren Theatre Collective.

Popular movements can promote Caribbean development by:
- acting as a stimulus for political and social change by becoming pressure groups or even revolutionary forces to foster awareness of important issues;
- demanding transparency and accountability by the government;
- promoting socio-economic development programmes beneficial to citizens, labour, family and the environment. For example, in Trinidad and Tobago the Highway Re-route Movement has demonstrated their concerns about, and expressed discontent at, the removal of citizens from their homes and the destruction of environmentally important wetlands and farmland to construct a highway. Also, the environmentalist group, the Fisherfolk Society, has aired views on recent blasting by Petrotrin and oil spills in Point Fortin, which have destroyed marine life, damaged mangrove swamps and created unemployment of fishermen;

- making citizens more conscious of their rights and duties; for example, to protect the environment as well as to protect human rights such as gender-oriented groups, which were formed to protect women against abuse, and to assert the right to be treated with equity and equality.

Popular movements can hinder Caribbean development by stirring up unrest, discord, damage and disruption, such as the Rodney Riots in Jamaica after Walter Rodney was banned from returning to the UWI in 1968, and the 1990 Jamaat Muslimeen attempted coup in Trinidad, neither of which achieved significant political or social changes.

Government Policies

Government policies can affect both human and economic development. Governments can use their powers to invest directly to develop new industries; introduce and enforce laws to provide protection to social groups or to the environment; provide public goods and services; and use taxes and incentives to achieve economic or social objectives.

How government policies can promote Caribbean development:

- By investing in business; Caribbean governments have become major employers, resulting in reduced unemployment.
- By improving technology, healthcare, education, agriculture and supporting the private sector.
- By improving labour relations and enactment of policies aimed at environmental protection and anti-pollution.
- By setting prices to prevent a 'black market' from developing.
- By adopting measures to help small to medium sized businesses, such as reducing the cost and time to import raw materials and export finished products.
- By establishing social programmes and improving infrastructure. Water and electricity are usually provided by government as public utilities. The fire, police, defence force and coast guard are also under government jurisdiction.
- By maintaining a safe environment for investors to open businesses.

Did You Know?

Taxing businesses is a way for governments to raise revenue, but transnational companies (TNCs) and multinational companies (MNCs) can often obtain preferential tax incentives to stay in the region. **Fiscal policies,** such as tax rebates, tax-free profits, tax-free loans or tax holidays, may attract both foreign businesses and local firms. Tax concessions are the preferred means to attract certain firms to promote investment. Corporate income tax holidays of 5 to 10 years can be granted for firms that export to, or are located in, a designated area known as an export processing zone (EPZ).

Key Term

Fiscal policy is the use of government spending or taxation to influence the economy.

Government policies can also hinder Caribbean development through obstruction of the setting up and running of new businesses with processes that take time and cost: making it difficult to get construction permits and permits to trade across borders; complex tax procedures; lengthy processes for getting electricity and water; or even registering property.

It could even be argued that government policies, or lack thereof, have hindered an active response to the process of globalisation because some governments in the region have been slow to provide support for sunset industries, in decline because of increased global competition, while at the same time neglecting the need to establish sunrise industrial activity as a replacement.

Making the Connection

The theory behind and concept of 'industrialisation by invitation' are looked at in more detail in Chapter 17 'Intellectual Traditions'.

Did You Know?

Industrialisation by Invitation

The 'industrialisation by invitation' policies put forward by economist Sir Arthur Lewis in the early 1950s placed focus on developing regional export markets due to surplus labour in the agricultural sector. This was used in the 1960s Operation Beehive in the garment industry in Barbados, which was successful at providing opportunities for economic growth. Foreign direct investment (FDI) created EPZs near to the ports of entry. Manufacturers could get duty-free imported raw materials, industrial quality infrastructure and leased space in buildings, thereby reducing costs for setting up factories.

There were several ways in which the policy of 'industrialisation by invitation' spurred or promoted Caribbean development:

- It led to the economic diversification of Caribbean economies from being based only on agricultural production of coffee, bananas and sugar into manufacturing.
- Light-manufacturing was greatly needed in Caribbean economies due to the lack of foreign investment and a reliance on the traditional industries of sugar processing and retail.
- The unemployment rate was reduced slightly, especially for women, who took advantage of the opportunity for employment in new areas of manufacture that also provided better facilities than the old sugar refineries.
- Some industries that have remained in the Caribbean contribute to regional exports (for example, Yankee Garments in Barbados has been in the region since 1962).

On the other hand, it can be argued that the policy of 'industrialisation by invitation' hindered development:

- Governments spent scarce resources developing the required infrastructure to attract foreign investors, including outfitting buildings with the needed utilities.
- Critical foreign exchange was lost to governments because of tax and other concessions.
- Due to a lack of stringent terms of agreement with the MNCs involved, reinvestment in the region was lower than anticipated and, once the financial incentives ended, the firms moved their factories to set up production elsewhere.
- Reduction of unemployment was not as widespread as hoped for. Companies' employment levels did not keep up with the increasing number of school leavers. In Jamaica, for example, the number of school leavers has overtaken the available places in manufacturing industries.
- Criticisms of EPZ industrial practices include gender discrimination through low wages, sexual harassment in the work place and breaches of labour laws.
- Salaries in industrial corporations were inclined to be low.
- Many light-manufacturing industries were assembly line operations in which the workers only created part of the product. Skills and knowledge acquisition were therefore limited.

- Environmental problems arose because of the operations of some of the firms; there are examples of chemical and pharmaceutical products polluting the soil with toxic waste.

Economic Factors

Distribution of Wealth and Resources

A key feature of Caribbean societies is the unequal distribution of wealth, income and resources among citizens. Some citizens, especially the elite, live in luxurious conditions, while other citizens live in poverty or abject poverty, as many do in Haiti. For various reasons, some countries have failed to adopt a policy of sustainable development that aims to provide social and economic equalisation for all citizens.

There are also disparities in wealth at a national level. Many Caribbean countries have limited energy and mineral resources. As such, they experience disadvantages in terms of trading with countries with more resources and so their expenditure is high on imports. In Haiti, due to the absence of resources, the economy is very dependent on a declining agricultural sector for most of its GDP.

Historically, the distribution of wealth is a legacy that has hindered development of the region. Under Crown Colony government, raw materials were extracted and exported to the metropole rather than developing flourishing local economies. Wealth was in the hands of a few planters, and its uneven distribution has been passed on through inheritance, maintaining in many places a stratified social system. Where a more equal distribution of wealth and resources can be achieved, the population is socially mobile and has access to a higher standard of living, including better social services such as healthcare. The Gini Index is a measure of the inequality of wealth distribution; a value of 0 means total equality and a value of 1 (or 100%) is complete inequality.

How the distribution of wealth and resources affect Caribbean development:

- Capitalism consolidates assets, both wealth and resources, into private ownership, which heightens disparities between rich and poor resulting in increased unemployment, low levels of investment, fewer opportunities and, for some, homelessness and living in abject poverty.
- From a human development perspective, poverty means more than just the lack of what is necessary for material well-being. Poverty of choices and opportunities suggests that poverty must be addressed in all its dimensions, not income alone. This further manifests itself in poor healthcare provision, the creation of slum and ghetto areas, and a resultant lower standard of living.
- Crime and social unrest increase as a result of poverty. This can act as a deterrent to foreign investors and tourists, meaning not only a fall in foreign exchange or revenue, but also still higher unemployment rates.
- The concentration of wealth and assets in the hands of the few can be perpetuated by corrupt practices such as bribery or **nepotism**, as has been alleged in Trinidad and Tobago, for example. A trend of low productivity among high-income earners can also emerge as wealth circulation among certain cadres provides little incentive for hard work.

Making the Connection

Chapter 15 'The Integration Movement' assesses some of the challenges faced by CARICOM and other trans-regional organisations and institutions due to economic and wealth differences between countries in the region.

Quick Facts

Some Caribbean Gini Index values (supplied by UN sources) are:

- Haiti – 0.61 (2012)
- St Vincent and the Grenadines – 0.60 (2004)

(For comparison, the US value was 0.41 in 2013.)

High levels of poverty can coincide with a high Gini Index, such as St Vincent and the Grenadines.

Low levels of poverty can also coincide with a relatively high Gini Index, such as Antigua and Barbuda 0.47–0.5 (2007).

Key Terms

Nepotism – the practice of those with power or influence to favour relatives or friends, especially by giving them jobs or contracts.

Capital flight – the large-scale exodus of financial assets from a nation due to events such as political or economic instability, currency devaluation or the imposition of economic policies that control capital and investments.

Brain drain – when a country loses its best workers due to 'push' factors such as economic or political conditions, or 'pull' factors such as better opportunities or the desire to seek a higher standard of living elsewhere.

Entrepreneurs – business owners who perceive needs and bring together the labour, materials and capital required to meet those needs, often in an innovative way. They seek to generate value through **entrepreneurial activity** by identifying and exploiting new products/services, processes or markets.

Entrepreneurship – creative and innovative action by entrepreneurs to establish an enterprise; the ability to discover, create or invent opportunities and exploit them to the benefit of society, which in turn brings prosperity to the innovator and his organisation.

Entrepreneurial drive – the strong desire behind entrepreneurial activities to achieve outcomes and opportunities for continuous improvement, innovation and new value creation.

• Uneven wealth distribution can lead to **capital flight**, in that wealth is concentrated in the hands of a few who can make personal decisions on what to do with it, and a **brain drain**. To help counter this, governments might be forced to borrow from international sources, which results in higher taxes and inflation.

Entrepreneurial Drive and Activity

There is a direct link between business and economic growth and development. If few persons are willing to take risks and open their own business, the concentration of wealth and economic power remains in the hands of a few big businesses. This has social implications, such as widespread poverty. Although the economic growth and development of a country depends largely on the productivity of its human resources, there must also be dynamic **entrepreneurs**. Entrepreneurs play a key role in an economy because they look for new ways to create products or do business.

More specifically, **entrepreneurial drive** and **activity** can promote Caribbean development in several ways:

• By creating employment (direct and indirect) and reducing the high unemployment levels in the Caribbean. For example, hotel projects in the Caribbean generate many local jobs.
• By meeting the growing demand for goods and services, thereby increasing **national income**, and paying taxes such as corporation taxes, which assist in funding government social services and programmes.

The reward for enterprise is profit, which can then attract FDI into the region, such as foreign businessmen investing in hotel-related business enterprises.

When entrepreneurial businesses grow at a fast rate, they often need to look to new areas, such as small towns rather than cities, to establish or extend their enterprises. This contributes to the development of peripheral regions and results in more balanced regional development.

Entrepreneurial drive and activity can support attempts made by Caribbean governments to reverse the unfavourable trade balance, with more goods imported than exported, by reducing dependence on foreign imports through establishment of **import substitution industries**. At the same time, the large-scale export of locally manufactured goods can earn much-needed foreign exchange for the country.

Spin-off business projects can be created. For instance, the construction of a hotel generates opportunities for small construction sub-contractors and perhaps sources of green energy, and opportunities for food vendors to profit from sales to construction workers.

Innovation has the potential to make Caribbean industries more competitive internationally. For example, through innovation in energy, the region's soaring energy bill and heavy reliance on fossil fuels could be decreased. Moves in this direction include the pioneering work of James Husbands on solar powered water heaters, which has reduced the dependence on electric heaters. Also, innovations in using solar panels to generate sufficient amounts of electricity could serve to lessen the dependence on oil.

Governments can assist and support **entrepreneurship** and small businesses by providing financial incentives such as grants and loans with low rates of interest. In Trinidad and Tobago tax concessions are offered for companies with approved small-business status. while in Jamaica shopper 'free zones' have been formed to assist struggling small businesses and vendors, with little or no tax paid to the state.

As well as financial support, government schemes and agencies together with NGOs from many sectors help to boost entrepreneurship by providing technical assistance, research and prototype development, secretarial services and mentorship.

Did You Know?

In Barbados, the aim of the Youth Entrepreneurial Scheme is to aid the launch of young self-employed innovators. Channelling the entrepreneurial qualities of youths who are unemployed onto an alternative path via self-employment can also help to reduce social tensions and unrest among those who may display deviant or criminal behaviours.

Conversely, restrictive or complex government regulations and policies can create or augment an adverse business environment for small entrepreneurial start-ups. Many policies are geared towards larger firms and not individual entrepreneurs, despite these making up the majority of businesses in the Caribbean. Export promotion within CARICOM is currently weak and there is little access to regional and international markets without high customs fees and tariffs.

Economic constraints can include factors such as a high cost of raw materials and productive equipment, which often have to be imported, high overhead costs and a variable price for the final goods or service. Low staff productivity and a high level of competition from low quality/cheap imports from the Far East can also put the business at risk of bankruptcy.

Global Conditions

As small, open economies, Caribbean countries are highly exposed to changes in international economic conditions. These can be changes in international markets, prices and interest rates. Most economic activities in the Caribbean are affected by **globalisation**. CARICOM and the CARICOM Single Market and Economy (CSME) represent a regional response to this.

Global conditions can hinder Caribbean development:

- Small economies or very small domestic markets can make countries economically dependent on foreign trade and overseas markets and investors. Foreign investment may be significant for employment in the short to medium term, but does not necessarily strengthen the institutions of a country for sustainable development.
- Changing international prices for goods and services determine Caribbean countries' economic fortunes. Many countries are dependent on imported goods from the metropole or Far East. In addition, economies dependent on commodity exports, for example Trinidad with its large oil and gas industry and smaller islands that depend on monoculture crops such as sugar or bananas, go from boom to bust depending on the international prices of their products. This volatility in important industries damages the long-term development of small economies because it increases risks and therefore deters investment in all other businesses.

Key Term

National income – goods and services produced in a country as well as those that are imported.

Quick Fact

Social services, including hospital services, education, health, entertainment, road repairs and construction, all benefit from sources of government income such as corporation taxes (usually 25–35% of profits) and licence fees paid by power and telecommunications companies.

Key Term

Import substitution industries – industries that reduce the dependence of a country on imported goods. An example is the manufacture of Carib Beer, which reduces the quantity of foreign brands imported.

Key Terms

Globalisation – the process of the economies and cultures of different countries coming together on a worldwide scale.

Making the Connection

Chapter 14 'Globalisation and Development' looks specifically at globalisation and its impacts on the Caribbean region in more detail.

- International interest rates, which are heavily influenced by the monetary policies of the world's largest economies, can also fluctuate suddenly, creating difficulties for indebted Caribbean governments and businesses when the rates increase.
- Increased international competition can have a negative impact on regional tourism. Tourism is also an industry heavily dependent on external factors: recessions in Europe and the USA and concerns about global security have resulted in a decline in tourist numbers to the Caribbean.
- Some Caribbean manufacturing businesses have found themselves unable to compete in their export markets with products from very low-wage 'emerging economies' of Asia, and, at the same time, have difficulties competing against powerful industrialised countries with far larger production capacity.
- Likewise, domestic producers can be put out of business by cheaper imports, or by consumers' preference for imported brand-name goods or foreign products.
- The growth of consumerism, fostered by globalisation, has consequences for areas such as the environment with a growth in vehicle ownership.
- Technological advances introduced from abroad in traditional manufacturing industries tend to replace all but skilled workers. Lack of opportunities, however, mean that many skilled workers migrate to where they are properly compensated, leading to a loss of skilled labour on the local market.

Global conditions can promote Caribbean development:

- By opening opportunities for Caribbean countries to pool their productive resources to capture new and wider markets globally.
- By providing opportunities for Caribbean businesses and entrepreneurs to respond to global demand for and interest in certain types of goods and products (e.g. the manufacture and export of 'natural' foodstuffs and beauty products, Caribbean music and associated merchandise).
- There is a wider choice of goods and services generally, which can be beneficial if the goods are produced locally. An increase in the availability of cheaper goods and services can benefit customers.
- Fewer international barriers provides avenues for employment and other economic opportunities for Caribbean nationals outside the region.
- Foreign investment often brings with it significant and much-needed technological know-how and support.

Tourism

The tourist industry is a major aspect of the economy of many Caribbean countries, which earns foreign exchange and other revenues for Caribbean governments. It has therefore been used extensively to promote development of infrastructure and social services.

The Contribution of Tourism to Development

1. **Employment:** tourism creates both direct and indirect employment for Caribbean people. Direct employment in tourism includes jobs in the hotel sector, restaurants, clubs and tourist attractions. Indirect employment is created via links with industries that support tourism, such as agriculture, transportation, construction, distribution of items to hotels and restaurants.

2. **Government revenue:** includes berthing fees for cruise liners and landing taxes for aircraft, taxes on goods and services bought by tourists, taxes on businesses in the tourist industry, head and departure taxes on visitors, import duties on items brought into the country for the tourist industry and taxes on wages of those employed in the industry. With this revenue, the government provides services such as health, sanitation and education.

3. **Direct foreign investment** in building hotels and marinas; opening businesses such as shops and malls increases trade and commerce.

4. **Development of infrastructure:** revenue generated is used to upgrade and construct roads, ports, airports, shopping centres, transport systems, parks, telecommunications and housing. Old and historic buildings are repaired. These developments improve general quality of life.

5. **Government expenditure:** Infrastructure, for example expanding airports and improving water supply and sewage disposal, not only benefits tourists but residents as well. These programmes encourage community tourism based around smaller family-managed hotels away from large resorts, which in turn promotes broader improvements in these systems.

6. **Stimulation of local cultural expression, performance and knowledge:** the tourist industry has produced opportunities for cultural expression for local people, for example, dance, music, food and craft. Caribbean nationals have also developed cultural and historic attractions, such as heritage trails, museums, historic buildings and plantations, to appeal to particular types of tourists. Cultural development occurs through learning about the local culture as local sites become tourist attractions and locals train as tourist guides. Establishing festivals (for instance, Carnival, CARIFEST) that attract tourists at specific times of the year promotes year-round employment for tourism workers.

Did You Know?

As well as cultural/heritage tourism, other types of tourism available in the Caribbean include:

- **Sports tourism:** Tourists have an opportunity to participate in land-based and marine-based sporting activities.

- **Ecotourism, or nature tourism:** Many tourists are attracted to the Caribbean by the sandy beaches, warm temperature and natural landscapes. Eco-resorts have been established in Belize and nature reserves set up in several locations, such as the Asa Wright Nature Centre, Trinidad. Tourism provides an incentive for the protection of such areas.

- **Cruise tourism:** Cruise tourists are exposed to different locations across the region. A potential benefit of this is that it will inspire people to return to their favourite and stay there longer.

Quick Fact

Figures produced by the World Travel and Tourism Council show the 2014 direct contribution of travel and tourism to the Caribbean region as 4.5% of GDP (US$ 16.1 billion) while the total contribution – including indirect (such as food, IT services or government infrastructure spending) and induced (such as clothing and equipment purchased by direct and indirect employees' contributions) – is calculated as 14.6% of regional GDP (US$ 51.9 billion).

Quick Fact

As of 2015, there were 22 UNESCO World Heritage Sites located in the Caribbean region, ranging from areas of natural beauty and importance (Blue and John Crow Mountains, Jamaica; Belize Barrier Reef Reserve System) to places of architectural and historical significance (Brimstone Hill Fortress National Park, St Kitts; Historic Bridgetown and its Garrison, Barbados).

Making the Connection

Sports tourism is investigated in Chapter 16 'Contributions of Sport to Development'.

7. Valuable **foreign exchange** can be generated for many Caribbean counties, which can be used to purchase or import foreign goods and repay international loans.

8. **A multiplier effect:** for example, through linkages to the local agricultural sector if tourists consume or demand local produce.

9. **An incentive to address social issues:** the desire to promote and develop tourism can provide governments with an added and urgent impetus to tackle social issues such as high crime rates and poverty.
   Tourism can also have a negative effect on Caribbean development:
   - It can result in great harm to the environment through waste management issues and damage to fragile ecosystems in countries where environmental monitoring and conservation is minimal.
   - There is a risk it could impinge on remote areas with significant numbers of indigenous people in countries such as Guyana and Belize, where it may negatively impact on their lifestyles, sacred rights and social structures.
   - There is capital flight due to profits being sent overseas to foreign investors and hotel-owners, or economic leakage of foreign exchange when money is spent on importing foreign food or materials for tourists.
   - Local resources and economic activities are used less for the development and benefit of local communities and more for the benefit of tourists; for example, investment in golf courses rather than affordable housing or agriculture.
   - Hotels and golf courses are frequently constructed on prime agricultural land, thus decreasing the amount of land utilised for producing food. This has negative repercussions for food security.
   - The import bill is high in Caribbean countries that import food for tourists. Hotels, in particular, may import a large quantity of foods to satisfy the preferences or tastes of their clients rather than support local agriculture.
   - The land where tourist resort facilities are constructed or developed becomes very costly and, in most cases, unaffordable for local residents.
   - The tourist industry can offer higher salaries and many workers leave the agricultural sector, resulting in an inadequate labour supply in that sector.
   - Governments are forced to invest heavily in infrastructure, such as roadway development, communication and historical sites, in an effort to encourage consistent support for the industry. In these instances, this leads to a decline in other sectors (such as health, public transport) because they are ignored, leading to the welfare of the locals being sacrificed for the national or regional good.

Challenges Presented by Tourism

Tourism presents two major challenges:

1. How to increase its benefits by increasing the volume of tourists and retained earnings generated.

2. How to minimise its costs, mainly economic; for example, by the inflating property prices.
   These challenges manifest themselves in the following ways:

- A lack of finance, or capital, and infrastructure to promote tourism, develop sites and maintain properties exists generally in the Caribbean.
- A broad range of rooms and hotel rates are needed to increase the volume of tourists by catering to different needs and budgets.
- Marketing, which is vital, requires a high degree of spending, which some governments, tourist organisations and hoteliers do not possess. While there are benefits to a regional approach to marketing, a challenge is to persuade tourists that each Caribbean country is unique.
- There is inadequate training provision in the region and a lack of trained personnel. This means some reliance on foreign institutions for training and the employment of foreigners to ensure the skilled and proficient work force required for a successful tourist industry.
- Heavy reliance on tourism for employment, and its seasonal nature, can create problems.
- An inadequate water supply and poor infrastructure can be an issue. The tourist industry needs a reliable and available supply of portable water that is protected from natural disasters such as floods or hurricanes. Therefore, countries must invest in water storage and purification systems.
- A natural or man-made disaster can adversely affect the tourist industry. Also, the Zika virus outbreak in 2015 in Dominica and The Bahamas had some effect on reduced visitor arrivals.
- The tourist industry is vulnerable to global conditions and any problems in the economy in Europe or North America could result in its failure. Many airlines are foreign owned and a shutdown of unprofitable routes can lead to a further drop in arrivals.
- Global terrorism may discourage people from travelling due to concerns about security or delays caused by security checks.
- Lack of direct air access to some Caribbean countries from major tourist markets results in difficulties for organising airlines to bring passengers in sufficient numbers. This can be because there are no scheduled carriers servicing the route or airports are too small to accommodate large aircraft.
- Emerging destinations that provide similar experiences at competitive prices, and are closer to traditional markets, pose challenges. There are emerging destinations also within the region. The challenge here is to ensure that these countries benefit from tourism without having a negative impact on the economies of those countries where tourism is already established.
- Non-standardisation of policies, regulations and fees across the region can promote intra-regional competition. For example, a lack of standardised fees and taxes paid by cruise operators when they dock their cruise ships can result in them looking for another, cheaper destination.
- Tourism is associated with negative social effects such as an increase in the sex trade, prostitution, illegal drugs, gambling and the spread of diseases such as HIV/AIDS.
- Recently there has been a high level of crime against tourists. The challenge is not only to provide adequate security, but also to deal with the issues which lead to crime. There have also been incidents of discrimination and racism perpetrated by tourists against locals.

Quick Fact

The CTO, in partnership with the Caribbean Hotel and Tourism Association, owns the Caribbean Tourism Development Company, a marketing and business development entity dedicated to promoting the Caribbean brand worldwide.

Key Term

Sustainable tourism – an approach in which all aspects of tourism (such as activities, programmes or policies) are environmentally, socio-culturally and economically sustainable and balanced. It promotes linkages to other sectors, such as agriculture and fisheries, manufacturing and services of all kinds to increase the added value to national economies.

Key Term

Technology – refers to improved techniques and processes of doing things. These can include machinery as well as software and business methods that add to efficiency and cost effectiveness or that better satisfy human needs and solve problems.

Some ways to overcome these challenges are:

- governments establishing and working with investors on programmes and initiatives that support sustainable development, such as the ecotourism sites being developed in Guyana and Dominica. Initially this may prove costly, but would be profitable in the long run;
- planners and government agencies committed to environmental protection and conservation, especially in the face of big business interests, so that the environment, including the marine environment, only suffers minimal damage, if any;
- offering diversified economic opportunities so that the tourist is not viewed as the only source of foreign exchange. Hotels should also diversify so that they have different activities to rely on when there is low occupancy.

Caribbean Tourism Organisation (CTO)

The CTO is the Caribbean's tourism development agency. Its aim is to position the Caribbean as the most desirable, year-round, warm-weather destination, with the slogan 'Leading Sustainable Tourism – One Sea, One Voice, One Caribbean'.

The role of the CTO in promoting or contributing to regional development:

- Monitors the industry's performance in the Caribbean region and collaborates with other regional tourist organisations, such as the Caribbean Hotel and Tourism Association, and hospitality training institutions.
- Provides a reliable body of knowledge via data collection, collation and research to planners, developers, policy makers, tourism practitioners and other stakeholders. It hosts conferences, meetings and workshops, publishes newsletters and produces other sources of information for members.
- Encourages member states to promote **sustainable tourism** development to harness the most effective use of natural, cultural, social and financial resources for national development on an equitable and sustainable basis, to provide a unique experience for tourists and to improve quality of life through partnerships between government, the private sector and communities. In this, it also has an input into and manages projects that address resources utilisation and preservation, energy efficiency and climate change.
- Markets the Caribbean as a single destination and serves to create a single voice internationally by promoting a strong Caribbean brand.
- Provides education and training for tourism workers by making a strong input into human resource management and education.
- Develops and promotes regional travel tourism programmes to and within the Caribbean.

Technological Factors

Use of Technology

The availability and use of **technology** in the Caribbean, as elsewhere, is a key factor in development. The Caribbean's economic and human development has been shaped by technologies over history. From the windmill used in the sugar industry to the computer, the Caribbean has seen a growth in its use. Modern technology started with the use of science and engineering applied to human problems. The most important technological changes at present, in terms of their effects on economic and human development, are in information and communications technology (ICT). The use of technology can have both negative and positive effects.

The use of technology promotes Caribbean development in the following ways:

- Creates new products and services, which influence economic growth and hence economic development. A good example of this is in communications with improved mobile phone services and high-speed and reliable internet. A 2009 World Bank report acknowledged that these are a major characteristic of economic growth and job creation.
- Helps Caribbean governments to devise strategies to solve problems. In island countries, the use of ICT is of great value.

Did You Know?

Mobile phone services and internet across the Caribbean have revolutionised personal and business transactions throughout the region:

- Mobile phone services can be used to access the internet, send and receive email and for internet banking, even to make online purchases.

- The internet can also promote Caribbean integration, and hence regional development, by enabling access to regional websites and newspapers, various government websites and the purchase of goods and services across the region.

- Improved communication across the region aids cooperation for business, economics, finance and response to disasters.

- Commercial and financial transactions are increasingly made using new forms of information technology, such as telebanking, internet banking, automated teller machines (ATM), debit and credit cards and mobile payments.

More students and workers are becoming trained in ICT as a basic requirement for work, study and leisure, and ICT is increasingly used to disseminate information and deliver online tuition.

Access to an increased information about products and services facilitates sound purchasing decisions.

The use of technology can also hinder Caribbean development in some ways. Today, stress is placed on efficiency/productivity that holds a competitive edge. This involves downsizing and automation, such as in the car production and garment manufacturing industries where automated processes have replaced the traditional, human-resourced production line. This leads to both an increase in unemployment and a preference for workers with technical skills who can adjust to rapid changes in technology.

There are several challenges to be faced regarding the use of technology in the region. There is still low internet usage across the Caribbean due to the high cost of personal computers and the patchy provision of high speed broadband services. Concerns about internet security and the risk of fraud and identity theft can also be an issue. In addition, dependency on foreign technology can stifle Caribbean creativity and innovation. These issues need to be addressed for further development to occur.

Quick Fact

The CSME is using ICT to establish online communities, share information and provide online training, thus assisting in economic growth and poverty reduction, provision of affordable healthcare and education.

Environmental Factors

Natural and Human-made Disasters

The region is susceptible to a variety of **natural or environmental hazards** caused by extreme climatic and geological impacts, such as earthquakes, volcanic eruptions, tsunamis, floods, landslides, drought and storms. They are hazards that can have devastating effects on the economies and people of the Caribbean, and have the potential to develop into **disasters**. Some of the environmental hazards are man-made and this is a result of mismanagement of the environment; for example, flooding caused by over farming and deforestation in Haiti, Guyana or Suriname. Industrial accidents, such as chemical or oil spills, pollution and soil erosion where improper farming techniques are used, are also examples of man-made disasters. Caribbean countries, with varying resources, skills and infrastructure, differ in their capacity to address the impact of disasters.

The impact of natural disasters has serious consequences for the economies affected, as they undo years of development: humans are injured or lose their lives and property is damaged. Migration is a common response and many families are consequently broken up. Poverty makes coping with these events and their consequences even more difficult because of a lack of cash savings and health and property insurance.

Disasters hinder development in the following ways:

- They can retard development in that they destroy raw materials or natural resources required for economic growth. These materials and resources are scarce in many parts of the Caribbean.
- They can easily have a negative impact on tourism, on which many Caribbean economies rely.
- Preparation for, and recovery from, such disasters can cost large amounts of money. Infrastructure is destroyed and this sets back economic growth by causing losses to businesses and halting many development projects to focus on rebuilding. For example, in 2015 Dominica was hit by Tropical Storm Erika and The Bahamas by Hurricane Dorian in 2019, setting back economic growth and halting many development projects in order to focus on rebuilding in both countries. This in turn increases unemployment and poverty and reduces productivity.
- They can cause disruption to water and electricity supplies, which uses up a country's emergency reserves. There are also risks of disease from contaminated water.

Due to the region's vulnerability to natural disaster, it has been suggested that disaster preparedness be part of the economic policy of the region and CARICOM established the Caribbean Disaster Emergency Management Agency (CDEMA) in 1991 to coordinate an immediate response to a disaster in a member state. A challenge faced by disaster relief efforts, and especially the supply of financial aid, is to ensure its equitable and proper distribution. In Haiti, for example, there have been problems in the past with government control over aid relief supplies.

Making the Connection

The role of technology as a facilitator of development is also discussed in Chapter 14 'Globalisation and Development'.

Quick Fact

Environmental indicators of development include air and water quality, proper waste management and alternative sources of energy such as solar energy and wind farms.

Quick Fact

The 2010 earthquake in Haiti killed about 250,000 persons. Because the country is economically poor, and so little or no development can occur, many of the population were still living in tents when Hurricane Matthew struck them in 2016.

Making the Connection

Natural hazards are investigated in Chapter 8 'Geographical Phenomena'.

Key Terms

Natural or environmental hazard – an entity in the physical environment that poses a threat or is harmful to humans or other life.

Disaster – an adverse situation or event that overwhelms local capacity and necessitates some form of external assistance.

Cultural Factors

In addition to the factors outlined above, the culture of the Caribbean can also have an impact on the development of the region. Attitudes, beliefs, values, priorities and outlook are all shaped by the experience of being socialised by institutions such as the family, religion, education and the media.

Some examples of how cultural factors can positively affect development include:

- the creation of cultural-based industries, such as in areas of goods, art, food and performance, are ways to showcase and express the unique Caribbean cultural identity. This both enhances a sense of cultural value as well as generating income.

- the celebration of unique Caribbean cultural forms serves to underpin human development and helps foster regional creativity and innovation.

- the role and relevance of education in developing creative thought and expression

- the role of the media in promoting positive images and views of regional cultural identity and achievements as opposed to those that are imported

- the development of a regional as opposed to a nationalistic outlook that can help establish the Caribbean as a whole as a player in the increasingly globalised world.

> **Making the Connection**
>
> Chapter 6 'Characteristics of Society and Culture', Chapter 7 'Identity and Social Formation', Chapter 9 'Societal Institutions', Chapter 10 'Arts and Popular Culture' and Chapter 18 'Roles and Functions of the Mass Media' all look in more detail at cultural factors mentioned in this section.

Making the Connection

Chapter 8 'Geographical Phenomena'

Chapter 12 'Concepts and Indicators of Development'

Chapter 14 'Globalisation and Development'

Exam Tip

'**Discuss**' requires an extended response defining key concepts, giving the facts, exploring related concepts and issues and presenting reasoned arguments. You must use detailed examples, but **not** necessarily draw a conclusion.

Check Your Knowledge

Discuss TWO factors that promote development and TWO factors that hinder development in the Caribbean.

Demonstrate an understanding of the following terms and concepts by defining and using them correctly:

- Caribbean
- development
- other concepts used will vary based on the factors of development selected

You must choose any TWO factors that promote and any TWO factors that hinder development in the Caribbean. You must also show the link between the factors chosen and development.

Here are some examples:

- Popular movements *promote* Caribbean development by:
    - influencing political and social changes by acting as pressure groups
    - demanding transparency and accountability by the government
    - promoting socio-economic development programmes of benefit to citizens, labour, family and the environment
    - making citizens more aware of their rights and duties.
- Tourism *promotes* Caribbean development by:
    - governments using revenue created by tourism to provide social services;
    - bringing in direct foreign investment through construction of hotels, resorts, marinas or malls;
    - promoting development of infrastructure by using revenue generated to construct and upgrade facilities and housing that improve quality of life;
    - improvements in infrastructure that are to the benefit of residents as well as tourism;
    - generating employment, both direct (such as hotels and attractions) and indirect (links to supporting sectors such as agriculture, transportation, construction);
    - stimulating local cultural expression or performance, thus promoting cultural development.

- bringing in foreign exchange, which can be used to purchase or import foreign goods and repay international loans;
- linking to the local agricultural sector, which can supply local produce to hotels and restaurants.

- The distribution of wealth and resources *hinders* Caribbean development by:
  - the historical legacy of uneven distribution of wealth inherited from colonial times;
  - inequalities between rich and poor, with wealth tending to be concentrated in the hands of a few, and increased unemployment, low levels of investment and homelessness and poverty for those at the other end of the scale;
  - increased crime and social unrest can retard economic growth and development as they deter tourists and investors, leading to not only a fall in foreign exchange or revenue, but also a high unemployment rate;
  - disparities in access to and quality of key services such as healthcare;
  - a lack of policies that aim to provide social and economic equalisation for all citizens, creating a barrier to achieving sustainable development;
  - an uneven distribution of natural resources across the region, resulting in countries with limited resources feeling disadvantaged in terms of trading with countries with more.

- Natural and human-made disasters *hinder* Caribbean development through:
  - damage and destruction to human life, property and infrastructure, which can both destroy existing development and retard future development;
  - destruction of scarce raw materials or natural resources; monoculture economies are especially at risk due to lack of diversity;
  - negatively impacting on tourism, a major revenue earner for many Caribbean countries;
  - the high cost of preparation for and recovery from such disasters;
  - disruption to the water and electricity supplies, which uses up a country's emergency reserves;
  - risk of disease from contaminated food and water;
  - social impacts, such as migration after a disaster (such as Montserrat).

A possible conclusion can be a summary of the main points provided in this essay.

Multiple-choice Questions

1. Which of the following represents gender inequality in the Caribbean?

    I.   Few women in politics

    II. Human trafficking

    III. Wage disparity

    A. I only

    B. I and II

    C. I and III

    D. I, II and III

2. Changing class boundaries has promoted Caribbean development in which of the following ways?

    I.   Improving the standard of living of persons in the working class as they become more socially mobile

    II. Harnessing the potential of members of society by providing universal education

    III. A new peasantry of mainly ex-indentures diversifying the economy by introducing additional crops such as rice, cocoa and coffee

A. I and II only

B. I and III only

C. II and III only

D. I, II and III

3. Political ideologies can promote development by:

A. De-sensitising the youths about political issues because they are the future leaders

B. Producing cadres of informed leaders with well-defined goals

C. Supporting cultural imperialism

D. Offering clear guidelines for social and economic diversification

4. Which one of the following is NOT an example of a popular movement?

A. CAFRA

B. WAND

C. CARIFTA

D. Environmental and social justice non-governmental organisations

5. Popular movements can promote Caribbean development in which of the following ways?

I. Acting as a pressure group to foster consciousness of significant social and political issues

II. Making citizens more aware of their human rights and to be treated with equality and equity

III. Stirring up social and political unrests to achieve political and social changes

A. I and II only

B. I and III only

C. II and III only

D. I, II and III

6. Which of the following statements is NOT a way government policies can promote Caribbean development?

A. Investing in foreign businesses to increase long-term employment

B. Improving labour relations

C. Enacting policies aimed at environmental protection and anti-pollution

D. Regulating prices to prevent black markets

7. A characteristic of wealth distribution in the Caribbean is:

A. The middle class are the uneducated members of society

B. The ruling class has experienced low quality housing and unemployment

C. The working class predominantly inherit wealth and authority

D. Many of the working class are prevented from owning businesses

8. One successful way the effect of entrepreneurial drive on the economy of the Caribbean can be increased is by:

A. Creating studios

B. Bringing in stakeholders

C. Encouraging skills training

D. Monitoring start-up costs

9. Caribbean countries can BEST combat adverse global conditions by:

A. Higher wages and taxes

B. Fees and import substitution

C. Diversification and integration

D. Diversification and industrialisation

10. Technology influences human development in the Caribbean in which MAIN way?

A. Many people buy mobile phones

B. Provides time management improvements

C. Brings in experts to tackle ITC related bugs

D. Provides training for locals so they can increase efficiency

11. Which of the following is a major aim of the Caribbean Tourism Organisation?

A. The creation of trade unions for the promotion of hotel workers' rights

B. Negotiations made with governments in building hotels on heritage sites

C. Workshops for human resources to make sure guests have quality service and return

D. Meetings aimed at harmonious partnerships among private sector financial institutions

Chapter 14

Globalisation and Development

After revising this topic, you should be able to:
- define and explain different forms of globalisation;
- describe the facilitators of globalisation and development:
  - World Trade Organization (WTO)
  - Economic Partnership Agreement (EPA)
  - International Monetary Fund (IMF)
  - World Bank
  - transnational organisations
  - technology
  - ideologies: social, gender, economic, political;
- assess and discuss the impact and response to globalisation in terms of:
  - industry and commerce
  - distribution sector
  - labour
  - technology
  - ideology
  - popular movements.

Syllabus Objective

Assess the ways in which globalisation affects development in the region.

Definition and Forms of Globalisation

Globalisation facilitates the connection and interdependence of economies resulting in the world becoming a 'global village'. This means that events occurring in one part of the globe can have a great impact on persons all over the world in a very short space of time. It is a multi-faceted concept. Four main aspects of globalisation are:

1. The social-cultural dimension: this encompasses the coming together and commercialisation of various cultures. Globalisation links different cultures, religions and forms of dress, for example.

2. The economic dimension: this entails **trade liberalisation**, the key facilitator of globalisation.

3. The technological dimension: this comprises the media and communications aspects that deal with a network of wireless technology, 3D, 4D and real time, effectively making the world a 'smaller place' in terms of communication.

4. The environmental dimension: this involves viewing the world's environments as one in which global warming and climate change occur.

Key Terms

Globalisation – the process of the economies and cultures of different countries coming together on a worldwide scale via advances in technology, communications, transport, commerce and trade liberalisation.

Trade liberalisation – the removal of laws and guidelines regulating trade, preferential treatment and the free movement of goods and labour.

Capitalism – an economic and political system in which a country's trade and industry are controlled by private owners for profit, rather than by the state. Capitalism is also characterised by a competitive environment.

At the root of all forms of globalisation is economic globalisation because it involves the advancement of **capitalism** to promote the free movement of trade and commerce. Harnessing market forces to achieve profit is the main force behind globalisation, and for businesses it means that the world has become a global market.

Therefore, to relate the process to economic development, we say globalisation involves the free flow of goods, capital, labour and technology around the world with an increasing dominance of local economies by international financial markets and **transnational corporations (TNCs)**. In a global economy, goods can be produced in many different places and transported anywhere in the world for sale. Of course, more powerful countries have a stronger voice, so they tend to exert more of an influence than smaller countries. The links are in many areas: trade, countries' economies, human culture and language, technology, communications, politics, the environment. Our ideas, foods, clothes and information, as well as migration, are shaped by this interaction with other people from other places. Shops in the Caribbean sell foreign products, such as vehicles manufactured by the Japanese company Toyota, while Caribbean products, such as Jamaican Blue Mountain Coffee, are exported across the world. Tourists travel to and from the Caribbean, investors from outside the region open joint ventures in Caribbean countries and Caribbean people invest overseas.

Drivers of globalisation include:
- communications technology: the internet, mobile phones and email;
- faster and cheaper air, road, sea and railway transport;
- capitalist national and international policies, such as trade liberalisation and liberalisation of **capital markets**.

Globalisation has:
- fostered global interdependence with major impacts on patterns of trade, investment, growth and job destruction/creation;
- created networks for creative and volunteer work;
- created new risks and opportunities;
- placed an increased emphasis on competition, efficiency and productivity;
- heightened the importance of market forces and market expansion as a contributor to economic development;
- made technological revolutions accelerate;
- placed a spotlight on good governance and **macroeconomic** policy;
- promoted the growth of the service industry;
- recognised intellectual property internationally (writers, songwriters, artists, inventors).

There has been much debate on the impact of globalisation on income equality, not just internationally, but also on a regional and national level. Many point to a widening income gap between rich and poor in both industrialised and developing countries, while others perceive more complex trends, such as a narrowing of the gap between industrialised and developing countries in the last years of the 20th century due mainly to exponential growth in Asia.

Key Terms

Transnational corporation (TNC) – also called a multinational corporation (MNC), these terms refer to any corporation or mega business that is registered and operates in more than one country at a time.

Capital market – the part of a financial system concerned with raising capital by dealing in shares, bonds and other long-term investments. International financial markets are now the main sources of international investment, replacing major government donors and development banks.

Key Term

Macroeconomics – the branch of economics concerned with large-scale or general economic factors, such as interest rates, national productivity, price levels, GDP or changes in unemployment.

Facilitators of Globalisation and Development

Figure 14.1 Multilateral agencies: countries A–E pay a quota into a multilateral agency and countries X and Y get loans or technical assistance

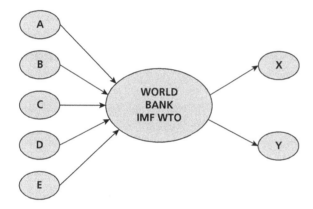

World Trade Organization (WTO)

The WTO, which deals with encouraging and facilitating trade worldwide, has its headquarters in Geneva, Switzerland. As part of a multinational trade agreement, it was formed in 1948 following a meeting of the world's most powerful leaders, including the United States, the UK and Canada, in Bretton Woods in 1944. It was agreed that for world economic growth to occur in the aftermath of World War II there was the need for a body to facilitate trade among countries, so they signed an agreement called the General Agreement on Tariffs and Trade (GATT). Since 1995 this agreement has been an institution called the WTO.

The functions of the WTO are to deal with the rules of trade among nations, handle trade disputes, provide a forum for fair trade negotiations and necessary sanctions, and offer technical assistance to developing countries. Some of the benefits of having such a body are the existence of a set rules governing trade that aid understanding between countries, liberalise trade, and increase income and growth stimulation. The rules can also make governments more transparent as their trade policies are monitored by the WTO.

Did You Know?

The objective of trade liberalisation is market access. To liberalise means to remove the barriers to trade between countries, either in the form of tariffs (taxes on foreign goods) or non-tariff barriers, such as import licences, excessive port fees, labelling requirements or the **payment of subsidies**. Subsidies act as trade barriers because they can reduce prices but still allow producers to make a profit, thus giving an advantage to those that receive them. Because of these types of barrier, free trade is difficult to achieve in reality.

Under WTO regulations, the market access one country grants to another must be automatically extended to all the other members. This can be restricted in certain sectors or activities, such as agriculture, deemed to be not yet ready for full liberalisation. This measure protects small, local industries. No preference should be shown to either local or foreign-owned service providers. This is aimed at providing a level playing field and letting the consumer (market) decide which company will get the business and thereby remain profitable. Unprofitable businesses will be forced to change.

The Impact of the WTO in the Caribbean

- The WTO supports development in the Caribbean, especially, through its efforts in poverty reduction and in the development of infrastructure.
- The challenge to Caribbean exporters is to make goods that are competitively priced for the local and overseas markets. Since 2000, Caribbean agricultural producers have faced competition from cheaper imports of, for instance, poultry, onions, carrots and melons.
- Another problem has been a drop in government revenue because of the reduction of tariffs that can be charged on imports.
- More manpower has to be used to monitor the standard of imported foods and goods so that the public is protected from low quality and the potential spread of disease.
- Through WTO trade policy reviews, Caribbean participants are obliged to maintain fair trade practices according to international standards.

Economic Partnership Agreement (EPA)

The EPA was signed in 2008. It was a joint agreement between 15 CARIFORUM States (CARICOM States and the Dominican Republic) and 27 European Union (EU) states to allow both groups to conform to WTO rules. In the case of the Caribbean the aim was also to facilitate economic growth and job creation.

The Impact of the EPA on the Caribbean

Allowances were made to remove customs duties on each other's goods. However, this could not be equalised because of the difference in levels of development.

Liberalisation of trade in goods meant that EU members could trade in Caribbean agriculture and fisheries: bananas, rice and sugar. Caribbean states bought fish; mainly cod, herring and sardines.

Liberalisation of trade, services and investment allowed for trade-related development cooperation, resulting in an upgrade in the capabilities of the

Key Term

Subsidy payments – the government provides finance to a sector of the economy or an industry to control supply and prices of commodities. For example, farmers may be paid a subsidy to either produce or limit production of certain agricultural commodities.

Caribbean countries' service providers in areas such as tourism, finance and business. Guaranteeing access to large EU markets has facilitated growth in the amount of services exported from the Caribbean. Travel was now facilitated to EU countries for Caribbean artistes, musicians and any other cultural practitioner. Other services could be provided, such as international law practice, nursing, fashion modelling, chef de cuisine and architectural services. The benefit of improving the environment through investment in Caribbean service sectors.

The EPA has been criticised by several CARICOM countries, who believe that it cannot really help in repositioning the Caribbean as a primary producer. Caribbean states with small economies have to compete with highly industrialised countries that have more resources and capital, while the Caribbean is still heavily reliant on these countries for financial and technical support.

International Monetary Fund (IMF)

The IMF is an international lending institution that was formed in 1945 by the UN after the Bretton Woods Conference. It aids globalisation and development by ensuring stability in the international monetary sector with regard to exchange rates of currencies. A stable financial state is important in avoiding crisis or uncertainty so that investors are happy to spend their money, resulting in economic growth, the maintenance of high living standards and a reduction in global poverty. It does this through monitoring the economic and financial policies of all 188 member countries. The governing of the fund is related to each country's position in the global economy. Each country pays a quota into the fund depending on what they can afford, and then these subscriptions are used to lend to other countries.

The IMF lends money to countries with financial problems – their expenditure is more than their revenue, or they have high international debts (balance of payment issues). These loans are short term because they must usually be paid back in less than five years. To help stabilise the economy, certain conditions concerning policy changes are imposed. These are called Structural Adjustment Policies (SAPs) and can cover:

- trade policy, such as removal of import quotas;
- tax reform, such as Value Added Tax (VAT);
- exchange rate control;
- austerity measures (higher taxes and lower government spending);
- currency devaluation to reduce balance of payments deficits;
- monetary policies, such as interest rates on savings in banks;
- product price control, such as removal of subsidies, food price rises;
- privatisation of state-owned industries and resources.

Quick Fact

IMF loans are intended to help countries resolve balance of payment problems (i.e. their international debts) while World Bank loans focus more on funding specific development projects.

The Impact of IMF in the Caribbean

Jamaica went to the IMF for a loan in the face of economic problems in 1977. The IMF called for some serious belt tightening, including privatisation of 18 public companies, the contracting out of several public sector services, currency devaluation and tariff reduction. Other Caribbean countries, such as Trinidad and Tobago, Guyana and Barbados, also received loans from the IMF during the 1980s and 1990s.

Several external factors, including the war in Iraq, the 2001 9/11 attack in the USA and the global recession, have had a negative impact on the Caribbean economies, especially with a decrease in tourist arrivals. Natural disasters have also affected several Caribbean economies. Since 2008, IMF loans have been taken out by Belize, Dominica, Grenada, St Lucia and St Kitts and Nevis. In 2010, Jamaica again needed a loan due to high foreign debt caused by the global economic recession. There was an agreement to privatise some state-owned businesses, but the social welfare programmes were continued, including the school feeding programme.

While repayment of these loans has proved difficult in the short term, strict monitoring is carried out to ensure national development in the long term, with an increased GDP. Some areas that need addressing are too many tax exclusions related to VAT and improved effectiveness in government by restructuring.

Did You Know?

The SAPs can be difficult and unpopular for a government who has to break the bad news to the population. Four main policies that have been introduced into the Caribbean are the devaluation of the national currency to increase exports, cutting social welfare programmes to reduce government spending, the possibility of job cuts or lay-offs in the public service and a pay cut or wage freeze throughout the private and public sectors.

Some negative impacts of the implementation of SAPs in the Caribbean include:
- a high debt burden on the economy;
- low levels of capital investment and private capital being moved out of the region (capital flight);
- a large price rise in consumer goods;
- cutbacks in further education.

The World Bank

The World Bank has the responsibility of issuing loans and credit options, trust funds and grants to assist in economic growth and poverty reduction. It works to facilitate the transfer of capital from rich countries to the poor countries of Africa, Asia and South America.

The World Bank comprises two development institutions: The International Bank for Reconstruction and Development (IBRD) and the International Development Association (IDA). The Caribbean gets aid from the IBRD, which helps the middle-income and less developed countries. It is open to its 187 member countries only, not to individuals. The headquarters are in Washington, USA. The bank began in 1945, and at first its focus was to finance the reconstruction of European countries after World War II.

Poverty alleviation was initially only done through loans to improve infrastructure, but has now branched into other social areas. Its stated aims are to end poverty (measured at below 3% living on US$1.90 per day) within a generation or by 2030, and to promote shared prosperity by increasing the income of the bottom 40% in every country.

The Impact of the World Bank in the Caribbean

Projects undertaken by the World Bank include: road, communications, power stations, water supplies, rural development, heath care and the use of ICT in education. The easy terms of the loans make them attractive to countries. The interest rate, or the cost of borrowing the money, is usually low as the repayment period may be as long as 40 years. Countries can alleviate poverty and not get into debt, which condemns future generations to high repayments. The bank may make the loan conditional on some aspect of social or human rights that may be lacking, such as becoming a democratic state or reducing corruption. It also provides analytical and advisory services and assists with **capacity building**. The World Bank and United Nations Development Programme (UNDP) facilitated the setting up of the Caribbean Development Bank (CDB) in 1970 to assist the region.

In 2011, St Lucia was approved a loan to repair Hurricane Tomas damage to the infrastructure and improve the island's vulnerability to disasters. In 2012, Haiti received loans to improve maternal and child health. In 2013, Antigua and Barbuda qualified for loans towards public sector reform through temporary employment and training programmes.

Transnational Organisations

Transnational corporations (TNCs) or multinational corporations (MNCs) are huge or mega businesses that operate across the globe with headquarters on every continent and employing many people at various branches around the world. The main headquarters is usually in a metropolitan or developed country such as the USA, the UK, France, Germany or Japan. These companies have huge domestic markets, so they can sell many products with low-cost mass production, low-cost mass advertising, low prices and global brand recognition or standards. Some examples are Coca Cola, Microsoft, Facebook, Apple and Burger King.

These organisations are business enterprises set up to make a profit. To ensure they are profitable they can move parts of their operation to regions where they can gain an advantage in their business. They are attracted to countries with a cheap labour force and a supply of raw materials where they can run manufacturing units and research into new product development. Tax breaks and lower labour costs offered by the Caribbean make the region an attractive source of investment or a good production location.

TNCs, which rely heavily on economies of scale, are fully integrated in controlling finance, markets and technology. In fact, they are usually technology driven. Key to their survival and growth are strategic takeovers or buyouts of other, smaller businesses that compete for customers in the marketplace. Another common strategy for expansion is to provide **foreign direct investment (FDI)** in companies. In this way, they accrue some of the profits of the company. This is good for both the company and the country where it is located because the TNC can provide needed capital. Typical areas of investment in the Caribbean are shipping, call centres and hotels. TNCs can also contribute to activities in the local community, such as sports and cultural festivals. The Irish-owned and Caribbean-based communications TNC, Digicel, has been a key sponsor of the West Indies cricket team. However, TNCs have also been criticised for exploitation of workers, poor labour practices, cultural clashes and foreign management that leads to economic leakage.

Technology

Technological globalisation occurs via media and communications, facilitating the shrinking of the world into a global village. Due to the

Key Term

Capacity building – a long-term process in which the resource capabilities of a country (human, technological, natural, scientific, institutional) are maximised by understanding the inherent obstacles to advancement and making the changes that will lead to the achievement of development goals.

Making the Connection

The role of the CDB in the region is examined in Chapter 15 'The Integration Movement'.

Quick Fact

Transnational corporations attempt to incorporate and reflect the culture of the region where they have established business. For example, KFC offers meals such as the Curry Rice Bowl on its menu in The Bahamas and Jamaica.

Key Term

Foreign direct investment (FDI) – a long-term investment in a company that is located in a different country from that in which the investor is based.

introduction of cable, internet, television, mobile phones and computers, globalisation has had a profound effect on other aspects of societies, such as their culture, identity, commerce and trade. Modern technology has increased both the speed of and how global communication occurs. Today, satellite transmissions have linked the Caribbean with other countries. This means international programmes, especially from the US, are accessible in the Caribbean and contribute to cultural diversity.

The internet and mobile technology have hastened globalisation. Access to smart mobile phone services and high-speed and reliable internet are features of economic growth and job creation. Mobile phone service providers such as Digicel provide the most modern global technology.

Internet across the Caribbean has also completely revolutionised education and business transactions. The University of the West Indies facilitates distance learning and online education with students in various parts of the globe taking part in online class sessions. Video conferencing and cyber consultations are also facilitated. Caribbean companies can access the global market using the internet and can market their products anywhere in the world.

Mobile phone services can be used globally to access the internet, send and receive email, for internet banking and to make online purchases such as e-tickets for air travel. The internet promotes the purchase of goods and services across the region without the need for cash or cheques.

Ideologies: Social, Gender, Economic, Political

Globalisation is an **ideology** that promotes the view that all social, economic and political activities must be liberalised to facilitate free movement of labour and trade. However, critics have argued that common social, economic and political activities are developed in richer industrialised countries, which have a strong influence over the ideologies of less wealthy nations, such as those in the Caribbean, through institutions including the mass media or financial and aid institutions, such as the IMF, the WTO and the World Bank.

Social ideologies

These include ideas about social equality and rights. They can differ across countries, but where there is commonality, such as in areas of equal opportunities, the roles of social institutions and the environment, it can create a connection and help break down barriers.

Many of the social institutions of the Caribbean are derived from models established under colonialism. The justice and legal system, including the law codes, of the English-speaking Caribbean, for example, is very close to that of the UK, and are governed by principles very similar to those that govern the systems of many industrialised Western nations, such as the USA. These links and similarities help facilitate the globalisation process.

Gender Ideologies

Gender ideologies relate to the role of women in society. The predominant global ideology associated with this is feminism, an international movement that seeks to achieve equality between the genders in all aspects of life: in rights, freedoms, opportunities and so on.

Economic and Political Ideologies

In 1948, the formation of GATT, after the end of World War II, underlined the division of political and economic thought into two main ideologies on economic and political issues.

The Soviet Union, with Russia at its centre, and its allies in the East believed in the communist philosophy of a centrally planned economy and state political control of a one-party state. Their economies were closed and they traded only among themselves. Other countries, including the USA, Canada, Japan and the industrialised countries of Western Europe, believed in the **market economy** and political democracy. Here, wealth was in the hands of private individuals as opposed to those of the state. This resulted in an intense conflict known as the Cold War between West and East, especially in the 1960s and 1970s, when each side attempted to attain influence over developing countries that had recently achieved independence and required an economic and political structure to achieve development.

The end of the Cold War was heralded by the collapse of the Soviet economy and the political break-up of the Soviet Union in 1991. In the late 20th century, the communist bloc faced many challenges with the global recession. This led to economic collapse among many communist and socialist countries, and popular discontent led to the collapse of many of the political regimes. Aid was sought, but there were strings attached; the terms of the proposed IMF rescue programmes involved the adoption of a liberalised economic model and political democracy.

The prevalent economic ideology is therefore based around free trade and open markets, and political democracy is the political system favoured by the foreign policies of powerful Western countries, particularly the US. Political reform, including moves towards democracy, is often a condition of financial aid from the IMF or World Bank.

The place of government in the management of economies has been much debated. Market fundamentalists, or advocates of **neoliberalism**, accept no external interference with the mechanism of the open market. However, others argue that, as the purpose of markets is to generate wealth, with no concern for collateral impacts, there exists an important role for governments to intervene where necessary. They highlight the significance for governments currently in the process of economic and social development to ensure the benefits are felt as widely as possible, especially regarding social concerns and needs, such as poverty reduction, environmental protection and labour rights, to name a few.

Impact and Response to Globalisation

Globalisation has had both a positive and negative impacts on Caribbean countries. These must be put in their proper context of the vulnerability and small size of the Caribbean states and the historic dependency of the region on wealthier and industrialised countries, particularly the ex-colonial powers. It should also be noted that the various stages of development of Caribbean states have led to different responses to globalisation.

Making the Connection

Feminism in the Caribbean is discussed in Chapter 17 'Intellectual Traditions'.

Key Term

Market economy – an economic system in which economic decisions and the pricing of goods and services are driven by the market, leading to increased productivity. Government intervention or central planning is minimal.

Did You Know?

The Cold War was a conflict which began in the mid-1940s, after the end of World War II, and ended in 1991 with the collapse of the Soviet Union. It was a clash of divergent beliefs and ideology: the USA advocated capitalism and the USSR advocated communism. These differences were the foundation of the protracted international power struggle as both superpowers sought dominance to expand worldwide by seizing every opportunity presented to it.

Key Term

Neoliberalism – an economic and political theory that views market mechanisms as the most efficient allocator of resources and driver behind economic decisions.

Figure 14.2 Some advantages and disadvantages of the Caribbean vis-à-vis globalisation

Advantages	Disadvantages
It is for the most part democratic with adherence to a system of laws, which conditions help attract investment	Small domestic markets, which make the achievement of economies of scale difficult
It has a relatively high level of education compared with other developing regions	Small domestic markets, which make the achievement of economies of scale difficult
It is to a large extent English-speaking, the language of most international commerce and communication, and is in close proximity to the US, the largest single market	A small resource base in terms of skills and natural resources; slowness or inability to adapt to the ever changing economic environment; vulnerability to natural hazards can cause loss of resources
It has been following economic liberalisation policies since the early 1990s, including reduction or elimination of capital controls	A high dependence on a small number of exports to limited markets coupled with a high dependence on imports, especially on imported energy
The relatively small size of the individual economies requires a correspondingly relatively small capital investment to stimulate economic growth and development	It lies outside established trading routes, making international transportation costly
Likewise, a relatively small increase in exports can have a large positive effect on per capita GDP	Small production units and economies vulnerable to economic shocks, which have adverse effects, even causing a rise in poverty; for example, the region is vulnerable to oil shocks, which will likely intensify as a result of increased global energy demands

Some view advantages, or positive impacts, of globalisation on the region as the following:

- An opportunity for Caribbean states to pool their productive resources in order to capture a wider global market beyond historic economic relationships.
- Increased availability of goods and services from both traditional sources, such as the metropoles, and newer, emerging Asian producers; under the terms of trade permits, large quantities of goods can be imported into the Caribbean at low prices.
- Providing potential new markets for goods and services produced in the Caribbean; one major potential growth area, given the location of the region, is in 'weightless' products such as IT expertise and innovation.
- Providing avenues of employment and economic opportunities for Caribbean nationals outside the region; this has led to improved standards of living in the Caribbean through remittances.
- Access to international financial markets through the removal of capital controls, which has increased the flow of external resources to the region; FDI often brings with it technological expertise.
- Transfer of technology that occurs between more technologically advanced countries and the Caribbean; for example, there is now widespread use of technology for financial transactions, and use of technology can also aid in making small-scale decentralised production in goods and services competitive.

On the other side, the following can be presented as disadvantages or negative impacts:

- Capital leakage to where the TNCs remit their profits; this, along with outflow of foreign exchange to buy foreign goods, can lead to currency devaluation and poverty.
- The imposition of first world ideology and cultural practices on Caribbean countries amounts to cultural imperialism.
- The weakness of the Caribbean in trade negotiations is reflected in the unequal outcomes that result from the trade liberalisation process.
- A continuation of the historical dependency on the metropole through preferential trading terms via the EPA, which can stifle impetus to establish new markets.
- The flooding of local markets by cheap foreign-produced goods, from Asia for example, make local products unavailable and so reduce consumer choice.
- The already limited export market for Caribbean products is further reduced because globalisation favours richer and more industrialised countries that have much larger productive capacities than the small Caribbean states.
- Local businesses that cannot compete in a liberalised environment are forced to close down; for example, car assembly in the Caribbean has ceased in the wake of easy access to imported second-hand vehicles.
- A lack of government regulation, controls and negotiation on how FDI is set up can mean that some investment does not amount to a long-term commitment to the region. Some TNCs, particularly food and hotel chains, may increase employment in the short or medium term, but do little or nothing to promote sustainable development.
- Heavy reliance on FDI and other forms of foreign investment can overexpose the region to global financial variations and crises.
- The introduction of technology leads to automation and downsizing of the manufacturing sector. Employment can also be limited to those who possess the necessary technical skills.
- The need for a cheap labour force and a tendency to exploit the labour market; especially women, who receive low wages compared with men. There has been particular criticism of labour practices in the EPZs.
- High labour mobility means TNCs and MNCs can locate their operations wherever best suits their business needs. This places the Caribbean in direct competition with other developing regions to entice investment.
- The decline of the production sector in the region and its replacement by the distribution sector results in foreign exchange being used to purchase more imports, causing a balance of payments problem.
- The 'brain drain' to overseas markets is accelerated.

The following are more specific areas and examples as to how globalisation has impacted the Caribbean region and local responses to it.

Industry and Commerce

Allowing the free flow of capital around the world makes everyone more connected. The region has become more sensitive to what is happening in the wider world. The prices that commodities are sold at are not controlled by individual countries, but are determined by the global

Making the Connection

You can find out more about EPZs in the section on government policies in Chapter 13 'Factors That Affect Development'.

Making the Connection

The role of the distribution sector is examined in a later section of this chapter.

market price. In the Windward Islands, there is evidence of this impact as they depend on one or a narrow range of exports, such as bananas. Other industries have also suffered from the inability to compete in export markets or with cheaper imports; for example, manufacturing (car assembly, garment manufacture, sugar cane processing), which in many countries (including Barbados, Jamaica, Trinidad and Tobago, St Vincent and the Grenadines and Dominica) has stagnated or declined since the 1990s.

Larger territories, such as Trinidad, Guyana, Jamaica and Barbados, have been more successful at diversifying their economies to new growth industries; for instance, to tourism. Increasing raw material demand, related to strong economic growth in Asia, is also likely to benefit regional producers of mining products – Trinidad (oil), Guyana (bauxite) and Jamaica (bauxite and alumina).

Did You Know?

In the late 1990s and early 2000s, small banana producers from the Caribbean and Africa, Europe, US multinationals and the WTO became embroiled in what was known as the Banana Trade War. Traditionally, African and Caribbean countries enjoyed advantageous trade terms with Europe for the import of their bananas, but this situation came under threat from the terms of the WTO invoked by US multinationals who controlled the Central and South American banana trade. The dispute lasted 15 years and ended with the dropping of high tariffs placed on the US companies' imports and compensation for the smaller producers. The situation placed the spotlight on both the dangers of economic specialisation and the power wielded by global corporations over institutions such as the WTO.

Since 2014, the prices of commodities have fallen; this means that the region has less to pay for its imports, but also gets less for its exports. Some FDI has been felt in the construction of hotels since 2015 and some firms have restructured operations in the region, including expansion and forming strategic alliances to put them on a better competitive footing, but these moves have not offset the overall result of high unemployment and falling standards of living.

In the Caribbean there is a small manufacturing sector with a small range of goods. Manufacturers have asked for 'stimulus packages', but the governments either do not have the funds or do not want to step in to bolster private ventures. Businesses in the agriculture sector, for example sugar and banana producers, are feeling most of the negative impacts of globalisation.

Being able to buy a product from somewhere across the globe can be a benefit to the consumer. Cheaper clothing from China is an example, as higher quality global branded clothing and shoes are both expensive and inaccessible for the poorest sections of the community. There is increasing Westernisation or cultural imperialism of the developing world coming from television and media, which influences consumers' buying choices; for example, Halloween and Thanksgiving are now both celebrated in the region.

Distributional Sector

The **distributional sector** is the commercial sector in the economy responsible for accessing, linking and supplying the network of wholesalers and retailers in the local market. The efficiency of the sector is crucial to ensuring that consumers have access to a wide variety of goods at competitive prices. It contributes to the overall growth and development of the Caribbean by providing employment and promoting entrepreneurship and local manufacturing. In a well-organised system, it manages and maintains the balance between demand and supply, thereby promoting efficiency in the market. It also contributes to the management of foreign exchange by sourcing goods at reasonable rates.

Many goods, such as cars, trucks, food, toys, and services consumed in the Caribbean region are not produced in the region, but imported. They are then sold to a wholesaler who can hold a large stock of items. These items are then ordered by a retailer or shop to sell them on to customers. The larger retail outlets are supermarkets and department stores, both of which stock a broad range of goods that are often foreign and not locally produced.

This influx of foreign goods has resulted in a growth in the distributional sector, while the productive sector in the Caribbean has declined. This can lead to an imbalance in payments and higher foreign exchange rates. The foreign competition has caused the closure of some manufacturing centres, which in turn can discourage new businesses.

Labour

With globalisation, there has been a reduction in labour and labour costs and a rise in unemployment. Productivity is now highlighted and this often means automation and downsizing as well as a preference for workers with technical skills. In the Caribbean, this trend has accompanied a downturn in certain industries, such as manufacturing, because of an inability to compete in global markets.

There is therefore imperative to ensure that the unemployed can re-enter the job market. An important requirement is the provision of retraining opportunities. A well-educated or well-trained workforce can foster a creative and enterprising society that can compete on the world scale. Education and training have to focus on relevance or importance, and also need to be adaptive and able to respond quickly to a dynamic and ever changing economic environment. New training has to take place relative to what skills employers need their employees to possess, and the training system needs to be flexible to respond to the new types of job opportunities evolving and old jobs being displaced. Governments, the private sector and trade unions all need to be aware of what skills are needed and this must be constantly updated. The Caribbean Single Market Economy (CSME) is an attempt to allow the free movement of skilled labour within the region and so facilitate an accelerated regional adjustment to change.

Another problem facing Caribbean economies is a 'brain drain', where skilled and talented people cannot find jobs in the region so they migrate to overseas markets. Diversifying the economy can provide different types of jobs and reduce out-migration.

Quick Fact

While on the surface a cheaper and wider selection of goods and services may be advantageous to the consumer and their pocket, the wider implications of not buying locally produced, but perhaps more expensive, goods should be considered, such as the decline of local manufacturing and other industries.

Key Term

Distributional sector – the sector of the economy that provides the necessary link between producers and consumers, within and across borders.

Making the Connection

Free Trade Zones as an aspect of 'industrialisation by invitation' policies are discussed in more detail in Chapter 17 'Intellectual Traditions'.

Quick Fact

Labour mobility is a feature of globalisation and liberalisation whereby labour is free to move to where there is work. It facilitates a more efficient allocation of resources and has been identified as a driver of innovation.

Technology

Modern technology is needed in existing industry to improve processes, including management, efficiency and product quality, in all sectors, such as agriculture, manufacturing and services. New technologies have affected manufacturing in the Caribbean, resulting in the creation of new industries. However, this has largely been driven by foreign-owned companies. On the one hand, new technologies have shrunk and eliminated other, more traditional local industries and the jobs associated with them (for example, in the car industry and garment manufacturing). On the other hand, the telecommunications industry has advanced in the Caribbean for the last 20 years, leading to opportunities for new services and diversification of old industries.

Technology is the most significant tool of globalisation because it has facilitated trade among countries on both small and large scales. For example, small- and medium-sized businesses can use the internet to seek customers by practising **e-commerce**. Many have or use websites designed to sell products. Items for sale on the internet include books, products in mail-order catalogues, printing, clothes and cars. Customers can also download software and recorded music to their devices. Services that are delivered electronically include insurance, banking and consultancies.

Some benefits of e-commerce include access to a wider market, lower costs of production because no 'bricks and mortar' selling outlet is needed and a 24-hour business day. Websites can, however, entail additional responsibilities for the users, a main challenge being security of payment, which must normally be verified by using a credit card plus a personal identity number (PIN) to prevent credit card fraud. However, some consumers in poorer households may not have access to the internet and credit card facilities.

Making the Connection

Discussions on the revolutionary nature of modern communications via satellite, internet, mobile phone services and network technology have been addressed earlier in this chapter.

Key Term

E-commerce – the production, distribution, marketing and sales, or delivery, of goods and services via electronic means.

Did You Know?

E-government is the use of electronic communications (the internet and worldwide web) to provide public sector services and information to the citizens of a country. The implementation of e-government produces a significant increase in government savings and a more efficient interface between government, business and the public, an important consideration in the context of increasing global competition. Caribbean countries are at different levels of development and implementation of e-government, with Barbados at the forefront.

Ideology

As part of its colonial past, the Caribbean has been influenced by the ideologies of the wealthier, industrialised nations in Europe, such as democracy and capitalism. The later 20th century saw the increased influence of the USA in Caribbean affairs. The region is strategically close to its borders and during the years of the Cold War became a focus for the ideological battle between the USA and communism, a situation heightened by the communist revolution in Cuba. Through multilateral agencies such as the IMF and World Bank, the US supported the economies of Caribbean countries via the provision of aid and finance, which worked to prevent the influence of communism spreading further in the region.

Since Independence, the Caribbean has also experimented with implementing socialism – in Jamaica, Guyana and Grenada. In the former, the financial cost of social reform proved too high for the economy to bear, while in the latter two countries, intervention by the UK and the US put an end to their attempts.

Globalisation has introduced new ideologies, to achieve a unified world stressing trade liberalisation. Free trade ideologies have impacted on small, vulnerable economies in the Caribbean region in the form of debts and reduced productivity and outputs. The granting of aid or loans from a multilateral agency is often accompanied by stipulations that the receiving country should instigate political or economic reform through SAPs, which takes it further in the direction of democracy, or a market economy along the lines of what has come to be known as the **Washington Consensus**.

Globalisation as an ideology has its opponents. Anti-globalists view trade liberalisation as a means for TNCs to exploit cheap labour without passing on significant material benefits to their workers. Other criticisms include pointing out the dangers inherent in the privatisation of industries that exploit natural resources and the environment and that privatisation and other measures create a small, local, wealthy elite with a vested interest in continuing labour exploitation. Non-governmental organisations (NGOs), such as the Caribbean Policy Development Centre (CPDC), have helped to point out the negative social consequences of the implementation of SAPs.

The CSME is intended as a regional response to the challenges of globalisation. Integration is seen as a strategy, if not a necessity, to aid the successful insertion of the region and its component parts into the global trading and economic system. It also recognises the need to strengthen trading links with non-traditional partners.

Popular Movements

Globalisation has resulted in the growth of movements within civil society that reflect the issues and interests of people, such as human rights and the environment.

Caribbean Association for Feminist Research and Action (CAFRA)

This is a regional non-governmental organisation that comprises researchers, activists and women's groups who are focused on bringing about change for oppressed women. The work of international women's groups have influenced the organisation's focus on addressing issues and fighting for the rights of women in areas such as the sex trade, tourism and human trafficking, as well as the impact of trade liberalisation on the poor generally and women in agriculture specifically. They receive funding from international non-profit organisations and local governments to finance projects and help them to promote sustainable development in the Caribbean. They also collaborate with regional interest groups by publishing magazines, hosting regional conferences and funding scientific research. International non-profit organisations and local governments grant funds to CAFRA for projects and help them to attain sustainable development in the Caribbean.

Making the Connection

Marxism, of which communism is the ultimate goal, and socialism are further investigated in Chapter 17 'Intellectual Traditions'.

Key Term

Washington Consensus – a set of 10 economic measures, including trade liberalisation, privatisation and tax reform, included in SAP packages promoted by the IMF and World Bank. In a broader sense, the phrase has come to refer to a strongly market-based approach (also referred to as market fundamentalism or neoliberalism).

Making the Connection

The CSME and its various challenges are discussed in Chapter 15 'The Integration Movement'.

Quick Fact

WAND is a unit within
the Consortium for Social
Development and Research
(CSDR) of the Open
Campus, UWI.

Key Term

**Non-governmental
organisations (NGOs)** –
not-for-profit organisations
that are independent from
governmental organisations
and are established for the
purpose of carrying out
social functions, mainly
via advocacy. They are
independently funded
through donations and
some are run primarily
by volunteers. Caribbean
NGOs operate various
projects in each island,
such as on Autism,
underprivileged support,
wildlife conservation and
HIV/AIDS education.

Quick Fact

CAFRA and WAND
are both dedicated to
encouraging women's
development through
education, outreach training
and research. They advocate
the implementation of
policies that benefit the
upward movement of
women and document how
these policies impact the
development of the region.

Quick Fact

International service
organisations that fundraise
to promote humanitarian
and environmental projects,
such as The Rotary Club,
have several branches
across the region.

The Women and Development Unit (WAND)

WAND was established in 1978 as a part of the United Nation's focus on the Decade for Women, with the goal of equality, development and peace. The unit's aim since has been to ensure gender equality and the full integration of women into the development process, by focusing on how women continue to be subordinated by culture, society and economic systems, particularly capitalism as reinforced through globalisation. It looks to influence policy and the provision of services by providing information and a point of view on women and their role in Caribbean development. It is committed to supporting and promoting women's development through training, research, documentation and community outreach.

Environmental and Social Justice NGOs

NGOs address issues such as human rights and sustainable development and act when, for instance, countries are slow to enact legislation directed at disaster mitigation or basic environmental indicators. Some international agencies active in disaster relief in the region are the Red Cross and the Salvation Army, while global environmental pressure groups, such as Greenpeace and Friends of the Earth, are also present.

The CPDC is the main regional umbrella body representing NGOs concerned with social development, providing them with a voice on several policy issues and concerns at both regional and international level. It aims to bring together NGOs, civil society and government for critical dialogue on a number of policy areas that touch on aspects of social justice, such as sustainable development, trade liberalisation, governance and participation, and capacity building. It also represents the views and concerns of civil society in its work with major stakeholders (policy makers, the private sector and trade unions) to formulate perspectives and programmes aimed at advancing regional social and economic development.

Regarding globalisation, CPDC's research and advocacy has shown how SAPs have adverse effects on the livelihoods of many Caribbean people; a fact now generally accepted by policy makers and multilateral agencies. CPDC advocates for the write-off of the Caribbean's external debt and a proportional increase in social spending. It educates its members about the many implications of trade agreements and global institutions for Caribbean development.

Opportunities for the Caribbean

Globalisation is an ongoing, dynamic process. The Caribbean therefore needs to position itself to deal positively with opportunities presented by further developments and to protect itself as far as possible against future economic shocks and threats, with human resource development and technology needing to be the focus.

Possible opportunities include:

- Identification of trading opportunities in new markets and in new areas, especially in the service sector, such as financial services, software development and corporate outsourcing, where use of English is often a prerequisite. Other advantages of the Caribbean include an accounting and legal system based on UK or US law and a steady supply of the required skills.

- Development of e-commerce services. The liberalisation of the telecommunications industry, technological developments and ongoing global internet penetration resulted in explosive growth in e-commerce, which has accompanied an increased need for producers to maximise efficiency in a very competitive global environment. This is being achieved through e-commerce by improved inventory/supply chain management and automated payment systems, for instance.

For the Caribbean to take advantage of these trends depends upon the upgrading and extension of telecommunications infrastructure, substantial provision of appropriate and focused training and appropriate legal infrastructure. Globalisation is largely technology driven and the Caribbean has been relatively slow to embrace technology. Thus, the region requires an aggressive strategy towards the adoption and development of technologies to increase productivity as well as an emphasis on maths, science and technology at all levels of education and training.

Another view is that the Caribbean should concentrate on its own 'back yard' and effectively cease trying to conform and fit in with the global picture. It should focus on strategies and policies that directly achieve human and social development over economic development, while intensifying the regional integration process; if necessary, at the cost of losing foreign aid and advantageous trade terms.

Check Your Knowledge

Examine FOUR ways in which globalisation has impacted on Caribbean development.

Demonstrate an understanding of the following terms and concepts by defining and using them correctly:

- globalisation
- Caribbean
- labour
- good
- service
- employment/unemployment
- prices of goods and services
- trade
- trade practices
- technology
- development

First explain the process of globalisation:

- Globalisation, through the principle of trade liberalisation, is a process that permits goods, services and brands produced in industrialised countries to enter the Caribbean in large quantities and at reduced prices (for instance, Tate & Lyle, Hilton Hotels and Kentucky Fried Chicken).

Clearly describe any FOUR of the following examples and demonstrate an understanding by giving specific examples. You must also make the link between globalisation and Caribbean development.

Some negative impacts are:

- The Caribbean cannot compete with more industrialised manufacturing regions, leading to business contraction and even businesses closing down.
- Local goods are displaced and the local production and manufacturing sectors suffer.
- Irregular local labour and services influences the volume of goods traded, resulting in an imbalance.

Making the Connection

Chapter 12 'Concepts and Indicators of Development'

Chapter 13 'Factors that Affect Development'

Exam Tip

'**Examine**' requires a detailed study in an extended answer, defining key concepts, stating the facts and exploring related concepts and issues.

- Balance of payments worsens for Caribbean countries due to shrinkage of productive sectors, their replacement by the distribution sector and foreign exchange being used to buy more goods from abroad.
- TNCs can locate labour wherever it is required (concept of labour mobility). Frequently this has led to the exploitation of the labour market.
- Despite many TNCs setting up businesses that may increase employment over the short and medium term, there are often no long-term sustainable development plans associated with this.
- An increased use of technology stimulates downsizing and automation, and results in increased unemployment.
- There is a brain drain or migration of skilled labour to overseas markets.
- Globalisation can have a negative effect on people's cultural confidence through the market being flooded with foreign goods that are in direct competition with those being locally produced for Caribbean consumers; for example, locally produced food items such as breakfast cereals compete directly with products from the metropole or US.
- Increased consumerism stimulated by globalisation can affect the environment; for example, through increased vehicle ownership and use.

Some positive impacts are:

- Lower prices of some overseas mass-produced goods have benefited the consumer in the Caribbean.
- Countries with mineral deposits (Jamaica and Guyana with bauxite and Trinidad and Tobago with oil) have been able to take advantage of an increased global demand for raw materials.
- There has been the creation of new trading opportunities, such as in service industries, e-commerce and the identification and exploitation of niche markets for locally produced goods.
- An influx of foreign investment provides much needed capital.

A possible conclusion is that you summarise the main points in your essay.

Multiple-choice Questions

1. Globalisation involves which of the following processes?

   I. Global warming

   II. Trade liberalisation

   III. Liberalisation of capital markets

   A. I only

   B. II and III

   C. I and III

   D. I, II and III

2. One way the WTO facilitates development in the Caribbean is by:

   A. Regulating the world currencies

   B. Having its head office in a developed country

   C. Monitoring government trade agreements to raise income and stimulate growth

   D. Regulating the day-to-day running of firms and households to maximise efficiency

3. The EPA benefits Caribbean countries MAINLY by:
    A. Negotiation by ministers on business trips
    B. Implementation of lower codes of standard
    C. Enhancing cultural and business sector services
    D. Gaining huge profits for large overseas-based businesses in the UK

4. Large or mega companies that have headquarters in one country and branches or subsidiaries in various countries are referred to as:
    A. Private corporations
    B. Macroeconomics
    C. Multinational corporations
    D. Mega stores

5. Which of the following is a characteristic of transnational organisations in the Caribbean?
    A. Consists of a parent company in Suriname or St Lucia
    B. Business is based on sales only and high volume
    C. Medium size makes it able to take advantage of privatisation
    D. May boost local employment, but can employ overseas personnel for management

6. The MAIN impact of globalisation on labour in the Caribbean is:
    A. Workers trained by a local firm may emigrate overseas to work in a related industry
    B. Waste products produced by production of oil and gas may endanger the environment
    C. Social factors may be excluded from fiscal discussions and negotiations at the country level
    D. Hiring of new staff can increase the efficiency and productivity by division of labour

7. Which of the following is a successful response by industry and commerce in the Caribbean to globalisation?
    A. Abolish state-funded education in tertiary institutions
    B. Export-led growth can create income and jobs and increase GDP per capita
    C. Structural adjustment plans recommended by international multi-laterals like the IMF
    D. Increase government spending and put a hold on interest rates to prevent banks from lending to small business

8. How have CARICOM countries responded to globalisation and the formation of mega-trading blocs?
    A. Elections held every five years
    B. Appeals to the British Privy Council
    C. CARICOM Single Market and Economy
    D. Caribbean Single Market and Economy

9. Which one of the following concepts BEST describes how events in one country can impact people in many other countries and the ways that politics, culture and economics transcend national borders?
    A. Global industrialisation
    B. Globalisation
    C. E-commerce
    D. Commercialisation

10. Which of the following is NOT a characteristic of globalisation?
    A. Trade liberalisation
    B. Increasing use of communications technology for commercial transactions
    C. E-commerce
    D. Workers receive higher wages

11. Globalisation is BEST defined as:
    A. Trade liberalisation
    B. The integration of cultures, governments, technologies and economies
    C. Cultural transmission via the mass media using satellite technology
    D. Workers receive higher wages

Chapter 15

The Integration Movement

Explain the ways in which the evolution of the integration movement in the Caribbean has influenced development in the region.

Quick Fact

The United States of America and the more recent European Union (EU) are all examples of states that have come together in different ways to pool resources and ideas of governance for the benefits of protecting their borders, improving local economies and sharing ideas on governance.

Key Term

Regional integration – a process in which states that share a common geographic location, history and/or political structure enter into an agreement in order to introduce coordination and increase cooperation through common institutions and rules. This integration is usually aimed at bringing together resources and talents and to unify systems of government to some extent in order to protect borders, increase efficiency and pool resources for its citizens.

After revising this topic, you should be able to:
- define and explain what is meant by regional integration or movement towards regional integration;
- describe the reasons for the evolution of the main institutions of regional integration from the 1950s to the present day and how they have influenced the development of the region;
- name and discuss the institutions that have contributed to the Caribbean integration movement;
- assess the achievements of and challenges faced by key regional institutions;
- describe and explain factors that hinder and promote regional integration.

What is Regional Integration in the Caribbean?

Reasons for Integration

The Caribbean is generally perceived as a natural regional entity and **regional integration** in the Caribbean refers to a series of attempts by Caribbean states to form a union in an attempt to create a political, economic, cultural or trade block that would better enable them to meet the needs of the Caribbean people and to provide combined political and economic weight to gain recognition and influence on the international scene.

Attempts at integration have been made because:
- individual states in the region are small, with little political or economic international clout;
- resources of individual states are limited;
- states have encountered similar problems and issues with trading partners;
- states share backgrounds historically and culturally and these similarities assist in the creation of partnerships among them.

The three main areas where integration has been attempted are:
- political integration or unity, particularly in the coordination of foreign policy;
- economic integration and cooperation, through the Caribbean Common Market (CARICOM);

- functional cooperation among states in areas of health, education, law, tourism, disaster relief, media, agriculture, financing and industrial relations.

The movement towards regional integration in the Caribbean is often seen as being initiated by Britain in the 1950s in the form of the West Indian Federation to promote Caribbean economic and political cooperation, while also easing the responsibilities Britain would have for her colonies as the 'Mother Country'. This 'union' also came at a time when many Caribbean nationals sought employment opportunities outside of agriculture, without having to travel too far (to Europe or North America) from their families and friends. Growing Caribbean industries, such as the petroleum in Trinidad and bauxite in Jamaica, also absorbed a large portion of the Caribbean labour force and gave confidence to workers that the Caribbean was a place of growing opportunities. It is for these reasons that many Caribbean nationals also saw regional integration as the bridge that would enable them to access the opportunities of their neighbouring islands without any political or even cultural barriers preventing transition or making it difficult.

The first attempts at regional integration were made by English-speaking territories, recognising the similarities between them. Many regional integration movements over the years have been responses to increased globalisation and the perceived need for smaller states to work together to protect their interests, economically speaking. They have also aimed to educate Caribbean nationals in matters of regional importance.

Factors that Hinder Regional Integration

Why, then, is the movement towards the development of the region socially, politically and economically through integration not as advanced as it could be? And why are organisations set up to promote integration so frequently unpopular in individual states? The answer lies in nationalism and diversity, which can result from, and manifest themselves in, the following ways:

- Territories are at different stages of development, which gives rise to differences in priorities and concerns about economic disparity, especially among the more developed territories who are reluctant to use their resources to support those that are less developed.
- Members of an organisation may be unwilling to cooperate for various reasons to do with protection of their own interests, autonomy, jealousies, competitiveness and so on.
- Conflicts exist between territorial and regional demands.
- Territories do not have the same currency.
- Territories do not have the same types or amounts of resources.
- Territories have incompatibile or different political systems.
- Territories have dissimilar economic policies.
- Territories have differences in their social and racial make up, giving rise to very basic differences in value systems, beliefs, approaches and priorities.
- Territories are scattered over the region.

Fundamental to all this is a varied understanding of what it actually means to belong to one Caribbean. Race and colour continue to define people and, as a result, create distinctions between them. Stratification along the lines of class has also created fundamental social divisions that stand in the way of a unfied outlook.

Did You Know?

Culture is a major unifying force within the Caribbean region. Shared cultural forms can help to create a bond between different territories. Music is a good example of this with musical forms such as calypso and reggae being played across the region. Similar foods, sayings, stories and so on are also shared. The holding of festivals such as carnival or CARIFESTA also brings people together and showcases shared cultural forms, albeit for a short period of time.

Making the Connection

The complexities surrounding the recognition of the Caribbean as an identifiable region, while also involving many diverse factors, is also reflected in the difficulties and contradictions that lie in the way of attempts to define 'the Caribbean' discussed in Chapter 4 'Location and Definition of the Caribbean'.

The Evolution of the Idea of Caribbean Integration

Figure 15.1 **A timeline of Caribbean regional integration**

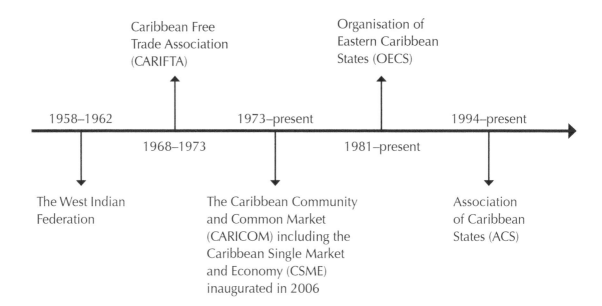

Quick Fact

There was a Senate and a House of Representatives along with a Governor General, a Prime Minister and 10 ministers. The federal seat of government was in Trinidad.

Key Term

Federation – a group of states under a central government, but with independence in internal affairs.

West Indies Federation

The West Indies Federation (WIF) came into being in January 1958 as an attempt to create a political union among British colonies, with the exception of Guyana, Belize, the Virgin Islands and The Bahamas. A regional economic committee was also set up to investigate means of achieving economic unity. Britain retained responsibility for defence, external affairs and financial stability.

The thinking behind the WIF involved:

* a desire to strengthen the movement towards self-government with the hope that the political union would eventually become independent of Britain (in the belief that small individual territories could only achieve this together as a group);
* a desire to strengthen internal and regional development by establishing federal institutions and supporting regional structures, for example the development of the University of the West Indies and the establishment of the Regional Shipping Service;
* the fact that **federation** was among the measures taken by the British government for better administration of the colonies and to save on administrative costs.

Elections for seats in the House of Representatives were held in March 1958 with the West Indies Federal Labour Party (WIFLP) supported by N.W. Manley, Eric Williams and Grantley Adams gaining more seats than the Democratic Labour Party (DLP) supported by Sir Alexander Bustamante and Sir Stanley Eugene Gomes.

This integration step was mainly a political one and it lasted only four years. The reasons for its failure were many:

- The masses were not educated in the meaning and importance of federation. Many did not understand what it meant or how it worked and this insecurity was played on by anti-federation politicians, such as Bustamante in Jamaica who argued that it was a ploy by the British to prolong colonisation.

- The federal government had very little or no authority as individual territories were unwilling to give up their own power and the largest territories of Jamaica and Trinidad and Tobago vied for leadership.

- There were insufficient communications (shipping, telephone, postal services) between the islands and unsuitable government and administrative structures imposed by the British.

- Envy and jealousy reigned among the states because of their varying degrees of economic development and prosperity and of the location of the capital in Trinidad.

- The insecurities of the smaller states persisted, as they feared the potential takeover of the organisation by Jamaica and Trinidad, especially after they proposed to prematurely change the constitution of the Federation.

- Disputes arose, especially between Jamaica and Trinidad and Tobago, over the movement of people from one territory to another, taxation and central planning.

After a referendum in 1961, Jamaica withdrew. After the withdrawal of Jamaica, Eric Williams, Prime Minister of Trinidad and Tobago, famously stated that 'one from ten leaves zero', and Trinidad and Tobago also withdrew because the withdrawal of Jamaica, which was one of the region's largest economies at the time, made the aims of the movement seem futile. The remaining eight territories tried to continue for a few years, but their attempt collapsed. As a result of its withdrawal, Jamaica itself embarked on the journey towards full independence.

> **Exam Tip**
>
> **'To what extent'** requires an examination of to what degree – lesser or greater – cultural diversity caused the failure.

Check Your Knowledge

To what extent to you agree with the statement that the cultural diversity of the Caribbean led to the failure of the West Indian Federation?

Demonstrate an understanding of the following terms and concepts:

- Federation
- Caribbean
- Cultural diversity
- Development

You must first introduce your essay, covering the following points:

- Define the concepts: culture, cultural diversity.

- Provide a very brief synopsis of what the Federation was, its aims and the year it was established (1958).

- Present a thesis statement declaring that your essay aims to examine whether or not cultural diversity affected its failure or if there were other reasons, for example more economic causes of failure.

Then examine each of the following areas and, at the end of each, answer the question: Did cultural diversity cause this issue?

- Lack of finance
  - Territories were at different stages of development. This led to differences in priorities and concerns about economic disparities. This must be mentioned as contributing to the failure apart from cultural diversity. The Federation suffered from a lack of finance. Dues were to be paid to the Federation, but they were inadequate; the amount collected could not help finance projects and activities. The currencies were different. Jamaica and Trinidad felt that too much financial responsibility was placed upon them. This resulted in alienation between the federal authorities and the local governing bodies.
- Seeking own interests
  - Trinidad and Tobago and Jamaica wanted to prioritise their own interests and they bickered over it. This contributed to the distrust the small islands had of the larger ones. The smaller islands felt that their interests would be sidelined. Trinidad and Jamaica did not want to give up their political power to the Federation. These larger countries also hosted most Federation buildings and offices. This led to the smaller islands feeling as if this was a show of how the decision making in the Federation would be pursued, with the larger islands being the focus and at the centre.
- Unrestricted movement
  - The West Indian Federation allowed unrestricted movement of islanders between the islands. The Trinidadian Prime Minister, Eric Williams, disliked this idea as he feared the poor would flock to Trinidad. He felt too many unskilled workers would enter the island leading to unemployment and overcrowded towns. This contributed to the shakiness of the Federation.
- The people spoke
  - Jamaica was not really interested in getting involved in the political union, despite being a member of the Federation. She held a referendum in 1961, allowing her citizens to vote on whether to stay or leave the union. The majority voted against staying a member, so she withdrew. This led to the final downward spiral and prompted the withdrawal of Trinidad from the doomed political union. Eventually, the Federation was disbanded in 1962.
- Political rivalry/distrust between the island states
  - There were disputes as to where the capital of the Federation should be. Barbadians felt that since the premier was Barbadian, the capital should be there. It was argued that Trinidad and Jamaica politically dominated the Federation. This contributed to the distrust between the island states.

The conclusion needs to agree or disagree with the statement. Was it more due to cultural diversity or for economic reasons?

Despite its ultimate collapse, the attempt at forming the Federation led to the development of politics in Caribbean territories in terms of strengthening the movement for self-government and facilitating the movement from colonialisation to independence via a united voice. It also contributed to the formalisation of ties among British Caribbean states that would form the foundation for future Caribbean unions. It was on this platform that CARIFTA was built.

Caribbean Free Trade Association (CARIFTA)

CARIFTA was created in 1968 following independence of a number of former British colonies – Jamaica, Trinidad and Tobago, Guyana and Barbados. These new states were concerned with issues such as nationalism, self-determination and economic development. It was in response to this last concern that CARIFTA was established.

The aim of CARIFTA was to promote economic and social development in the Caribbean region by encouraging free trade among members. This meant the removal of custom duties, taxes and licencing arrangements that had prevented greater volumes of trade among the territories for goods produced within the region. Membership comprised the former members of WIF plus Belize and Guyana.

CARIFTA faced a number of challenges:
* High unemployment rates and poverty in some member states and a wide disparity among members in terms of per capita income hindered an even distribution of economic benefits.
* A lack of authority and the means to implement regional decisions.
* Leadership issues, with Trinidad and Tobago and Jamaica once again vying for the position of leader.

Successes included the establishment of the Caribbean Development Bank and the CARIFTA games, but it failed to meet its main aim of facilitating free trade among member states. These member states decided to expand and deepen cooperation by forming CARICOM.

Caribbean Community and Common Market (CARICOM)

CARICOM was created by the Treaty of Chaguaramas, signed on 4 July 1973 by Jamaica, Trinidad, Barbados and Guyana. It began operation on 1 August 1973. Currently, membership includes CARIFTA members as well as Haiti and Suriname.

CARICOM was conceived as a stronger form of integration than CARIFTA, with three pillars: economic integration (a common market in goods); functional cooperation (for example in health and education); and foreign policy coordination. By the 1980s economic integration had stalled and so in 1989 the Revised Treaty of Chaguaramas established the Caribbean Single Market Economy (CSME). A new governance structure was put in place and the Caribbean Court of Justice created. Security was added as the 4th pillar of integration in 2007. The CARICOM Single Market was officially inaugurated in 2006, but completion of the Single Economy is still to be achieved.

The aim of CARICOM is to be both an economic and a political force in the Caribbean, promoting economic, political and human development. Its stated strategic priorities for 2015–2019 were:
* building economic resilience (stabilisation and sustainable economic growth and development);
* building social resilience (equitable human and social development);
* building environmental resilience;
* building technical resilience;
* strengthening the CARICOM identity and spirit of community;
* strengthening governance.

It aims to achieve these through activities such as:
* improving economic development by extending free trade and free movement of skilled workers through the CSME. Although free

Quick Fact

CARICOM is aided in functional cooperation throughout the region through the collective participation of community and associated institutions, such as the Caribbean Development Bank, the Caribbean Learning and Knowledge Network and the Caribbean Examinations Council.

trade had been established under CARIFTA, it did not succeed in facilitating the free movement of labour and capital or in coordinating agricultural, industrial and foreign policies;

- the formulation of the Caribbean Court of Justice as a local final appellate court that would nullify appeals to the Privy Council in England. This court has already successfully tried and judged cases involving disputes among member states and citizens of member states; the most high-profile being the Shanique Myrie case of 2013;
- enabling functional cooperation in areas such as health, education, culture, broadcasting, transport, meteorological services, technical assistance and disaster management;
- establishing common policies in dealing with non-member states and transnational cooperation.

Did You Know?

Jamaican Shanique Myrie claimed damages against the state of Barbados because when she arrived at the airport in Barbados she was not only denied entry into that country, but also detained overnight in a cell in the airport, sexually molested and deported to Jamaica the following day. Myrie was awarded BDS$77 240 by the Caribbean Court of Justice, which ruled that her treatment in Barbados ran contrary to the rules of the revised Treaty of Chagaramas. The ensuing outcry led to a move to clarify the parameters of the CSME and prompted Jamaica and Barbados to act quickly in resolving any ill feelings citizens of either nation might harbour against each other.

Organisation of Eastern Caribbean States (OECS)

The OECS was established in June 1981 by the Treaty of Basseterre to formalise various aspects of economic cooperation and promote unity and solidarity between seven newly independent island states in the Eastern Caribbean. Following the collapse of the WIF, two caretaker bodies were created: the West Indies Associated States Council of Ministers (WISA), in 1966, and the Eastern Caribbean Common Market (ECCM), in 1968. As the islands gained their independence from Britain, it became evident that there was need for a more formal arrangement to assist with their development efforts, so the OECS was established.

The OECS is now a nine-member grouping comprising Antigua and Barbuda, Commonwealth of Dominica, Grenada. Montserrat, St Kitts and Nevis, St Lucia and St Vincent and the Grenadines. Anguilla and the British Virgin Islands are associate members. The mission of the OECS is to be a major regional institution contributing to the sustainable development of the member states by supporting their involvement in the global economy and assisting them to maximise the benefits from their collective resources. Its stated objectives are:

- to promote cooperation between member states and on a regional and international level;
- to promote unity and solidarity among member states and defend their sovereignty and independence;
- to support member states in realising their responsibilities and obligations to the international community;
- to coordinate a joint foreign policy as far as possible;
- to promote economic integration among member states.
- to provide a forum for and facilitation of common policies.

The OECS has a central bank, its own currency and even a shared judicial system that is funded from a pool formed by the member countries. These accomplishments, though no easy feat, were facilitated by the striking commonalities among the small islands that are geographically close and share a similar history of development. These smaller Caribbean islands face the same issues (being small states with limited land) and also acknowledge that the free movement of people will not only lead to a more fluid sharing of resources, but also help to maintain a tourism product where visitors can travel along the island chain without hinderance.

Association of Caribbean States (ACS)

This grouping was formed in 1994 by the Treaty of Cartegena to enhance cooperation within the Greater Caribbean region and is made up of English, Spanish, French and Dutch speaking territories, with the secretariat located in Trinidad.

It states its five main areas of concern as:

- To preserve the environmental integrity of the Caribbean Sea that is shared by the peoples of the region and to promote sustainable development of the region.
- To promote sustainable tourism across the region.
- To support and strengthen regional economic cooperation and integration through increased trade (raw materials and finished products) and investment, thereby improving the economic competitiveness of the region.
- To establish strategies for dealing with natural disasters, both in terms of disaster relief and dealing with the longer term economic consequences.
- To improve intraregional transport links in order to promote closer relations and provide a base for effective cooperation.

Its main areas of action are:

- working on the Sustainable Tourism Zone of the Caribbean;
- facilitating language training;
- working on the Caribbean Sea initiative;
- coordinating an annual Business Forum of the Greater Caribbean;
- defending the interests and treatment of small economies;
- updating building codes;
- strengthening disaster agencies.

> **Quick Fact**
>
> The ACS is the world's fourth largest trading bloc and by 2016 comprised 25 nations of the Caribbean region and three associate members.

> **Making the Connection**
>
> Globalisation is explained and discussed in Chapter 14 'Globalisation and Development'.

> **Making the Connection**
>
> The overall aims of CARICOM are discussed in the section 'The Evolution of the Idea of Caribbean Integration' above.

Did You Know?

The differences between CARICOM and ACS are:

CARICOM:	ACS:
• Mainly the English-speaking Caribbean (15 members, approx. 13 million people)	• Represents the Greater Caribbean (25 members, three associate members, approx. 237 million people)
• Focus is integration	• Focus is cooperation
• Aims to be a Single Market and Economy (CSME)	• Is a zone of cooperation (current focus on trade, transport, sustainable tourism and natural disasters)

Achievements and Challenges of Caribbean Organisations and Institutions that Promote Integration

The movement towards regional integration has given rise to a number of organisations and institutions whose remit is to encourage cooperation and coordinate functions across the region, thus supporting regional development. Many of these are facing challenges posed both from within the region and from without as the forces of globalisation erode the boundaries that define the region they serve.

The Caribbean Community and Common Market (CARICOM)

Achievements

- Reaching out to and incorporating other regional groups into the fold (OECS is now considered a sub group of CARICOM).
- The establishment of the Caribbean Single Market Economy (CSME), the main aim of which is to create links between Caribbean economies and enable economic needs to be met where there is a shortfall in one state. For example, the CSME allows Caribbean professionals to travel freely to CARICOM states on their CARICOM passports. This is beneficial to countries whose industries may be lacking a particular group of artisans or professionals.
- Free movement of capital.
- Larger market for individual member states. Manufacturers and merchants are now able to market and sell their products and services to a wider customer base. They are not limited to the consumers in their native country and, through CARICOM and the CSME, their products are now able to reach consumers and customers throughout the region.
- Better negotiations with trading partners through the Caribbean Regional Negotiating Machinery (CRNM).
- Better border control with the establishment of a CARICOM passport.
- Improved economic strength as resources are pooled. In areas such as disaster preparedness and aid relief this has meant improved economic assistance and functional cooperation, as seen in the effort commissioned by the group in 2004 to help those states worst hit by Hurricane Ivan.
- The creation of the Caribbean Court of Justice (CCJ) and the movement towards establishing it as the final appellate court of the region.
- Stronger persuasive voice in global matters.
- CARICOM creates a stronger Caribbean unity and identity with the promotion of Caribbean industries, produce and services. CARICOM also promotes trade among regional members. Industrialists, merchants and consumers of goods and services are encouraged to source products and services within the Caribbean instead of looking

Making the Connection

The achievements of and challenges for CSME specifically are looked at in more detail later in this chapter.

to other global markets outside the region. For example, Trinidadian producers of snacks and packaged drinks enjoy a healthier market share of the Jamaican snack and drink/juice market than those North American manufacturers that are more popular in other parts of the world.

- Creates a better understanding and appreciation of diverse Caribbean cultures as continued regional integration leads to increased interaction between people of different Caribbean island states.
- Benefits the talents of individuals and member states as musicians, poets, writers and artists can travel freely on their CARICOM passports to those other Caribbean states that wish to experience their artistry or work.

Challenges

As with previous attempts at creating integration, CARICOM has had to face challenges such as:

- Difficulties in implementing regional goals due to a lack of authority across the region and insufficient tools of governance and implementation.
- Differences and disparities in economic resources between member states.
- Individual members pursuing political and economic development strategies that deviate from the aims and objectives of CARICOM.
- A lack of shared impetus across the region due to 'nationalistic' attitudes and no overriding desire to see the bigger picture among member states.
- Functional inefficiencies due to a reluctance to pool resources. Some specific examples of issues and challenges faced by CARICOM and, by extension, the CSME are:
- There is a balance of trade deficit between states, with some states exporting more goods into other countries than they are allowing in. This 'uneven trade' has affected the relationship between Trinidad and Jamaica over the years where Jamaicans feel the Trinidadian government restricts the flow of Jamaican goods into Trinidad, while Trinidadian manufactured products have almost nil policy restrictions preventing them from reaching Jamaican consumers. These imbalances in trade have also hindered the creation of transregional companies and businesses.
- The ideal of a common currency for Caribbean states has not been achieved beyond OECS. This would also help to promote ease of travel for tourists who would only have to contend with one currency.
- The ideal of free movement of labour between member states is an area where the reality affects different states in different ways. There is a fear of mass immigration among Caribbean states that are politically and economically stable. The fear is that mass immigration to their country will lead to a social and economic strain on their resources. As a result, rigid systems are put in place in countries such as Trinidad and Tobago and Barbados to restrict the flow of Caribbean immigrants.

Quick Fact

The ACS is the world's fourth largest trading bloc and by 2016 comprised 25 nations of the Caribbean region and three associate members.

Did You Know?

Statistics show that the majority of CARICOM nationals seeking entry into Barbados between 2007 and 2012 came from Trinidad and Tobago, St Lucia and St Vincent and the Grenadines and that just over 600 nationals from these states were refused entry. Comparatively, more than 2,000 Guyanese and approximately 1 500 Jamaicans were refused entry to Barbados over the same period. This apparently discriminatory trend is reflected in Trinidad and Tobago, as statistics show that more than 300 Jamaicans were refused entry in 2015 alone. Thus, despite CARICOM's intent of free movement of Caribbean nationals between member states to promote economic and social cooperation, it has yet to be fully achieved.

- Some Caribbean leaders are still wary about the benefits and usefulness of CARICOM. The Jamaican JLP political party, for instance, has often openly questioned the need for CARICOM, and its various arms such as the CCJ, with leader, Andrew Holness, suggesting in 2016 that Jamaica establish its own final court. He, like many Jamaicans, believes that CARICOM's policies can interfere with sovereignty of an independent state and the need to act in the country's best interests.
- The full integration of Haiti and Cuba, two historic and important countries in the region, into CARICOM has still to be achieved after years of talks.
- On an international level, CARICOM also faces the challenge of inserting the economies of its members into the global economy.

Did You Know?

Haiti and Cuba are seen by many Caribbean states as liabilities to the CARICOM movement. Haiti eventually gained CARICOM membership on 3 July 1997. However, it was still excluded from the common market as many Caribbean leaders expressed fears that the poverty in Haiti would lead to a mass migration of Haitians to other Caribbean states, with a resulting economic burden. There was also the view that Haiti's internal political turmoil might be difficult to ignore and could pull other member states unwillingly into the problem.

Regarding both Haiti and Cuba, there was major concern that political affiliation with these states could lead to animosity between CARICOM and partners outside the Caribbean that view them as failed states with many human rights breaches and which constantly ignore international laws.

The University of the West Indies

The University of the West Indies was founded in 1948, and started with the Mona campus in Jamaica, at the suggestion of the Moyne Commission, as a solution to the lack of training facilities for skilled workers in the region. The three campuses today continue to bring solutions to issues facing the Caribbean, although there are challenges along the way. It is an Associate Institution of CARICOM.

Achievements

- Offering a curriculum that is relevant to the needs of the region.
- Inclusion of Caribbean gender studies in the Faculty of Social Sciences as a way of promoting the inclusion of women in Caribbean development.

- Having distance learning as a solution for many working Caribbean people who seek training and an education in order to advance social mobility.
- Producing skilled personnel in business, government and industry, and people who are committed to the region by developing science and technology.
- Training professionals (doctors, teachers, lawyers and so on) of the future to work in both public and private sectors to meet the needs of the region.
- Producing research which contributes to development of the private sector and which helps in solving society's problems.
- Raising levels of innovation and entrepreneurship in the region.
- Breaking down barriers and dispelling ignorance and prejudice of and towards other nationals.
- Acting as a forum for regional integration by uniting scholars, academics and intellectuals in the common purpose of serving the Caribbean.

Challenges

- Strong competition from foreign universities that offer degrees by distance teaching.
- Can be costly for faculties of medicine and law. The university has been finding it difficult to lower the cost of these programmes to increase the enrolment of future Caribbean doctors and lawyers.
- Contributing states sometimes lag behind with their required contributions, leading to a depletion of funds to pay lecturers and procure items/tools necessary for the teaching of some programmes.
- Still no full integration of programmes across campuses. Students still have to travel across the region for some programmes that are offered only on a specific campus.

Did You Know?

The University of the West Indies was initially established as an agricultural science school (which is why the faculty of natural sciences on the Mona campus is the oldest faculty) at a time when agriculture was the main driver of Caribbean economies. This was also the period of colonisation, and many thought that an agricultural education was most suited for the Caribbean Black students because some professions, such as law and medicine, were reserved for wealthy Whites and mixed race students who could travel to England for tertiary studies.

Caribbean Examinations Council

The Oxford and Cambridge examination bodies were formerly used to evaluate and test secondary school students before they entered into the world of work, or moved on to further their studies. Thus, there were two British examination bodies attempting to prepare local students to fill positions in the local workplace. This arrangement was untenable as the region sought a workforce equipped to address the issues unique to the Caribbean. It was on this premise that, in 1972, the Caribbean Examination Council (CXC®) was formed. It is a Community Institution of CARICOM.

Achievements

- Offers secondary-level certification, advanced proficiency diplomas and associate degrees.
- Ensures that the education of Caribbean people is geared towards the needs of the region, thus fostering economic development: examination by the region, of the region and for the region.
- Syllabus reflects learning from a Caribbean perspective.
- Creates employment opportunities: administrators, curriculum officers, measurement experts, content specialist markers, supervisors, examiners.
- Finance is kept in the region rather than going to the UK as foreign exchange.
- Creates interaction among peoples of the region: regional integration, awareness of commonality, a sense of brotherhood.

Challenges

- Many candidates from across the region still yearn for a more diverse evaluation, especially where languages are concerned. It is believed that continued focus by the CXC® on using standard English as the official language for responses to exam questions is discriminatory.
- CXC® text books and revision guides, especially for the social sciences, tend to use more examples of and references to the larger Caribbean states. The cultural and geographical references to the smaller states are minimal.
- CXC® is currently transitioning to become fully online with its communications and evaluation tools. Many schools in the region, however, have not yet found the resources to procure the equipment that would enable them to coordinate with the CXC®.
- While most tertiary institutions in extra-regional societies accept CXC® results, there are some that still require results from qualifying exams in their own regions before a student can be admitted. Many still refuse to fully recognise CXC® passes as adequate.

Did You Know?

Local examination bodies and institutions also have to contend with competition from overseas institutions that have gained accreditation to operate online schools in various Caribbean territories. Many Caribbean students flock to these institutions whose programmes are sometimes significantly cheaper than native schools and are marketed to be more universally accepted than our own. This is especially appealing to a region with a culture of migration. For example, the University of London's law courses are immensely popular in the Caribbean because of the convenience of its self-study programme (the University of the West Indies law course is not as flexible) and the fact that its qualifications are universally accepted, with students who complete the whole course being able to practise law throughout the British Commonwealth.

The West Indies Cricket Board

Cricket was once the most popular sport among English-speaking states and territories and could boast of being the only area of successful regional integration. The unification of Caribbean states into one team, challenging the likes of our former colonial masters, excited and satisfied the resilient spirit of Caribbean people and created a united Caribbean identity on the international scene. So important was the sport to the region, that the West Indian Cricket Board (WICB) was formed to promote the development of the game and to accept new talent to ensure the replenishment of cricketing talent. It also acts as the oversight body for all cricket related matters in the region.

Achievements

- Develop and promote West Indian cricket for the benefit and enjoyment of the West Indies people, clients and other stakeholders.
- A role in the development of a regional identity as well as an economic contribution to the region through staging competitions, for example the Cricket World Cup.
- The promotion of different formats, for example 20/20, in a bid to futher popularise the game, especially to those that may find the longer Test format a bit too slow.
- The creation of a West Indian cricket hall of fame to celebrate the likes of Brian Lara, Sir Garfield Sobers, Sir Frank Worrell and Courtney Walsh, who are recognised the world over as some of the game's best-ever players.

Challenges

- Discord between the West Indies Players Association (WIPA) and the WICB regarding compensation packages for matches and the seemingly biased recruiting methods of the board have led to a string of disappointing performances from the team in recent times.
- Funding is increasingly becoming a problem as the sport is not as popular as it used to be and has a weak spectatorship and viewership compared to other sports.
- Funding and sponsorship issues have been a major issue with the WICB. This has been a major setback for the board as they are not able to fully carry out their mandate to expand and develop West Indian cricket without adequate funding.
- Lack of funding from sponsors has been blamed on an increasing lack of interest in cricket among Caribbean nationals, and both these factors have led many talented Caribbean players to look to the more lucrative cricketing nations of India and Australia, which have vibrant and exciting cricket leagues of their own.
- Many players have claimed that the WICB has not done enough in organising and funding local competitions in a bid to discover and promote cricketing talent.

Quick Fact

Programmes offered by CARIMAC: Diploma in Media and Communication; Bachelor of Arts in Media and Communication; Bachelor of Arts in Journalism; Bachelor of Arts in Digital Media Production. At post-graduate level: MAs in Communication Studies and Communication for Social and Behaviour Change.

Did You Know?

The 20/20 format of the game (also known as T20) was introduced in 2003 in England and has become a favourite among younger West Indian cricket fans. It is a shortened version of the game that usually lasts a maximum of three hours, which is achieved by having limited overs (a maximum of 20) per game. This format is considered by many as the most exciting. As a result, many West Indian players have gone to play in 20/20 leagues in India, Australia and England where the format is hugely popular and brings in a lot of money.

Caribbean Institute of Media and Communication

The Caribbean Institute of Media and Communication (CARIMAC) was established in 1974 to provide media personnel with a professional grounding along with a Caribbean orientation, while also ensuring that Caribbean media and communications worked to aid Caribbean development through the transmission of information.

Achievements

- Producing graduates who are immediately relevant to media and communication services.
- Producing graduates who are adaptable to a rapidly changing media and communication environment, and who have the skills to be immediately competent in this environment.
- Provides research, consulting, product development and training in media and communication for private and public sector entities across the region.
- Works with a growing list of government development agencies and community-based organisations to develop media and communication applications for critical development challenges.

Challenges

- A major challenge faced by the Institute is the size and condition of its building and it is attempting to expand the premises. The need for more space is critical. The current building was initially designed for an annual intake of 31 students. The current intake is four times as many.
- The basic facilities for students are overstretched. The laboratories and studios do not provide a physical environment that is conducive to efficient teaching and learning. The physical problems also affect the staff.

Caribbean Single Market and Economy

The CARICOM Caribbean Single Market and Economy (CSME) is the heart of CARICOM's economic integration. CARICOM lists the benefits of CSME as:

- better opportunities to produce and sell goods and services competitively and to attract investment;
- greater economies of scale; increased competitiveness;
- full employment and improved standards of living.

  Its ultimate goal is to provide the foundation for growth and development through uniting markets to allow for restriction-free commerce and movement of labour and capital among its members.

Achievements

- Goods are being traded in free market conditions.
- People of approved categories are moving freely. For example, skilled labourers who are in possession of the CARICOM passport have been allowed entrance to other Caribbean states to ply their trade. This includes musicians and entertainers.
- Capital is moving, with an increased inflow of new capital, entrepreneurship and technology.
- Larger market opportunities for a wide range of goods and services. Trinidad and Tobago, for example, has found a large market for its

cheese, potato, banana and peanut snacks in Jamaica, where these snacks are often purchased rather than similar Jamaican manufactured snacks because of their cheaper prices and what many believe to be more attractive packaging.

- Greater opportunities for travel, study and work in CARICOM countries resulting in increased employment opportunities and improved standard of living.
- Greater economies of scale as many industries can now benefit from cheaper production costs by procuring goods important to their businesses that are cheaper to produce in other member states. Many companies, such as Carib Cement Company, which is located in Jamaica but partially owned by the Trinidadian government, will procure material and goods from Trinidad and other parts of the Caribbean that can lower production costs. Some Jamaican companies are even known to operate branches in Trinidad because of cheaper energy costs there.
- Pan-Caribbean brands, strengthened competitiveness, lower consumer prices, creation of regional companies, increased opportunities to invest through direct stock ownership or mutual fund investments.

Challenges

CARICOM still faces many challenges in its quest for economic integration through the CSME:

- There is still no common currency for members of CARICOM, which hinders attempts at a free market economy. The experience of the OECS also indicates that a common currency can produce a broad (macroeconomic) stability, which aids the economy of individual economies (microeconomies) within it. Also, many who travel to the region, for both business and tourism, often get frustrated with trying to exchange currency according to the countries they visit.
- The disparity in performance of individual markets creates tensions between member states and makes it difficult to achieve an equal balance of trade between them.
- Smaller and poorer countries harbour concerns about the ability of their businesses to compete with those of larger and richer ones in the local market.
- The local market, due to similarities in goods and products from across the region, presents limited scope for growth. Focus therefore needs to placed on external rather than intraregional trade.
  The World Bank has identified five important issues for CSME:
- Increase productivity.
- Expand trade openness.
- Improve public investment in infrastructure and education.
- Reduce the size of government.
- Maintain macroeconomic stability.

Regional Security System

The Regional Security System (RSS) was established in 1982 when Barbados, Antigua and Barbuda, Dominica, St Lucia and St Vincent and the Grenadines decided on the heels of the Grenada Revolution to sign a memorandum of understanding to commit to the protection of the Caribbean in response to security threats and political instability.

Achievements

- The security arrangement provided for cooperation in areas such as natural disasters, combating threats to national security, pollution control, maritime policing duties, smuggling prevention (including drugs and weapons), search-and-rescue operations, immigration, customs and excise control, and fisheries protection.
- Restored democratic government in Grenada.
- Teamed with US and British intelligence in establishing a protocol on how to prevent and deal with oppressive and violent governments, groups or invading forces. The RSS assisted police in the 1990 attempted coup in Trinidad.
- Pooled funds to implement systems to thwart the trafficking of drugs, guns and contraband in the region.

Challenges

- Lack of funding.
- Some territories have an issue with the USA involvement in the region under the guise of being part of the RSS.
- Because not all CARICOM member states are part of the RSS, there are large gaps in the security of the region that have been used as transshipment points for drugs and illegal guns from South America heading to the United States.
- No clear mandate on how to deal with cyber crimes and money laundering.

Caribbean Development Bank (CDB)

Achievements

- This Associate Institution of CARICOM aids both economic and social development by encouraging investment in programmes such as education and poverty reduction through loans to undertake these projects.
- It plays a major role in promoting the region to potential investors both from within and outside, since there are many nations competing for investment dollars. It also plays the role of middleman by helping connect potential investors with businesses and projects that are in need of investment.
- The CDB provides expert and technical advice to the banks and member countries in the region by helping with complex projects where nations lack expertise, and also determines the feasibility of projects.

Quick Fact

TVET – defined by UNESCO as those aspects of the educational process involving, in addition to general education, the study of technologies and related sciences and the acquisition of practical skills, attitudes, understanding and knowledge relating to occupation in various sectors of economic life.

Key Term

BMCs – **B**orrowing **M**ember **C**ountries affiliated to the Caribbean Development Bank. These regional members are not only allowed to borrow funds for the development of their states, but they are also allowed to take part in the decision making of the bank through their voting rights.

Did You Know?

Projects funded by the CDB in 2015 include drinking water in St Lucia, energy in Anguilla, transportation in Turks and Caicos Islands, drainage in Barbados, education in Belize, Haiti, Grenada and St Kitts and Nevis (Technical Vocational Educational Training; **TVET**).

Challenges

- The current levels of poverty are too high and the pace of poverty reduction is slow in many **BMCs**. Hence, there is continuing need for strong social protection systems and strategies for accelerating the pace of economic growth and poverty reduction.

- The current level of debt accumulation in BMCs is generally too high and there is a continuing need for growth-sensitive financial and debt adjustments in the economic policies of most BMCs.
- BMCs require substantial technical and financial assistance, in some cases for extended periods, because of the negative economic consequences of large debts, together with the potential challenges and risks of implementing the CSME.
- Repositioning BMCs in the context of trade liberalisation and globalisation will require high levels of budgetary resources.

Multiple-choice questions

1. 'One from ten leaves zero' was a response to
   A. Jamaica's withdrawal from the West Indies Federation in 1961
   B. Jamaica's withdrawal from the West Indies Federation in 1962
   C. Trinidad's withdrawal from the West Indies Federation in 1958
   D. Trinidad's withdrawal from the West Indies Federation in 1961

2. One of the reasons for the failure of the West Indies Federation was
   A. Britain wanted to grant the islands independence
   B. The lack of resources in the smaller islands
   C. The distrust the larger islands had for the smaller ones
   D. Jamaicans were uninterested in the union

3. The treaty that was signed in Chaguaramas on 4 July 1973 established
   A. CARICOM
   B. CARIFTA
   C. CSME
   D. ACS

4. CARIFTA was formed in response to
   A. Concerns over economic development in independent islands
   B. Concerns about islands gaining independence from Britain
   C. Concerns over the disbanding of the Federation in 1962
   D. Concerns over the smaller islands wanting to establish their own associations

5. One of the chief aims of the ACS is to
   A. Focus on cooperation
   B. Focus mainly on the English-speaking Caribbean
   C. Focus on integration
   D. Focus on becoming a member of the CSME

6. In the mid 20th century, the aim of the University of the West Indies was to
   A. Train West Indian Black students in agriculture
   B. Train all West Indians in the field of medicine
   C. Train all West Indians in the field of law
   D. Train West Indian Whites and mixed race students in the field of agriculture

7. Which of the following is not an achievement of the RSS?
   A. Restored democratic government in Grenada
   B. Assisted police in the 1990 attempted coup in Trinidad
   C. Provided funds to aid in curbing the trafficking of drugs in the region
   D. Improved public investment in infrastructure and education

Chapter 16

Contributions of Sport to Development

Evaluate the importance of sports to the development of the region.

After revising this topic, you should be able to:
- explain how sport generates income for the region;
- understand and describe the relevance of health and fitness to development;
- identify educational opportunities provided by sport in the Caribbean;
- explain how sport contributes to Caribbean identity;
- recognise how sport engenders discipline and morale;
- show an awareness of the importance and potential of sport tourism.

Sports have been a major source of enjoyment for Caribbean people since the Amerindians. Both the Maya and the Tainos enjoyed a ballgame, called Batos by the Tainos, that was common to both cultures. The game was a popular spectator sport that was played in large open spaces that were common features among Amerindian settlements geared at accommodating large crowds.

While sporting activities of any kind were too much of a luxury for the enslaved plantation workers of the Caribbean, the Europeans brought with them various sporting activities that were part of their traditions. Colonisation and creolisation resulted in Caribbean people developing an appreciation and love for these European sports, such as horse racing, cricket, soccer/football, track and field, tennis and most

Exam Tip

When considering this topic, it is important to remember to look beyond medals and individual achievements of sporting stars to evaluate how the Caribbean's involvement in international sporting competitions and the establishment of regional sport programmes has contributed to the economics, culture and social and educational development of Caribbean society.

Figure 16.1 Contributions of sport to the development of the Caribbean

Development of Caribbean economies and culture	+	Generaton of income
Sport tourism	+	Employment
Government investment and recognition	+	Industries emerging (Sporting goods etc)
Sports sponsorship and endorsement deals	+	**International recognition**
Caribbean identity	+	Mass media
Sports events and competitons	+	Sports programs and education
Educational opportunities	+	Development of talent
Discipline and morale	+	**Health and fitness**

types of water sports, including swimming and water polo. In embracing these sports, Caribbean sportspeople and athletes have often excelled in their performance and have developed distinct and flamboyant styles of playing games, such as in cricket.

The significance of sports is not restricted to areas of leisure and entertainment. Facets and aspects of 'sports' run through Caribbean politics, economies and society, as summarised by Figure 16.1. Sports contribute to the region on many different levels; from boosting economic development through income generation to supporting human development in the form of improving health and fitness and as a source of self-esteem.

Generation of Income

Next to tourism and music, sporting activities have become a major contributor to the economies of Caribbean states by providing employment through the collection of taxes, spectator fees and sports venue rental and from the marketing and sale of sporting merchandise. Tourism specific to sport is an important adjunct to this.

Taxes

- Sporting activities have contributed to government income through the collection of taxes and tariffs from sporting goods coming into the country.
- Sporting professionals and athletes also contribute to government coffers, and, by extension, to the economic and infrastructural development of the Caribbean, via direct PAYE and other forms of income taxes.

Employment and Earnings

- The traditional income earning fields in sports include athletes earning from participation in various events and the employment of coaches, officials who monitor sporting events and members of sporting oversight and regulation bodies.
- Money coming in from spectators through the staging of national sporting activities contributes to the widespread employment of workers who maintain and run these facilities before, during and after sporting events.
- Governments and private owners of sporting arenas and complexes earn when their venues are used for events. The National Stadium, the Catherine Hall Sporting Complex in Montego Bay, Jamaica, and the Barbados National Stadium all have to be rented for use of track and field and football events.
- Many earn a living by entering some of the new and highly sought after sport-related occupational fields. Physiotherapy (a physiotherapy degree programme was recently introduced at the University of the West Indies, UWI), sports medicine, rehabilitation technicians/spa directors, nutritionists and promoters are just some of the fields that have become popular following on from the success of Caribbean athletes in various sporting activities.
- The owners and operators of sport wellness facilities also earn greatly from both recreational and professional athletes. Gymnasium and spa

---

Making the Connection

Take note of the links between sports and our historical development, Chapter 5 'The Historical Process', sports and our cultural identity, Chapter 7 'Identity and Social Formation', sports and Caribbean unification, Chapter 15 'The Integration Movement', and the promotion and broadcasting of Caribbean sports across the region, Chapter 18 'Roles and Functions of the Mass Media'.

Quick Fact

Since his record-breaking feat at the Olympic Games in 2008 in Beijing, China, Usain Bolt has achieved an estimated net worth of over US$30 million. His earnings have come from appearance fees for the European track and field circuit, and also an estimated US$10 million per year in endorsement fees. The number of people employed by Bolt as coaches, handlers and business advisors, who have earned from his success as an athlete, should also be considered.

operators charge fees for use of their facilities and these are increasingly in demand resulting from the successes of Caribbean athletes.

Media and Advertising

- The Caribbean's various media outlets earn large sums of money per year from the broadcasting and advertising of sporting events. Caribbean television media buy the rights of popular sporting events and air them exclusively on their own stations in order to secure viewership and earn from advertising spots bought around the airing of these events.

Did You Know?

Television Jamaica (TVJ), one of the Jamaica's largest media outlets, The Caribbean Broadcasting Corporation in Barbados (CBC), The Grenada Broadcasting Network (GBN) and the Caribbean Communications Network from Trinidad and Tobago are all examples of television channels that partner with the Olympic and World Championship committees to buy exclusive rights to the showing of all World Championship and Olympic content during the staging of the games (for example, in 2011 and 2012 respectively) in the knowledge that interest in and viewership of the expected successes of Caribbean athletes would be high in the region and among the diaspora. These stations hope to gain from advertising spots around events that would fetch a premium price considering the large viewership via television and internet streaming, thus illustrating the economic viability of sports in the region.

Key Term

Endorsement – a form of support or approval. Athletes often endorse companies or products and are usually paid by the company for doing so.

- Sports merchandising and **endorsements** have become fast-growing industries in the Caribbean, especially with the increasing popularity of athletes from the region. CXC® Track and field stars Usain Bolt, Asafa Powell and Shelly Ann Fraiser-Price, cricketer Chris Gayle and swimmer Alia Atkinson are all signed to major beverage and sporting goods brands. This type of advertising often generates more income for athletes than taking part in sporting events.

Making the Connection

Sport tourism is discussed in more detail later in this chapter.

Tourism

The success of Caribbean athletes and teams in international sport has in turn drawn in international competitions and spectators from abroad. These, combined with the emerging niche tourism market that offers packages based around water sports, hiking and so on, have created a relatively new source of income for the region.

Health and Fitness

Sporting activities form part of the programmes that help to ward off lifestyle diseases such as diabetes, high blood pressure, heart disease and cancers that plague people all over the world, including the Caribbean. Good health forms one of the bases for human development as it is necessary for full empowerment of the individual. Health problems caused by inactivity and lack of exercise can negatively affect productivity and economic growth because when people are ill, it can slow their performance as well as lead to absence from work.

These forms of lifestyle diseases can also put a strain on the health sector of Caribbean states. The cost of treatment of these diseases can drain any health ministry's budget as they would need to procure expensive equipment and personnel.

Sporting activities often form part of primary healthcare programmes that deal with the implementation of preventative measures to negate the impact of ill health on Caribbean economies. Sports have also helped the programmes of many rehabilitation centres that use sport in an interactive way to help heal accident victims or victims of violent crimes. This has helped productive people who suffer from crippling illness or other physical or even mental setbacks brought on by accidents to be rehabilitated and continue to make their contributions to the growth of Caribbean society.

Sporting activities have over the years been a main pillar in the formal education system of many Caribbean countries. It has even been a Caribbean Examinations Council (CXC®) subject for the past decade. Physical Education (PE), as it is called in many schools, has helped to introduce children to the importance of physical activity and the mental and physical benefits of engaging in competitive sports.

Educational Opportunities

It is widely known throughout Caribbean secondary schools that taking part and doing well in a sport at school level can open opportunities for students to earn scholarships and bursaries to attend Ivy League universities in foreign countries. These scholarships have given many Caribbean athletes the opportunity to access a tertiary education and expand their exposure to new forms of coaching to help them transition into being professional athletes.

Did You Know?

Universities and colleges in the US award approximately US$1 billion each year to 150 000 student athletes from across the globe. With some colleges requiring only a minimum of five CSEC® subjects for eligibility to a scholarship financing full-time studies, many Caribbean students attend these institutions and represent them in competitions at college level. Most scholarships require students to train for a minimum of three hours per day, leaving them with time to properly pursue the academic side of their studies. Many of these graduates return to the region to pursue careers in various areas, having utilised sport to acquire an education that they otherwise could not afford.

New courses and educational opportunities have opened in many fields in the Caribbean as a result of the contribution of sports. Examples of these courses are the physiotherapy degree now offered at the University of the West Indies, the focus/specialisation of sports medicine in many of the region's tertiary institutions and numerous coaching certification programmes now offered to fill the demand for coaching staff.

Did You Know?

According to the World Health Organization, in a 2015 fact sheet on non-communicable disease (NCD), physical inactivity is a leading contributor to the development of these kinds of illnesses, which include various forms of cancers and cardiovascular diseases. The Pan-American Health Organization outlined in a 2001 report that NCD contributes to 70% of the total burden of diseases in the Caribbean and Latin America. Both of these reports can be used to stress the importance of sports as a means of preventing the occurrence of NCD among people, including in the Caribbean.

Quick Fact

A 2013 World Bank Study on NCDs in the Caribbean showed that the prevalence of these types of illnesses led to lower tax revenues and lower returns on human capital investment.

Discipline and Morale

Making the Connection

Through its contributions to health, individual empowerment, self-discipline, morale and so on, sport in its various forms and aspects positively affects human development. Chapter 12 'Concepts and Indicators of Development' looks more closely at various definitions of development and how it can be measured, including human development.

Sportsmen and women throughout the region are often admired for their commitment to improvement in their respective fields. This is because of the discipline that it takes to commit to specialised diets and extensive training programmes that help on the road to becoming a better athlete. Sport is often viewed as a character-building activity because of this required commitment in order to succeed, along with the need to perform in the spirit of fair play.

Teamwork is a major part of all sports, even those involving individual events. Being part of a team teaches athletes to respect the rules of the sports in which they are competing, the style and abilities of their teammates and the professional advice of the coaching staff. The discipline and respect engendered by sport can be used to inculcate similar attitudes and approaches among the young, especially those deemed to be 'at risk' from involvement in crime, drug-taking and so on. A number of schemes have been established to promote sport and its benefits among the young, and to deter them from risky or anti-social behaviour.

Did You Know?

Examples of sports youth programmes are:

- **The Ballaz Liberty Park Turf initiative in Jamaica:** sponsored mainly by Jamaican manufacturing giant LASCO Ltd and launched in 2016, the initiative involved the construction of two miniature artificial football (soccer) turfs. It aims not only to promote physical activity and talent development in football, but also to develop and boost the morale and social and mental character of children through promoting discipline and dedication in sports.
- **The Caribbean Healthy Lifestyle Project:** began in Jamaica with the promotion of netball among girls in order to engender social responsibility, leadership skills and an appreciation of the benefits of healthy living, it has now extended to both genders, other parts of the Caribbean and other sports.

Did You Know?

Sport can be a form of social and economic empowerment. It is one of the main ways in which men and women who would not normally have access to opportunities provided by wealth and education can be upwardly mobile in the Caribbean. Track stars Veronica Campbell-Brown and Grace Jackson, cricket legend Vivian Richards and soccer/football star Dwight Yorke are all examples of athletes whose talents gave them the resources and recognition to enable them to rise in the social strata of the Caribbean. This is another way in which sport can have a positive effect on human development.

Involvement in sports is used by businesses such as those in the private sector in Jamaica, where employees work together and compete in teams for prizes in Business House sporting competitions. The aim is to boost staff morale through representation of their organisation and to promote teamwork, which is important for any organisation to be successful. Thus, the acquisition of discipline and morale through the extension of sports competitions into the world of business can contribute to training employees in the importance of commitment, team work and health and fitness, which in turn will have a positive impact on productivity.

Development of a Caribbean Identity

The Caribbean is known globally as a major source of sporting talent; especially in the areas of track and field, cricket, football/soccer and, more recently, swimming (following the emergence of the record-achieving swimmers, George Bovell III and Alia Atkinson). As a result of this association with famous athletes, Caribbean nationals are fast becoming known for their athletic prowess. The association has become part of our Caribbean identity.

This attribution has become so widespread that secondary school students often list sports as their extra curricular talents to gain entrance into prestigious foreign universities and colleges, knowing that university recruiters often identify Caribbean nationals as sportsmen and women. Caribbean athletes have filled vacancies for talent in various leagues and sporting competitions across the globe because recruiters and sporting scouts often offer Caribbean nationals scholarships and positions on professional teams.

Some Caribbean countries have shaped an identity and an association with certain sports because of their continued success in that field. For example, Cuba is known for its boxing programme, Jamaica for its track and field programme and its stars, Trinidad and Tobago are known to produce excellent footballers and the Dominican Republic is known for producing baseball players. With individual territories identified for excellence in specialised fields, athletes can focus on developing and perfecting their prowess in one area, thus increasing their likelihood of doing well in a particular sport.

The sport the Caribbean first excelled at globally was cricket. The West Indies cricket team was eventually formed in the 1900s after the West Indian Colonies put together teams on a regular basis to challenge visiting English teams. This led to the development of a West Indies cricket programme that challenged England's dominance in the sport, and it was this challenge that put the team on the map in the world of cricket. Although individual territories have their own cricket programmes and national teams, it is under the title of 'The West Indies' that the region becomes most recognisable in the sport. This has led many within and outside the region to identify the Caribbean as a cricketing society.

Track and field, like cricket, has become a sporting area that the Caribbean is known for because of the strong challenges and celebrated victories against North American and European countries, which have had longer established track and field programmes and more resources to invest in them. 'Greats' such as Arthur Wint, Donald Quarry and Merlene Otty, of Jamaica and Oto Boldon, of Trinidad, were the first major challengers against 'big name' athletes from other parts of the world. These early successes have been built upon by successive generations of Caribbbean athletes with the result that the Caribbean is now known as the 'track and field factory' of the world. Consequently, many athletes and coaches travel to the Caribbean to experience and study best practice in our track and field programmes.

Making the Connection

Other aspects of Caribbean identity are investigated in Chapter 7 'Identity and Social Formation'.

Making the Connection

The role of the West Indies Cricket Board in Caribbean integration is described in Chapter 15 'The Integration Movement'.

Quick Facts

Recogition of the Caribbean as a major talent pool of athletes is shown by the selection by other nations of Caribbean athletes to represent them at club and national level football and athletics. Examples are Dwight Yorke, Johnny Barnes, Donovan Bailey, Lindford Christie and Sanya Richards-Ross.

Did You Know?

The Caribbean is one of the first regions to have consistently produced and promoted female athletes, who sometimes do better than their male counterparts in international competitions. Athletes such as Merlene Otty, Juliet Cuthbert, Grace Jackson-Small and Deon Hemmings have all outshone their male counterparts in their respective events; a feat that many other nations have yet to experience. The association with, and identity of, the region as a powerhouse in creating great female athletes has empowered many Caribbean women to pursue careers in their respective fields.

Sport Tourism

Sport tourism is a fast-growing dimension of visits to the region. Sports fans and even athletes visit to watch or take part in major sport events held in the Caribbean. These visitors spend money on accommodation, food, entertainment and souvenirs that help to support local Caribbean economies.

The success of Caribbean athletes in the 2008 Beijing Olympic Games put the spotlight on track and field as an area that could be exploited in terms of tourism. Its significance is not just in the staging of events; sport tourism also has the potential to bring attention to the emerging state-of-the-art training facilities now being built all over the Caribbean. One such training facility, the Usain Bolt Track at the UWI Mona campus, continues to attract athletes from all over the world who visit to get a feel for the conditions under which Caribbean track stars train. Visitors also flock to the facility to get a glimpse of the record-breaking athletes. This product has major potential for growth and could possibly help to boost the region's tourism industry in the traditionally slow summer period, which would be around the time when most Caribbean track and field competitions take place.

Sport tourism is not only about spectators and participation on a professional or high-order level, however. There is also much tourism across the region associated with recreational activities that could be classed as sports: in areas such as water sports, for example surfing, diving, sailing and fishing; and outdoor 'adventure' activities, such as hiking, mountaineering and white-water rafting. All these require a local level of expertise in support and training as well as the provision and maintenance of specialised equipment, and so make a contribution to local economies.

Key Term

Sport tourism – refers to travel that involves either observing or participating in a sporting event. As the concept develops, different forms of sport tourism are being identified and it is generally accepted to include participation in sports for recreational purposes and visiting famous sporting locations as well as spectatorship of or participation in an actual competitive event.

Key Term

Sponsor – a person or organisation that pays for, or contributes to the costs involved in staging, a sporting or artistic event or financially supports an individual or team in return for advertising.

International Recognition

The global recognition in sports brought to the area by Caribbean successes has been accompanied by significant monetary sports investment from private **sponsors** seeking to benefit from the attention their companies receive by being associated with popular sports and athletes. Examples are sporting goods giant Puma as the official sponsor of the Jamaican 2012 and 2016 Olympic teams, and Digicel as the official sponsor of West Indian cricket. This recognition has also created scholarships for student athletes and professional opportunities abroad for Caribbean athletes and coaches.

Sport tourism, too, has benefited from the international attention brought by Caribbean sporting success, as international media, sports enthusiasts, spectators and athletes visit the region to satisfy their curiosity about its sports programmes or to see their favourite athletes.

This recognition is fueled by the high profile of record-breaking performances of Caribbean athletes on YouTube® and other forms of social media, and by Caribbean media outlets broadcasting and streaming regional and international sporting events of interest to those outside the region, in particular the diaspora.

The international recognition of the Caribbean in the field of sport, of its high-performance athletes and world-ranking teams in track and field, cricket and soccer/football in particular, serves to promote not only the region's sporting achievements but also the region as a whole.

Check Your Knowledge

Discuss FOUR contributions from sport to the development of the Caribbean.

Demonstrate an understanding of the following terms and concepts by defining and using them correctly:

* development
* tourism
* sport tourism
* regional/Caribbean identity.

You must discuss FOUR of the points below, arguing how sports contribute to the development of the Caribbean and making sure to draw examples from Caribbean countries.

* **Sport tourism:** huge events, such as golf, water sports, cricket (including the 2007 World Cup), football and athletics, attract very large crowds to the region. Marketing the Caribbean as the number one sporting destination will result in sporting fans spending a lot of money on food and travel, thus generating income and contributing to economic development. For example, both the private and public sectors can develop golf courses to world-class standards to host international competitions at local venues that have a unique Caribbean brand.

* **International recognition** brings media attention to the region, such as when Jamaican track and field star Usain Bolt became the first athlete in the world to win three consecutive gold medals for the 100 metres, 200 metres and the 4 × 100 metres relay race at the Rio Olympics in 2016. His photographs were on billboards in Times Square, New York, London, Beijing and Rio. Keshorn Walcott of Trindad and Tobago, a javelin thrower, also won his second Olympic medal (bronze) at the Rio Olympics.

* **A sense of morale and discipline:** participation in sports requires discipline and can, for example, control behaviour in hyperactive children as well as promote teamwork. In times of civil unrest and political instability, sports can serve as a way of boosting or raising morale.

* **Generation of income or wealth:** professional sportsmen and women earn incomes that can contribute to social and economic

Making the Connection

Chapter 11 'Caribbean–Global Interactions'

Chapter 12 'Concepts and Indicators of Development'

Chapter 13 'Factors that Affect Development'

Exam Tip

'**Discuss**' requires an extended response defining key concepts, giving the facts, exploring related concepts and issues and presenting reasoned arguments. You must use detailed examples but **not** necessarily draw a conclusion.

development. Sport is tied to a global marketplace via media coverage, and advertising and television rights earn money for the Caribbean.

- **Provides educational opportunities:** as a field of study, a co-curricular activity and a way of attaining further education. Sports have been introduced into the school curriculum as PE and as a CXC® CSEC® examination, which expands students' career choices. Sports scholarships are an opportunity for higher education in the United Kingdom and North America. Sports scouts travel to the Caribbean to search for talent. There has also been an upgrade of sporting facilities in schools, improved teaching and learning resources and professional development for teachers. These have helped to boost economic growth.

- **Development of health and fitness:** mentally, physically and psychologically. Exercise and diet control diseases such as hypertension, diabetes and heart disease, which negatively affect the sustainable growth and development of the economy through high medical costs, decreased productivity and loss of life.

- **A representation of national and Caribbean identity:** cricket, for instance, defines us because it acts as a unifying force among Caribbean people, facilitating integration: the team is selected from across the Caribbean and represents independence from colonial powers, especially when the team wins games against England. When the Jamaican football team won the qualifying round of the World Cup, the Prime Minister announced a national holiday and pride in the team extended to the region as a whole. The entire Caribbean and the diaspora supported Usain Bolt at Rio in 2016 when he won three Olympic gold medals for Jamaica.

- **On the other hand, you can argue the following:**
  - Some Caribbean countries lack the proper infrastructure and capital to develop sport tourism. Some Caribbean governments may not view sports as a priority because of other pressing issues, such as poverty and the environment.
  - Wealth and income can only be generated from sports if there is capital investment by Caribbean governments, who need to build state-of-the-art facilities and more local sporting centres and sports colleges, provide government grants for sports in national budgets and formulate government policies to oversee and enforce sports processes that conform with international laws.
  - Many recipients of sports scholarships do not return home after completing their education abroad because of lack of training facilities/infrastructure and employment opportunities. Some represent the country where they reside rather than the Caribbean.
  - The contributions sports can make to health varies from one country to another based on diet and other factors, including the conditions under which sporting activities occur (e.g. presence of dust, absence of equipment, degree of financial support and level of infrastructural development or facilities). The general infrastructure and the rate of poverty within a country directly affect health and fitness and development.
  - Far from being a source of Caribbean and diasporic identity, sports can bring feelings of insecurity and divisiveness as individual Caribbean countries compete against each other. This was evident in preparation for the Cricket World Cup in 2007 when countries bid for the finals to be held in their specific country.

- **Conclude** the essay by summarising the different arguments.

Multiple-choice Questions

1. The success of Caribbean athletes in the Olympics has contributed to ALL of the following EXCEPT
   A. Growth of spa directors
   B. Growth of nutritionist agencies
   C. International recognition
   D. Divided loyalties for Caribbean athletes among Caribbean nations

2. Which of the following sports can be considered indigenous to the Caribbean?
   A. Football
   B. Batos
   C. Track and field
   D. Croquet

3. The Olympic athlete who placed the spotlight on the Caribbean at the Beijing Olympic games in 2008 is
   A. Ato Boldon
   B. Usain Bolt
   C. Chris Gayle
   D. Alia Atkinson

4. Cricket can be considered all of the following EXCEPT
   A. An indigenous game to the Caribbean
   B. A game brought to the West Indies by the British
   C. A sport once considered 'a gentleman's game'
   D. A sport that integrates the Caribbean and the diaspora together

5. The involvement of the mass media in sports coverage encourages all of the following EXCEPT
   A. It promotes integration among Caribbean people
   B. It promotes pride for all athletes aired on television
   C. It spurs economic activity within islands that air these events via the various mass media forms
   D. It encourages individual islands to be loyal to their own athletes during aired sporting events

6. Which of the following is the most important reason to develop sport tourism in the Caribbean?
   A. It encourages tourists to visit the islands freely
   B. It encourages hotels to improve on their accommodations
   C. It contributes to the growth of the small Caribbean economies
   D. It encourages the growth of stadia in the islands

Chapter 17

Intellectual Traditions

After revising this topic, you should be able to:

- define the terms: Pan-Africanism, Négritude and Rastafari;
- identify the pioneers of Pan-Africanism, Négritude and Rastafari and explain their contributions to the movement;
- discuss the contributions of Pan-Africanism, Négritude and Rastafari to the Caribbean region;
- assess the impact of different schools of political and economic thought on development of the region, in particular Industrialisation by Invitation, Marxism/Neo-Marxism and Dependency Theory;
- explain how Caribbean feminist thought and the theories of gender impact on development in the region;
- discuss the significance of Indo-Caribbean thought in the region;
- assess the contribution of the indigenous perspective on development.

To fully understand the idea of intellectual traditions that have acquired importance in the Caribbean, it is important to know why these intellectual traditions developed from the 1850s onwards. The Caribbean people had been:

- subjected to systems of oppression (encomienda, slavery, indentureship, colonialism);
- left with no voice and no means of redress for the injustices they faced;
- becoming increasing vocal about the social injustices and oppressive treatment that they faced;
- fighting to change the untenable situation that they lived in.

As the second half of the 19th century progressed, the wave of persistent criticism against the systems that were in place became more strident and organised. Scholars began to articulate the conditions of the people in their writings, producing works that highlighted the social, political and economic conditions and in many instances providing solutions to these problems. These writings, which touched all aspects of Caribbean life, were important in expressing Caribbean thought and for providing political, social and economic ideas when, later, leaders devised plans for their countries' development.

With the opportunity for Caribbean nationals to study abroad, many became more aware of the oppressive and limited nature of development that existed in their homelands. Many of these students assumed the role of activists and advocates as they attempted to create strategies to bridge the divide that existed and which was perpetuated by the socio-economic conditions.

Syllabus Objective

Assess the significance of Caribbean thought to the development of the region.

Quick Facts

Writers with Caribbean roots who articulated the condition of their people include René Maran (born in Martinique of Guyanese parents) who won the Goncort Prize, an award for French novelists, in 1921.

Some early Caribbean home-based scholars include T.A. Marryshaw of Grenada, who became managing editor of the newspaper *The West Indian* in 1915, and Anténor Firmin, a Haitian anthropologist, politician and writer.

Afro-Caribbean Thought

In different parts of the world, the circumstances that the same group of people face can evoke different reactions. In the case of Africans and those of African descent, their reactions to their circumstances have led to Pan-Africanism, Négritude, Rastafari and Garveyism. The political actions which they have generated tend to reflect not only the situation of the time, but also the countries where these reforms took place and the tools they used to institute these changes.

During the second half of the 19th century, a wave of criticism began among West Indian writers who spoke out about the injustices of colonialism, underdevelopment, social inequality and racial discrimination. This movement led to a rise in Black awareness and the establishment of ideologies that shaped the political and social landscape in both the Caribbean and the international community. The evidence of this Black consciousness and assertiveness is seen in:

- Pan-Africanism
- Négritude
- Rastafari.

Pan-Africanism

Pan-Africanism is a philosophy based on the belief that Africans and people who are of African ancestry have a commonality of goals and other links. The movement encourages harmony and unity among Black people in order for them to achieve their shared objectives. A key aspect of Pan-Africanism philosophy is an understanding and promotion of Black Power or unity among Black people, which advocates a sense of racial pride and self-esteem.

Pan-Africanism developed as a response by African people and people of African descent to the treatment and oppression of their forebears during colonisation and slavery. The idea of Pan-Africanism is said to have begun in America during the mid-1800s. It is a belief that African peoples, including those on the continent of Africa and in the diaspora, share a common history and a common destiny and that they have an interdependence which is manifested in the creation of political institutions.

Based on these beliefs, it is important to understand that Pan-Africanism:

- developed out of the need to combat the confines of slavery and colonialism;
- is entrenched in the idea that all people of African ancestry have common interests and so must be unified and celebrated;
- has as its main vision the creation of a unified African nation where all Africans in the diaspora can live.

Pan-Africanism and its Contribution to Development in the Caribbean

In the first half of the 20th century, the typical Caribbean worker was faced with poor remuneration and deplorable housing and living conditions. There was limited self-government with no social services, few workers' rights and, in some cases, high unemployment. Resistance to these conditions during the 1930s and beyond led to a mass movement in the Caribbean, fuelled by the ideology of Pan-Africanism, as workers sought to have these issues addressed. The end results were:

- public awareness of the plight of Black people, especially in the Caribbean and USA;
- increased international cooperation among Black people;
- the emergence of some radical leaders;
- an awakening of the workers' class consciousness;
- the formation of grassroots political parties;
- the labour movement becoming a political issue, with labour strikes and protests;
- the formation of formal labour movements such as the Trade Union Congress, the Jamaica Workers and Tradesmen's Union (JWTU) and the Oilfield Workers' Trade Union (OWTU) of Trinidad and Tobago;
- the formation of nationalist movements and a move towards socio-economic and political independence.

Figure 17.1 provides some information on some of the main Caribbean leaders of the Pan-African movement and Figure 17.2 presents the impact of the movement on the region.

Key Term

Black Power – the political slogan that represents the ideologies of equality and racial pride, and the establishment of Black political and cultural institutions aimed at the promotion of the interests of all Black people.

Figure 17.1 **Key Pan-African Leaders of the Caribbean**

Henry Sylvester Williams (1869–1911)

- Born in Trinidad, was a lecturer who spoke out against the oppression that Africans and their descendants faced.
- In 1897, while studying in Britain, formed the African Association, later renamed the Pan-African Association, to expose the injustices that African people faced and to promote their interests.
- Organised the first world Pan-African Conference in London in July 1900, attended by representatives from America, Ethopia and Lybia and important figures such as W.E.B. Du Bois and Alexander Walters of the African Methodist Episcopal Church.
- Established Pan-African Associations in Jamaica and Trinidad in 1901; launched a journal called *The Pan African* in the same year.

Marcus Mosiah Garvey (1887–1940)

- Born in Jamaica, formed the Universal Negro Improvement Association (UNIA) in 1914.
- UNIA sought to improve the standard of living for people of Black African descent in North and South America, Europe and the Caribbean, and became one of the biggest organisations in the history of the Pan-African movement.
- Called the Black Moses, proclaimed the need for the establishment of an independent Black economy within a White capitalist society and in 1919 established the shipping company, the Black Star Line, and the Negro Factories Corporation to encourage Black economic independence.
- With worldwide circulation, his weekly newspaper, *The Negro World* (which included pages in Spanish and French), worried colonial officials and they retaliated by banning it from their colonies.
- Was investigated for mail fraud in connection with the inappropriate sale of Black Star Line stocks and was eventually deported from the US.
- On returning to Jamaica in 1925, found that racial discrimination and capitalism hindered the Black people there. These same issues affected other English-speaking colonies, including Barbados, Grenada and Trinidad. He reconstructed the UNIA to address the specific issues of the workers.

(continued)

Cyril Briggs (1888–1966)

- Born in Nevis, he was a Black nationalist, civil rights activist, journalist and member of the American Communist Party.
- In 1918, he began publishing his own journal, *The Crusader*, and, in that same year, he founded the African Blood Brotherhood (ABB), which would later serve as the link between Black communities and the Communist movement in the US.
- The ABB was founded upon the ideas of Garveyism, which sought to promote Black nationalism, and supported equal rights for Black people.
- The ABB had a large contingent of supporters, including many Caribbean-born political activists.
- He offered an alternative to Garvey's movement and became involved in an open, ongoing dispute with Garvey; he criticised the capitalist nature of 'Garveyism', and later cooperated in the mail fraud investigation against him.

George Padmore (1902–1959)

- Born in Trinidad, his name at birth was Malcolm Ivan Meredith Nurse.
- Worked in Germany as the head of the International Trade Union Committee of Negro Workers (ITUC-NW) during the 1930s.
- Wrote *Life and Struggle of Negro Toilers*, which dealt in some depth with working conditions of Black people around the world.
- Initially critical of people such as W.E.B. Du Bois and Marcus Garvey because of his communist ideology, he later wrote for Du Bois' *Crisis*.
- Moved to London in 1934, and dedicated his time to writing about Pan-Africanism and African independence.
- Was influential in planning the Fifth Pan-African Congress in Manchester, UK, in 1945.
- Wrote *Pan-Africanism or Communism?*, which was published in 1956 and considered his most significant work.

Walter Rodney (1942–1990)

- Born in Georgetown, Guyana; received his PhD in African History at the age of 24.
- Presented a paper, 'African History in the Service of Black Liberation', at the Congress of Black Writers Conference in Canada in 1968.
- Was banned from returning to Jamaica where he held an academic post at UWI the same year and this led to rioting in Kingston, known as the 'Rodney Riots'.
- Published the book, *How Europe Underdeveloped Africa*, in 1972; a direct result of his involvement in the African Liberation Struggles.
- Influence is seen in the Caribbean through the idea of 'Black Power', the movement he promoted; in May 1970, Maurice Bishop led a Black Power demonstration in Grenada.

Figure 17.2 The impact of Pan-Africanism

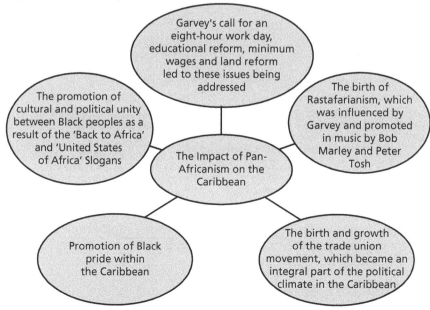

Quick Facts

Other Pan-African figures include:

- Cyril Lionel Robert (C.L.R.) James of Trinidad
- Norman Cameron of Guyana
- Rosie Dougal of Dominica
- Leonard Timoshenko Hector of Antigua
- Amy Ashwood Garvey and Dr Theophilus Edward Samuel Scholars of Jamaica.

Opposition to the Caribbean Pan-African Movement

The main interest groups in the Caribbean who opposed the Pan-Africanism movement in the Caribbean were the White planter-merchant class and those of mixed, Asian and Middle-Eastern descent who recognised the potential far-reaching impact of the movement:

- They saw Pan-Africanism as a disruption or attack on their interests in terms of the social, political and economic situation.
- In particular, the White planter-merchant class viewed education and enlightenment of the former-enslaved peoples as causing the disintegration of colonialism.

These interest groups were mostly involved in manufacturing and trade. Yet more opposition interest groups included shopkeepers, business owners, small-scale farmers and landlords. All these groups offered resistance to the movement because it would mean a restructuring of the class system.

Quick Fact

While Henry Sylvester Williams is credited with coining the idea of Pan-Africanism, it was the influence of W.E.B. Du Bois and Garvey that concretised the movement. They supported and promoted the objectives and beliefs of the Pan-African movement, establishing it on the international scene.

Négritude

The **Négritude** movement began as a literary movement in France among French-speaking Africans and Caribbean intellectuals and writers who were living there. It was in response to their objections to French colonial rule and the concerted effort to integrate them into French society. The various Négritude movements around the world developed because of shared concerns and interests among Black people.

Key Term

Négritude – a literary and ideological movement led by French-speaking Black intellectuals, writers and politicians and adopted as part of Pan-African ideology. It is a consciousness and promotion of Black pride, and an awareness and appreciation of the cultural and physical aspects of African heritage.

Did You Know?

Négritude began in France. The French sought to assimilate the cultures of those within their boundaries, including their colonies, and the people affected objected to these efforts. To combat this, the Black populace in France and the colonies began to make attempts to recover and reclaim their history, their culture and their national identity. The Négritude movement is one example of the literary expression of Pan-Africanism.

Figure 17.3 **Some founders of the Négritude movement**

Léopold Sédar Senghor
(1906–2001)

- Born in Senegal
- Poet, playwright, teacher, politician
- Was put off by the 'cultural arrogance' of the French he met while studying in France
- Helped to launch *L'Etudiant Noir* (*Black Student*) in 1934, which was used to promote the idea of Black intuitive thought
- First president of independent Senegal

Léon Damas
(1912–1978)

- Born in French Guiana
- Editor, poet, diplomat
- The first Black writer to do in-depth work on the effect of colonisation on the consciousness of the oppressed
- Poems addressed the negros' problems of self-identity, which stemmed from French colonisation racism

Aimé Césaire
(1913–2008)

- Born in Martinique
- Poet, teacher and statesman
- The Négritude movement's most prominent spokesman
- His poems *Cahier d'un retour au pays natal* (*Notebook of a Return to the Native Land*) *Soleil cou-coupé* (Cutthroat Sun), in 1948, were used to criticise the French colonial oppressors

The Basic Ideas of Négritude

- Emphasis on the importance and dignity of African traditions and its people.
- The richness of African life should be advanced over the insensitivity and materialistic nature of the Western culture.
- Africans must utilise their own cultural traditions to determine how they operate in the modern world.
- There must be the restoration of Black Africans' cultural identity.
- Writers must use African subject matter and, in doing so, promote a longing for political freedom.

The Objectives of Négritude

- To promote the fierce pride and spirit of the African people and to use Africa as the foundation for establishing a cultural and ethnic identity for Black peoples.
- To neutralise the persistent notion of Black inferiority and to promote Black independence instead.
- To use the arts and literature to promote the concept of Blackness.
- To eradicate the barriers that existed between Black students of the numerous French colonies and, by extension, all people of Black descent.
- To promote an acceptance of the Black identity by the oppressors, and more specifically the European imperial powers.

The Impact of Négritude on the Caribbean

- Its beginning in French Martinique, with political activist Aimé Césaire, was the basis of protest against French colonialism.
- Damas' poems decried the practice of slavery, colonial assimilation, the rejection of one's cultural identity and discrimination. His writings are said to be the 'manifesto of the Négritude movement'.
- Franz Fanon, also of Martinique, supported the decolonising efforts and used his writings to achieve social justice for the oppressed. His extensive writings on the effects of colonialism on the human psyche and colonised people influenced the decolonising efforts when they began in the Caribbean.
- It focused on the advancement of Black consciousness and led to the renewal of Black pride and self-worth through literature, poetry and other forms of entertainment.
- It influenced many Caribbean writers, such as Derek Walcott, Claude McKay, Patrick Chamoiseau and Jean Bernabé.
- Embraced more in Haiti and Cuba than in the Commonwealth Caribbean, Négritude is seen in the acceptance of the movement's ideals by Jacques Roumain, the founder of the Haitian Communist party.

Quick Fact

Négritude was also influenced by the Harlem Renaissance, which occurred in Harlem, New York City, from the 1920s to the mid-1930s. It was a literary, artistic and intellectual movement that kindled a new African-American cultural identity. It is the most influential movement in African-American literary history.

Quick Fact

The origins of the term 'Négritude'

In 1934, Aimé Césaire, Léopold Sédar Senghor and Léon Damas founded the journal *L'Étudiant Noir*, which was used to promote the Pan-Africanist literary and cultural movement later named 'Négritude' ('Blackness' in French), which was coined by Césaire in his book, *Cahier d'un retour au pays natal* (*Notebook of a Return to the Native Land*, 1939).

Did You Know?

The terms Pan-Africanism and Négritude are applied to different movements where common ideas are expressed about how African populations should perceive themselves. Garveyism took on a more complete Pan-African perspective, as it sought an African-ruled nation for all Blacks, while Négritude was a movement that sought to promote African culture.

Making the Connection

Chapter 5 'The Historical Process'

Chapter 6 'Characteristics of Society and Culture'

Chapter 7, 'Identity and Social Formation'

Exam Tips

'**Discuss**' requires an extended response defining key concepts, giving the facts, exploring related concepts and issues and presenting reasoned arguments. You must use detailed examples but **not** necessarily draw a conclusion.

'**The extent to which**' wording requires you to evaluate something by measuring the degree to which it is reliable, valid or useful.

Check Your Knowledge

Discuss the extent to which the ideologies of Pan-Africanism altered the lives of African descendants in the Caribbean.

Demonstrate an understanding of the following concepts by defining and using them correctly:

- Pan-African movement
- Society
- Culture
- Intellectuals

- Values
- Ideology
- Trade union
- Descendants

- First define Pan-Africanism:
  - State what Pan-Africanism is and where it has its origins. Make mention that Pan-Africanist leaders, in particular Marcus Garvey, had a vision of instituting Black pride in all Black peoples throughout the globe. This vision is what altered the lives of African descendants throughout the Caribbean – politically, economically, socially and culturally.
- Present the ideologies of Pan-Africanism and state for each how it altered the lives of African descendants in the Caribbean.
  - **Political**: To unite Africa:
    - Pan-Africanists wanted to unite all displaced Africans from the diaspora into one space – Africa. Pan-Africanists blamed the dispersion of descendants on colonialism. In this way, they could face all problems that plagued Black people on a united front. In the early 1900s, awareness of the ideologies of the movement in the region was improved by setting up local branches of the Pan-African Association in the Caribbean, in which Henry Sylvester Williams was instrumental.
    - Though the overall vision of a united Africa never happened, the thoughts of political freedom from the imperialists was brought to the fore at the fifth Pan-African Congress in Manchester in 1945, of which George Padmore was one of the organisers. The attendees were emerging Caribbean and African leaders who took the idea of condemning imperialism back to their homelands with them, making this a turning point in the political history of both the Caribbean and Africa. The talk and push for independence in the Caribbean by these attendees had proved successful by the 1960s, in particular in the British Caribbean, where Black people were free to determine their own affairs.

- Added to this, the call to direct their own affairs was seen in the working men's riots of the 1930s in the Caribbean. The delegates of the fifth Pan-African Congress encouraged disgruntled workers in the Caribbean to fight for better working conditions and against discrimination in the work place. This contributed to the growth of the trade union movement during that era – altering the working lives of working Caribbean Black people.
- Later, in the 1960s and 1970s, the teachings of academics such as Walter Rodney triggered an increased political awareness across the Caribbean, especially among working-class Black people.
- **Social**: To improve lives of Black society:
  - Apart from instilling Black pride and uniting all Africans, prominent Pan-Africanist Marcus Garvey aimed to improve the lives of all Black people. He felt that Black people should realise their true worth and use the necessary resources to lift themselves out of poverty, discrimination and oppression by the imperialists. He established the Universal Negro Improvement Association (UNIA) to achieve this aim. He also formed Universal African Black Cross Nurses.
- **Economic**: To achieve Black economic independence:
  - One of Garvey's main ideas was the establishment of an independent Black economy within the wider global economy. To this end, he established the Black Star Line shipping company and the Negro Factories Corporation. This independent Black economic activity and entrepreneurship provided exemplars and inspiration for Black people for what could potentially be achieved within a White-dominated economic climate.
  - Walter Rodney, on the other hand, prompted by his strong views on the capitalist colonialist oppression of Africa, argued for a socialist template for development and was especially critical of the post-independence middle-class proponents of capitalism in the Caribbean and their continued economic reliance on the metropole. These beliefs transferred into reality under socialist governments of the late 1970s and the 1980s in Jamaica, Guyana and Grenada.
- **Cultural**: To promote Black pride in their African culture:
  - Connected to his vision of a Back to Africa movement, Garvey encouraged all Black people in North America and the Caribbean to embrace their heritage/culture lost during the days of slavery. He awoke the Black consciousness in the Black diaspora through his newspapers, making Black people aware of who they are – a race oppressed by the Western culture. Other Pan-Africanists, such as Padmore, also used publishing as a way to transmit their messages and ideas across the Pan-Africanist world. This led to literary works and poems on such themes, clearly seen in the works of Caribbean authors today.
- The **conclusion** must then declare, based on the evidence, the extent to which Pan-Africanism altered the lives of African descendants in the Caribbean.

Did You Know?

The relationship between Pan-Africanism and Négritude

Négritude is foremost a cultural and intellectual movement, mostly influential in Black Francophone regions, while Pan-Africanism is a broader political, cultural and intellectual phenomenon reaching from the USA and the Caribbean to Africa. Both were born in situations where Africans from Africa, North America and the Caribbean experienced some form of colonialism or imperialism. In addition, both were responses to compliance on the part of the oppressed Black people with colonisation and discrimination. Both movements sought to condemn colonialism, and to encourage Black people's acceptance of themselves and deny the control that the Western world had over their lives. Another link is that both promoted political solidarity among Black peoples all over the world.

Key Term

Rastafari – a social and religious movement that originated in Jamaica. It includes the veneration of Haile Selassie, the former Emperor of Ethiopia, as the Messiah and its beliefs are based in Judaism and Christianity, with an emphasis on Old Testament laws and prophecies.

Did You Know?

The Rastafari movement coincided with the birth of reggae, the music form from Jamaica that had inspiration for the youth as its objective. It was out of this that reggae icon, Bob Marley, emerged and became one of the most popular advocates of Pan-African ideas and ideology in the second half of the 20th century. His songs are said to have done more to promote the actual problems of African liberation than anyone before or after.

Rastafari

The **Rastafari** movement, or Rastafarianism, emerged as a popular movement in response to people's need for an organisation that was free from state control. Rastafari was influenced by Marcus Garvey and adherents are of the belief that he was the second John the Baptist.

Leonard P. Howell, a Jamaican who initially worked with Garvey in the United States, is credited with being the first Rasta. He authored the first book about Rastafari philosophy, *The Promised Key*. His promotion of the divinity of Haile Selassie as the Black Messiah helped to establish Rastafari as a religion.

The Rastafari movement has some fundamental components:
- It is a religious movement among Black Jamaicans.
- It teaches that Black people will eventually be redeemed.
- It claims that Black people will return to Africa.
- It venerates Haile Selassie as the Messiah.
- It incorporates the ceremonial use of marijuana.
- It forbids the combing and cutting of hair.
- It calls for a specific diet: natural foods, an 'Ital' diet (saltless diet), no red meat, no processed food.

Table 17.1 **The impact of Rastafari on the Caribbean**

One of the leading cultural trends in the Caribbean and the world: • Seen in the dreadlock hairstyle, a distinctive style of dress (sandals or no shoes, caftans, turbans, ethnic African-style jewellery) and the sporting of red, green and gold colours.
Influenced the political climate of Jamaica during the 1970s and beyond: • Prime Minister Michael Manley used Rastafari icons, language, symbols and, in particular, the message of reggae artists such as Bob Marley to show that he had connected with the poor Jamaican masses and the Rastafari.
• The 1976 elections saw reggae musicians articulating the issues of class and race; Rastafari symbols, language and appearance being used by both political parties (PNP and JLP).
Promotion of the consciousness of Black pride and Black religion.
One of the latest and most popular Afro-Caribbean religions of the late 20th century. Its appeal lies in its Afrocentric focus, and its rituals, belief system and reggae cultural revolution especially attract a wide cross-section of generations.

Economic and Political Thought

Leaders in the Caribbean have drawn on different **schools of thought** to utilise a variety of **political** and **economic** ideologies to develop the countries that they have led. Even after the Second World War, the region was still dominated by Great Britain and the United States, which supported the **capitalist system** that was in place. In addition, France and Britain faced financial trouble as their economies had weakened, leading to a dependence on the US. When the Caribbean countries later received independence from Britain, they were faced with:

* a very dissatisfied population;
* ridding themselves totally of the shackles of colonialism;
* instituting a political system that achieved democracy;
* creating individual paths to development;
* addressing the issues of poor healthcare, education and other social issues that would have an impact on their economy.

The economic conditions and political instability in the Caribbean during the 1960s and the decades leading up to the 1990s were worsened by:

* countries experimenting in and embracing political ideologies (in particular, democratic socialism);
* an increase in violence and migration;
* the collapse of the Soviet Union in the late 1980s, as it provided aid to some countries, including Cuba, in the form of financial support and market availability;
* Jamaica's imposition of a new tax on foreign bauxite companies, which drew the ire of the US government and foreign companies;
* economic problems resulting from increases in oil prices;
* Caribbean countries having no recourse but to borrow from the International Monetary Fund (IMF).

In an effort to resolve the issues facing their countries, political leaders chose economic reforms that were rooted in the ideologies of Marxism, Neo-Marxism and the Dependency Theory. These leaders sought to encourage investment in the Caribbean to address the high unemployment levels, to promote local and foreign investment and to strengthen the industrial sector.

Key Terms

Political thought – the study of questions, theories and ideologies concerning concepts of power, justice, rights, law and other issues to do with government; how they have come about and how effective they are.

Economic thought – the study and formulation of economic theories and ideologies. There are different 'schools' of economic thought which comprise various economic thinkers who share or have shared a common perspective on the way economies work.

Capitalist system (capitalism) – an economic system based on private ownership of the means of production and their operation for profit in competitive conditions.

Making the Connection

The achievement of independence in the Caribbean is covered in Chapter 5 'The Historical Process'.

Industrialisation by Invitation

Faced with a series of uprisings in the 1930s, which were a result of protests against persistently high levels of poverty (indicated by high employment, poor housing and a sugar industry that could not provide the needed jobs and which caused extensive property damage, loss of lives and racial division), Caribbean leaders were forced seek practical yet sweeping solutions. In the 1950s, St Lucian economist, Sir Arthur Lewis, devised an economic model, later referred to as '**Industrialisation by Invitation**', as the solution for governments to address the issues that countries faced.

Key Term

Industrialisation by Invitation – an economic development strategy where foreign investment is invited into the region by offering incentives and concessions to stimulate capital (economic resources) and entrepreneurship.

Quick Facts

Industrialisation by Invitation is also known as 'The Lewis Theory'. The esteemed economist, Sir William Arthur Lewis, recognised that the Caribbean needed to stop depending on an agricultural sector that had a history of very low productivity and seek other avenues to develop local industries and ultimately promote economic self-reliance. He was knighted and won a Nobel Prize in Economics.

Figure 17.4 **How industrialisation by invitation works**

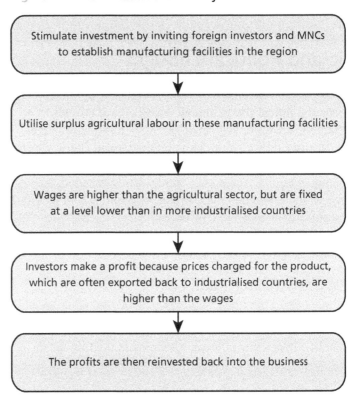

Stimulate investment by inviting foreign investors and MNCs to establish manufacturing facilities in the region

Utilise surplus agricultural labour in these manufacturing facilities

Wages are higher than the agricultural sector, but are fixed at a level lower than in more industrialised countries

Investors make a profit because prices charged for the product, which are often exported back to industrialised countries, are higher than the wages

The profits are then reinvested back into the business

The results are:
- lower unemployment
- less reliance on agriculture and a more diversified economic base
- increased productivity and exports
- stimulated industrial growth
- ultimately higher wages in both the agricultural sector (as surplus labour is absorbed in industry) and in the new industrial sector as profits are reinvested
- a transfer of knowledge, technology and skills to the region.

Industrialisation by Invitation in the Caribbean

A model Lewis was able to refer to when formulating his theory was Operation Bootstrap, which had been implemented in Puerto Rico from the 1940s onwards.

Did You Know?

Operation Bootstrap

- The initiative was geared at transforming the agrarian economy to an industrial one.
- Incentives, such as tax concessions, grants and low wage rates were offered to US and multi-national companies to establish manufacturing facilities.
- In the first stage, domestic US investments grew, stimulated by tax incentives, and then, in the second stage, there followed substantial foreign investment.
- Between 1960 and 1978 the total US investment in Puerto Rico increased from US$1.4 billion to US$20 billion. This resulted in:
  - a high living standard among Caribbean countries, with a per capita GDP that was three times that of other Caribbean countries;
  - substantial investment in the education sector, which is seen in the country boasting the highest tertiary enrolment rate in the Caribbean.

  Puerto Rico, however, was in a unique situation as it pursued this industrialisation strategy. Although the ensuing neglect of rural areas led to an increase in population and poverty levels in urban areas, the fact that Puerto Rico was a territory of the United States meant that ease of labour migration to the US alleviated the stress of unemployment problems, and welfare payments from the US helped to control increases in poverty.

Quick Fact

Despite developing its human capital through investment in education, this has not converted to actual employment for many Puerto Ricans. Instead, the country continues to face a significantly high level of unemployment among graduates and persistent migration to the United States.

An example of part of the Commonwealth Caribbean implementing policies that reflect the principles behind Lewis' model is Jamaica, where an initiative called the 'Ten-Year Plan of Development' was issued in 1947 but revised in 1951. It offered monetary incentives, such as tax holidays, duty-free importation of raw materials and tariff protection, and invited North American companies, such as Alcan, Reynolds, Alcoa and Kaiser, to conduct mining in the country.

In the 1960s, the country invited investment in banking and insurance. In the 1970s, the generation of capital from investments allowed the government, led by Michael Manley, to introduce policies such as the establishment of rural health schemes, free secondary and higher education, a national minimum wage, equal pay for women and food subsidies.

Did You Know?

Between 1972 and 1976 the Jamaican government took on a more actively socialist approach, nationalising (with compensation) all of the foreign-owned utility companies. It went on to purchase Barclays Bank and acquire sugar factories, financing the ventures through deficit spending and huge increases in the levy on bauxite production. This increase led to a dispute between the aluminium companies and the government. In the end, it led foreign companies to develop new resources elsewhere, resulting in a decline in new investment in Jamaican bauxite. By 1980, Jamaica's gross national product had declined to some 25% below the 1972 level. Due to rising foreign and local debt, the government sought International Monetary Fund (IMF) financing from the United States and others.

Other examples of Industrialisation by Invitation in the Caribbean include Trinidad, in the natural gas manufacturing industry in the 1950s; and, also in the 1950s, 'Operation Beehive' launched by Barbados, which was implemented in the garment industry.

Making the Connection

The impact of 'Industrialisation by Invitation' on Caribbean economies and development is assessed in more detail in Chapter 13 'Factors that Affect Development'.

Key Term

Marxism – the political, economic and social theories developed by Karl Marx and Friedrich Engels, which support the principle that the struggle between social classes is a determining factor in economics and that there should eventually be a classless society.

Quick Fact

The concept of Marxism was developed as a result of Marx's analysis of economic development during the Industrial Revolution of the mid-19th century. In his Communist Manifesto (1848), Marx was critical of the capitalist mode of production and the consequences for individuals in such societies.

Advantages and Disadvantages of Industrialisation by Invitation

Advantages:
- Provided an impetus to diversification, and investment in light industry in particular.
- The creation of Free Trade Zones (FTZs): areas usually located near a major port, which provided unrestricted and duty-free trade. An example is Montego Bay Freezone in Jamaica.
- The creation of Export Processing Zones (EPZs): zones where buildings and services concerning a specialised industrial estate were erected. They enjoy concessions such as no taxes and duties. In 1997 there were 51 EPZs in the Caribbean, 35 of which were located in the Dominican Republic.

Disadvantages:
- Despite the theory behind the concept, unemployment remained high in many places.
- EPZs have a reputation for low wages and poor working conditions.
- Detachment of these industries from the domestic economies.
- A large labour force, but with employees earning low wages and remaining low-skilled.
- Reinvestment in the region was lower than anticipated and, once the financial incentives ended, firms moved their factories and set up production elsewhere.

Marxism

Karl Marx's Communist Manifesto of 1848 provides the arguments for **Marxism**. It presents criticism of the capitalist system where the factors of production are in the hands of the wealthy or the bourgeoisie and they exploit the working class, or the proletariat, because the profits they receive are much greater than the wages they pay. Marxism has political, economic and social tenets, and predicts the inevitable overthrow of capitalism by communism:
- All societies are made up of social classes.
- Industrial societies have two main classes – the bourgeoisie and the proletariats.
- These two classes will always be in conflict.
- Political change is the only way the workers' rights can be upheld, so that they will eventually own the means of production. The workers (proletariats) must therefore rebel against the bourgeoisie and overthrow them.
- In order for them to rebel, the masses of workers must become class-conscious (develop an awareness that they are being exploited by the capitalists). Western religion exists to condition the masses to accept their social position.
- After the revolution, workers will establish a classless society. All men will be equal.
- The state, or the government, will become redundant and disappear.

Figure 17.5 Elements of the capitalist society, according to Marx

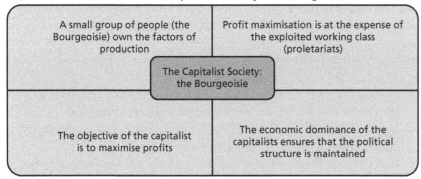

The impact of Marxism on the Caribbean

While Marxism was a popular theory, political thinkers in the Caribbean embraced the Neo-Marxist ideology. Neo-Marxists believe that:
* the capitalist class has control of the mass media, the security forces and the political machinery;
* the capitalist class uses the superstructure to strengthen its dominant position in society.

Leaders in the Caribbean, such as Forbes Burnham and Cheddie Jagan of Guyana, Michael Manley of Jamaica, Fidel Castro of Cuba, Maurice Bishop of Grenada and Desi Bouterse of Suriname, were influenced by the ideology of Marxism and **Neo-Marxism**.

In Jamaica and Guyana the socialist experiment failed because of heavy debt burden. In Grenada, the socialist experiment failed because of internal conflict and the overthrow of Maurice Bishop in 1983.

Marxist ideology also had an impact on:
* C.L.R. James of Trinidad and Tobago, a leader in the Pan-African movement, political activist and historian;
* Walter Rodney of Guyana, a political activist, historian and author of the renowned book, *How Europe Underdeveloped Africa*;
* Trevor Monroe of Jamaica, a politician, political scientist, labour activist and author of *The Politics of Constitutional Decolonization*.

Figure 17.6 The influence of Marxism in the Caribbean

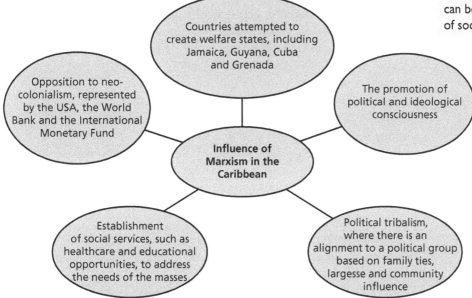

Quick Fact

A denial of an awareness of the true nature of the capitalist system is what Marx refers to false consciousness. This denial leads to an acceptance of the system, an unwillingness to criticise it and how it functions, and an aversion to making any attempt to change the existing state of affairs.

The Dependency Theory

The **Dependency Theory** puts forward the idea that developed nations actively under develop the Third World countries through the various ways they interact. The Dependency Theory:

- originated in the Third World;
- incorporates some Marxist concepts;
- proposes that economic activities in the wealthier countries tends to lead to serious economic problems in the poorer countries;
- focuses on the issue of inequality and attributes the inequality of the poorer countries to the developed nations;
- states that, as the developed nations' power and wealth grows more quickly than that of the developing countries, the gap increases between the two.

Figure 17.7 **The structure of Dependency Theory**

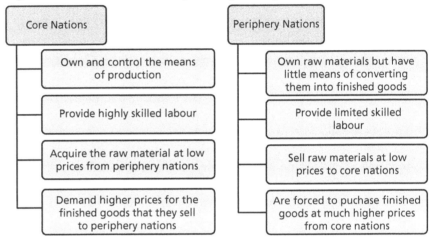

Key Term

Dependency Theory – a theory that seeks to explain how the economic development of a developing or Third World state is determined by external influences (political, economic and cultural) and how they relate to the national development policies of that state.

Quick Fact

Walter Rodney in his book, *How Europe Underdeveloped Africa*, was formulating his own ideas of Dependency Theory.

Key Term

Feminism – the theory that women and men should be treated equally in the social, political and economic landscapes. Feminism does not seek to establish female rule or dominance, but rather it seeks to establish equality of the sexes. In this way it challenges the patriarchal order, which subordinates female to male.

Caribbean Feminist Thought and Theories of Gender

Feminism is a sociological perspective (concept) that is concerned with the experiences of women, especially in addressing the inequalities that they face in their social, political and economic lives. The birth of feminism began in the late 19th century, when middle- and upper-class women in Europe began to demand the right to vote and to enjoy political equality.

The feminist movement in the Caribbean began in the 1960s, and this was as a result of the push by women in the USA during that time as they sought to achieve racial and social equality. Males exerting their economic and political influence, and being the primary decision makers, had led to a disparity between genders now being questioned.

The objectives of feminism are to:

- promote the recognition of the rights of women;
- achieve gender equality;
- eradicate the exploitation of women;
- create a climate where all women are treated with dignity and respect.

The Impact of Feminism in the Caribbean

In an effort to eliminate the domination of males, legislation skewed to males and bias against females, feminists sought to address the issues through:

- the establishment of the rights of women;
- the demand for gender equality;
- lobbying for legislation to protect women; key among them being rape laws, labour laws and property rights;
- empowering women through education.

Making the Connection

The impact of feminism can be seen in the establishment of the Caribbean Association for Feminist Research and Action (CAFRA), which is discussed in Chapter 14 'Globalisation and Development', while the role of gender in the development of the Caribbean region is discussed in Chapter 13 'Factors that Affect Development'.

Feminist organisations in the Caribbean include:

- The Women Speak Project – provides a medium through which women can highlight their stories of discrimination;
- CODE RED for Gender Justice – provides a haven for all women, regardless of sexual orientation, to discuss issues such as relationships, love and family;
- National Organization of Women (NOW) – focuses on women's rights issues in Barbados, including economic justice, pay equity, women with disabilities, women's health and body image and reproductive rights;
- Sistren in Jamaica – uses drama to explore issues of women's oppression. The group hosts a workshop to encourage inner-city women to develop skills needed to establish their own small businesses;
- Belize Rural Women Association (BRWA) – formed to provide health education for rural women and leadership training in the establishment of small businesses for women.

The establishment of such groups provides the women of the region with the motivation and confidence to achieve empowerment and attitudes of independence.

Did You Know?

Two sociologists who have focused on the roles of women in the Caribbean are Patricia Mohammed, who has done work on women of East Indian descent, and Rhoda Reddock, who has investigated the role of Caribbean women in history.

Indo-Caribbean Thought

Indo-Caribbean thought refers to the ideas that evolved out of the shared experiences of Indians across the Caribbean. Indo-Caribbean people are Caribbean nationals who have East Indian ancestry. Indo-Caribbean thought is a response to the experiences of the Asians who, in the late 1800s, were contracted to work on Caribbean plantations and were forced to endure the strict terms of their labour contracts. Their response to the hardships they experienced was expressed in:

- the writing that expressed their culture as it adapted to the Caribbean lifestyle;
- the birth of Indo-Caribbean thought;

Quick Fact

In Dependency Theory the First World country is known as the *centre* or the *core*, and the Third World country is known as the *periphery*. While political and economic events in the First World will have an impact on the politics and economics of Third World countries, the political and economic events of the Third World countries have little effect on the First World countries.

Quick Facts

Feminism can be conceived in different ways and there are many different approaches to feminist theory, each with their own particular emphases; such as liberal feminism, radical feminism, Marxist feminism, eco-feminism or post-feminism.

Key Term

Indo-Caribbean thought – a unique school of thought that developed among the Caribbean people with roots in Asia; it was created out of expressions of culture and responses to the oppression that they experienced from contractual strictures during the indentureship period.

Quick Fact

Feminism, in its fundamental challenge to patriarchal societal structures, beliefs and attitudes, presents a particular challenge to women of the Indo-Caribbean community, which is itself founded on and structured around strongly patriarchal traditions.

- demonstrations and strikes in protest of their living and working conditions;
- some leaving their positions and returning to their homeland;
- some leaving the plantations at the end of their contracts and embarking on independent farming;
- preserving their culture through traditions, such as the Hosay and the Phagwa (Holi) festivals;
- the creation of associations, such as the East Indian National Association (EINA) in 1897 and the East Indian National Congress (EINC) in 1909, to address oppressive immigration policies.

In places with a large East Indian presence, there have been issues of polarisation between Africans and East Indians stemming from inter-community rivalries on the plantations. Not only did the arrival of East Indian workers keep wages low, but plantation owners exploited the social and cultural differences between the two groups to their own advantage. Africans also resented the East Indians being given land once they were freed from their contracts; they had not been given this privilege.

The focus of Indo-Caribbean thought was therefore on the retention of their identity and, at the same time, the establishment of their right to citizenship, in particular in the face of rivalries with the African community.

Retention of identity:

- Continuation of religions – Hinduism and Islam – and maintenance of rituals, behavioural codes and so on related to these (though there was abandonment of the caste requirement in some areas as there was intermarriage between Muslims and Hindus).
- Continuation of material culture such as food, music, festivals, etc.
- Reinforcement of endogamy (marriage within a specific group as determined by that group's customs and rituals).
- Setting up communities on the land they were granted after the end of their contracts.

Making the Connection

Indentureship and the experience of the Indo-Caribbeans on the plantations are presented in more detail in Chapter 5 'The Historical Process'.

Strategies to achieve citizenship and a sense of belonging:

- They set up businesses and sought educational opportunities, which, in fact, resulted in facilitating ongoing social integration as well as upward social mobility.
- They established political parties along ethnic lines. The existence of parties representing different ethnic groups has proved socially divisive in Guyana in particular, but also in Trinidad and Tobago and Suriname.

Did You Know?

Authors who have written about Indo-Caribbean thought and culture include the following:

- V.S. Naipaul – a descendant of Hindu Indians who had immigrated to Trinidad as indentured servants. He initially wrote comic portrayals of Trinidadian society before moving on to highlight political themes and colonial and post-colonial societies.
- Samuel Selvon – Trinidadian-born novelist and short-story writer of East Indian descent, known for his recreation, in vivid detail, of the lives of East Indians in the West Indies and elsewhere.

- David Dabydeen – Guyanese author of four novels, three collections of poetry and several works of non-fiction and criticism. His writings explore Indo-Caribbean issues such as focusing on the historical tensions that existed between indentured Indian workers and Guyanese of African descent.
- Clem Seecharan – a Guyanese writer and historian of the Indo-Caribbean experience, now based in the United Kingdom, who teaches a course on the history of East Indians in the Caribbean and on the history of West Indies Cricket.

Indigenous Perspectives

Indigenous people refers to the Amerindians: the Tainos and the Kalinagos. The pervasive view, historically, that these groups were inferior and helpless has led to concerted efforts to change this misconception. The need arose for this reversal of perceptions because Europeans:
- depicted the Tainos as naive and helpless;
- portrayed Kalinago society as violent and cannibalistic and which should therefore be eradicated;
- dismissed the history of the Amerindians as well as the Africans;
- lacked any interest in the indigenous peoples, claiming that they had become extinct, or that those that remained were not 'pure' Amerindian.

To dispel these erroneous notions, and acknowledge their contributions to the region's history, development and culture, West Indian writers began to present literature that:
- established the history of these people;
- highlighted their cultural contributions to the region;
- showed their influence and contribution during the encomienda system and beyond.

Some writers that have been influential in highlighting the contributions of the indigenous people are:
- Hilary Beckles – *Black Rebellion in Barbados*
- Richard Hart – *The Slaves Who Abolished Slavery*
- C.L.R. James – *The Black Jacobins*
- Walter Rodney – *A History of the Guyanese Working People*.

Did You Know?

The indigenous people in Belize, Guyana and Dominica have faced issues related to social, economic and political marginalisation. Typically, in Guyana the two major ethnic groups focused on are the Indo-Guyanese and the Afro-Guyanese while the Amerindians are ignored. They are treated separately because they reside in remote areas in the interior of the country. Sadly, they live in poverty and seclusion, almost as an outcast group.

Multiple-choice Questions

1. The main objectives of Pan-Africanism are to
   I. Promote Black consciousness, Black pride and a sense of nationalism
   II. Raise the awareness of African people about gender equality
   III. Repatriate Africans back to Africa
   IV. Pursue justice for Black people
   A. I, II and III only
   B. II, III and IV only
   C. I, III and IV only
   D. All of the above

2. Pan-Africanists such as W.E.B. Dubois and Marcus Garvey promoted the message of solidarity among people of African heritage through
   A. Books and newspapers
   B. Scholarships and African values
   C. Controversial meetings and African nationalism
   D. Support and adoption of African owned businesses

3. The merchant class in the Caribbean resented the Pan-African movement because they felt that it
   A. Supported the need for African independence
   B. Posed a threat to the system of colonialism
   C. Exploited the Africans and their descendants
   D. Promoted the exploitation of free labour

4. The Négritude movement arose because
   A. There was an absence of dominant cultures of the colonies, which led to a loss of identity among the colonisers and the colonised
   B. It threatened the social and economic status quo that existed during the period of exploitation
   C. The colonial powers promoted their culture in the colonies and forced the Black people to deny theirs
   D. People of African descent saw the need to promote national political involvement

5. One objective of the Négritude movement was to
   A. Combat the perception of Black superiority
   B. Explore the rich heritage of African-Americans through arts and literature
   C. Get rid of their responses to the hardships they experienced
   D. Promote the acceptance of the Black identity

6. Rastafari has been established as a religion due to the work of Leonard P. Howell, who
   A. Rejected the idea of hair cutting and combing
   B. Wrote about the religious movement among Black Jamaicans
   C. Venerated Haile Selassie, the Emperor of Ethiopia, as the Black Messiah
   D. Encouraged the youths to strive for political and economic change in Jamaica

7. When the state takes full control of banks, mass media, literature and industrial production, it represents
   A. Socialist reforms
   B. Attempts at job creation
   C. Attempts at equally distributing resources
   D. Attempts at boosting the economy with governmental policies

8. The 'periphery', which sells its raw materials cheaply to the 'core', then purchases the manufactured raw material from the same 'core' at a high price, falls into the
   A. Dependency Theory
   B. Neo-Marxist Theory
   C. Industrialisation by Invitation
   D. Periphery law

9. Evidence of feminism in the Caribbean is seen in the establishment of
   A. The East Indian National Association (EINA)
   B. The Caribbean Association for Feminist Research and Action (CAFRA)
   C. Women in Control Association (WICA)
   D. Trinidad and Tobago Women Suffrage Association (TTWSA)

10. The move to reverse efforts to negate the legacy of the cultural contributions of the Indo-Caribbean people led to the
   I. Incorporation and maintenance of the cultural practices of the colonial powers
   II. Production if literary works that detailed how their culture adjusted to the Caribbean lifestyle
   III. Staging of festivals indigenous to the Amerindians and East Indians
   IV. Creation of associations, which sought to address harsh immigration policies
   A. I, II and III only
   B. II, III and IV only
   C. I, III and IV only
   D. All of the above

Chapter 18

Roles and Functions of the Mass Media

After revising this topic, you should be able to:
- identify the ways in which the mass media provides information and how this can affect development;
- recognise the role of the mass media in the provision of entertainment;
- evaluate the role of the mass media in the construction of national, regional and diasporic identity;
- describe the role of the mass media in the promotion of cultural experience and exchange;
- understand the concept of cultural imperialism and possible responses to it;
- assess the role of the mass media in the promotion and defence of rights and citizens.

The main role of the **mass media** has traditionally been seen as the widespread dissemination of various types of information and entertainment – to inform, educate and entertain. Its various forms include:
- electronic or broadcast media, comprising film, radio, recorded music and television;
- print media, which includes newspapers, magazines, journals and books;
- digital media, which comprises the internet and forms of mobile communication (email, social network sites, websites, internet based radio and television;
- outdoor media, involving various forms of advertising and infographics displayed on billboards, posters, signs and so on.

The foundation of the modern concept of 'mass media' really began in the 18th century with the advent of high-circulation broadsheets or newspapers, although the term 'the media' was not used until the 1920s. The 20th century saw the growth and expansion of mass media driven by technology, first radio and television, later boosted by the advent of satellite broadcasting, and then the dawn of the 'internet age'.

However, mass media has a deeper function than the simple provision of news, information and entertainment. It also has a role to play in society; for example, in the promotion of social and cultural identity and in the provision of a 'voice' for the disadvantaged. In these and other ways it therefore has an impact on the development of the region.

Syllabus Objective

Critically analyse factors which impact mass media's contribution to the development of the region.

Key Term

Mass media – technology intended to reach a large (or mass) audience. It is the main means of communication used to reach the vast majority of the general public. The most common platforms are newspapers, magazines, radio, television and the internet.

Quick Fact

Some schools of thought do not include local or specialist forms of media under the umbrella of mass media – for example, those covering specific forms of sport – as these forms, by their local or specialist nature, do not have a large enough audience to be classified as 'mass'.

Provision of Information

The media provides information at different levels, in many forms (for example news reports, articles, documentaries, blogs, investigative journalism) and for various purposes (for example education, exposure of deficiencies, advocacy of a point of view, promotion, entertainment). All of this information helps to fill a knowledge gap, which, in turn, serves to empower those who receive the information and enables them to make informed decisions based on it, thus directly contributing to the advancement of human development. In the Caribbean, information can touch on local or national events, affairs and issues, those that involve the region as a whole and those that affect the global community.

Of course, the flow of information is mostly one way, from source to audience. The advent of the internet, with social media sites and blogs, has in many ways created a counter-movement to this with its emphasis on participative involvement. However, it should be noted that media outlets are businesses, often owned by large corporations, or have some element of government ownership or control, and so the information provided by television, radio and newspapers (including online versions) is likely to have been filtered, or even censored, in some way by the prevailing policy and views of the ownership. There will always be an editorial choice on what information is broadcast and the angle taken. Through this selectivity, the media play a significant role in creating perceptions and influencing how the public thinks about issues.

Freedom of expression is enshrined in the constitutions of most Caribbean nations, especially the English-speaking Commonwealth. However, freedom of the press, specifically, is not and many journalists are campaigning to have this and free access to official information included. Cuba is the most prominent exception, where all media is state controlled and freedom of speech and journalism are allowed only if they 'conform to the aims of a socialist society'. However, there have been instances of official interference with press coverage across the region, such as in Trinidad and Tobago, where there is a history of clashes between members of the media and the government, and also in Guyana where there is evidence that the government has attempted to exercise control over parts of the media by refusing to grant new radio broadcasting licences and to use state advertising revenue as a tool of media reward or punishment.

Key Term

Libel – the written or broadcast form of defamation, which is the act of damaging a person's reputation (distinguished from slander, which is oral defamation). It renders the offending person or entity (perhaps a newspaper, magazine or political organisation) open to a lawsuit for damages by the defamed person who can prove the statement about them was a lie.

Did You Know?

Journalist organisations, such as the Association of Caribbean Media Workers (ACM) and its national affiliates from across the Caribbean, have campaigned for many years for a review or repeal of stringent **libel** legislation, which they claim stifles the ability of the press to report on issues without fear of repercussions, and for free access to official information, which many governments are reluctant to grant. They have expressed the belief that free access to information 'has the potential to be a net contributor to development through better informed citizens benefitting from a free exchange of information, opinion, analysis and debate'.

Areas of Information Provision

Events

At a local level, these could include elections, political speeches outlining policy, cultural festivals, crimes, instances of pollution or racism and so on. Regionally they could include trade events, Caribbean Community (CARICOM) summits or sporting events. International press agencies provide information on, and coverage of, international events such as conflicts, outbreaks of epidemics, such as the SARS or Zika viruses, and international sports competitions.

Trends

Locally and regionally, these would include issues such as rising crime rates (for example, in Jamaica and Trinidad and Tobago), tourism, health issues and education. The media can provide information about, and educate people on, global issues, elements or aspects which may have a more local impact. A case in point is the environment, where an appreciation of global diversity and an awareness of the various threats to the environment on a global scale could heighten awareness of environmental issues closer to home. Other examples would be economic trends, such as exchange rates, levels of investment and trade balances, and the fight against diseases such as HIV/Aids, which would also have a local impact.

> **Quick Fact**
>
> International press agencies include organisations such as Associated Press (AP), Reuters and the British Broadcasting Company (BBC).

Did You Know?

The Caribbean Broadcast Media Partnership (CBMP) on HIV/AIDS, founded in 2006, unites broadcasters from 24 countries in the region's first coordinated media response to the pandemic. It provides a framework for sharing information and resources to expand HIV/AIDS-related programming and public education activities across the Caribbean. Information is delivered free of charge across a variety of platforms and formats, including public service announcements, entertainment, news and public affairs programmes and online resources. The combined work of the CBMP, the Pan Caribbean Partnership (PANCAP) against HIV/AIDS and ministries of health across the Caribbean has resulted in more than 70,000 people in 21 countries being tested through this initiative.

In March 2007 the CBMP launched its campaign 'LIVE UP: Love. Protect. Respect.', the first media-led campaign on HIV/AIDS to reach across the entire Caribbean. Through radio and television public service ads, its own website, Facebook page and YouTube® channel it aims to inspire audiences, especially young people, to consider what is within their power to do to stem the spread of HIV/AIDS.

Institutions

Information about local institutions and the services they provide is fundamental for equal access to these services for all. Regionally and internationally, the media plays an important role in providing information to, and educating people on, both pan-regional institutions, such as CARICOM and the Caribbean Court of Justice, and international institutions, such as WHO (World Health Organization), WTO (World Trade Organization) and the IMF (International Monetary Fund), which may well impact on their lives in some way.

Political and Economic Affairs

Information on government policy, especially local government, helps to inform individuals' opinions and allows them to assert their rights and access any benefits owed to them through aspects such as welfare. Information on the local economy can assist in the effective management of small businesses. When it comes to elections, publicising the rights of citizens, the individual party manifestos and the processes involved empowers people to participate on a free and fair basis.

Goods and Services

Advertisements, although always promoting a certain product, underpin the concept of freedom of choice. The media can also serve to highlight and advise on new goods and services available as well as provide critiques of existing ones.

Entertainment

Making the Connection

Chapter 16 'Contributions of Sport to Development' looks at how advertising at and around sports events generates income via the media.

The provision of entertainment by digital and print media, either through direct access to programming by both broadcast and digital media or through information to enable access to events (reporting, advertisements, etc.) is an important function of the mass media.

As with information, forms of entertainment can be categorised as local, regional and international. Local forms include local cultural festivals and sporting events, media coverage of which usually encourages commercial sponsorship. Larger cultural events, such as Carnival in Trinidad and Tobago, could be classed as regional or even international, as could the Caribbean Song Festival. The advent of satellite technology has opened up the region to international sources of entertainment, with major international sports competitions such as the Olympics, the Football World Cup, the NBA from the US and various cricket internationals proving popular across the region as well as cultural events including the Grammy Awards and the Oscars.

Entertainment has a role to play in human development by promoting one's well-being through relaxation and stress release. Also, the concept of edutainment – educating through entertainment – can be an effective way of communicating important messages, for instance about health, lifestyle, the environment, social behaviour and the economy, in an entertaining and relevant way. In this way, the media can exert a positive influence in the human development of individuals by providing an equitable information source, open to all, which empowers them to make choices and enhance their productivity.

Forms of entertainment promoted by mass media, both local and international, have also proved to be successful exports of the region. Musical forms, such as Reggae, Calypso and Ska, and artistes, such as Bob Marley and Rihanna, have enjoyed international recognition and success.

Construction of National, Regional and Diasporic Identity

National Identity

Mass media provides a fundamental service in the promotion of a national identity. This was critical in both the run up to independence – with newspapers giving column space to proponents of anti-colonialism and nationalism, such as Claude McKay and C.L.R. James – and then to the fledgling Caribbean states following independence, when newly-formed governments became actively involved in the ownership of media outlets and the screening of content they broadcast in order to bolster national consciousness and patriotic dedication. The recognition that a strong cultural identity would strengthen a sense of pride and unity led Jamaican leader Michael Manley to establish the Jamaican Cultural Development Committee shortly after independence, with radio and TV spotlighting the cultural activities it promoted.

State ownership of media has been eroded over time and by advances in technology, which have made the setting up of independent television and radio stations much easier than previously. The extension of local radio and television stations and regional newspapers into remote areas has helped to connect isolated and often indigenous communities with the rest of the population as well as provide them with a voice in national affairs. The United Nations Educational, Scientific and Cultural Organization (UNESCO) has provided funds to establish radio stations in these kinds of areas, such as Radio Toco in remote north-eastern Tobago.

Regional Identity

Most Caribbean-based mass media is country focused. Regional news providers, such as the Caribbean News Agency (CANA), which belongs to the Caribbean Media Corporation (CMC), have been established to provide a focus on news at a regional level, but they have found it difficult to compete with international press agencies. The Caribbean Broadcasting Union (CBU) was set up in 1970 by CARICOM as a not-for-profit association of public service and commercial media broadcasters with the intention of promoting integration. With content contributions from its members, it created several regionally syndicated programmes of which CaribScope, a cultural magazine programme, enjoyed particularly wide viewership. Its commercial operations, including television production, merged with CANA in 2000. The Caribbean still lacks a pan-regional television or radio station, the existence of which would help cement a feeling of regional identity and provide a huge boost to the integration effort.

Making the Connection

The integration movement, and the various institutions and organisations that are working towards increased integration in, and a common identity across, the region, are investigated in Chapter 15 'The Integration Movement'.

Diasporic Identity

Those in the diaspora risk losing or diluting their identity as they struggle to settle in a foreign land. The local media, especially in areas with a large Caribbean population, can help ease this process by providing Caribbean focused content: music, cuisine, news and so on. Increasingly, programmes are being broadcast from the Caribbean itself to diasporic communities. CaribVision, for example, was launched by CMC in 2006 and broadcasts a variety of programming including news and current affairs, sports, drama, sitcoms, soaps, entertainment and lifestyle shows across the region, to parts of Latin America, to the East coast of the USA, to Ontario and Quebec in Canada and to the United Kingdom.

Promotion of Cultural Experience and Exchange

The media has served to facilitate the promotion of various forms culture, both within and outside the region. Technological advances have helped to extend the reach of information with, for example, the internet allowing local cultural events, such as the Antigua Carnival, as well as regional ones, such as the Caribbean Song Festival, to be advertised and broadcast across the region and beyond. Media coverage has also served to provide a platform for artistes and art forms, which has helped to boost cultural industries, such as music, dance, art and drama. The media is also a means to showcase diasporic Caribbean culture with the promotion and coverage of carnivals held by emigrant communities in London (the Notting Hill Carnival) and Leicester in the UK, Toronto in Canada and Atlanta in the US, to name a few.

Exposure to different forms of culture, not just for those outside the region but also across the Caribbean, helps to foster an acceptance of diversity, which in turn can help the integration process. It is, however, a two-way process and influences from outside the region and traditional Caribbean culture and society come to bear in, for example, fashion, music, dance, religion and social attitudes and roles. Television is the most powerful cultural influence, with the majority of programming originating from outside the region, although radio also plays a role in playing non-Caribbean music and broadcasting fundamentalist Christian programmes from the US.

Responding to Cultural Imperialism

Key Term

Cultural imperialism – the culture of a large and powerful country having a great influence on another, less powerful country. Cultural imperialism can involve forced acculturation or a voluntary acceptance of the foreign culture.

The dominance of the US mass media in the Caribbean, especially cable TV programming, has been viewed as a form of **cultural imperialism**. The view is that US programming has imbued the Caribbean population with US attitudes, perspectives, values, culture and beliefs at the expense of traditional native Caribbean ones. These include language, religion, family structure and relations and so on. There is also some evidence that the aspirational, but ultimately unreal, lifestyle portrayed in many US soaps has fuelled a desire, especially among the young, to emigrate.

There are those who argue against this, pointing out that, despite US media influence, the Caribbean has a history of emigration and a strong element of free choice is in play – just because someone enjoys listening to foreign music, is entertained by foreign dramas and likes to follow global fashion trends, it cannot be argued that they may not still retain their fundamental and distinct Caribbean identity.

Despite this, the shadow of cultural imperialism still makes it imperative for some kind of movement to help counter the media dominance of the US. The borderless nature of broadcast technology makes it difficult to physically block US broadcasting, and the commercial gain from airing popular US shows would cause reluctance to do this. Therefore, alternative solutions need to be found. Some possibilities are:

- the increased generation of indigenous high-quality programming to compete with US imports;
- educational initiatives to inform people of the 'real world' as opposed to the ideal or the sensational as portrayed in many programmes;
- more analysis and communication of this to increase general awareness of the impact of media influence and how it can shape attitudes and perceptions;
- the establishment of **watchdogs** to highlight inaccuracies and bias in US and other news reporting;
- the establishment of a coordinated regional policy on the media that focuses on both national and regional development in order to counter the influx of foreign influences.

Key Term

Watchdog – a person or organisation that monitors companies, governments, and so on, to ensure that they are not doing anything illegal or wrong.

Promotion and Defence of Rights and Citizens

Despite issues surrounding how much press freedom is actually enjoyed by the Caribbean media, commercial considerations and corporate or government influence, the media still has a significant role to play in the promotion and protection of people's rights – political, social and economic – and thus help to counter breaches of social justice that infringe people's rights and impede development.

This can be done in the following ways:

- Investigative reporting serves to expose and make public shortcomings in government and societal institutions.
- Talk shows and phone-in shows on television and radio give, often marginalised, people a voice to express their dissatisfaction or experiences of discrimination or disadvantage. Often individual problems can be remedied as a result of this exposure.
- The media is in a position to highlight problems faced by groups or individuals and subsequently keep the problem alive and to the forefront of public awareness even if it is against the interests of powerful groups.
- The broadcasting of programmes and discussions on issues such as racism, gender and lifestyle choices helps to spotlight them and to provide a means to air the main arguments and points of view surrounding them.
- The defence of basic democratic freedoms, such as the right to peaceful protest, the right to take industrial action, the right to freedom of information, the right to freedom of worship and so on, through coverage, reporting and discussion is a key role of the media.
- Providing information on people's legislative rights, consumer rights or social rights serves to empower citizens.

Making the Connection

The concept of social justice and how breaches of it can affect development are discussed in detail in Chapter 19 'Social Justice'.

Making the Connection

Chapter 12 'Concepts and indicators of Development'

Chapter 13 'Factors that Affect Development'

Exam Tips

'**Discuss**' requires an extended response defining key concepts, giving the facts, exploring related concepts and issues and presenting reasoned arguments. You must use detailed examples but **not** necessarily draw a conclusion.

'**The extent to which**' wording requires you to evaluate something by measuring its reliability, validity or usefulness.

Check Your Knowledge

"Press freedom can both inhibit and spur development in the Caribbean region."

Using examples, discuss the extent to which you agree with this statement.

1. Demonstrate an understanding of the following terms and concepts by defining and using them correctly:

- Mass media
- Freedom of the press
- Identity
- Print media
- Electronic media
- Development
- Ethnocentric
- Freedom of speech
- Libel

- Newsworthiness
- Globalisation
- Internet
- Television
- Truth reporting
- Journalistic integrity
- Cultural imperialism
- Colonialism
- Political interference

2. Define the term 'press'.

- Discuss what press freedom entails, the rights of the press and the arguments for why the press should be free. On the other side of the coin, journalists have a responsibility to present fair, objective and accurate reporting of events (truth reporting).

- Press freedom also involves unrestricted broadcasting both from within and outside the region. Governments have responsibility for control of local media and so become the 'gate keepers'.

- Freedom of Information Acts, covering how citizens obtain facts from government departments, exist in some countries, including Jamaica, Guyana, Trinidad and The Bahamas. Only draft Acts exist elsewhere.

3. The extent to which press freedom can retard or inhibit development – discuss at least four of the following points:

- **Political interference**. Censorship demonstrates that the press is not free to report different opinions of stories and events. Press freedom is compromised by government ownership and control of stories or news. Also, accusing journalists of libel can stifle the press. The policies and laws of a country can hinder or influence how the mass media operate.

- Syndicated news and foreign-based programmes have **North American or Eurocentric cultural values**. A lack of restrictions on these, coupled with a lack of 'home grown' alternatives, means they are free to spread cultural imperialistic ideologies to Caribbean people that can only serve to hinder development.

- Historically, the Caribbean has been **dependent** on the metropole or colonial powers for goods and services, food and fashion, which has served to stunt creativity and innovation and so retard development. Continued reliance through the influence of mass media will exacerbate this.

- Journalists may have their **interests deflected**. This may be to create 'sensational' stories that attract attention and increase sales.

- If the press focuses too much on **sensational news reporting** of issues, such as crime and violence (and do not balance their reporting), this will have a negative impact on development. People will be afraid to travel to Caribbean countries, resulting in lack of foreign investors and a reduction in tourists.

4. The extent to which press freedom can spur or promote development – you also have to debate at least four of the following points:

   - The press can play a crucial role in developing a national identity by promoting cultural events and local movements, such as The Barbados Reggae Festival, Tobago Jazz Experience, Caribbean Fashion Week, Pagwah, Carnival, Parang and sporting events. Electronic media play a large part in this. Also, press support for, and coverage of, CARIFESTA and the CARIFTA games promotes regional solidarity.

   - Sports that take place on the international stage are televised globally and serve not only to boost tourism and create employment, but also our sporting heroes are introduced to the world. This contributes to cultural exchanges and in turn promotes culture building and a 'oneness' in the Caribbean.

   - When electronic media advertises the Caribbean as a tourist destination to the world, this contributes to its development because tourism generates foreign exchange/revenue, which in turn increases countries' gross domestic product (GDP).

   - Through the internet, globalisation is harnessed as the Caribbean is part of a global village. Globally, people are now privy to what occurs in the Caribbean and can take an interest.

   - Press freedom is vital for the democratic process of communicating with the people in which they receive knowledge about the actions of international, regional and local government agencies regarding their development.

   - The press can play a key role in acting as a watchdog or pressure group, for example, when the press brings sensitive issues such as undemocratic political leanings and an increase in crime and violence to the public's attention. This creates awareness and policies to deal with the issues.

   - The press can aid development by educating the public on environmental issues such as hazards.

   - Some Caribbean media houses have merged to create larger regional entities, for example One Caribbean Media, so they have more money for investment. This in turn allows them to extend their reach both within and beyond the region.

5. Your conclusion must be clear and based on your analysis. You must also indicate the extent to which you agree with the statement and why.

Multiple-choice Questions

1. Which of the following is NOT a role of the Caribbean mass media?

    A. To expose the Caribbean region to all forms of entertainment – local and foreign

    B. To provide foreign and regional news on all important events to the Caribbean public

    C. To allow Caribbean governments to assist in choosing what the public is exposed to

    D. To encourage freedom of expression and speech

2. One benefit of the Caribbean region being exposed to North American media is

    A. It can inform Caribbean citizens about global events

    B. It can stifle Caribbean culture

    C. People may prefer to watch foreign-based channels over local ones

    D. It allows for cultural imperialism

3. Call-in programmes are beneficial for all of the following reasons EXCEPT

    A. They allow the Caribbean people to practise freedom of speech on important issues

    B. They are a way for the public to air views on political issues

    C. They build on national harmony

    D. They provide a means for Caribbean politicians to take note of the feelings of the electorate

4. Which of the following broadcasting news agencies was established by CARICOM to provide regional news in 1970?

    A. CaribScope

    B. CANA (Caribbean News Agency)

    C. CaribVision

    D. CBU (Caribbean Broadcasting Union)

5. Which of the following are threats to mass media in the Caribbean?

    A. Government supervision and cultural imperialism

    B. Cultural imperialism and freedom of speech

    C. Censorship and competition between regional broadcasting agencies

    D. Socialist ideals and lack of censorship

Chapter 19

Social Justice

After revising this topic, you should be able to:
- understand different concepts of social justice, such as recognition of natural (or human) rights, welfare and mutual advantage;
- describe and explain various forms of discrimination: ageism, gender discrimination, racism, classism and discrimination on the grounds of sexual orientation;
- recognise how police brutality breaches ideas of social justice and impacts on development in the Caribbean;
- discuss how indicators of development are affected by breaches of social justice in terms of levels of social inequality, productivity levels, quality of life and democratic rights, and understand how they are affected.

Concepts of Social Justice

What is Social Justice?

Social justice is the idea of enabling human beings to access their **inalienable** natural rights (human rights) and legal rights afforded them by legislation, international treaties, court orders, law of **equity**, **common law** or customs. Social justice differs from legal justice in that the latter follows a list of rules or laws of a country to mete out punishment or compensate the injured, while the former is about concepts of equality and fairness, which legal justice plays a part in protecting.

Did You Know?

While human rights are differentiated from legal rights, it is important to note that the human rights of Caribbean citizens are entrenched in the **constitutions** of Caribbean states and so are supported by legislation that enforces sanctions if any entity, group or government should infringe on the human rights of others.

The concept of social justice began during the 18th-century Enlightenment, but was formally recognised on a global scale in the middle of the 20th century when concern for protecting the vulnerable became a major driver towards the UN Declaration of Human Rights, which stated that all people should be treated equally regardless of race, class, nationality, gender, sexual orientation or age.

Syllabus Objective

Formulate reasoned responses to issues of social justice within your community.

Key Terms

Social justice – a concept promoting equality, fairness and valuing diversity through just distribution of wealth, opportunities and privileges in a society.

Inalienable – a right or an item that cannot be taken away under any circumstances. Inalienable rights are those rights that all human beings are entitled to. Examples are the right to life and the right to own property.

Equity – deals with fairness, justice and what is considered reasonable conduct or what is morally correct. Equitable decisions are often used by a judge to ensure the preservation of people's natural rights where the rigid application of the law may penalise those seeking justice.

Common law – is any law, including those of the Caribbean Commonwealth, that emanates from a judge's ruling or custom.

Constitution – a body of laws and guidelines that establish the legal and political parameters of a state.

Quick Facts

The implementation of social justice often involves principles of equity. For example, in a world based on equality (all having the same status, rights and opportunities) every citizen is expected to pay taxes. However, some individuals with disabilities may be exempt because their condition has made it difficult for them to earn a living. This is an example of **equity** (fairness) in action.

Making the Connection

The formalisation of humanistic-based concepts such as social justice has gone hand-in-hand with the move towards more people-focused concepts of development. See Chapter 12 'Concepts and Indicators of Development'.

Quick Facts

During the 18th century, the European Enlightenment initiated the debate of equal rights and justice for all human beings, which helped to inspire the French Revolution. The messages of the Enlightenment, that all men were equal and free, inspired the 'mulattos' and Black enslaved of the Haitian Revolution to fight for their inalienable rights.

Key Term

Rule of law – a legal principle that states that we are all subjected to the same standards and directives outlined in legislation.

Social Justice in the Caribbean

"We want justice!" is often the cry among people when they feel that their rights are being neglected or the benefits that they are due are allotted elsewhere or simply denied to them. This was the cry among the protesters of the Morant Bay Rebellion of 1865, who sought help from the British government to allay the effects of the devastating 1860s drought, and among Barbadian citizens during the May 2016 protest against Freudel Stuart's DLP (Democratic Labour Party) handling of the country's affairs.

The need for social justice also becomes evident when the **rule of law** is neglected and some people live above the law while others become victims of it. In the Caribbean, it has been known for politicians to escape imprisonment for criminal activities, while the poor are pursued and imprisoned for alleged crimes such as using obscene language, being in possession of small quantities of medicinal or ceremonial marijuana or resisting arrest.

Society's call for justice is not just a Caribbean trait, it is a worldwide demand by those who feel they are being ignored or taken advantage of, which is why world governing bodies have established international laws and oversight committees to ensure that people's inalienable human rights as well as their legal rights are not denied.

The Role of Social Justice

The main role of social justice is to:
- make sure that people's unalienable human rights are not denied, neglected or legally overlooked by governments, industrialists, armed forces and others in pursuit of power, wealth or any other personal or national ambitions;
- ensure that all groups, regardless of race, class, nationality, religion, gender, sexual orientation or political views, are viewed and treated equally under the laws that govern their territory;
- enable equal access to all resources and opportunities to which a citizen of a country is legally entitled;
- empower people to gain access to an improved quality of life, such as clean air, habitable living spaces, acceptable medical care and a valuable education;
- ensure that governments, religious leaders, businesses, industries and all those given the responsibility to care and provide for people, carry out their responsibilities effectively and without **prejudice**;
- promote the implementation of legal systems and sanctions that will minimise corruption and discrimination that may lead to the marginalisation, unfair treatment, ill health and death of vulnerable groups.

These ideals of social justice to empower and protect can only be facilitated within a state if legal systems, governments and international bodies protect a citizen's natural rights and oversee the equal or equitable distribution of material needs and other forms of social support through administration of systems of welfare or the application of concepts such as mutual advantage.

Natural Rights

Natural rights, sometimes termed **human rights**, need to be upheld if social justice is to function, and are supported by the highest forms of law in most countries. These rights are enforced and even entrenched in modern constitutions to ensure that no group can claim dominance over another through the use of force or institutionalised **discrimination** leading to the lowering of the social or economic status of the disadvantaged group, or even its disappearance. In the British Commonwealth Caribbean, for example, the various constitutions of British former colonies include a section that outlines the natural rights of its citizens called the Bill of Rights.

Many countries are signatories to international treaties on human rights that mean their citizens automatically have access to their human rights without it needing to be specifically recorded in law. However, the practical implementation of these principles is very much dependent on individual government action.

Did You Know?

The Universal Declaration of Human Rights (UNHDR) is a document that was drafted by representatives from countries all over the world at the United Nations General Assembly in December 1948. This established that human rights must be protected. Some of these human rights include the right to life and freedom, the right to freedom of religion, the right to a nationality, the right to a fair and public hearing and the right to own property.

The Functions of Natural Rights

The main functions of natural rights are to:
- protect human beings from enslavement and forced labour systems;
- protect the legal rights of citizens by ensuring that they have equal access to the judiciary system and a fair public hearing in the event that they are accused of crimes;
- protect the economic and social rights of all citizens and promote equal access to education, employment opportunities, amenities and the right to own property;
- underpin international laws giving citizens of a country civil and political rights, which include **the franchise** and the right to enter public office;
- protect ethnic groups from being marginalised or debased by systems established by dominant groups to try to prove or reinforce their superiority over others. This is to ensure the protection of indigenous cultures and practices of all ethnic groups.

Did You Know?

Slavery is an example of how an ethnic group's culture and racial identity can be systematically destroyed in the pursuit of economic gain. This has happened in the Caribbean to the extent that the descendants of enslaved Africans still live with the negative connotations and stereotypes associated with their ancestors. African descendants still own considerably less property and fewer businesses compared to the descendants of White colonialists, and even their fellow Chinese and East Indian plantation labourers. Also, African culture is still considered inferior and African descendants have less access to employment and other opportunities because of the negative stereotypes that influence their employability.

Key Terms

Prejudice – this is any baseless assessment made of an individual or group to show one's disapproval, hatred or disdain. For example, people may dislike the inclusion of the poorer classes in a country club because they are used to only seeing upper class people taking part in club activities.

Natural rights (also called **human rights**) – rights that are naturally conferred at birth and which are considered inalienable because denying them can never be justified. Examples are the right to life, the right to own property and rights to health, clean water and food. Freedom from discrimination is also an inalienable right.

Discrimination – any form of unjust, hurtful, harmful or belittling action, perception or statement made against individuals based on negative stereotypes of the individuals' or groups' race, religion, culture, gender, age, health or nationality. For example, assuming that someone who is HIV positive is either promiscuous or homosexual is a form of discrimination.

Key Term

The franchise – the right given to an individual to vote in a general election. This right was conveyed to all Jamaican citizens over the age of 21 in 1944 (and subsequently extended throughour the region), when universal adult suffrage was granted. The voting age was later changed to 18 because it was thought to be unjust to draft 18-year-olds for war, yet deny them the right to vote.

Making the Connection

Chapter 5 'The Historical Process'

Chapter 7 'Identity and Social Formation'

Chapter 9 'Societal Institutions'

Chapter 17 'Intellectual Traditions'

Exam Tip

'**Discuss**' requires an extended response defining key concepts, giving the facts, exploring related concepts and issues and presenting reasoned arguments. You must use detailed examples but **not** necessarily draw a conclusion.

Check Your Knowledge

Discuss the extent to which the notion of natural rights in the 18th century altered the political, economic and cultural landscape of the Caribbean society up to the present day.

Demonstrate an understanding of the following terms and concepts by defining and using them correctly:

- Natural rights/human rights
- Plantation society
- Social stratification
- Caribbean society
- Discrimination (race/racism and colour)
- Institutionalised slavery
- Slavery (African)

- Indentureship
- French Revolution/Haitian Revolution
- Abolition
- Emancipation
- Independence
- Political, economic, cultural landscape

1. You must first:
   - Establish the time frame given in the question – 18th century to the present.
   - Give a definition of natural rights and give reasons for its popularity during that time period. Where did this notion of natural rights filter from? Mention the French and the Haitian revolutions and ideas of liberty, fraternity and equality.

2. You must describe the following THREE areas in the 18th-century Caribbean and make a comparison, if any, to the present day. Discuss whether any change has been due to natural rights coming to the forefront. Remember to trace change through the centuries:
   - Political:
   - In the 18th-century colonies, rights were held by the White plantation owning class (who qualified as the 'citizens' at that time) only, and power remained in the hands of the colonial **elites** until independence in the second half of the 20th century. Enslaved people had no rights, being chattel, and later indentured labourers had very few rights, which were often denied to them by plantation owners. Revolts by the enslaved were partly inspired by ideas of natural rights (Haiti being the only successful one). In the British Caribbean, even after emancipation, the franchise was denied to most of the population vecause of the imposed property requirements. Ideas of rights and justice were also behind the labour unrest of the early 20th century leading up to independence. Universal adult suffrage was not achieved until 1944 onwards.
   - Today, natural rights are enforced and entrenched in modern constitutions whereby citizens are given civil and political rights including the franchise and the right to enter public office. The constitutions of British former colonies have a section outlining the natural rights of its citizens called the Bill of Rights.
   - The legal rights of citizens are protected by ensuring that they have equal access to the judiciary system and a fair public hearing should they be accused of crimes.
   - The legal systems and governments protect a citizen's natural rights and oversee the equal or equitable distribution of material needs and other forms of social support through systems of welfare or the application of concepts such as mutual advantage.

- Cultural:
  - Plantation society/slavery resulted in an ethnic group's cultural and racial identity being systematically destroyed in the pursuit of economic gain. In modern Caribbean society social justice is upheld to ensure that no group can claim dominance over another by the use of force or institutionalised discrimination/racism resulting in the lowering of the social or economic status of the disadvantaged group, or even its disappearance (as with genocide of the Amerindians).
  - In modern Caribbean societies, ethnic groups are to some extent protected from being marginalised or debased by systems previously established by dominant groups who attempted to prove or reinforce their superiority over others.
  - Discuss what **equal access to education** (as a basis for new class formation and upward mobility) and social amenities has meant in modern Caribbean societies compared to plantation/enslaved society.
  - Discuss how in the Caribbean descendants of enslaved Africans still feel the impact of the negative stereotypes and social stratification (discrimination) associated with their ancestors. Racial tensions still exist in modern Caribbean society based on race and colour.
- Economic:
  - Mention the plantation system, style of production, forced labour and treatment of workers prior to Enlightenment ideas and the abolition of slavery. Compare the systems of production after the ideas were filtered into the Caribbean to the present day (trades unions, rights of workers, establishment of small businesses, etc).
  - Argue how modern Caribbean societies promote equal access to employment opportunities and the right to own property. However, Caribbean descendants of enslaved Africans still own significantly less property and businesses compared to the descendants of White colonialists, and Chinese and East Indian plantation labourers.
- Your conclusion should assess whether natural rights did alter the political, cultural and economic landscape of the Caribbean. You can argue to a lesser or greater extent.

Welfare

Welfare systems are a means of promoting social justice through distribution of resources according to need. Traditionally, welfare systems have been established to aid those citizens who fall below the poverty line, those with special needs, the unemployed, citizens with serious medical issues and orphaned and neglected children.

How Welfare Works

Welfare systems are usually state funded and operated. The financing of these programmes is usually generated from a pool of funds from contributors who are taxpayers.

Contributions to welfare programmes are usually not voluntary, and many Caribbean governments deduct contributions from the salaries of taxpayers before they receive their net pay. These types of deductions are called PAYE (Pay As You Earn) contributions. In the territory of Jamaica, for example, these include:
- Education Tax (used to finance public schools).
- National Insurance Scheme (NIS) contributions (paid into a pension scheme that gives beneficiaries access to money upon retirement).

> ### Key Term
> **Welfare** – the distribution of resources through social programmes designed to aid vulnerable groups to gain access to the basic necessities needed to live; for example, food, shelter, clothing.

- National Housing Trust (NHT) contributions (responsible for providing low-interest-rate mortgages and building low- to middle-income housing for contributors).
- National Health Fund (NHF) contributions (gives contributors access to healthcare and medication for illnesses that are expensive to treat).

Modern welfare systems and programmes have, however, gone a step further in providing aid that gives needy citizens of a country access to material (food, clothing, housing and currency) and non-material benefits (education, medical care, training) that enable them to have access to a standard of living comparable to the average and acceptable standard of living of that country.

Modern welfare systems may extend to state-run job agencies, agencies set up to advise and care for pregnant teens and abused women, and even some that are approved by the government but funded privately (**NGOs**) that support, for example, AIDS sufferers, homosexuals and drug abusers.

The Impact of Welfare on Development

Welfare programmes operate on the understanding that the more wealth is equally distributed among the citizens of a country, the better the chances of the disadvantaged to make a meaningful contribution to the development of the state. For example, when the state promotes training and education among disadvantaged youth, their chances of being employed will increase, likewise those with special needs can also be educated to help themselves and society in whatever capacity they are able.

Arguments that welfare programmes support development include:
- Access to education up to tertiary level not only trains and prepares future taxpayers and professionals for the world of work, but also creates grateful and responsible citizens who will in turn contribute to helping other disadvantaged members of society, easing the government of that responsibility.
- Creating systems that enable people to gain employment also helps to create a more stable Caribbean society. Those employed are better able to take care of their families without state funds being needed to provide for them.
- Healthcare programmes under the welfare system help to combat illnesses that can impact the productivity of the workforce.

Critics of welfare point out that the system can lead to dependency on the state and that it is open to abuse, for example by those unmotivated to find work. In addition, welfare programmes can be seen as a strain on a country's economy and the main cause of public debt and overspending. They are often cut or significantly reduced when austerity measures are implemented by international loan agencies such as the IMF upon entering into a loan agreement with an indebted nation.

Mutual Advantage

The idea behind **mutual advantage** is that citizens requiring help from a welfare programme need to reciprocate in the form of an informal contract in which they undertake to use the advantages of welfare to lift themselves out of poverty and thus eventually make a contribution to society or the economy.

Key Term

Non-governmental organisations (NGOs) – privately funded, non-profit agencies that seek to address social, political and economic issues. One of their key roles is in working to eradicate poverty and social issues in underdeveloped countries. Examples in the Caribbean region are OXFAM and the CHASE Fund.

Did You Know?

Contributions made to the University of the West Indies by Caribbean governments is a form of welfare programme. They contribute more than half of a student's tuition for most courses, giving a wider cross-section of the population access to a tertiary education that they would not normally be able to afford.

Key Term

Mutual advantage – a concept which involves an unwritten contract of reciprocation between the state and citizens seeking to gain benefits from its welfare system.

How does Mutual Advantage Work?

Supporters of mutual advantage see it as a means of protecting the resources of the state from those who:
- seek to benefit from state resources without having to make a contribution;
- exaggerate their disabilities, illnesses and misfortunes as a strategy to live off the state;
- rely on the state to deal with the consequences of their own life choices and behaviour (such as being promiscuous, knowing the state is obligated to take care of any unwanted children, or abusing drugs, knowing that the state will provide rehabilitation).

Below are some examples of how mutual advantage can be put into practice:
- Many Caribbean countries make arrangements for unemployed people on welfare to gain training in a skill as a condition for continuing to receive benefits. One example is the HEART Trust of Jamaica where low-cost and highly subsidised skills training programmes are offered to working and unemployed people, which include employment to allow students the opportunity to practice their newly acquired or improved skills while earning a living.
- Pregnant teenagers may be encouraged to use contraceptives in a controversial bid to encourage young girls to take responsibility for their actions and bodies.
- Women in abusive relationships who are being housed by state-funded women's centres may be encouraged to end their relationships, move out on their own and are even sponsored with the resources to do so in a bid to prevent the reoccurrence of abuse and continued reliance on the state.
- Those with special needs may be trained in programmes that enable them to seek employment or start their own businesses in order to earn a living.

The Impact of Mutual Advantage on Development

The stringent systems of monitoring, training, educating and keeping account of beneficiaries of welfare programmes have led to the rehabilitation and introduction of many productive members of society. Many argue that mutual advantage is a more fair and productive extension of welfare as it is based on merit (only those who are judged by their actions or attitude to be deserving receive support) and a commitment by the recipient to produce a positive result.

Welfare vs Mutual Advantage

The protection and promotion of natural rights, a welfare system to meet the needs of underprivileged citizens in order to promote equality, and the implementation of the concept of mutual advantage to promote a mutually beneficial relationship between state and recipients based on merit and reciprocation are all reflections of social justice in practice. However, some view mutual advantage as counter to social justice as the 'agreement' involved is unequal, being imposed on one side by the other.

There is much debate about the different concepts of fairness embodied in the ideas of unconditional welfare, seen as the most effective means to achieve equality, and mutual advantage, seen as a way to help promote the responsible use of state funding while heightening the effectiveness of welfare programmes. Many argue that the model of mutual advantage is in opposition to welfare rather than an extension of it, as it demands a contribution (in some form) from beneficiaries. They also argue that mutual advantage favours those who are able to invest long term in training, for example, and not those whose needs are more immediate. Others argue that, when examined on a practical level, many welfare programmes can lead to wasteful spending, which in turn can contribute to government debt and thus increase unemployment and poverty.

Discrimination

Discrimination is often, but not always, the result of prejudice. Prejudices may arise out of a person's limited understanding of a culture, race or organisation; prejudice stereotypes emerge when this limited understanding leads to a negative generalisation of racial or social groups. An example of prejudice is where immigrants are blamed for a country's economic woes because they make demands on state resources and welfare benefits.

In the Caribbean, the most common forms of discrimination are on the grounds of age, gender, race and class. There is also an intense discrimination against alternative sexual lifestyles, seen as a threat to traditional conservative Christian values, that has gained the attention of international organisations and media. Discrimination in all these forms represents a breach of social justice.

Ageism

This type of discrimination has become more intense in this technological age when many believe that it is difficult and even impossible for some elderly people to adapt to emerging technologies that have become important features of the modern workplace and lifestyle.

Ageism in Practice

Ageism is a firmly **institutionalised** form of discrimination that is often overlooked in many areas of work and society.

Ageism in employment is common:
- in redundancies, it is widely accepted that the older members of the workforce are laid off or put on early retirement before other staff members;

- the wording of job advertisements often only associates youth with value and potential, for example by stating a company is seeking "young, energetic and dynamic individuals for the post of …";
- the aged are often blamed for static growth or lack of new ideas in an organisation. Younger employees are often used to attract younger customers, thus assuming that the elderly are not appealing;
- employers often believe costs in production time and money lost to illness, training and providing healthcare and other benefits are higher for older workers.

Ageism can also appear in other contexts, such as aspects of social or cultural life or government policy:

- Older people are often excluded from social activities because of the notion that they will not be able to appreciate current music, games and dress.
- Many governments focus on researching illnesses and providing healthcare solutions for the young 'productive' members of society. That the 'geriatric generation' will eventually be afflicted with diseases and disabilities is generally accepted as a natural part of aging that cannot be ameliorated.

Gender Discrimination

Gender discrimination in the Caribbean has its origins firmly grounded in the culture of the region where gender prejudices are entrenched. For example, the idea (itself a stereotype) that all Caribbean men will abandon their families at some point, leaving a broken home led by a single mother, comes from the assumption that plantation owners not allowing marriages and families has somehow implanted a negative view of family life among Caribbean men. This is, however, a sexist assumption as there are many other factors that could lead to the break up of families.

The prevalence of Christianity, Islam and Hinduism in the Caribbean, all of which involve a tradition that females should submit to males, is also a contributing factor to sexist ideas.

Gender Discrimination in Practice

Most sexist and gender-biased remarks tend to be directed at women. This is because Caribbean men have historically viewed women as the weaker sex in the European, East Indian and West African traditions of men being the head of their households and the women the homemakers. Other sexist notions directed at women are:

- Men are scientifically proven to be stronger – this is evident where women are rejected as potential employees in industries where the work is physically demanding. Historically, recruiters of Asian immigrant labourers mostly recruited men, believing that women would not adjust well to plantation labour.
- Men are better at industrial and engineering jobs – many factories and engineering companies still prefer to employ men because employers believe that they are better able to handle the equipment.
- Women should not become religious leaders – this notion is still prevalent in the Roman Catholic church where women cannot become priests. The Caribbean Islamic community and most Rastafarian orders also still refuse to accept female leaders.

Key Term

Gender discrimination, also known as **sexism** – any form of discrimination based on general expectations and assumptions of an individual's gender rather than their talents, achievements and contributions to society.

Key Terms

Racism, or **racial discrimination** – actions based on the belief that an **ethnic** group is superior (or inferior) to another because of their biological or cultural differences. Racist views are so prevalent and widely accepted in the Caribbean that it can be difficult to identify these discriminatory acts.

Ethnicity – being part of a uniform and cohesive national or cultural group that is defined by a common race, language, history or religion.

Classism, or **class discrimination** – any form of discrimination against the poorer people of a society who are commonly classified as the 'lower' social class. This classification in itself is an indictment of their cultural forms and lifestyle, not just economic position, through the use of the term 'social' to define it. We see this at work in society where the Black Caribbean culture is often viewed as inferior because it emanates from the 'lower class' structure.

Making the Connection

Caribbean feminist thought and theories of gender are looked at in Chapter 17 'Intellectual Traditions'.

Making the Connection

Chapter 5 'The Historical Process' and Chapter 7 'Identity and Social Formation' discuss the plantation system and its legacies.

- Women should not earn more than their male counterparts – this comes from the ideology that women should generally play a lesser role in the workplace and the notion that men should be the main breadwinners in families.

Did You Know?

Women began to enter male-dominated industries and fields such as medicine, heavy industry and full-time farming after World Wars 1 (1914–1918) and 2 (1939–1945) when they had to replace men who had gone to fight. The realisation that they were as capable as men at most jobs lead to the prevalence of the feminist movement in the 1960s when many women demanded that they be treated as equals to men and some asserted that women were better than men at many tasks.

Racism and Class Discrimination

Ethnicity and class are closely linked in the Caribbean. The influence the plantation system has had on the economic development of the Caribbean's racial groups cannot be understated. Today, those of European descent still control most of the economic infrastructure (for instance, factories or machinery) and natural resources such as land. Likewise, the Chinese and Indians, who could afford to open businesses in plantation society, play a significant role in commerce. The Black peoples, whose ancestors were enslaved unpaid labourers, artisans and poor peasant farmers, also continue to carry that legacy in today's society. So, a class pyramid representing the various races during the plantation period and one showing modern Caribbean society would look quite similar.

Did You Know?

Racism in the Caribbean is an example of institutionalised discrimination. For example, because most people of the lower class in the Caribbean are of African descent, many find the idea of a Black billionaire surprising and may even question how he/she came upon their wealth. Reports of a homeless, poverty stricken man of Chinese or European descent would be met with equal surprise, but only because people of these races are usually associated with being wealthy.

Racism and Class Discrimination in Practice

Racial prejudices and stereotypes result in probably the most destructive type of discrimination because it affects a wider cross-section of Caribbean society than any other form. As the lower economic stratum of society is largely made up of people of African descent, race and **class discrimination** are in many ways inextricably linked.

- Black culture (literature, music, language and religious forms) has been discriminated against in the Caribbean because it emerged from a race that historically was thought to be intellectually and biologically inferior: indigenous or creole languages based on Amerindian or African culture are secondary to the primary European-based languages spoken in the islands; European dress is mainly seen as acceptable in formal settings, such as for work or Christian worship, while traditional African, indigenous or even East Indian and Chinese clothing is usually worn as costumes during cultural festivals or cultural holidays.

- The implicit acceptance of an historically entrenched association of Caribbean people of African descent with criminal activity, violence and deviance has discouraged many from examining further and remedying the causes of their disadvantaged economic situation that has led to the high incidence of crime and destructive behaviour among Black communities.
- As a result of the association of Caribbean people of African descent with poverty, financial institutions and others can be cautious of doing business with them. In the past this led to a difficulty in accessing loans and getting backing for establishing small businesses, which helped perpetuate the cycle of poverty among Black communities in the Caribbean. In recent years governments, such as that of Trinidad and Tobago, have provided assistance and incentives to help people of all ethnic groups to establish small businesses. However, statistics from the private sector in Jamaica and Trinidad and Tobago still reveal that more stringent processes are applied to mortgage and loan applications from the Afro-Caribbean community.
- The largely Eurocentric education system in force in the Caribbean has contributed to negative perceptions of non-European cultures through its lack of coverage of thriving indigenous African and Asian societies before European intervention. Social issues affecting the Afro-Caribbean community, such as high levels of crime and violence and single-parent families, are frequently highlighted in history and social studies text with negative connotations, and have led to commonly held negative stereotypes.

Discrimination on the Grounds of Sexual Orientation

This emerged as a social issue in the Caribbean at the beginning of the 21st century, with increased exposure to liberal ideas via the internet and cable TV, and is increasing in intensity with growing numbers of support groups and NGOs, for example The Jamaica Forum for Lesbians, All Sexuals and Gays (JFLAG), that concern themselves solely with protecting gay rights.

Caribbean governments face problems dealing with these issues because territorial laws (for example, the Buggery Act of Jamaica) and many Caribbean citizens (who are conservative Christians, Muslims or Hindus) are against any act of homosexuality, and consecutive governments choose to ignore the issue in a bid to maintain popularity among the people.

How Forms of Discrimination can Affect Development in the Caribbean

As a result of living in such a **plural society**, the danger of discrimination inevitably becomes a feature. This discrimination can negatively affect development in Caribbean states in the ways outlined below.

Age Discrimination

- Failure to recognise the contributions that older people can bring to the workplace excludes potential experience, expertise and connections.
- Companies may also fail to benefit from the possible reduced labour cost of hiring the elderly who are often open to working part-time or doing consultancy work in return for a fraction of the pay for full-time employees. This would be especially useful for growing small businesses that need experienced and knowledgeable workers, but may not be able to employ them full-time.

Key Term

Discrimination on the grounds of sexual orientation – commonly termed homophobia, this refers to discrimination against individuals who engage in sexual acts with a partner of the same sex. These individuals are part of what is known as 'the gay community'.

Key Term

Plural society – a society in which people of different classes, races, religions and so on coexist but continue to have their different traditions and interests.

- The cultural heritage of the Caribbean is of utmost importance to the economy as It Is a major draw for tourists and locals who pay to attend various shows featuring traditional music, dance and art. Neglecting the oral traditions and other contributions the aged can make to this sector can be to the detriment of many tributary industries that rely on it.

Gender Discrimination

- Discrimination against women in the workplace, for example, receiving less pay than men even though they are equally qualified, and being overlooked for promotions and sidelined from certain types of jobs, has an immediate negative economic impact on a society where single-parent (predominantly female) families are prevalent.
- Sexist attitudes can deter women from starting their own businesses as many Caribbean people are of the view that male doctors, lawyers and engineers, for example, are superior to their female counterparts.
- Sexist attitudes and discrimination against women who refuse to conform to the sexual stereotypes expected of them in the workplace result in many qualified women failing to achieve their true work potential and, therefore, their full potential contribution to the economy.
- The expectations of men that women should be docile and submissive have led to the physical, sexual and verbal abuse of women at home (domestic abuse) and in the workplace (sexual harassment). Considerable welfare resources have had to be spent on dealing with the effects of these types of abuses.

Racism and Class Discrimination

- Many conflicts in the Caribbean, starting with the Morant Bay Rebellion and continuing with the Caribbean-wide riots of the 1930s, were the result of racism and classism and led to considerable economic loss among Caribbean economies.
- Racial tensions resulting from racist views have led to political divisiveness in Caribbean countries, such as Guyana where the electorate has tended to vote along racial lines rather than for the most qualified and proven leaders. Guyana today remains among the poorest, least developed Caribbean nations.
- Many of the Caribbean's African descendants have not had the opportunity to contribute on a large scale to the region's economy because of lack of funding and access to resources due mainly to racial and class discrimination. Banks and financial institutions would rather invest in capital-rich clients, who happen to be mostly White and mixed raced people who can trace their ancestry back to the planter class. Afro-Caribbeans have contributed to the region's economy, but mainly in terms of small businesses.

Discrimination on the Grounds of Sexual Orientation

- Violence against those who practise alternative sexual lifestyles has led foreign governments to withhold grants and bursaries to Caribbean governments in a bid to force their hands to ameliorate this social issue. In 2011 David Cameron, then Prime Minister of the UK, threatened to withhold aid from countries that have anti-gay records or legislation only weeks before a visit to Jamaica, known for its strong anti-gay stance.

Quick Fact

Many small businesses established by people of African descent are very small scale. Many are starved of funding and statistics show that most end up failing before reaching their fifth anniversary of operation.

- Private investors and companies have also pulled financial support from local musical talents and artistes who promote violence against the gay community in songs and interviews.

Police Brutality

The role of the police should be to serve the community as part of the machinery to implement legal justice, which in turn should promote and uphold natural rights and social justice. However, instances of **police brutality** undermine this role and their relationship with the community.

Police brutality tends to be against those groups that are already vulnerable and socially disadvantaged, especially the young males belonging to them. This was the case of Mario Deane who died in 2014 following a severe beating in his cell after being taken into custody for possession of a marijuana cigarette. The police claimed that Deane behaved aggressively when a surety came to bail him, and as a result was sent to his cell. As a result of Deane's death, the Jamaican government passed legislation allowing individuals to possess two ounces of the drug. Deane's death was blamed on a system that targets the poor while the rich break laws and are exonerated because they either are not pursued by the police or can afford capable legal council.

Police brutality has led to a serious distrust of law enforcement in the Caribbean. Instances of corruption and of partisanship, of association with political factions, which in turn can also be linked to criminal gangs, for example in Trinidad and Jamaica, work to exacerbate this mistrust. This in turn has made the investigation of crime, especially violent crime, difficult as potential witnesses and perpetrators refuse to cooperate with law enforcement. A number of kidnappings in Trinidad and Tobago, for instance, have not been solved because citizens and victims have been reluctant to share information with the police about the perpetrators.

With spiralling crime problems and people calling for a solution, many Caribbean governments find it a difficult task to rein in the use of excessive force among police officers while at the same time issuing a strong deterrent to criminals. Some governments have established agencies to investigate police brutality. In Jamaica, which registers the highest yearly rate of police killings in the English speaking Caribbean, for example, the Independent Commission of Investigation was established to investigate police shootings and acts of excessive force within the Jamaica Constabulary Force (JCF).

Increased brutality and unaccountability by those meant to protect results in general fear and apathy among the population, which in turns leads to lower productivity. The negative international press puts off potential tourists to the region and this issue has also resulted in foreign investment being withheld in an attempt to force Caribbean governments to act.

> ### Key Term
>
> **Police brutality** – the use of excessive and unnecessary force on civilians beyond what is considered safe or humane. This includes all acts where the police use unnecessary violence to manage conflicts or to detain a citizen. Any action where police are verbally abusive or use their power and authority to coerce cooperation from citizens can also be categorised as police brutality.

Breaches of Social Justice Affecting Indicators of Development

Development can be affected by breaches of social justice and can be held back by inequality in a country. The Human Development Paradigm can be used to summarise and measure the ways in which breaches of social justice can have a negative effect on human, economic and sustainable development. It places human development within the context of economic and sustainable development and lists four essential pillars for development, which are based on principles of social justice. These pillars are Equity, Productivity, Sustainability and Empowerment.

- Equity – people must have access to equal opportunities. For people to be able to participate in and benefit from economic and political opportunities, all barriers to these opportunities must be eliminated. If not, there is a high level of social inequality.
- Productivity – people must be enabled to increase their productivity and participate fully in the process of income generation and employment for which they are renumerated in some form. In this way, economic growth depends on the implementation of the principles of social justice that underpin human development. If they are not implemented, productivity levels will be low.
- Sustainability – access to opportunities for all must be ensured not only for the present generation but for future generations as well. Therefore, all forms of capital (physical, human and environmental) should be replenished in order to ensure an equitable **quality of life** for all.
- Empowerment – development must be implemented by the people, not just for them. Therefore, people must participate fully in the decisions and processes that shape their lives. The most effective way to do this is by granting people their **democratic rights** and allowing them to assert them. Where democratic rights are impaired, development will also suffer.

Of the four pillars, equity is the most important as the others rest upon this. When the implementation of the principles of social justice that lie behind these pillars is compromised, levels of development will be adversely affected.

Levels of Social Inequality

Social inequality by definition is in itself a breach of social justice as it involves the uneven distribution of wealth within a country and the existence of unequal opportunities and conditions for different social groups. It occurs when the people in a country are divided into groups based on race, gender, class, sexual orientation, age, ethnicity and educational achievements. Usually White males who are graduates of a university are at the top of the social hierarchy.

The main aspects of inequality that form barriers to economic and social opportunities are living conditions, education and healthcare. The measure of social inequality as reflected by income distribution is the Gini coefficient, which can show if there is a high level of wealth concentrated in the hands of a few.

Productivity Levels

The productivity of a population gives an idea of the average output per worker in a country. Each person's contribution to the country's income is commonly indicated by GDP (gross domestic product) per capita. Any factor that impacts on human resources can influence this measure. For example, reducing the number of sick days by offering employees health benefits is a way to improve productivity.

Key Terms

Quality of life – the overall wellbeing of an individual life, including income and emotional state.

Democratic rights – a situation where a constitution sets rules regarding citizens having basic human rights and political and religious freedom.

Quick Fact

The concept of equity is based on the idea of fairness. If all people are treated fairly, they have access to the same (equal) opportunities.

Making the Connection

Indicators of development and the Human Development Paradigm are examined in more detail in Chapter 12 'Concepts and Indicators of Development'.

Productivity is not just about good business management. It can be affected by various forms of discrimination, such as on the grounds of age, gender and disability, as well as by social injustices, such as the lack of good, relevant and affordable education and the lack of healthcare, all of which lower the productivity potential of various individuals.

Quality of Life

The quality of life is the degree to which one is satisfied with one's life. If the GDP per capita is high, it means the majority of people should have enough income to enjoy a comfortable and healthy life. The HDI (Human Development Index), however, reflects a better picture of quality of life because it has a social (life expectancy and adult literacy) as well as an economic dimension. A person who has a healthy lifestyle with a balanced diet, exercises regularly and avoids harmful drugs should lead a long enjoyable life. Further benefits come with good familial relationships, a stable community life and access to education and employment, enabling them to build their family and country. Social inequalities can result in the opposite for many people, with a reduced quality of life involving poor education and job opportunities, low income, poor levels of housing and nutritition, and vulnerability to crime.

Democratic Rights

Democratic rights are those rights associated with choosing and participating in government, at both a local and national level. Good governance is the indicator of development associated with this and involves a free and fair electoral process with elections held regularly, transparency in the processeses of government and decision making based on consensus.

Good governance also involves how, once in power, a government functions to the equal benefit of all, the degree of political participation allowed to those not in power and openness of the political culture, in that opposition is permitted to exist and express itself unhindered. Corruption, inequitable distribution of resources and welfare, exclusion from the decision-making process and suppression of freedom of expression are all examples of how citizens' democratic rights can be impaired.

In the past, not all Caribbean people were allowed to vote, only those owning property. Adult suffrage or every man and woman over 21 (lowered to 18 in the 1970s) being able to vote was introduced in the Caribbean between 1944 and 1953. Democratic elections are usually held every five years and transfer of political power is mostly smooth. There have been some accusations of ballot box tampering or bribery, but this is not widespread. There are issues of social injustice, however, through political corruption. An example of this is when elected officials hire political appointees or party supporters without the required qualifications. Also occurring is nepotism, where persons in authority hire or award government contracts to relatives.

When people are dissatisfied with the current conditions, they have the freedom to vote for different leadership. One exception is Cuba, which has had a one-party Communist regime since the 1950s and the majority of political candidates are state recommended.

Multiple-choice Questions

1. Which of the following rights is most important in a socially just society?

   A. Freedom from an 8-hour working day

   B. Police brutality in the low income areas of a country

   C. The punishment for wrongdoers if they cannot afford lawyers

   D. Protection of children from abuse even if it is at the hands of their parents

2. One way a breach of social justice is likely to lower the quality of life is

   A. Women getting better good jobs in the private sector

   B. Politicians bribing voters by offering cash during elections

   C. Minorities being unemployed

   D. Sponsorship of events by alcoholic drink manufacturers

3. When there are breaches in social justice, development is affected. Which statement(s) BEST reflects this?

   I. Lowering of productivity when minority groups are marginalised

   II. Blocking of roads by residents because they are unemployed

   III. Riots and protests by Black people in society when they are unfairly targeted by the police

   A. I only

   B. I and II

   C. I and III

   D. I, II and III

4. The successful fight for social justice in the early 19th-century Caribbean was seen among

   A. The enslaved Haitians of Hispaniola

   B. The enslaved of the Morant Bay Rebellion

   C. The enslaved of the Christmas Revolt

   D. The East Indians on the sugar estates furing the Indentureship era

5. The Gini coefficient

   A. Measures the disparity in income distribution in a country

   B. Measures the inefficiencies of the healthcare system in a country

   C. Measures the inefficiencies of the education system in a country

   D. Measures the level of social injustice in a country

6. All of the following indicate poor governance in a country except

   A. Infrequent elections

   B. Transparency in decision making

   C. The views of the electorate are ignored

   D. Corruption during the electoral process

7. The Caribbean island where most of the political candidates are state recommended is

   A. Barbados

   B. Tobago

   C. Jamaica

   D. Cuba

8. The practice of forcing a senior female member of a workforce into early retirement is referred to as

   A. Sexism

   B. Discrimination

   C. Prejudice

   D. Ageism

9. The assumption that all Caribbean men eventually abandon their families is called

   A. A sexist assumption

   B. A Eurocentric assumption

   C. An ethnocentric assumption

   D. A prejudicial assumption